Becoming a Professional Reading Teacher

The Psychology and Psycholinguistics of Literacy Skills

or *evidence-based instruction* are often heard. The student teacher is urged to exercise caution in drawing conclusions from studies that claim to be "scientific research" and are published in journals. Throughout the book, illustrations are provided to show that whereas the "scientific" data may be reliable, the interpretation of these data can be subjective. Cattell's studies on word recognition (discussed in Chapter 2) form a case in point. Furthermore, what appears to be a finite truth at the moment eventually turns out to be a tentative conclusion that has to be modulated as more evidence accumulates with time. For example, the current view is that phoneme awareness training in conjunction with the teaching of alphabetic knowledge is more effective in improving reading skills than phonemic awareness training alone (which was once believed to be the most effective method).

Throughout the book, an effort has been made to keep technical terms to a minimum. Care also has been taken not to overwhelm the student with too many citations of scientific studies. Research is cited mainly to support statements and conclusions that are counterintuitive and controversial. To expose undergraduate students to journals in the field, reading assignments are suggested at the end of each chapter. Furthermore, to relate the theory presented in the chapters to practical experience, brief assignments at the end of each chapter require the student teacher to interview teachers or interact with students.

REFERENCES

Bernstein, A. (2005, April 7). Lou Gerstner's classroom quest. *Business Week.*

Gibbon, P. (2002). *A call to heroism: Renewing America's vision of greatness.* New York: Grove/Atlantic.

Levine, A. (2006). *Educating teachers.* Retrieved November 27, 2007, from http://www .edschools.org/teacher_report.htm

National Commission on Excellence in Education. (1983). *A nation at risk: The imperative for educational reform.* Washington, DC: U.S. Department of Education.

No Child Left Behind Act of 2001, PL 107-110, 115 Stat. 1425, 20 U.S.C. §§ 6301 *et seq.*

U.S. Department of Education (2003). *Meeting the highly qualified teachers challenge: The Secretary's Second Annual Report on Teacher Quality.* Washington, DC: Author.

Acknowledgments

We express our appreciation to Sarah Shepke, Acquisitions Editor at Paul H. Brookes Publishing Co., who was a source of encouragement for publishing this book. The literary quality of the book has been considerably enhanced by the help of Senior Production Editor Nicole Schmidl, and we are much indebted to her.

knowledge in instruction, and be competent in assessing and evaluating children's progress in literacy acquisition. The book is divided into three parts and the chapters in each section are designed to provide the essentials necessary to meet these three prerequisites.

Section I deals with the psychology and psycholinguistics of literacy skills. In Chapter 1, literacy skills are defined, and the factors that influence acquisition of literacy skills are organized under the Component Model of Reading. This model presents a comprehensive picture of learning to read and write and draws the student teacher's attention to not only cognitive factors but also psychological and environmental factors. Special attention is paid to the psychology of the reading process. A great deal of the information we have about the reading process comes from studies that have been carried out under the rubric of experimental design. The information processing branch of cognitive psychology has contributed much to our knowledge of the reading process by conducting studies that have utilized experimental design. Such studies also have led us to consider reading as an aspect of linguistics. In this section of the book, the psycholinguistics of spoken and written language presents the background knowledge essential for understanding literacy processes. This section also deals with the growth and development of spoken and written language skills.

Section II addresses the application of the knowledge presented in Section I. The chapters in this section of the book deal with the instructional strategies necessary for developing literacy skills and describe specific instructional methods, along with numerous activities, for classroom use. Following the Component Model of Reading, the chapters in Section II present topics such as phonological awareness, phonemic awareness, word recognition, vocabulary, and comprehension. Instant word reading (also known as sight word reading) and its relationship to fluency is given objective treatment. This section of the book addresses the issues of what to teach and how to teach.

Most of the material presented in Section II is meant for teaching children who do not experience unusual difficulty in learning to read and write. The greatest challenge the professional reading teacher will face is assisting some children who find it difficult to learn to read and write. The nature of reading difficulty experienced by these children is presented in a separate chapter, which takes an objective look at terms such as *learning disability* and *dyslexia*. Specific methods that are used to teach children who experience learning difficulties are presented; however, it is noted that these methods are equally applicable to all beginning readers.

Section III focuses on testing and assessment. Formal and informal methods of assessment are described in some detail. In addition, leading standardized tests of literacy are described and compared with each other with reference to their strengths and weakness. Teachers are also urged to use qualitative assessment procedures, which often lead to direct instruction.

Additional resources for the student appear in the form of end-of-book appendices. Appendix A is a glossary of terms commonly encountered in literacy articles and texts; glossary terms also are bolded at first mention in *Becoming a Professional Reading Teacher*. Appendix B offers an overview of basal readers. Appendix C presents information on technology assistance and software designed for literacy instruction.

An additional skill expected of the professional reading teacher is the ability to critically examine literacy-related issues. Phrases such as *scientifically based finding*

Preface

For more than 100 years, acquisition and instruction of literacy skills such as reading, writing, and spelling have received much attention from American educators. In recent years, literacy instruction has received added consideration because of the passage of the No Child Left Behind Act (NCLB) of 2001 (PL 107-110). Although NCLB aroused a great deal of self-examination and has generated much activity, another aphorism that has emerged at the heels of NCLB is "No teacher left behind" (Gibbon, 2002) or "No great teacher left behind" (Bernstein, 2005). Gibbon, after noting that teachers are the key for NCLB to succeed, concluded the success of NCLB depends on commitment from highly qualified teachers. Expressing a similar view almost a quarter of a century earlier, the publication *A Nation at Risk: The Imperative for Educational Reform* (National Commission on Excellence in Education, 1983) recommended the engaging of qualified teachers and the setting up of rigorous educational standards in teacher-preparation programs to stave off the crisis. *Meeting the Highly Qualified Teachers Challenge: The Secretary's Second Annual Report on Teacher Quality* (The Standards-based Teacher Education Project; U.S. Department of Education, 2003) is more specific and has proposed three requirements teacher preparation programs should meet. The programs should be designed to ensure that 1) teachers know their subjects, 2) teachers know how to teach children at high levels, and 3) teachers know how to assess student learning. In a more recent report, Levine (2006) made several recommendations that are similar in tone. One of his salient recommendations is that education schools should be transformed from ivory towers into professional schools that train professionals.

A general definition of *profession* is a disciplined group of individuals who adhere to high standards and possess special knowledge and skills derived from education and training of a high caliber. Furthermore, professionals are prepared to exercise this knowledge and skill in the interest of others. When applied to the teaching profession, this means that teachers should possess special knowledge, that they should apply this knowledge in their professional practice, and that this knowledge has been acquired from education and training of a high level. This description very succinctly characterizes *Becoming a Professional Reading Teacher*. The textbook in your hands is designed to facilitate the accomplishment of these expectations.

A frequently expressed view is that anyone with a certain degree of motivation, whether he or she has received any specialized education and training or not, can enter a classroom and teach children. In other words, teaching is not a profession that requires education and special training of a high level but is more of an art. This book takes issue with this viewpoint and argues that teaching, particularly teaching of literacy skills to children, requires a high level of expertise that comes from professional training. This book champions this belief and the title reflects it.

Becoming a professional teacher requires that three conditions are met. The professional reading teacher should posses a thorough knowledge of the foundations of literacy and literacy acquisition, have mastery over the application of this

About the Authors

P.G. Aaron, Ph.D., is Professor in the Department of Educational and School Psychology at Indiana State University in Terre Haute. He received his doctoral degree in educational psychology from the University of Wisconsin–Madison. He is a recipient of the Albert Harris Award of the International Reading Association for research in reading disabilities and of the Distinguished Coffman Professorship at Indiana State University. In addition to writing many research articles, he is the author of the book *Dyslexia and Hyperlexia: Diagnosis and Management of Developmental Reading Disabilities* (1989, Kluwer Academic Publishers). With Malt Joshi, he coauthored *Reading Problems: Consultation and Remediation* (1992, Guilford Press) and coedited *Handbook of Orthography and Literacy* (2005, Lawrence Erlbaum Associates).

R. Malatesha (Malt) Joshi, Ph.D., is Professor of Literacy Education at Texas A&M University in College Station, where he teaches courses and conducts research on assessment of and intervention for reading and spelling difficulties, as well as literacy and orthography. He is the editor of *Reading and Writing: An Interdisciplinary Journal.* Since the mid-1980s, he has received funding from the North Atlantic Treaty Organization (NATO) to direct international institutes in Europe, the last one being in Italy in 2004. His papers have appeared in *Neuropsychologia, Journal of Learning Disabilities, School Psychology Review,* and *Psychological Reports.* His most recent publication, coedited with P.G. Aaron, is *Handbook of Orthography and Literacy* (2005, Lawrence Erlbaum Associates); this book examines the writing systems of approximately 25 languages and how these systems affect literacy acquisition.

Diana Quatroche, Ph.D., is Associate Professor and Chair of the Department of Elementary, Early, and Special Education at Indiana State University in Terre Haute, where she teaches undergraduate and graduate courses in reading and language arts. She received her master's and doctoral degrees at the University of Pittsburgh, where she specialized in reading. She has experience teaching elementary school, supervising school reading programs, and coordinating Title I reading programs.

Contents

What Are Literacy Skills?
When Are Literacy Skills Acquired?
Do All Children Acquire Reading Skills at the Same Rate?
What Factors Influence the Acquisition of Literacy Skills?
The Component Model of Reading

The Psychology of Reading
History of Literacy Instruction in the United States
Approaches to Literacy Instruction: Today's Major Players

The Importance of a Knowledge of Linguistics
Linguistics and Psycholinguistics
Components of Spoken Language
The Influence of Language on Reading and Writing Skills

Basic Concepts Involved in the Study of Writing Systems
Origins and History of Writing Systems
Written Language Is as Natural as Spoken Language
Written Language Is Not Merely Speech Written Down
The Influence of Written Language on Spoken Language

Prereading Skills: Print Awareness, Emergent Literacy,
    and Invented Spelling
Developmental Sequence of the Components of Spoken Language

Major Approaches to Beginning Literacy Instruction
Promoting Listening Comprehension Skills in Preschoolers
Strategies for Fostering Print Awareness
Strategies for Developing Phonological Awareness

Paul H. Brookes Publishing Co.
Post Office Box 10624
Baltimore, Maryland 21285-0624
USA

www.brookespublishing.com

Typeset by Integrated Publishing Solutions, Grand Rapids, Michigan.
Manufactured in the United States of America by
Sheridan Books, Inc., Chelsea, Michigan.

Scripture taken from the New King James Version®. Copyright © 1982
by Thomas Nelson, Inc. Used by permission. All rights reserved.

Some material on pages 34–35 from Redd, T.M., & Webb, K.S. (2005). *A teacher's
introduction to African American English.* Urbana, IL: National Council of Teachers
of English. Copyright 2005 by the National Council of Teachers of English. Used
with permission.

Some material on page 205 from BLACHOWICZ, C., & FISHER, P. TEACHING
VOCABULARY IN ALL CLASSROOMS, 3rd Edition, © 2006, p. 12. Adapted by
permission of Pearson Education, Inc., Upper Saddle River, NJ.

Library of Congress Cataloging-in-Publication Data

Becoming a professional reading teacher / by P.G. Aaron ... [et al.].
    p. cm.
  Includes bibliographical references and index.
  ISBN-13: 978-1-55766-829-5 (hardcover)
  ISBN-10: 1-55766-829-9 (hardcover)
  1. Reading teachers—Training of—United States.   2. Reading—United States.
  3. Psycholinguistics.   I. Aaron, P. G.

LB2844.1.R4B44 2008
428.4'071—dc22   2007048047

British Library Cataloguing in Publication data are available from the British Library.

2012   2011   2010   2009   2008
10   9   8   7   6   5   4   3   2   1

Becoming a Professional Reading Teacher

by

P.G. Aaron, Ph.D.
Indiana State University
Terre Haute

R. Malatesha Joshi, Ph.D.
Texas A&M University
College Station

and

Diana Quatroche, Ph.D.
Indiana State University
Terre Haute

·P·A·U·L·H·
BROOKES
PUBLISHING Co.®

Baltimore • London • Sydney

CHAPTER 1

Introduction to Literacy Skills and Their Acquisition

Summary

This chapter defines literacy skills and deals with two major questions relating to these skills: When are literacy skills acquired? What factors influence the acquisition of literacy skills? In this book, *literacy* is defined as the ability to read and write and use written language effectively. Literacy skills emerge very early in life, as early as 3 years of age or even earlier in some children when they show a tendency to scribble. Literacy skills are therefore believed to emerge rather than be learned. Many factors influence literacy acquisition. These factors are grouped under three domains—**cognitive, psychological,** and **ecological**—and are represented in the **Component Model of Reading**. An understanding of these components guides teachers in helping poor readers become better readers and good readers become skilled readers.

Main ideas presented in this chapter

1. *Literacy* is a comprehensive term that refers to an ability to read, write, and conduct any other activity related to written language.

2. All children do not acquire literacy skills at the same rate.

3. Literacy acquisition is affected by three factors, which are the cognitive, psychological, and ecological domains of the Component Model of Reading.

4. The ability to decode the written word and comprehend written language are two components that make up the cognitive domain of the Component Model.

5. To comprehend written text, the reader should be able to decode written words instantly and automatically. Thus, **fluency** is an important characteristic of a good reader.

6. Motivation and interest, **learning styles, teacher expectation**, and gender differences are components of the psychological domain of the Component Model. These factors also affect literacy acquisition.

7. Home environment, dialectical differences, and peer influence also have an effect on literacy acquisition. These are placed under the ecological domain of the Component Model.

8. African American English is a **dialect** which is linguistically as intricate as **Standard English.**

9. Parents play an important role in influencing children's literacy acquisition and, eventually, children's performance at school.

10. Successful teaching depends on the teacher's ability to understand the nature and role of the different components described in the Component Model.

What Are Literacy Skills?

According to the United Nations Educational, Scientific and Cultural Organization (UNESCO; 1953), literacy is the ability to identify, understand, interpret, create, communicate, and compute, using printed and written materials associated with varying contexts. Literacy involves possessing levels of proficiency necessary to function in society. Some definitions of literacy include proficiency in the use of spoken language as well as written language. In the future, literacy may even include the ability to use computers to communicate. In this book, we adopt the traditional definition of literacy, which is the ability to read and write and use written language effectively.

There is general agreement about what reading is; it is extracting and constructing meaning from written language. Writing, conversely, is expressing one's thoughts and ideas using the written language as a medium. Disagreement, however, arises over how to teach young children to read and write. According to Hittleman (1988), "Reading and writing are learned within the context of all subject areas, not as separate skill subjects" (p. 4). In contrast, a report by the American Federation of Teachers (1991) stated that "well-designed, controlled comparisons of instructional approaches have consistently supported these . . . practices in reading instruction: direct teaching of decoding, comprehension, and literature appreciation; systematic and **explicit instruction** in the code system of written English" (pp. 7–8). The validity of these two different descriptions of reading instruction is not easy to determine because it is not known whether they are aimed at students of the same age. Hittleman's statement is most likely aimed at mature readers; the statement by the American Federation of Teachers obviously was made with beginning readers in mind.

The lack of specificity of the target student population is one source of the perennial disagreement among reading educators about how to teach reading. The issue regarding reading instruction is, therefore, intimately related to the question of when children *begin* to acquire literacy skills. This book, therefore, examines this question in some detail. In the past, the onset of literacy skills acquisition was usually discussed under the topic of reading readiness. Traditionally, it was believed that children were ready to learn to read when they entered first grade, at about 6 years of age (Durkin, 1993). During the 1920s and the following decade, this belief was reinforced by theories derived from the psychological concept of **mental age** and the biological principle of maturation. The thinking followed these lines: Until a child reaches the appropriate mental age, learning to read is considered all but impossible and attempting to teach such children unproductive because mental age is primarily determined by maturation, which is under biological control. This view has practical implications. For instance, many years ago, Washburne, a superintendent of the Winnetka school system in Illinois, urged his teachers to keep track of the mental ages of the children in their classrooms and not to attempt to teach them to read and write before they had reached the mental age of 6½ years (Washburne, 1936).

However, it was soon realized that mental age may not be a reliable correlate of reading ability and, therefore, educators could not depend on mental age alone as an indicator of reading readiness. Furthermore, even in the first grade, children with a wide range of mental age could be seen. Considering these facts, it was proposed that even if a child was not likely to profit from reading instruction, he could be prepared and made ready to receive such instruction at a later date. This gave rise to the concept of reading readiness and eventually resulted in the development of readiness programs in kindergarten classes. Readiness programs did not teach reading directly but included activities such as handling books, looking at pictures, naming the objects in the pictures, listening to stories read by the teacher, and receiving an occasional smattering of alphabetic instruction. A reading readiness program may also have included auditory, visual, and perceptual activities. The distinction between readiness programs and reading programs, however, remained blurred.

When Are Literacy Skills Acquired?

Two studies published in the 1970s (Chomsky, 1970; Read, 1975) reported that many preschool children show a strong tendency to try to produce words they know by "writing" them down. This indicates that children as young as 3 and 4 years of age do have some concepts about writing and written language. Very young children's knowledge about writing and reading may be unrefined and vague, but these studies showed that even at a young age, children are eager to deal with language in its written form. Observations of children by other investigators have confirmed and extended these conclusions. For instance, on the basis of her studies of children ages 2 through 7 years, DeFord (1980) concluded that "learning to write is initiated tacitly, as in oral language" (p. 162). It has also been noted that children pick up clues about the writing system that is prevalent in their environment. For instance, Harste and Burke (1982) reported that the scribbles of 4-year-old Arabic children resemble Arabic script, whereas the scribbles of American children resemble English script.

A realization of very young children's ability to make a close connection between writing and speech in the absence of formal instruction led to the coining of the term *emergent literacy* (Teale & Sulzby, 1986). Earlier, Marie Clay (1966), an educator from New Zealand, had introduced the term *emergent reading* in her doctoral dissertation. Emergent literacy is not a formal theory of instruction but a description of young children's understanding, however vague, of the nature of written language. Nevertheless, the term implies that parents and early childhood teachers should create opportunities for children at home and at school to exploit the potentials presented by emerging literacy. As the descriptor *emergent* suggests, a desire to write and read is manifested at a very early age, and at this age children need not be formally taught reading and writing. Indeed, formal instruction during the preschool years may have a negative effect on the emergence of early literacy pursuits. However, this early desire to write and read should be supported and nurtured. As the term indicates, once literacy skills emerge, they do not cease to grow; they continue to progress throughout an individual's life.

Despite general agreement among educators regarding the concept of emergent literacy, the relationship between the reading skill level of children in the primary grades and the type of reading instruction that should be provided continues to be a source of disagreement. At times, the debate over instructional methods has been characterized as hostile. The instructional theories proposed by some educators have beginning readers in mind and include specific strategies for teaching fundamental skills to these children. Other approaches attach little or no importance to individual difference in skill level and are intended for all children. A corollary to this conflict is the observation that a majority of reading research has involved children who, in spite of being in second or third grade, have skills very similar to beginning readers. In contrast, many reading educators who write about reading instruction disregard the distinction between poor readers and good readers or between beginning and mature readers and have the entire population of children in mind. These differences in target population result in recommendations that are mutually disagreeable to those who stress skills instruction for beginning readers and those who focus on literacy appreciation for more mature readers.

The following example illustrates this controversy. In 1997, the U.S. Congress established the National Reading Panel (NRP) and commissioned it to conduct a thorough study of the research and knowledge relevant to early reading development and instruction. The NRP published its findings in 2000 and one of the many conclusions it presented was that its review of research showed that systematic **phonics** instruction makes a more significant contribution to children's growth in reading than do alternative programs. Some educators, however, have expressed dissatisfaction with the panel's recommendations. Yatvin (2000), a member of the panel herself, criticized the NRP's findings by stating that the panel tried to set higher standards for research, comparable to those used in medical research. She added that the panel did not address the fact that such research is applied to the treatment of disease or deficiency, not to the processes of typical, healthy development, which for most children characterizes learning to read. In fact, of the 38 studies the NRP reviewed, 65% dealt with children with reading problems and 27% involved children who were described as having a reading disability. The general conclusion arrived at by the NRP, therefore, is heavily based on children with reading difficulties, whereas Yatvin's comment about the NRP report is that it should include all children regardless of their reading skill. When reading teachers read reports by committees and articles, they must be aware of the skill level and maturity of the students for whom the recommendations are made.

Do All Children Acquire Reading Skills at the Same Rate?

To say that there are noticeable differences in the rate at which children acquire literacy skills is to state the obvious. What is not so self-evident is that children fail to make progress for different reasons. Some young children learn to read and write spontaneously, very much like the way they learn to speak. Other children learn these skills with some effort under parental and teacher guidance. Still others find it extremely difficult to learn to read in spite of strenuous efforts by teachers. In today's American education circles, children who fail to acquire reading and writing skills despite having no other impairments are considered to have a "reading disability." In contrast, children who lag behind in acquiring all cognitive skills, including reading, are described as "slow learners." Such a distinction is difficult to maintain and does not have much instructional utility. Research has failed to demonstrate a distinction in reading-related processes between children diagnosed with a reading disability and those who are considered slow learners. For instance, both groups have deficiencies in phonological skills, which result in difficulties with decoding and spelling.

The fact that some children find it difficult to learn to read was observed and reported by European physicians as early as the latter part of the 19th century. Physicians were the first to study and write about reading disabilities because reading was considered primarily a **visual process**; therefore, the ophthalmologist was the first professional to be consulted when a child was having difficulty reading. In 1896, British physician Pringle Morgan published a report in a medical journal about a 14-year-old healthy boy, Percy, who was referred to him by the boy's teacher because he had failed to learn to read in spite of many years of schooling. In his report, Morgan noted that Percy could not read even common monosyllabic words and at times could not spell his own name correctly. However, his oral language skills were good, and his teacher thought that he would have been the smartest lad in the school had the instruction been entirely oral. Percy experienced no difficulty in math and was able to correctly solve algebraic problems. For want of a better term, Morgan called Percy's condition **congenital word blindness**, which indicated that the problem was an inborn condition. Soon, many other reports like Morgan's appeared in medical journals both in the United Kingdom and the United States. Influenced by their professional background, physicians tended to explain this type of reading difficulty in neurological terms, modeling their reports after those of adult neurological patients who had lost their ability to read due to stroke.

Inspection of educational journals published in the United States during the late 19th century and early 20th century reveals that few articles of that period made reference to reading difficulties in children. The focus of educational research at that time was on the details of the reading process and identifying the most effective methods of teaching reading. The situation, however, began to slowly change in the late 1920s, when educators began to study and write about reading difficulties in children (e.g., Bronner, 1917; Fernald & Keller, 1921). Even though the nature of these difficulties resembled those in the situation described by Pringle Morgan, many educators chose to explain these difficulties in educational terms. An example is a report by Gates (1929), who gave detailed case histories of eight children and attributed their difficulties to deficiency in word analysis and phonetic analysis.

The development of **standardized tests** in the 1920s not only confirmed the reality of reading difficulties in children but also gave a reasonably accurate picture of the prevalence of reading difficulties. Over time, two opposing viewpoints emerged for explaining the source of reading disabilities, with physicians favoring constitutional etiology and educators preferring psychological, sociological, and linguistic factors. In spite of these differences of opinion, it came to be recognized that reading skills varied dramatically among children and that individual differences in reading achievement were to be expected.

During the later part of the 20th century, widespread public recognition of reading difficulties emerged. Important milestones in this development were the coining of the term *learning disabilities* by Samuel Kirk (1963) and the subsequent official endorsement of the condition by the government through the Education for All Handicapped Children Act of 1975 (PL 94-142). As a consequence of these developments, difficulties in learning to read came to be recognized as a legitimate topic of educational investigation. In its 1983 report titled *A Nation at Risk*, the National Commission on Excellence in Education noted that the literacy skills of American youth were very poor and that nearly 13% of all 17-year-olds could be considered functionally illiterate.

Concern about children's reading accomplishment has become quite intense in recent years. With the advancement of technology, it has come to be realized that "the U.S. economy demands a universally higher level of literacy achievement than at any prior period in history and that literacy demands are likely to increase in the future" (RAND Reading Study Group, 2001, p. 3). Realizing that the reading levels of schoolchildren remained stagnant during the later half of the 20th century (nearly 20% of elementary school children in the United States cannot read at a basic level, and nearly 60% read below the proficiency level; National Assessment of Educational Progress, 1995), the federal government, state governments, and some private agencies have investigated children's literacy acquisition and literacy instruction in schools.

Regardless of the controversy that prevails among educators and researchers about reading education, one thing is clear: There is a great deal of difference in the rate at which children acquire reading skills, and this results in a striking variability in children's reading skills. Nearly one out of five children in the classroom may need special help from a reading teacher to attain satisfactory levels of literacy. This poses the greatest challenge for the professional reading teacher.

What Factors Influence the Acquisition of Literacy Skills?

A knowledge of the factors that promote and impede literacy acquisition is essential for teachers who wish to accelerate students' acquisition of literacy skills and to help those who are lagging behind to move forward. No single factor is responsible for children's acquisition of literacy skills or for their failure; rather, a variety of factors contributes to children's literacy development. The following section presents the most salient of these factors. The model of reading set forth in this text, known as the Component Model of Reading, is useful for organizing the factors that influence the acquisition of literacy skills into a coherent format. The theoretical framework on which this reading model is based is derived from the following works: Aaron, 1995; Aaron, 1997; Aaron and Kotva, 1999; Gough and Tunmer, 1986; and Joshi and Aaron, 2000.

The Component Model of Reading

In the context of this reading model, a component is defined as an elementary and independent process that operates on other internal cognitive processes (Sternberg, 1985). What qualifies a cognitive process as a component is its elemental nature and its independence from other mental processes. An example of an elementary operation of the reading process is decoding written words. The independent status of a process can be evaluated by subjecting it to the criterion of double dissociation. One analogy that can be used to explain the dissociation concept is the functioning of the automobile, which has several components: the fuel system, the electrical system, the transmission system, and so on. Each of these components is independent from the other components because one of these components can break down, leaving the others intact. When a component, regardless of what it is, fails to function normally, the automobile is disabled. Likewise, a child will read poorly if any of the components of reading, such as decoding or comprehension, fails to develop typically.

There is overall agreement that at the cognitive level, reading is made up of at least two components: decoding and linguistic comprehension. Fluency, or speed of reading, is claimed by some researchers to be yet another component, but its independent status is not clearly established. The implications of the componential nature of reading is that one component can develop at a typical rate while the other component, independent of the first, lags behind. For example, a child might fail to develop optimal decoding skills yet show typical listening comprehension skill; another child's decoding skills might develop typically but listening comprehension may lag. As a result, there are four different kinds of readers: those who have impaired decoding skills but typical linguistic comprehension; those who have typical decoding skills but poor linguistic comprehension; those who have impairments in both decoding and comprehension skills; and those who have satisfactory decoding and comprehension skills. Apart from these cognitive factors, there are also extrinsic factors that can hold back the acquisition of literacy skills.

Factors influencing the acquisition of literacy skills are organized into three domains within the Component Model. These three domains are

1. The cognitive domain
2. The psychological domain
3. The ecological domain

Although the cognitive domain satisfies the two requirements of a component— elemental nature and independence from other cognitive processes—the other two domains do not satisfy these requirements nearly as well. Nevertheless, the Component Model provides a framework for teachers to navigate their course through various assessment decisions and meet the instructional needs of the children in their classroom. The Component Model is used here as a means of coherently organizing the several factors that affect literacy development. The important thing to remember is that students can fail to acquire satisfactory levels of literacy skills because of deficiency in any component in one of these three domains. It follows, then, that in order to enable students to attain satisfactory literacy skills, the deficient area must first be identified and then remedial instruction targeting the deficient area implemented. A study by Catts, Hogan, and Fey (2003) demonstrated the success of such an approach. The three domains of the Component Model of Reading and their constituent components are shown in Figure 1.1.

The Cognitive Domain

The initial idea of the componential nature of reading comes from a proposal by Gough and Tunmer (1986) in the form of a simple mathematical formula:

$$RC = D \times LC$$

RC = reading comprehension, D = decoding of the printed word, and LC = linguistic comprehension (in this case, listening comprehension). This means that decoding and comprehension are two components of the cognitive module of reading.

According to Gough and Tunmer, if D = 0, then RC = 0. Likewise, if LC = 0, RC = 0. That is, if a child's decoding skill is zero, his or her reading comprehension is zero; if a child's listening comprehension is zero, his or her reading comprehension is also zero. In other words, a child who cannot decode the printed word cannot read and understand, and a child who cannot listen and understand also cannot read and understand. The model formula as used in this textbook is slightly modified from the one shown above. The modified formula is RC = WR × LC, where RC = reading comprehension, WR = word recognition, and LC = listening comprehension. The difference between the modified formula and the original one proposed by Gough and Tunmer is that **word recognition** replaces **decoding.**

Word Recognition

Word recognition (WR) is made up of two subprocesses: decoding and instant word reading (sight word reading). After a child's decoding skills reach a certain level, recognition of familiar words becomes fast and automatic, a skill also referred to as sight word reading. This text uses the term *instant word reading* instead of *sight word reading* because the latter term implies that visual processes are mainly responsible for quick recognition of the written word. However, studies show that phonological skills play a major role in decoding, which is a precursor to instant word reading (Ehri, 1998). In other words, whereas a few words can be

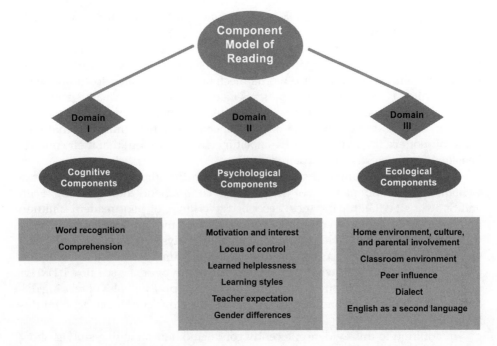

Figure 1.1. The Component Model of Reading.

read by using visual memory, a large sight vocabulary depends on well-developed decoding skills. Visual memory has a limited capacity, perhaps not exceeding a few hundred words, yet a mature reader can recognize more than 80,000 words instantly. Obviously, the instant recognition of this many words cannot be accomplished by visual memory alone.

Comprehension

Comprehension is a generic term that includes both listening comprehension and reading comprehension. Studies have shown that these two types of comprehension are highly correlated and that they are mediated by the same cognitive mechanisms (Jahandire, 1999).

The validity of the original simple view of reading was demonstrated by Hoover and Gough (1990) in a study of 254 bilingual (English-Spanish) elementary school children. The investigators found that a substantial proportion of the **variance** in reading comprehension was accounted for by the product of decoding and listening comprehension (first grade, 71%; second grade, 72%; third grade, 83%; fourth grade, 82%). Subsequent studies by other researchers showed that decoding and listening comprehension do not make an equal contribution to reading comprehension at all grade levels; decoding makes a greater contribution in first and second grades, whereas comprehension makes a greater contribution in the upper grades (Rupley, Willson, & Nichols, 1998).

Independence of Word Recognition and Comprehension

The independence of word recognition and comprehension is also supported by studies from neuropsychology (Marshall & Newcombe, 1973) and developmental psychology (Frith & Snowling, 1983). For instance, in Marshall and Newcombe's study, some patients with stroke misread the word *father* as "dad" and *garden* as "flower," which indicated that their comprehension was relatively intact but that their decoding skills were impaired. The converse pattern was seen in other patients, who tended to pronounce words mechanically but failed to comprehend their meaning. For example, these patients read the word *sale* as "Sally" and *listen* as "Liston." When asked what these words meant, they answered that it was the name of a girl and the name of a boxer, respectively, which indicated that they could pronounce the written words—albeit mechanically—but that their comprehension of these words was impaired.

Likewise, developmental studies have shown that the ability to pronounce written words is independent of the ability to comprehend their meaning. Frith and Snowling (1983), for instance, described two kinds of poor readers: children with average or above average IQ who can understand spoken language quite well but have difficulty with written language (i.e., dyslexia) and some children with **autism** who are precocious readers and can sound out written words but cannot comprehend well what they have read (i.e., hyperlexia; see Box 1.1). Hyperlexia and dyslexia are often considered to occupy opposite poles of reading difficulty. Thus, these two conditions show that reading difficulties can arise for different reasons.

In addition to this evidence, recently conducted neuroimaging studies show that decoding and comprehension tasks activate different parts of the brain, indicating that there are separate neurological substrates for decoding and comprehension processes (Shaywitz, Mody, & Shaywitz, 2006). What is relevant from an educational perspective is that assessment of the components of cognitive domain and instruction that targeted the weak component produces improvement in children's literacy skills (Aaron, 1995; Aaron, 1997; Aaron, Joshi, Boulware-Gooden, & Bentum, in press; Aaron & Kotva, 1999; Joshi & Aaron, 2000).

Data from genetic studies also add to the evidence that word recognition and comprehension are independent processes. Keenan, Betjemann, Wadsworth, DeFries, and Olson (2006) reported that their genetic study of dyslexia in identical

---

Box 1.1. **The syndrome of hyperlexia**

The **syndrome** of hyperlexia is a developmental disability in which children show extraordinary word recognition skill in conjunction with very poor comprehension. Hyperlexia is marked by three features: 1) learning to read words at 3 or 4 years of age in the absence of formal instruction, 2) exhibiting compulsive behavior and rituals when reading words, and 3) comprehending both written and spoken language very poorly. Frequently, but not always, this condition is associated with autism.

There are also some precocious children who can decode written material very well and also comprehend it quite well. Teachers should be careful not to mistake these precocious readers as having hyperlexia. Hyperlexia is marked by extreme deficiency in comprehension of both spoken and written language, and for this reason, very young children with good decoding skills should have their comprehension assessed. As with dyslexia, hyperlexia can vary in severity.

and fraternal twins showed that there is substantial and significant genetic influence on individual differences in both reading and listening comprehension. In this study, word recognition and listening comprehension each accounted for significant, independent genetic influences on reading comprehension.

As noted at the beginning of this chapter, reading fluency and vocabulary knowledge are two important correlates of reading skills. Nevertheless, they are not accorded status as components in the Component Model of Reading.

Fluency

As noted previously, some researchers consider the speed with which written words are named, known as fluency (a correlate of instant word reading), to be a factor independent of decoding skill (e.g., Bowers & Newby-Clark, 2002; Wolf, Goldberg, Cirino, Morris, & Lovett, 2002). Although the importance of speed of processing information is well recognized, its independent nature has not been settled. In a recent study that analyzed data collected from more than a thousand 5- to 10-year-old children, Konold, Juel, McKinnon, and Deffes (2003) reported that **processing speed,** along with vocabulary knowledge, made independent contributions to reading. However, other studies have indicated that speed of processing contributes only a negligible amount of independent variance to reading comprehension. This likely is so because instant word recognition is closely associated with reading speed, and instant word recognition is accomplished by processing the written word automatically and at a very fast rate (Adlof, Catts, Hogan, & Little, 2005; Cho & McBride-Chang, 2005; Hawelka & Wimmer, 2005). This makes it difficult to separate reading speed from instant word recognition ability and assign speed an independent status. For instance, can a child who is a fluent reader be a poor decoder? Conversely, can a child who is a poor decoder be a fluent reader? Neither possibility is likely. Vukovic and Siegel (2005) investigated the independent nature of fluency and concluded that the existence of poor readers who are deficient in naming speed but not in decoding has not been documented. This means that fluency marks a stage in which the reader has developed from a plodding decoder into a swift instant word recognizer. Instant word recognition and speed of reading, therefore, are not treated as two different components in the Component Model.

So, what is the final word on fluency? When children begin to read, they tend to focus on letters and **syllables** rather than on words in order to decode. By about the third grade, they are able to process bigger chunks of words and identify words instantly and automatically. Once children become instant word readers, they become fluent readers. When they reach this phase, they do not have to invest attention in decoding words but can focus on the meaning of the text. The ability to read words instantly and effortlessly, therefore, is a prerequisite for good reading comprehension. In one study, Vaessen, Gerretsen, and Blomert (2007) studied Dutch children in order to evaluate the "double-deficit **hypothesis,**" which states that poor readers have deficits in two different areas: decoding and naming speed. After testing 162 children with dyslexia, the investigators found that nearly 90% of the slow readers also had decoding difficulties and concluded their results do not support the double-deficit hypothesis.

The results of the previously mentioned studies should not be taken to mean that speed of processing is unimportant. The fact that fluency and fluency training have received much instructional attention underscores the important role fluency plays in reading instruction. Teachers should provide abundant opportunities for children to read, which will increase their fluency.

Vocabulary Knowledge

Whether vocabulary knowledge is independent of reading comprehension is a question similar to that of reading speed and decoding. That is, can a child have limited vocabulary knowledge but still have good comprehension? Though **vocabulary knowledge** is essential for comprehension, the precise relationship between the two is not well understood. Reflecting on this issue, Beck, McKeown, and Omanson (1987) asked, "are people good comprehenders because they know a lot of words, or do people know a lot of words because they are good comprehenders" (p. 147).

Attention

Yet another ability, the capacity to maintain consistent, sustained attention, also facilitates reading performance. But is attention independent of reading skills so as to be considered an independent component? Similar to fluency and vocabulary, attention is not considered a component of reading. That is, can children with limited reading skills attend to the text they are reading, and can children who have difficulty attending do well on tasks of text comprehension? Even though this question cannot be answered satisfactorily at this point, clearly there is an intimate relationship between reading performance and sustained attention. In addition, it is clear that children pay attention to materials they find interesting and fail to maintain attention when they find the reading material difficult or uninteresting. Research indicates that inconsistent attention can contribute to poor performance on reading tests and, conversely, that poor word recognition skills can make the reader's attention wander (Aaron, Joshi, Palmer, Smith, & Kirby, 2002). Simple techniques for differentiating reading difficulties caused by decoding deficits from reading difficulties caused by inconsistent attention are described in Chapter 9. Strategies for improving the reader's attention are also presented in that chapter.

Instructional Implications of the Component Model of Reading's Cognitive Components

As stated previously, reading performance is influenced by many factors, some cognitive in nature and others psychological or environmental. Although classroom teachers can influence the cognitive factors and, to a lesser degree, some psychological factors that mediate reading, some of the environmental factors will be beyond their influence. However, being aware of the source of students' poor reading performance—whether it is cognitive, psychological, or environmental—can help teachers understand the nature of the reading problems. With respect to the cognitive features of the Component Model, teachers have three functions to perform:

1. With typically achieving children, make certain that all components are functioning optimally, and nurture and foster associated skills during regular classroom instruction.

2. When a child encounters difficulty in learning to read, first identify which component(s) is the source of reading difficulty.

3. Design instructional procedures specifically aimed at improving the efficiency of the weak component.

The Psychological Domain

The psychological domain of the Component Model contains several components: motivation and interest, **locus of control,** learned helplessness, learning styles, teacher expectation, teacher quality, and gender differences. Many of these factors have been developed as theoretical concepts, and the tools that have been designed to assess them vary in reliability and validity. Teacher observation and judgment, therefore, are important in evaluating the role that psychological variables play in children's literacy acquisition. Based on their observation and judgment, teachers can adapt their literacy instruction to lead to optimal outcomes.

Motivation and Interest

Wittrock (1986) defined *motivation* as the process of initiating, sustaining, and directing one's own activity. Motivation leads children to read, and reading becomes an alluring activity when children find it interesting. Psychologists classify motivation broadly as extrinsic or intrinsic. External factors that motivate children to read are rewards, such as gold stars and verbal praise from the teacher. Intrinsic motivation comes from within the child; the child is motivated to read because of the satisfaction it brings. External rewards are difficult to administer consistently with a large classroom of children. Furthermore, external rewards may backfire when they are not continuously and consistently delivered. For example, in a study of kindergarteners (Deci, Koestner, & Ryan, 1999), one group of children was given rewards for drawing with crayons, an activity that very young children do naturally. Another group of kindergarten children, the control group, did not receive any rewards for playing with crayons. After a month, the experimenter stopped rewarding the first group of children. Not surprisingly, there was a significant drop in the drawing activities of the children in this group, which demonstrates that internal motivation provides a more reliable incentive for activities such as reading and writing than external rewards. As much as possible, teachers should try to make use of children's internal motivation rather than rely on external rewards for cultivating good reading habits. It should be noted, however, that other studies show that extrinsic rewards have a complex relationship with motivation and may not operate as "killers" of internal motivation (Cameron & Pierce, 1994).

How can teachers motivate children to be interested in learning literacy skills? There are four principles teachers must keep in mind when attempting to increase children's motivation for engaging in literacy-related activities. They are

- Interest
- Need
- Value
- Goal

Interest   Children should come to understand that interesting stories are hidden behind the "scribbles" in a book and that one can discover these stories by reading them. Teachers can foster this understanding by reading stories aloud to children, particularly those with characters and story lines with which children can empathize. In his simple but highly useful book *Best Books for Building Literacy for Elementary School Children*, Thomas Gunning (2000) offers brief descriptions of a selection of **read-aloud books** featuring characters or events with which children can readily identify. For example, Eric Carle's (1987) book *Have You Seen My Cat?* is about a boy searching for his lost cat. Teachers can interest children in the story by asking how many children have cats or dogs at home, how they would feel if the pet got lost, and what they would do to find it. A useful source for selecting books according to reading level and content, in addition to Gunning's book, is *The Read-Aloud Handbook* by Jim Trelease (1989). Every year, the October issue of *Reading Teacher* also publishes lists of books preferred by children and teachers.

Gunning (2000) suggested that the read-aloud practice meet three conditions:

1. Children must see the value in reading.

2. They should see that reading brings enjoyment and satisfaction.

3. The book chosen should be one that children would want to read themselves and feel confident in doing so.

Other principles to be observed in reading aloud include setting up a purpose for listening, drawing children's attention to the pictures and illustrations in the book during reading, and asking questions and leading a discussion during and after reading. It is also important to set a fixed time of about 20 minutes during the day for reading aloud so that children learn to look forward to this time. Additional information about read-aloud books and how to make use of them can be found by accessing http://www.trelease-on-reading.com (look under "The Treasury" of read-alouds).

Other means of motivating readers recommended by Gunning are doing cooperative group activities, participating in book discussions, voting for favorite authors, and participating in on-line chats with authors. The class can also be divided into groups to read books, then retell the stories they have read to the entire class. Children can write their own "stories," which can be assembled and made into books with their own names printed as the authors. Although children in kindergarten and early first grade may not be able to write much on their own, they can draw pictures and perhaps write their own first name for their books. A computer can be used to decorate the books. All of these activities can increase children's interest in books and motivate them to read.

Need   A powerful motivating factor in learning to read is need, or seeing the necessity for reading and writing. Scholars of linguistic history believe that during prehistoric times, most spoken and written languages developed to fulfill the immediate needs of the society. Some 2,000 years before the Christian era, Sumerians found that human memory was inadequate to store information about the numerous trading activities that were transacted in their society. A better means of storage, therefore, became a necessity, and writing emerged as a device to fulfill this need. It is not unreasonable to conclude that when children feel a need to communicate, they will be interested in learning how to read and write. As much as possible, the need-based tasks chosen to motivate children should be authentic.

Some principles should be observed in motivating children to read and write:

• Literacy tasks and activities should be authentic and meaningful for children. These include activities such as writing letters to friends, parents, and even the classroom teacher; reading recipes and making simple foods following the instructions; and writing in journals for personal reflection. Children can also be encouraged to communicate with one another through writing. Children with keyboarding skills can use e-mail for this purpose.

- An activity will be motivating to children if it is challenging but not beyond their skill.

- Students should be given some degree of autonomy in choosing the literacy task.

- Students should not be evaluated rigidly for their performance on literacy tasks that are designed to motivate reluctant readers.

- A supportive atmosphere enables students to ask questions and the teacher to provide encouragement to keep children attentive to the tasks they have chosen to accomplish (Tracey & Morrow, 1998).

We implemented a project called "Drop everything and write" in a fourth-grade classroom (Joshi, Aaron, Dean, & Rupley, in press). For 20 minutes each day, children were asked to communicate with their classmates through written notes; no talking was allowed during this period. At the beginning of the project, children were reluctant to write notes to one another, but toward the end of the semester they felt more comfortable as they got used to writing. There was a comparison group in which written communication was not imposed and children were allowed to talk with one another. Pre- and posttests showed that the reading skills of the treatment group improved significantly when compared to that of the control group and that they used more words and wrote in longer and grammatically more complex sentences than they did at the beginning of the study. The "Drop everything and write" technique is similar to the dialogue journals described by Bode (1989), Isaakson, (1992), and Wollman-Bonilla (1989).

Here are some additional ideas for creating a need for children to read and write:

- Establish pen pal dyads. A pen pal need not be outside the classroom; he or she could be a classmate or even the teacher.

- Set up class dramas, in which each child is given a simple script that he or she has to read, memorize, and use during the staging of the play.

- Ask children to complete a project such as constructing a map, executing a drawing, or assembling a model by reading and following written instructions.

These projects should be adjusted to match children's reading skills.

Value   Children will readily see the value in being able to read and write when they are able to communicate with one another through writing or reading stories on their own. They will also enjoy a sense of accomplishment when their own "stories" are assembled into small books.

Goal   In collaboration with the teacher, children can set up literacy goals, such as writing one letter per week, reading one book in a month, or assembling a toy following instructions. Goals could be set up for all of the activities described in this section. Setting up such goals creates a need for communication.

Locus of Control and Learned Helplessness

The two psychological concepts of locus of control and learned helplessness are closely related. Rotter (1966), who introduced the concept of locus of control into the psychological literature, classified it into two discrete categories, external and internal. When an individual feels that events in his or her life are the result of chance, luck, or fate or are under the control of others, he or she feels that the location of control is outside his or her person. When an individual feels that outcomes are the consequences of his or her own actions, the locus is said to be internal. This variable is believed to have significant influence on children's behavior. For instance, Coleman and his co-researchers (1966) studied almost half a million children and found that a belief that they have no control over their future was a major correlate of low school achievement.

Reliance on factors such as chance, luck, and fate can produce inconsistent outcomes and, often, failure. Continued failure can lead to learned helplessness. In one of his experiments, Seligman (1975) placed dogs in a confined area and randomly administered electric shocks. The shocks were administered again and again, and there was no way for the dogs to escape or avoid the shock. Later, when the dogs were given an opportunity to escape the shock by moving only a short distance, none of the dogs did so. They had given up and had learned to be helpless. Cognitive psychologists have theorized that when children are punished repeatedly or experience failure again and again, they begin to think that things are beyond their control and that no matter what they do, nothing is going to change. Thus, they learn to be helpless. This can lead to a lack of interest and effort by children. In the long term, they expect to not succeed and then fulfill their own prophecy by failing.

An instructional strategy that can help students avoid learned helplessness is changing the instructional environment from ego-involving situations to task-involving situations. An ego-involving situation is governed by notions such as capacity, competition, grades, and success or failure. In contrast, a task-involving situation is characterized by factors such as interest, cooperation, team performance, and goal achievement. Studies show that in ego-involving situations, students who perceive themselves as having low ability are unlikely to seek assistance because they see help-seeking as evidence of their own weakness. In contrast, the same students freely seek assistance in task-involving situations because they view help-seeking as a demonstration of their effort to accomplish the task.

How can teachers help children develop self-confidence and take control of their own learning? The best thing teachers can do is to create opportunities for all children to be successful. They can adjust assignments to the ability of each child, for instance, by decreasing the number of words to be spelled or by providing additional time to complete assignments. Tasks may be set up in such a way that children see them not as occasions for competing among themselves or as pass/fail situations but as a means of determining whether they have mastered the relevant basic skills.

Learning Styles

The term *learning style* describes a learner's disposition that interacts with certain environmental factors to produce optimal learning. It refers to reasonably stable patterns of behavior that indicate learning preferences. According to Carbo (1983) and Dunn (2000), who are leading proponents of designing instruction around learning styles, there are four dimensions of learning styles: cognitive, affective, physiological, and psychological. The cognitive component includes factors such as cognitive style (e.g., impulsive versus reflective) and **modality preferences** (e.g., auditory versus visual). The affective component includes personality characteristics such as anxiety level, expectancy, and level of motivation. The physiological component includes gender differences, daily rhythms (e.g., morning versus afternoon person), and dominant brain hemisphere (left brained versus right brained). The psychological component includes factors such as self-concept, locus of control, and sociability (e.g., loner versus a group person). Because the idea of matching the method of instruction with learning style is intuitively appealing, the notion of learning style has received much attention. For instance, take the cognitive component of modality preference. Some learners are described as auditory learners, some as visual learners. This means that there are differences among children in their preferences for one modality over the other in the way they receive information, and for an optimal outcome instruction should match these modality preferences. That is, information should be presented in auditory form to auditory learners and in visual form to visual learners. The auditory/visual modality preference is also linked to cerebral processes, as auditory learners are considered to be left brained and visual learners to be right brained. Advocates of learning styles claim that reading achievement improves significantly when reading programs match individual learning styles.

There are several problems associated with the concept of learning styles. One is that there are no reliable instruments to assess children's learning styles. For instance, even if the concept of left-brained and right-brained learning has scientific validity, it is not an easy matter to decide who is left brained and who is right brained. Simple questionnaires developed by learning style advocates do not effectively distinguish the two; it requires sophisticated neuroimaging techniques. Furthermore, the two conditions—right brained and left brained—are not mutually exclusive. All children, as well as adults, use both sides of their brains to carry out mental activities.

A second difficulty with learning styles is that is it not easy to determine whether a child is an auditory learner or a visual learner. If teachers match reading instruction with auditory/visual modality differences, they will be teaching some children only by using visual aids and other children only by talking to them. However, it is known that optimal learning occurs when *all* the modalities are utilized. Literacy instruction via multisensory learning makes use of this principle.

In spite of the many claims made by advocates of learning styles, research findings on the effectiveness of matching teaching with children's learning styles are not compelling. Some researchers (e.g., Cronbach & Snow, 1977; Stahl, 1988) have found no evidence of useful interactions between student preferences and instructional treatments. Adams (1990) cited eight separate reviews of the literature, all of which concluded that matching beginning reading methods to different learning styles is not a solution to reading difficulties. The notion that teaching children through their preferred modality improves reading has also not proven to be true (Kavale & Forness, 1987). As Johnston and Allington (1991) wrote, "Individualized remedial instruction differentiated on the basis of learning style has received no more support than that based on modality preferences, though it continues to receive considerable popular press" (p. 994). Finally, it would be physically impossible to accommodate the many varieties of learning styles that might exist in a classroom. For instance, how should teachers accommodate "morning" children and "afternoon" children?

Learning style is not to be confused with individual differences in children. Children do differ in family background, in the first language and dialects they use, in interests, in ability level, and in anxiety level.

Are there any lessons to be learned from the concept of learning styles and individual differences? Following are some suggestions for dealing with these differences:

- Children in the early elementary grades need a lot of hands-on activities and learn best when they can move around freely. Therefore, classrooms should be structured so that small-group activities and class projects can be conducted in designated areas.

- Some children with autistic traits have difficulty in retaining auditory information, such as the names of letters of the alphabet. Such children have been observed to learn better when written words are associated with pictures. Once these children have learned whole words, they find it easier to identify the letters in these words. Eventually, the letters of the alphabet can be introduced to these children.

- All children benefit when they can see, hear, and talk about the literacy materials being used in a lesson. This is the multisensory instructional foundation of teaching literacy skills.

Teacher Expectation

The concept of teacher expectation refers to inferences teachers make about students' future behavior and achievement, based on what the teachers know about the students at present (Good & Brophy, 1994). These expectations affect student outcomes because teachers, either consciously or unconsciously, tend to behave according to their expectations, and students tend to respond accordingly and fulfill these expectations. Teacher expectations can work in two ways: They may be positive or they may be adverse. Expectations come from different sources, such as teachers' lounge conversations ("I feel sorry for you; Johnny will be coming to you next year"); students' physical appearance (clean and well-groomed versus sloppy and poorly dressed), students' ethnicity, students' dialect, and gender differences. These expectations are formed early in the academic year, sometimes on the very first day of class and sometimes even before that if teachers have been discussing students. Once teachers form expectations of their students, they may expect the students to sustain the behavior that fits the expectations and fail to note any changes in the students. Although teachers may not be conscious of their expectations and behavior toward students, their behavior nevertheless communicates these expectations to students. Some examples of teacher behavior resulting from expectations are shown in Box 1.2. In this box, *high-expectation students (HES)* refers to students for whom the teacher has high expectations and *low-expectation students (LES)* to students for whom the teacher has low expectations.

Children pick up teachers' subtle cues and conform to their expectations. Although it is unavoidable that teachers will form expectations, being aware that they exist can help teachers change their behavior, if necessary. Teachers can incorporate the following ideas proposed by Good and Brophy (1994) to minimize the negative effects of their expectations of students. (Also see Box 1.2.)

Box 1.2.   Teacher behavior that reflects preformed expectations

1.   Giving less time to LES to answer questions.
2.   Asking HES more questions than LES; calling on LES less often.
3.   Using inappropriate reinforcement; giving high praise to LES even when they answer simple questions correctly; overpraising minor successes.
4.   Demanding less from LES.
5.   Praising, recognizing, and acknowledging LES less often.
6.   Responding to failures of LES with pity and sympathy.
7.   Showing less acceptance of ideas from LES.
8.   Failing to give feedback to LES as to why their answer was not correct.
9.   Accepting low-quality and even wrong answers from LES.
10. Exhibiting less smiling and other friendly interactive gestures with LES.
11. Making less eye contact with LES.
12. Seating LES farther from the teacher's desk.

From Good, Thomas L. & Jere E. Brophy *Looking In Classrooms*, 10/e; Published by Allyn and Bacon, Boston, MA. Copyright © 2008 by Pearson Education. Adapted by permission of the publisher.

- Be aware that expectations of others are formed, often unconsciously, and that this does influence one's behavior.
- Keep expectations for individual students current by monitoring their progress closely; be flexible enough to alter expectations.
- Place more importance on current performance than on past performance.
- Set flexible goals on an individual basis.
- Stress the continual progress of each child rather than how he or she compares to the rest of the class.
- Emphasize feedback rather than pass/fail evaluation.
- Recognize and reward students for real progress, not trivial attainments.

Teacher Quality

According to Tuerk (2005), who has addressed the issue of teacher quality with reference to the No Child Left Behind Act of 2001 (PL 107-110), studies show a statistically significant and substantial relationship between measures of teacher quality and student achievement. Although educators generally agree that teachers are the most important determinant of student achievement, there is little agreement on what is meant by teacher quality (Berry, Hoke, & Hirsch, 2004). One view of teacher quality holds that teaching is a complex skill requiring formal, specialized preparation; another view is that intelligent people with adequate subject matter background knowledge can perform as good teachers. Those who support the first position note that subject matter knowledge is necessary but not sufficient; teachers must also demonstrate a professional level of skills in classroom management, development of lessons that meet standards, student assessment, interpretation of test scores, teaching of children with special needs, student motivation, and utilization of technology for teaching. The report of the National Commission on Teaching and America's Future (2003) emphasized teacher education, state licensing, professional accountability, and compensation as strategies to enhance teacher quality.

Those who de-emphasize teacher preparation argue that many teachers know *how* to teach but not *what* to teach. Research shows that student poverty and geography are associated with differential access to highly qualified teachers and that this differential access is associated with student performance on achievement tests (Tuerk, 2005).

These observations show that a sound knowledge base is essential for competent teaching. This would include an understanding of the following:

- Sound grasp of the basic principles of the psychology of reading
- Understanding of **linguistics** directly related to literacy
- Appreciation of the psychology of students and learning

Gender Differences

Whether boys and girls differ in literacy and mathematical abilities is a question that has interested educators and psychologists for a number of years. As early as 1917, British physician Hinshelwood reported that more boys than girls had reading difficulties. This gender difference was observed by many other investigators over the past century. Feingold (1993) and Hedges and Nowell (1995) reported that girls read, write, and spell better than boys and that more boys have reading and other language-related problems, such as stuttering. In 1974, Maccoby and Jacklin published the results of their review of more than 2,000 studies of sex differences in their book titled *The Psychology of Sex Differences.* They concluded that gender differences had been observed in four areas: verbal ability, mathematical ability, spatial ability, and physical aggression. Girls showed an advantage over boys in verbal ability; boys, on average, were better in math and spatial tasks.

Maccoby and Jacklin's study, however, has been criticized for several reasons. The major criticism is that some of the studies included in the review were weak and, therefore, could have biased the authors' conclusions. However, when Hyde and Linn updated the Maccoby and Jacklin study in 1988, they found that females showed greater verbal ability in 75% of the nearly 165 studies they analyzed. They also found that gender differences were larger for general measures of verbal ability and speech production. It is important to keep in mind, however, that 25% of these studies did not find a gender difference. It also should be noted that these studies were based on statistical averages, and findings do not apply to individual children. There are many boys with superior language ability and many girls who have superior math ability.

After analyzing 46 **meta-analysis** studies, Hyde (2005) proposed the "gender similarities hypothesis," concluding that the genders are more similar than different even though small differences can be found in certain areas, such as mathematics. Within the area of mathematics, some small differences can be seen, with girls being slightly better in computation and boys being slightly better in problem solving. Even in areas of difference, however, developmental factors must be taken into consideration because the differences seen in children of elementary school age are much smaller than those seen in high school students.

Although the final word about gender differences in general abilities in language and mathematics is not yet in, reports of gender differences in reading disabilities are less equivocal. A higher incidence of reading disability in boys is readily seen, although the reason for this is disputed. There are two possible explanations. One is that there are potential cerebral hemispheric differences in the brains of the two sexes. That is, in female brains the language-handling areas are distributed in a diffuse manner in the two hemispheres, whereas in male brains the language areas are limited to the left hemisphere. This means that in females, more area of the brain is allocated to language tasks. There is, however, a trade-off. In the male brain, the area not allocated to language is used for mathematical and spatial abilities. Several clinical studies and some brain imaging studies show some support for this hypothesis. For instance, Clements, Rimrodt, Abel, Blankner, Mostofsky, Pekar, et al. (2006) used functional magnetic resonance imaging to study males and females and found that males had more left **lateralization of the brain** during phonological tasks and showed greater bilateral activity during the visuospatial tasks, whereas females were more right lateralized during the visuospatial tasks. This means males have more brain area allocated for simultaneous functions, such as processing pictures and geometrical patterns, and less area for sequential functions, such as processing **phonemes** in words. That is, instead of processing letters in words, they tend to process words holistically as though they are pictures. Females show the opposite pattern of processing. This conclusion, of course, should be interpreted that the differences between the two sexes in brain functioning are relative and not absolute.

The second explanation for gender differences in reading is an environmental explanation. In U.S. culture, there is a perception that reading, writing, and other literary pursuits are "girlish" interests; math and athletics are considered to be "boyish" interests. Sanders (2002) has pointed out that art, languages, and music are considered feminine subjects in school, whereas math, science, and technology are considered masculine subjects. In addition to general cultural perceptions, it has also been noted that boys who act aggressively and are restless more than girls are likely to attract the attention of teachers more often than girls. This may play a role in the greater number of boys referred for diagnostic evaluation for learning disabilities than girls.

Regardless of the varying viewpoints on the reasons for gender differences in language skills, it must be noted that the average 11th-grade boy writes at the same level as the average 8th-grade girl, and that boys' reading skills are lower than girls' at all grade levels. These data have not changed for the past 30 years (National Center for Education Statistics, 2000, p. 18). (See Box 1.3.)

It should also be pointed out that even though a gender advantage has been reported for boys in math, studies (e.g., Hedges & Nowell, 1995) have shown that girls receive better grades than boys on classroom math tests. They score lower than boys, however, on standardized tests of math achievement. Furthermore, the gender differences in language abilities are not as great now as they were some 20 years ago (Jacklin, 1989).

Why is a knowledge of gender differences important for professional reading teachers? Though the basic principles of motivation and instruction do not differ for boys than for girls, there is a possibility that gender stereotypes relating to literacy skills can influence teachers' expectations and thus affect instructional practice. Research on whether female and male students receive equal attention from instructors dates back to the beginning of the 20th century. In a recent examination of this topic, Jones and Dindia (2004) selected 32 studies for meta-analysis. They

Box 1.3. Do girls have better reading skills than boys?

Since the early 20th century, researchers (e.g., Hinshelwood, 1917) have reported that more boys experience reading difficulties described as dyslexia than girls. The number of elementary-age boys who struggle with reading significantly exceeds the number of girls who experience such difficulties. In a summary report of studies conducted at the University of Colorado examining the role of genetic and environmental factors in reading disability, Olson (2002) reported that when individuals with dyslexia were stratified on the basis of severity of reading impairment and IQ, there were more males than females in the groups with severe reading difficulties. This ratio decreased when the degree of reading difficulty was less severe; nevertheless, there were more males than females at all levels of reading disability. This report was based on 2,690 identical and fraternal twins, among whom at least one in each pair had a reading disability. The report also noted a strong genetic influence on phoneme awareness and word recognition skills. However, it is important to remember that genes do not operate in isolation but interact with an individual's environment to find expression. With favorable environmental conditions and proper remedial instruction, the severity of reading problems could be considerably mitigated.

In a review of the available research literature, Halpern, Benbow, Geary, Gur, Hyde, and Gernsbacher (2007) concluded that there are no simple answers to the complex questions about sex differences in science and math and that biological constraints, early experience, educational policy, and cultural context each have effects. In turn, these effects interact in complex ways.

concluded that although male students are the main participants in total interactions and negative interactions with teachers, teacher–student interactions are shaped by other factors, such as the social climate in the classroom, teachers' sex and race, and student behavior. The best way to avoid such gender-based expectations is to be aware that these studies of gender differences deal with averages and not individuals. That is, teachers cannot look at an individual child and conclude that "he is a boy, so I cannot expect much from him in reading, writing, or spelling" or "she is a girl, so she ought to be a good reader." In every classroom, there are boys who excel in reading and writing as well as girls who outperform boys in math.

What should the professional reading teacher know about gender differences regarding literacy?

- The best way to avoid gender-based expectations is to be aware that results of gender studies deal with averages and not individuals.
- In every classroom, there are boys who excel in reading and writing and there are girls who outperform many boys in math.

The Ecological Domain

The ecological domain of factors influencing literacy acquisition includes environmental factors, such as home environment and culture; dialectal differences; bilingualism; classroom environment; and peer influence. Many of these variables overlap with the psychological domain and thereby interact with other variables to influence instructional outcomes.

Home Environment, Culture, and Parental Involvement

It is known that a vast proportion of the difference in academic achievement seen among students and schools could be explained by the following factors: quantity and quality of reading materials in the home, number of pages read for homework, number of days absent from school, number of hours spent watching television, the educational level of parents, and the presence of two parents in the home. Home environment, of course, is closely related to social class, which some educators feel is more important than school environment for academic achievement. Rothstein (2004) put it this way: "The influence of social-class characteristics is probably so powerful that schools cannot overcome it, no matter how well trained their teachers and no matter how well designed their instructional programs. . . ." (p. 107). Several research studies also indicate a strong relationship between home environment and children's later reading achievement. Typical of these studies is the one reported by Grissmer, Kirby, Berends, and Williamson (1994), who found that students whose parents were not high school graduates scored significantly below students whose parents were college graduates on reading achievement tests. This study also found a relationship between family income and reading achievement. Maternal age was also a factor in reading skill; children of older mothers scored higher in reading.

A study by Molfese and Molfese (2002) supports these findings. These investigators followed 113 children from age 3 through age 10. They classified factors in the home environment into two categories: proximal variables and distal variables. Proximal variables included the availability of learning materials in the home, parent–child communication, parental modeling, and warmth and acceptance. Examples of distal variables are maternal IQ, parental educational level, parental income, and family income. The investigators found significant correlation between both proximal and distal variables, on the one hand, and reading performance of children on the other. Also, environmental measures gathered at preschool age were better predictors of reading scores in elementary grades than such measures obtained during later years.

These observations, however, do not mean that a child born into a family of good education and wealth will automatically be a good reader, nor that a child born into poor circumstances necessarily is destined to fail at reading.

Home environment affects children's reading performance in two ways. One is parental commitment to and involvement in children's learning, demonstrated through such activities as joint storybook reading, playing word games, visiting libraries, and so on. A longitudinal study conducted by Baker, Fernandez-Fein, Scher, and Williams (1998), which surveyed parental activities such as joint book reading, independent reading, playing games involving print, and library visits, found that such home experiences involving print prepared children for learning to read words when they entered school.

The second way home environment can affect children's literacy attainment is the potential difference between the home culture and the school culture. Culture here is used in the broad sense to include parental attitudes and behavior. An instance of discord that can arise due to differences in culture is the dissimilarity that can exist between home and school. These differences may be in child discipline, presence and frequency of literacy activities, how people in the environment relate to one another, and other areas. Imagine a child who spends her first 5 years in a home environment where there are no books, parents do little or no reading, the television is on all day and the child is free to watch as much as she wants, there is no fixed bedtime or eating time, and the child receives little discipline. At age 6, the child enters school, where the classroom is filled with books and other literacy-related materials; reading is an activity many other children are engaged in; there is a fixed timetable for the entire class to follow; and the child has to wait her turn, share materials, and get along with her peers. These two environments—the one in which the child has spent most of her formative years, and the new academic environment with its rules of cooperation and consensus—are markedly different. It is little wonder some children find it difficult to adjust to the classroom environment.

One of the challenging tasks for teachers is to discover what students already know about reading and writing, how they value these activities, whether there are differences between the home and school environments, and how to be sensitive to cultural differences. A number of authors have pointed out the importance of culturally relevant instruction. Philips (1972), for example, reported that Native American children were more comfortable working together in small groups than working alone. Similarly, native Hawaiian children have been found to be responsive to oral reading and cooperative responding, which reportedly enhances their oral language skills and subsequent reading achievement (Au, 1980).

One way to minimize the differences between the school and home is to involve parents, as much as possible, in the instructional processes. Keeping parents informed of children's performance through personal notes or newsletters throughout the year can help keep communication channels open. A letter describing the goals and procedures of the classroom as well as important dates about classroom and school activities can be sent home on the first day of school. Noting that children tend to succeed when schools and families work together to support learning, Neuman (1999) recommended several activities to increase communication and cooperation between school and home and involve parents in their children's education. These activities include homemade books, literacy-related prop boxes, and book clubs. A homemade book is a family album that encourages parent–child–teacher partnerships in literacy activities. Children gather newspaper pictures, family photographs, and their own drawings and paste them on sheets of paper and bind them into an album. Parents are asked to write simple captions under each picture. Children then bring these homemade books to school and read them to their peers in the classroom. In addition to promoting parental involvement, this activity helps children learn about other families and cultures.

Literacy-related prop boxes contain sets of related objects designed to stimulate literacy related to family and cultural interests such as birthdays and vacations. A box might contain written jingles and songs, children's drawings, toys, and other personal artifacts. The box can also contain simple storybooks relating to children's cultures. Parents are asked to be actively involved in the development of the boxes.

According to Neuman (1999), parent–child book clubs are very popular. Once a week, parents visit the school at a designated time and read a book with their child. If parents are unable to attend or cannot read, the classroom teacher, the librarian, or another child can do the reading. Parents are also encouraged to take a book home, read it along with their child, and return the book the following week.

Parent–teacher–child conferences provide another opportunity for involving parents in children's education. Although most conferences are pleasant experiences for both parents and teachers, this is not always the case. Many parents of young children feel frustrated when their child is not making progress at school. This can lead parents to explain away their child's difficulty by rationalizing the problem or denying that anything is wrong. They may blame the difficulty level of the textbooks, the amount of homework assigned, or even the teacher for his "unrealistic" demands or his method of teaching. Teachers should anticipate such encounters.

Teachers can encourage parental cooperation with these strategies:

- Make parents feel that they are part of a team with the teacher, rather than adversaries, with the mutual goal being the welfare of the child.

- Involve parents in projects such as those mentioned earlier—creating homemade books, putting together and using literacy-related prop boxes, and participating in book clubs.

- Hold regular, supportive parent–teacher–child conferences.

Peer Influence

The influence of peers on children's behavior is well recognized in the psychology literature. The term *cohort effect* captures the essence of peer influence. People in general, and young children in particular, are much more influenced by the interests and behaviors that prevail among individuals who are close to them in space and time. Teachers can capitalize on the positive benefits of students' working together by organizing students into small groups for learning. It is beneficial to include some students who show genuine interest in literacy-related activities. Reutzel (1999) recommended several formats for grouping students. For present purposes, the following peer group formats are suggested.

1. *Flexible groups:* These are temporary groups created and disbanded as the need arises. Groups are given different assignments during different meetings, and the teacher periodically supervises their activities.

2. **Literature circles:** Students are formed into groups to read trade books or literature books they have selected. All members of the group read copies of the same book. The teacher briefly explains the contents of each book so that each group can decide which book to select for study. The teacher keeps track of the reading and writing activities assigned to each group. At the end of the activity, each group gives a presentation on what the members have read. Over a period of time, each member in each group is required to give a talk on what has been read.

3. *Cooperative learning groups:* As with literature circles, students in cooperative learning groups work on assignments together, but the teacher may select the assignments for each group. All members in the group receive the same grade for their combined efforts. The teacher should assign students to groups carefully, taking into consideration their ability, personality, friendships, and interests. The teacher also should be aware of the fact that some students, when put together, are more likely to engage in nonproductive behavior and disrupt the efforts of the group. If this occurs after groups have been assigned, the teacher may have to reassign some students to different groups.

4. *Peer tutoring:* By observing students and reviewing their performance on classroom activities and tests, the teacher determines individual student needs for tutoring. Peer tutoring groups are formed by pairing students with more advanced skills with those who need assistance learning material. The teacher should, however, be careful not to pair students with such a wide discrepancy that both the skilled reader and the weak reader get frustrated and the pairing activity becomes a problem.

Classroom Environment

Young children are quite active and become restless and lose concentration if they are required to sit quietly for a long time. Therefore, the classroom should be arranged to provide plenty of opportunities for movement, action, and interaction with peers and the teacher. To promote literacy learning, the classroom should also be rich in literacy materials. Roskos and Neuman (2001) reported that ample space allocation, a flexible room arrangement conducive to active learning, and accessible materials and learning tools have a positive influence on children's literacy learning. The classroom space should have designated areas for specific functions: a shared reading area, bookmaking and writing area, collaborative writing and peer learning area, individual reading/teaching area, and the classroom library. In addition, a computer space should be available.

For optimal teaching and learning, students can be seated in a semicircle so that the distance between teacher and student is the same for all students. The result is that no student always sits in the front part of the classroom and no student is always at the back of the classroom. This arrangement not only promotes interaction between the teacher and all of the students but also minimizes discipline problems.

The classroom environment includes the number of students in the room. Though the idea that academic achievement is higher when there are fewer students in a room seems to be logical, this has been challenged by some researchers. Some studies have not found significant differences in student achievement between larger classes and smaller classes (Hoxby, 2000; Sanders, Wright, & Horn, 1997). One of the reasons for this unexpected finding is that these studies have failed to control for mediating processes in the classroom, particularly in teacher–student interactions. A majority of these studies, if not all, have compared the academic achievement of students from large classes (usually more than 30) with the academic achievement of students taught by the same teachers when the class size was reduced (usually less than 20). What is overlooked in these studies is the tendency for teachers who had taught larger classes for a number of years to continue to use the same instructional strategies they had used for teaching larger classes when teaching smaller classes. Thus, the reduction in class size did not result in changes in instructional method and had little or no effect on student achievement. Thus, smaller class size, in and of itself, does not appear to enhance student achievement unless teaching styles are altered to take advantage of the smaller group. Sanders et al. concluded that it is the teacher and not the class size that makes the difference.

The connection between class size and teaching style was explored in a study by Blatchford, Moriarty, Edmonds, and Martin (2002). In their longitudinal study of more than 10,000 4- to 7-year-old children, they observed teacher–child interactions in British schools. Their description of such interactions in small classes of 15 children is instructive. In smaller classes,

> There was lightness about the activities and a good deal of humor. . . . The teacher spent little time on control and there was little need to keep children on task. . . . There was a very noticeable contrast with the situation in another school . . . in a large class of more than 30, interactions with the children were a continuous battle to keep their attention on task. As a consequence, the teacher was severe; and the children subdued. (p. 102)

Qualitative analysis of the observational data showed that in larger classes, there was less individual attention, contact, and feedback and fewer individual reading opportunities compared with the interactions in smaller classrooms. The percentage of teaching time in smaller classes was 76%, compared with 70% in larger classes. Observation also showed that in smaller classes, children interacted more often with their teachers than in larger classes. The children were more likely to be the focus of a teacher's attention in a smaller as opposed to a larger class. On average, the number of teacher-initiated interactions was about 212 times in smaller classes, compared with 143 times in larger classes. Research studies have also reported that small class size does improve reading achievement of elementary school children (Costello, 1992; Nye, Hedges, & Konstantopoulos, 2000).

In almost every school, class size is beyond a teacher's control. Fiscal conditions generally dictate class size. However, if a teacher is fortunate to have 20 or fewer children in the class, she should take advantage of the situation by individualizing instruction as much as possible.

Dialect: Standard English and African American English

Dialect is a regionally or socially distinctive variety of language characterized by a particular accent, set of words, and even grammatical structures. Even though it is relatively easy to distinguish between a dialect and a language, the difference is largely a matter of degree. The criterion used for distinguishing between a dialect and a language is this: Individuals are considered to speak different languages if they do not understand each other. In contrast, they are considered to speak different dialects if they can understand each other, even if not perfectly. There are exceptions to this general rule. For instance, Swedish, Norwegian, and Danish are considered to be separate languages even though speakers of these languages can understand each other. Conversely, Mandarin and Cantonese are considered dialects of the Chinese language even though the speakers of one are largely unintelligible to the speakers of the other.

People who speak the same dialect are said to belong to the same speech community. A single dialect, which is usually spoken by a majority of people, comes to predominate as the official or standard form of the language. It also is usually the written form of that language. Thus, Standard English (SE) is the English dialect spoken by a majority of people, not one that possesses a set of highly developed linguistic features. Standard English is also known as Academic English and School English, terms that do not have a sense of status attached to them as does SE. Although written language is relatively stable, spoken language, including SE, varies from place to place and over long periods of time. According to Wolfram and Schilling-Estes (1998), the number of U.S. dialects ranges from 3 to 24, depending on the researcher. The three basic dialects are New England, Southern, and Western/general America.

This discussion of dialect differences and reading instruction will focus on African American English (AAE), the most widely known English dialect. It is also known as Vernacular Black English and Ebonics. Although there are variations of AAE from one region of the country to another in sound production and stress patterns, the syntactical structures among the different AAE dialects can be similar, suggesting that these dialects are rule based.

AAE dialect is thought to have its origin in pidgin and Creole forms of language (Traugott, 1976). Pidgin emerges when two groups of people who speak mutually unintelligible languages develop a telegraphic communication system in which the vocabulary of one language is made to fit the grammar of the other language. As a result, speakers of pidgin languages develop their own system of **phonology,** with utterances that are in active voice and are almost bereft of complex grammar. Eventually, over a generation or two, formalized grammar develops, at which point the informal pidgin becomes the grammatically formal Creole. Creole depends on the geography and the history of a people; there is English Creole, French Creole, Portuguese Creole, and Spanish Creole. Pidgin English may have originated when people were brought from the West African coast to the Caribbean islands and the United States. According to Malstrom (1973), the verb structure of Creole can still be seen in modern AAE, but its vocabulary is mostly English.

Sociolinguists who have studied AAE in great detail, such as Baratz (1973), Labov (1973), and Traugott (1976), have concluded that the phonological and grammatical features seen in AAE are not random aberrations but represent systematic changes. AAE is, therefore, a rule-governed system of communication.

Influence of Dialect on Phonology and Grammar   What should professional reading teachers know about AAE? First, they should recognize that some of its phonological variations can also be seen in the speech patterns of SE speakers. For example, some speakers from the Midwest (e.g., Indiana) do not always differentiate between allophones of /a/ and /e/ sounds and tend to pronounce the words *Mary, marry,* and *merry* the same way. Furthermore, some of the omissions seen in AAE that result in variations from SE are actually elimination of redundancies. For example, the plural *s* and the tense marker *ed* are redundancies when the number and tense are contextually indicated, as in "I have three ball(s)" or "Yesterday I skipp(ed) school." In some languages these plurals are not at all indicated by inflections. Also note that in SE, words such as *put* and *hit* do not carry past-tense markers; words such as *say* and *come* are not marked by *ed* to indicate past tense. Baratz and Povich (1967) assessed the speech responses of a group of 5-year-old African American children in a Head Start program to pictures. They found that the children were not delayed in language acquisition but that they had learned the linguistic structures of AAE. It is also important to recognize that African American children's use of AAE varies and that many children and adolescents can switch back and forth from AAE to SE as the occasion demands.

For these reasons, AAE is considered by many linguists to be a legitimate linguistic system. Even though AAE differs from SE in some respects, it is not a deficient linguistic system. Redd and Webb (2005) pointed out that grammatical features of AAE are not errors; they simply conform to a different set of rules than Standard Written English does. Nevertheless, such dialectal variations can result in deviations in spelling and **syntax**. It is also worth remembering that everybody has a dialect.

After reviewing studies of AAE, Malstrom (1973) reported that AAE has some phonological and grammatical features that differ from those of SE. The following phonological variations mark the AAE dialect. These changes in pronunciation can change words, which in turn can affect spelling and comprehension of SE sentences for AAE speakers. The following selections represent some of the variants seem in the AAE dialect.

- The disappearing /r/: The phoneme /r/ disappears before **vowels** or consonants: guard → *god*; sore → *saw*; court → *caught*; Paris → *pass*; terrace → *test*

- The disappearing /l/ in word-final position: toll → *toe*; tool → *too*

- Consonant cluster reduction. Consonants such as /t/, /d/, /s/, and /z/ are simplified when they occur as digraphs (two consonants pronounced as two distinct sounds), particularly at the end of words: past → *pass*; meant → *men*; mend → *men*; hold → *hole*

- Alteration of sequence of elements in a cluster: axe → *aks*; six → *skis, sick*

- No distinction between /i/ and /e/ before nasals: going → *goeng*; ring → *reng*

- Alteration of pronunciation often resulting in **homonyms** (different words with similar pronunciation). Labov (1973) listed a number of such homonyms characteristic of AAE: pin → *pen*; tin → *ten*; since → *cents*; death → *deaf*; found → *fond*; pound → *pond*; cheer → *chair*; poor → *pour*; boil → *ball*; oil → *all*

  AAE is also marked by the following grammatical variations:

- Omission of the verb form of *be* in certain sentence patterns: *He old* for "He is old" and *Dey runnin* for "They are running." The verb *be* is also used in ways not seen in SE: *He busy* for "He is busy now" versus *He be busy* for "He is habitually busy" (Stewart, 1973).

- Omission of possessive suffix: *My fahver frien* for "My father's friend"

- Use of different pronouns (pronouns used indiscriminately for subject and object): *Him know us* for "He knows us"; *He father* for "His father"

- Differences in verb construction: *He working* or *He be working* for "He is working"

- Grammar affected by omission of final consonants: you'll → *you*; he'll → *he*

- Nouns not marked for plurals: three miles → *three mile*

- Generalization of plural marker *s*: *childrens, foots, mens*

- Noun–verb agreement often not indicated: *The boys was there; She have a book; They was going*

- Past tense may not be marked by *ed* when it does not create a consonant cluster: walked → *walk;* called → *call;* passed → *past;* picked → *pick.* However, *came* and *went* are used correctly, indicating that phonological variations, not variations in meaning, lead to such utterances.

- Differences in preposition use: *He over to his friend house* for "He is over at his friend's house"; *He teach Wilson elementary* for "He teaches at Wilson elementary"

In summary, syntax refers to a pattern of arrangement of linguistic units in a sentence. To a large extent, phonology is also rule governed. The preceding discussion shows that even though expressions in AAE may differ from those in SE, they are not random productions but follow a consistent pattern. The syntax and phonology of AAE, therefore, is structured and rule governed as much as SE. As noted previously, AAE grammatical features are not errors; they simply conform to a set of different rules from SE (Redd & Webb, 2005). Additional examples of AAE, adapted from Redd and Webb are shown in Table 1.1.

Some AAE-speaking children use spelling variations. O'Neal and Trabasso (1973) studied 149 African American and European American children age 7–11 years to see if dialect affects spelling. African American and European American children were matched for grade level and home background. The investigators administered a spelling test consisting of 128 words classified into the following four categories: 1) words whose spelling would not be confused by speakers of either SE or AAE (e.g., *tear/year*), 2) words that would be confused by speakers of SE but not by AAE speakers (e.g., *are/or*), 3) words that would be confused by speakers of AAE but not by SE speakers (e.g., *coal/cold*), and 4) words whose spellings would be changed by speakers of AAE but not by SE speakers (e.g., *throw/throat*). The spelling test was presented in two formats: an isolated list of words and embedded words in sentences.

Results showed that spelling improved with age for all children. African American children produced more spelling errors for AAE-confusable words (Category 3) than did European American children. This suggests that some of the spelling errors of African American children can be attributed to the phonology of AAE. It was concluded that phonological representations do correlate with spelling and that phonological differences in spoken language can lead to differences in spelling. The investigators also noted that all children made fewer spelling errors when the words were presented in sentence context than in isolation. This indicates that, in addition to phonology, meaning also plays a role in spelling. Fountain (2006), in her study of fourth-grade African American children, found the following errors: health → *helf;* wealth → *welf;* collapsed → *collapes;* startled → *startle;* asked → *aksed;* going → *goin;* singing → *singin.*

Dialect: Implications for Instruction Phonology plays a major role in spelling and for this reason, the AAE user is prone to peculiar spelling patterns. Charity, Scarborough, and Griffin (2004) administered sentence imitation and reading tests to 217 urban African American children in kindergarten through second grade. The researchers hypothesized that greater familiarity with SE, as indicated by children's ability to imitate spoken SE sentences, would be associated with reading skills. They found that African American children varied widely in the extent to which they could correctly reproduce SE sentences, and higher familiarity with SE

Table 1.1. Examples of African American English and Standard American utterances

Feature	African American English	Standard English
Absence of plural *s*	two boy	two boys
Absence of possessive *s*	Natasha house	Natasha's house
Absence of singular *s*	She walk.	She walks.
Emphatic *s*	I loves my baby.	I love my baby.
	I gets excited.	I get excited.
	For money, I looks.	For money, I looked.
Absence of possessive form	they ball	their ball
Absence of *is* and *are*	They happy.	They are happy.
Suffix dropping	I look for him yesterday.	I looked for him yesterday.
	They have work hard.	They have worked hard.
Addition of *had*	We had played.	We played.
Unconjugated *be*	He be here tomorrow.	He will be here tomorrow.
	We gon win.	We are going to win.
Morpheme changes	He finna go.	He is about to go.
	You don't poseta . . .	You are not supposed to . . .
	I liketa drown.	I almost drowned.
	It's a school there.	There is a school.
	They got people there.	There are people in there.
	Here go my picture.	Here is my picture.
Absence of *is* and *are* and use of *be*	He talking.	He is talking right now.
	He be talking.	He keeps talking on and on.
	He be steady talking.	He usually talks.
Absence of *has*	He been sick.	He has been sick.
Verb after *have*	She had went.	She had gone.
Use of *done* and *bin*	She done finish.	She has already finished.
	He bin finish.	He finished long ago.
Negatives	I ain't lying.	I am not lying.
	Can't nobody beat us.	Nobody can beat us.
Inversions	Why I can't play?	Why can't I play?
Use of *by*	I got a black eye by him.	He gave me a black eye.
Double subjects	My friend, he likes me.	My friend likes me.
Absence of pronoun	That's the man was here.	That's the man who was here.

From Redd, T.M., & Webb, K.S. (2005). *A teacher's introduction to African American English* (pp. 113–120). Urbana, IL: National Council of Teachers of English. Copyright 2005 by the National Council of Teachers of English. Used with permission.

was associated with better reading achievement as assessed by tests of word identification, decoding, and comprehension.

The literacy skills of many African American children, particularly those who come from poor circumstances, are often reported to lag behind those of their peers. Dialect is proposed to be one of the causal factors for this discrepancy. Knowledge of the dialects spoken by children in the classroom will help professional reading teachers in their efforts to teach literacy skills. Following are some suggestions for working with students who speak AAE.

- Telling students that they have to use SE because that is the only way to succeed in life may not motivate them to use SE. In contrast, telling students that it is good to know SE because a majority of the people in the country use it and that the textbooks are written in SE is likely to be agreeable to many students.

- It is helpful for teachers to have an understanding of the words that can and cannot be phonetically distinguished by students who speak AAE (e.g., *book* and *look* versus *pin* and *pen*). This can help students in spelling. Teachers should also be sensitive to grammatical errors related to dialect and draw students' attention to the nature of these errors.

- Teachers should avoid telling students, "The way you have spelled the word is wrong, and this is the right way to spell it." It is more pragmatic to say, "Look, you have spelled the word differently, but this is the way the word is spelled in our textbooks." The same principle applies to sentences that reflect the influence of AAE syntax.

Teachers can readily understand the difficulties with reading experienced by many students learning English as a second language, but they may be baffled by the difficulties encountered by students who speak AAE. However, as Stewart (1973) pointed out, AAE speakers have difficulties of their own. Whereas the differences between English and another language (e.g., Spanish) are usually clear cut, the many similarities between AAE dialect and SE make it difficult to tell exactly where one leaves off and the other begins. This makes it difficult for students to know what is acceptable and not acceptable in the classroom. For students who are used to AAE and colloquial forms of SE, the teacher's speech may be baffling as well.

Teachers of literacy are said to fall into one of three camps of instructional policy toward dialect variations: eradicationist, pluralist, or bidialectalist (Gilyard, 1996). Eradicationists believe that AAE is an obstacle to learning and do not believe it should play any part in the classroom. Those in the pluralist camp wish to educate society in general about AAE and make it, along with SE, an acceptable legitimate linguistic form. Bidialectalists, although recognizing the legitimacy of AAE, accept that SE is a prerequisite for success in life and, therefore, teach students to switch from AAE to SE and to use SE when the circumstances demand it. The last option appears to be the most pragmatic and is acceptable to the majority of teachers.

In their book *A Teacher's Introduction to African American English*, Redd and Webb (2005) described five different approaches for instructing children who rely primarily on AAE for communication.

1. The traditional approach: This instructional philosophy promotes full immersion in SE, both in conversation and in writing. The teacher models SE and actively discourages the use of AAE, intervening when its influence appears. Extensive use is made of group learning, in which AAE students are partnered with SE students.

2. The second dialect approach: In this approach, SE is taught as a second dialect to children who are AAE speakers. Teachers highlight the differences between SE and AAE and encourage children to switch codes from one dialect to another—that is, to use AAE or SE, whichever is appropriate for the situation. SE is used extensively in classroom conversation, reading, and writing.

3. The dialect awareness approach: This approach helps students gain an appreciation of variations in dialects and is used to dispel any student beliefs that some dialects are inferior to others. Teachers discuss the nature of dialects, their differences and similarities, and the different dialects of the English language itself. Eventually, teachers draw students' attention to the contrasting

features of SE and AAE. As noted earlier, children who produce AAE-based spelling and writings are told not that they are wrong but that there is another way of using language, the one seen in textbooks.

4. The culturally appropriate approach: Although similar to the dialect awareness approach, this approach is more likely to include curriculum and methodology filled with information about African American culture. Curriculum materials include writings by African American authors as well as stories and history written about African American people. Whenever possible, teachers switch between AAE and SE and draw students' attention to the contrasting features of the two dialects.

5. The bridge approach: Instructional methodology that follows this approach is based on the belief that students whose native language is not English catch up with native speakers of English very quickly when they are taught school subjects in their native language. Teachers may start using textbooks written in AAE, followed by books written in a mixture of AAE and SE, and finally those written entirely in SE. An example is the *Bridge Readers* (published by Houghton Mifflin), which, at present, have been discontinued. The teacher may also draw students' attention to **Old English** writings, which have a dialectal flavor, to impress upon children that dialect variations are a common part of life. Admittedly, this approach would be difficult to implement in classrooms in which African American children constitute a minority.

Regardless of the approach teachers may prefer to use, certain general principles apply to instructing students who speak a dialect or a language other than English. Teachers should be able to distinguish between errors of pronunciation and errors that reflect a lack of understanding of concepts and their meaning. For example, the child who reads *When I passed my test, I was happy* as "When I pass my test, I happy" may not have learned that *ed* and *was* are markers for past tense. The child's attention, therefore, must be drawn to the grammatical significance of these markers. It is suggested (e.g., Labov, 1973) that if an oral reading error reflects only a difference in pronunciation, correction may not be necessary. If, however, such a reading error reflects a lack of understanding of the concepts involved, correction may be necessary.

Teachers should try to create an explicit awareness in students of the differences between SE and AAE. It should be noted that children who read extensive SE material outside the classroom are able to edit AAE patterns out of their schoolwork more successfully than those who do not read or write outside the classroom.

Teachers should not become frustrated if children's progress in learning SE is slow, because changes may not emerge quickly and easily. Students spend more time with their family and friends than at school, and AAE is the passkey for them to reenter their peer group when they go home each day. For further resources on dialect, please see Box 1.4.

English as a Second Language

Bilingualism is not a rare phenomenon; many people in the contemporary world are bilingual. Many people are also trilingual. Bilingualism exists in degrees. A student may come from a home in which only a language other than English is spoken or from a home in which both languages are used to various degrees. It is stating the obvious to say that a student whose native language is not English will face difficulties that are not experienced by a student whose native language is En-

Box 1.4. Resources for understanding dialect

The topic of dialect is so important that we provide the following sources to help teachers gain further understanding of dialects and their influence on literacy:

Adger, C.T., Wolfram, W., & Christian, D. (2007). *Dialects in schools and communities*. Mahwah, NJ: Lawrence Erlbaum Associates.

Charity, A.H., Scarborough, H.S., & Griffin, D.M. (2004). Familiarity with School English in African-American children in its relation to early reading achievement. *Child Development, 75*(5), 1340–1356.

Craig, H.K., Thompson, C.A., Washington, J.A., & Potter, S.L. (2004). Performance of elementary-grade African American students on the Gray Reading Tests. *Language, Speech, & Hearing Services in Schools, 35*, 141–154.

Green, L. (2004). *African American English: A linguistic introduction*. New York: Cambridge University Press.

Kamhi, A.G., Pollock, K.E., & Harris, J.L. (1996). *Communication development and disorders in African American children: Research, assessment, and intervention*. Baltimore: Paul H. Brookes Publishing Co.

Labov, W. (1995). Can reading failure be reversed: A linguistic approach to the question. In V.L. Gadsen & D.A. Wagner (Eds.), *Literacy among African American youth: Issues in learning, teaching, and schooling* (pp. 39–68). Cresskill, NJ: Hampton Press.

Mufwene, S.S., Rickford, J.R., Bailey, G., & Baugh, J. (Eds.). (1998). *African American English: Structure, history, and use*. London: Routledge.

Redd, T.M., & Webb, K.S. (2005). *A teacher's introduction to African American English*. Urbana, IL: National Council of Teachers of English.

Rickford, J.R. (1999). *African American English: Features, evolution, educational implications*. Malden, MA: Blackwell.

Treiman, R. (2004). Spelling and dialect: Comparisons between speakers of African American English and White speakers. *Psychonomic Bulletin & Review, 11*, 338–342.

Washington, J.A., & Craig, H.K. (2001). Reading performance and dialectal variation. In J.L. Harris, A.G. Kamhi, & K.E. Pollock (Eds.), *Literacy in African American communities* (pp. 147–168), Mahwah, NJ: Lawrence Erlbaum Associates.

glish. These difficulties can arise from differences between English and other languages in phonological, syntactic, and pragmatic aspects. Depending on the age of the student, phonology of the English language may pose difficulties, with older students finding it more difficult to master than younger students. In addition to phonology, prosody (stress and intonation patterns) also pose challenges. It is well recognized that younger children acquire prosodic skills much more readily than older students and adults. The phonology of the English as a Second Language (**ESL**) learner can influence his English spelling and morphology, as it does in the case of the user of AAE dialect. If a particular phoneme is not present in the student's native language, it is very likely that the student will not perceive that particular phoneme. This can lead to spelling errors because these phonemes may not be represented in a student's native language. Teachers can minimize phonology-based spelling errors by drawing students' attention to the phonological differences between their native language and English.

An additional source of difficulty for ESL students is the syntactical differences between languages. English follows a somewhat rigid word order with SVO (subject, verb, object) pattern, as seen in the sentence "The boy read the book." In Spanish, syntax does not always follow this format. For example, "Hableron de Juan" literally reads "Spoke about Juan," which means "They spoke about Juan." Similarly, "¿Que' dijo Susana?" literally reads "What said Susana?" meaning "What did Susana say?" English also does not indicate gender through morphemic affixations, as Spanish and many other languages do. For example, the English **morpheme** *friend* does not indicate reference to a male or a female. In Spanish, however, *amigo* represents male singular; *amiga* represents female singular. Because of these differences, word-to-word translation of one language into another would be an inefficient way of learning (or teaching) a second language.

The nature of **orthography** (spelling) also has some influence on the acquisition of literacy skills. The relationship between spelling and pronunciation is not straightforward in English, whereas Spanish has almost a one-to-one relationship between spelling and pronunciation. For this reason, English orthography is described as *opaque*; Spanish orthography is described as *transparent*. That is, knowing the names of the 26 letters of the English alphabet is not much help in pronouncing or spelling most English words; in Spanish this is not so. In general, review studies show that English-speaking children take almost one additional year to learn to read fluently compared with children who speak languages such as Spanish and Finnish, languages whose orthography is more transparent than that of English (Joshi & Aaron, 2006). The opaque nature of English orthography, therefore, can be expected to pose additional difficulties for ESL students.

Even though vocabulary development may pose less of a problem to ESL students than phonology and syntax, ESL students' English vocabulary may not coincide with the English vocabulary spoken in the classroom. This is so because the English vocabulary used by ESL children at home (if it is used) is usually limited to domestic referents, such as food, household materials, care of siblings, and household duties. In contrast, words encountered by ESL students in the classroom usually are academic in nature. For this reason, standardized tests of English vocabulary may not provide an accurate measure of ESL students' vocabulary knowledge.

Teachers of foreign languages advise that the best way to learn a second language is through immersion in a language-interactive (conversational) environment. Peers of ESL students can provide such an environment and offer a good resource for acquiring SE skills. Group activities can be used successfully for this purpose. Teachers can pair an ESL student with an English-speaking student, who reads a sentence from the textbook and then asks the ESL student to repeat what was heard without looking at the textbook. However, teachers must help English-speaking students accept and welcome ESL students as partners in their activities. Though admittedly the acquisition of reading and writing skills is far more difficult for ESL students than for native speakers of English, written language can actually be of help to students learning English. This is because written language is formal and standardized and spoken language is informal and colloquial, with numerous variations and subtleties. Furthermore, reading and writing activities allow children more time to decode and comprehend language, whereas listening and speaking are fast paced. Thus, reading and writing can be helpful in language instruction. These activities, however, should not replace conversational opportunities for ESL students.

Research studies indicate that students' rate of learning a second language is highly correlated with their level of proficiency in their native language. That is, ESL students who are proficient in their native language are likely to have less difficulty in learning a second language than ESL students whose level of proficiency in their native language is low. Thus, there appears to be a linguistic intelligence that cuts across languages. ESL students' level of proficiency in their native language can, therefore, provide useful information to teachers as to what to expect of the students' performance in English. It is possible to come across a few ESL students in every classroom who may experience an unusual degree of difficulty in acquiring English literacy, despite teachers' best efforts. Such children may be similar to English-speaking children who have reading disabilities. This situation would raise the question of whether the difficulty experienced by the ESL student is due to English not being his or her native language or to the presence of a language learning disability. An assessment of the ESL student's skill level in his or her native language can be helpful in resolving this issue. If there is a marked difference between the student's skill level in his or her native language and English, this could be due to the student's limited exposure to English. Conversely, if the student has limited skill in his or her native language as well, a disability may be suspected. This observation suggests that methods of instruction (e.g., component model–based instruction) used for English-speaking students are equally applicable to ESL students with a disability in learning English.

Children acquire any language quite readily by using it. For this reason, teachers should create opportunities for ESL students to use English in conversation in the classroom. English-speaking peers are a good source for interactive instruction. By creating a sense of empathy during the beginning of the school year, teachers can prepare English-speaking students to accept and welcome ESL children.

Assignments for the Student Teacher

1. Observe one or two preschool children and collect their inventive writings.

2. Visit a first-grade classroom at the beginning of the year. Observe and note how many of the children can already read simple words.

3. Observe and note how many children in first grade do not yet know the names of all the letters of the alphabet.

4. Converse with a child of a minority group in a classroom for about 10 minutes. Notice and report any phonological and grammatical variations in the child's speech.

5. Make a study of the arrangement of the classroom you have visited. Does it satisfy the plan recommended in this chapter? If you were the teacher, what changes would you introduce?

6. Observe the classroom you visit for the following features: class size, number of times the teacher initiates interactions with children, and number of times the children initiate interactions with the teacher.

7. Select three or four children in the classroom. Observe and record, in 1-minute intervals, how much time each child spends on reading and writing tasks.

Reading Assignment

Read one of the following articles, discuss it, and write a one-page summary. These articles can be obtained at your college library or downloaded by accessing the library's electronic holdings.

Blair, T.R., Rupley, W.H., & Nichols, W. (2007). The effective teacher of reading: Considering the "what" and "how" of instruction. *The Reading Teacher, 60*(5), 432–438.

Darling, S. (2005). Strategies for engaging parents in home support of reading acquisition. *The Reading Teacher, 58*(5), 476–480.

Perkins, J., & Cooter, R. (2005). Evidence-based literacy education and the African American child. *The Reading Teacher, 59*(2), 194–198.

CHAPTER 2

The Psychology of Reading and the History of Literacy Instruction in the United States

Summary

This first part of this chapter deals with the psychology of reading, describing the principles of behavioral and cognitive psychology as they apply to reading and literacy instruction. For example, the chapter explains the roles of short-term memory (**STM**) and long-term memory (**LTM**) in the reading process. Piaget's constructivism and Vygotsky's zone of proximal development and **scaffolding** are described in the context of literacy acquisition. The chapter also touches on metacognition and **schema** theory, illustrating their uses in day-to-day literacy instruction. The chapter's second part traces how literacy instruction has changed along with the U.S. political, religious, social, and cultural climate. Readers will see the roots of contemporary opposing views on teaching reading and writing.

Main ideas presented in this chapter

1. Principles of **behavioral psychology** and cognitive psychology can be successfully applied to classroom instruction.
2. Young children have a limited memory capacity; instruction should take this fact into account.
3. Letter–sound knowledge is a precursor to instant word recognition (sight word reading).
4. Decoding is the conversion of printed words into their respective pronunciations. An inability to decode impedes reading comprehension.
5. Metacognitive skills help readers monitor their own comprehension and self-correct reading errors.
6. According to Piaget, maturation and experience are necessary for learning; thought comes first and language is a vehicle to express it.
7. Vygotsky emphasized language and its role in learning. Zone of proximal development and scaffolding have a direct bearing on teaching reading to children.
8. U.S. reading instruction has vacillated between a skills (phonics) approach and a meaning approach.
9. The National Reading Panel (NRP)'s report inspired the No Child Left Behind Act of 2001 (PL 107-110). Policies such as accountability and national standards are closely linked to this legislation.
10. Reading specialists disagree about how to teach reading and writing because people differ in the way they define and carry out research.

The Psychology of Reading

Psychological theories that have attempted to describe and explain how humans learn can be placed into two broad categories: behavioral and cognitive.

Behavioral Theory

Behavioral theory emphasizes environmental factors as the primary elements that facilitate learning. Behaviorists, in general, consider reading to be an aspect of behavior and, therefore, regard the laws of learning derived from behavioral theories to be applicable to reading. The roots of behavior theory can be traced to associationism, which proposed that stimuli and responses are bound to each other and strengthened when followed immediately by **reinforcers.**

Reinforcers

Skinner (1957), a leading behaviorist of the 20th century, carefully studied the role of reinforcers (rewards, feedback, and punishment) in learning and came to consider reinforcement to be an important factor in learning. Learning takes place when a stimulus, such as the written word, becomes associated with a response, such as the pronunciation of the word or the comprehension of its meaning. Reinforcers promote such associative learning so much so that when the stimulus occurs again, the same response is likely to follow.

Reinforcers can be broadly defined as consequences of behavior. Some consequences of behavior, such as a child's receiving a piece of candy for giving the correct answer to a question, are pleasant and, therefore, make the child repeat the behavior that has been reinforced. Other consequences, such as being reprimanded for disrupting the class, are unpleasant and result in the learner's not repeating the behavior that was associated with negative consequences. Reinforcers can be tangible or abstract. Examples of tangible reinforcers encountered in the classroom are praise by the teacher, recognition by classmates, and attention given to the child. Chocolate bars, gold stars, and stickers are also tangible reinforcers often used by teachers. An example of an abstract reinforcer is feedback. When a child reads a story, enjoys it, and feels good about having accomplished the task of reading, the child has experienced feedback that is rewarding. He is likely to repeat the behavior when another occasion presents itself. Notice that this form of reinforcer is not only abstract but also, as discussed in Chapter 1, intrinsic.

In general, teachers should strive to provide ample opportunities for intrinsic reinforcement and minimize the use of extrinsic reinforcers. As it is impossible to praise every child for every accomplishment, teachers must devise learning opportunities for children to generate their own intrinsic rewards. One such opportunity is sustained silent reading. For a specified amount of time during the day, children read stories of their own choosing. This can be rewarding for children who enjoy this type of activity.

Contiguity

Behaviorist psychologists have identified contiguity as a factor that facilitates associative learning. The term *contiguity* means togetherness. In the context of reading, there are two kinds of contiguities: temporal and spatial, or togetherness in time and space, respectively. Things that occur together in time and space are likely to be learned together. For example, a student experiences temporal contiguity by receiving immediate feedback from the teacher as to whether the student's answer to a question was right or wrong. When the teacher writes a word on the chalkboard next to its definition, students experience spatial contiguity. These two concepts, reinforcer and contiguity, suggest that reading teachers should give feedback to learners as much as possible and as often as possible and that such information should be delivered promptly.

When students' assignments are promptly evaluated, this immediate feedback will yield better results than delayed feedback. Computers can be used effectively for providing immediate feedback when children are in the process of acquiring word recognition skills, vocabulary knowledge, and comprehension skills.

Social Learning Theory: Modeling and Think-Alouds

A variation of the behavioral theory of learning is referred to as social learning theory. Numerous studies conducted under the rubric of social learning theory show that modeling has a tremendous influence on behavior in general and reading in particular. Social learning theory proposes that behavior changes when the environment changes. Peers in the classroom are one such environmental factor. That is to say, if several children in the classroom overtly display an interest in reading, other children who are behind in reading are likely to emulate their peers. The teacher is the prime model in the classroom and, therefore, her enthusiasm for reading can have an infectious effect on children. The teacher can also encourage children to openly express their enjoyment of reading.

An instructional technique called think aloud is a simple tool that applies the idea of modeling to the teaching of reading. **Modeling and think-alouds** go together in that the teacher models ideal reading behavior while talking aloud about what is going on in her mind as she is engaged in reading. For example, as the teacher reads along, he or she may come across a word, pause, and say, "I don't know what this word—*pacify*—means; let me take a look in the dictionary. Oh, it means 'calm, quiet.'"

The teacher can also model the proper use of prosody and intonation. Prosody refers to the acoustic (sound) properties of speech, including intonation, stress, and pause. Intonation refers to variation in pitch. Prosody is involved in syllables, words, phrases, and clauses. Consider the sentence "You are going to school." By stressing the word *you* or the word *school*, the meaning of the sentence is changed. Furthermore, by a rising intonation or a falling intonation of these words, the sentence can be changed into a question. Prosodic features are of diagnostic value because when a student reads a sentence in a monotone without regard to prosody, it indicates that she is not comprehending the meaning of the sentence. Proper use of prosody in oral reading indicates that the reader *is* comprehending the meaning. The teacher should use the think-aloud technique as often as possible to teach children how to read with appropriate prosody and intonation.

Think aloud is also useful for teaching students how to use specific strategies for comprehending what they read. A method of teaching reading comprehension that uses modeling is **reciprocal teaching**. In reciprocal teaching, the teacher first models reading for small groups of children, using the think-aloud technique. The teacher may think aloud about the purpose of his reading and what he already knows about the topic he is going to read, he may periodically stop and ask himself if he is comprehending what he has read so far, and eventually he summarizes what he has read. Once students have mastered these steps, they take turns emulating the teacher's behavior. Reciprocal teaching is described in greater detail in Chapter 8.

So far this discussion has stressed learning situations that are rewarding for students. But what happens when unpleasant consequences arise as part of literacy instruction? Certainly, when a child repeatedly gets Ds or Fs in reading and on spelling tests, it can cause a great deal of unpleasant feelings. Psychologists and educational philosophers have long held that learning should be a pleasant experience, and unpleasant experiences should be avoided. In addition to failing grades, other situations that routinely take place in classrooms can be unpleasant for some students. For instance, reading aloud to their peers can be a frightening experience for some children, particularly for those who have weak word recognition skills. Although this form of round robin reading may benefit some readers, it can be a humiliating and painful experience for poor readers. The teacher must be careful in using such a reading practice on a regular basis. Repeated failure can create a lasting dislike for reading.

The teacher should try to minimize painful feedback by changing the demands of the task to suit individual children's capabilities. Reading and writing can be made into task-oriented assignments rather than ego-oriented assignments. In task-oriented assignments, the goal is to see that the student has mastered the skill; in ego-oriented assignments, the goal is to see how well the student compares with other children. Another potential solution is to make use of group work, to which all students can contribute without being singled out.

Cognitive Science

In contrast to behaviorist theory, cognitive theory assigns more importance to innate factors as mediators of learning. Cognitive psychology has two sides, an experimental side and a clinical side. Experimentally oriented cognitive psychologists study variables such as iconic memory, STM, LTM, executive memory, **mental lexicon,** schema, metacognition, and procognition by conducting controlled experimental studies. (These features of cognition are described in the following section). In fact, the psychology of reading is one of the major areas extensively studied by experimentally oriented cognitive psychologists, because reading is seen as a window into the mind. Many of the studies cited in this book have been conducted by cognitive psychologists. In contrast to experimental cognitive psychology, clinical studies obtain information primarily from observing children, asking them questions, and analyzing their answers. Scholars such as Piaget and Vygotsky have written extensively about learning and education, their ideas derived primarily from clinical studies.

Experimental Cognitive Psychology

To understand what happens during reading, cognitive psychologists have constructed a model that views the processing of information as though it proceeds in stages, starting with the initial input when the eyes encounter the printed word. This stage-based model of processing information is only a model and describes one way of looking at how humans read. In reality, during reading or listening many aspects of memory, such as STM and LTM, operate simultaneously rather than in a rigid sequence. For example, you can recognize a written English word instantly but may not be able to read a word written in Arabic. This shows that what is stored in your long-term memory (in this case, English) springs into action the moment you look at a word. Reading is an interactive process in which all levels of memory work in concert. Nevertheless, for ease of illustration, the reading process will be examined one stage at a time.

Iconic Memory   The first stage of input in the reading process, in which a visual image is transformed into a nerve impulse, is referred to as iconic memory, or sensory memory. Sperling studied the nature of iconic memory in 1960 by conducting a series of experimental studies using the tachistoscope, which flashes an image on a screen for a fraction of a second. From these studies, he concluded that the duration of iconic memory is only about one fourth of a second and that its storage capacity is limited to about 12 items. (Although the capacity of iconic memory in young children is much less than the 12 items typical of adult capacity, it expands as they grow older.) Thus, a word would be retained in iconic memory for a very short time and then would either be transferred to STM or be forgotten. It follows, then, that humans can process about 240 words per minute. Some skilled readers may be able to read as many as 300 words per minute, but the physiological as well as cognitive systems of the body have clear limitations and are not designed to handle many more words within that amount of time. Individuals who claim that they can read thousands of words in a minute either already know the subject matter they are reading or they merely skim the material. Incidentally, humans can also process only about 300 spoken words per minute.

The first stage in reading has been studied extensively in an effort to discover whether the nature of the unit of reading is the letter or the word itself. In other words, do readers process all the letters in a word, or is the word itself processed as a single unit?

This is an important question because it has implications for reading instruction. Naturally, if words are the units used for reading, then whole word reading instruction would be the most appropriate method for teaching reading. In contrast, if readers process the letters in the words when they read, then instruction that focuses on the letters of the alphabet would be the most effective means of instruction.

Cattell, an experimental psychologist, tried to answer this question as early as 1886. Cattell collected accurate measurements of the time it took to name a letter and to name a common word and found that both tasks take about the same amount of time, about 200 to 300 milliseconds. He interpreted his data to mean that it is the word and not the letter that is the basic unit of reading. This interpretation had a major impact on reading instruction in the United States at that time and led to the abandoning of the alphabetic method of instruction. In its place, the whole word, or look-say, method was promoted. In this method, children were first taught to read selected groups of words rather than the letters of the alphabet. In the look-say method, letters of the alphabet may be introduced, but only after children have learned to read a number of words by sight. The look-say method of reading instruction became well entrenched in American schools during the latter part of the 19th century, primarily because of Cattell's findings (see Box 2.1). However, even in those days many experienced teachers felt that this method left many children at a disadvantage and that children should be taught the letter–sound relationships first.

More recent experimental studies have confirmed Cattell's finding that common written words can be named as fast as individual letters (Aaron et al., 1999). So the possibility that words are recognized by processing the constituent letters

---

Box 2.1.　James McKeen Cattell (1860–1944)

James McKeen Cattell was one of the first Americans to receive a Ph.D. degree in psychology. The training he received in Leipzig, combined with his native ability, made him a leading researcher in the field of experimental psychology. As a result, he was well respected as a scientist and his findings had a widespread influence in the United States.

in a serial fashion, one by one, can be ruled out because a word can be named as fast as a letter can be named. If word recognition proceeded on a letter-by-letter basis, word naming would take longer than letter naming.

Are individual words then recognized as patterns, as Cattell believed? Three decades of empirical studies have shown that words are *not* read as single units (Massaro & Jesse, 2005). Eye-movement studies using computers have shown that readers do process almost every letter in a written word unless the word is a highly familiar one or an article or a conjunction. If attention were not paid to the individual letters in words, readers would confuse word pairs such as *hit/hut, chair/choir, grow/grew,* and *health/hearth,* which differ from each other by only one letter.

Confirmation of this statement comes from a study by Just and Carpenter (1987), which required college students to read passages presented on a computer screen. The students' eye movements were monitored as they read. The researchers replaced a letter in some words with another letter, which resulted in spelling errors. They found that as the reader's eye swept along the written sentence, it would pause whenever it encountered a spelling error, regardless of the position of the misplaced letter in the word. This was seen as evidence that readers sample almost every letter in the word when they read and that individual letters in the word are the unit that is processed.

Cognitive psychologists who have tried to find a definitive answer to the question of whether the basic unit used in reading is the word or the letter manipulate written words in two ways: transposition (e.g., read → *raed*) and substitution (read → *reod*). Using this technique, Grainger and Whitney (2004) found that text with letter transpositions is much easier to read than text with letter substitutions. They believed this demonstrates that specific letters in words are critical for identifying the word. But research shows that reading words in which letters are altered takes more time compared to reading unaltered words (see Box 2.2). As noted previously, common observation shows that unless readers sample the letters in words, they cannot correctly distinguish among words such as *beat, beet, bent, brat, blot, boot,* and *belt,* which differ in only one or two middle letters.

How written words are recognized is an important question, because some educators believe that letter–sound association is unimportant for learning to read. If this is the case, phonics would be irrelevant to reading instruction.

Box 2.2.   Are words read as wholes?

The argument that the word and not the letter is the unit in reading is sometimes advocated by citing the following message that appeared some time ago on the Internet and was widely circulated:

"Cdnuolt blveiee taht I cluod aulaclty uesdnatnrd waht I was rdanieg. The phaonmneal pweor of the hmuan mnid. Aoccdrnig to a rscheearch at Cmabrigde Uinervtisy, it deosn't mttaer in waht oredr the ltteers in a wrod are, the olny iprmoatnt tihng is taht the frist and lsat ltteer be in the rghit pclae. The rset can be a taotl mses and you can sitll raed it wouthit a porbelm. Tihs is bcuseae the huamn mnid deos not raed ervey lteter by istlef, but the wrod as a wlohe. Amzanig huh? yaeh and I awlyas tghuhot slpeling was ipmorantt. If you can raed tihs, psas it on!!"

Rayner, White, Johnson, and Liversedge (2006) have pursued this issue and obtained the following results by administering reading tasks to college students. The investigators presented sentences with altered spellings on a computer monitor and noted the amount of time the eye fixates on single words and how often the eye regresses to take a second look at words. These data show that manipulation of letters in words increases both reading time and regressive eye movements (see Table 2.1).

In another study, Rayner and Kaiser (1975) found that students in grade 6 took almost twice as much time to read passages when letters were altered in the middle position of words as compared to passages in which such alterations were not made. The students also committed twice as many errors when they read altered text than when they read standard text. As these data show, the statement in the Internet message in Box 2.2 that "the human mind does not read every letter by itself, but the word as a whole" is not correct. Instead, the apparent ease with which we read some misspelled words is because we can guess many familiar words provided there are sufficient cues, such as letters in the beginning and at the end of words. This is known as top-down reading. Notice the words in Box 2.2; if the initial letters are removed, guessing the words is almost impossible. Children in early elementary grades are not familiar with many words and, therefore, cannot guess these words. In contrast to top-down reading, they depend on bottom-up reading.

If letters and not words are the basic units of processing, this presents a dilemma. Research shows that readers do not recognize words by processing constituent letters one by one, in a serial fashion. Research also shows that almost all the letters in written words are processed. How can these two apparently contradictory findings be reconciled? In addition to processing words in a serial, letter-by-letter fashion or processing them as single units, there is another possibility. This is referred to as **parallel processing.** Studies show that readers sample each letter in a word and that all the letters in a word are processed simultaneously, in parallel (McConkie & Rayner, 1975; Rayner, 1998; Rayner & Pollatsek, 1989).

Parallel processing can be compared to the process involved in face recognition. When you look at a person, you do not process facial features in a sequence— eyes, then nose, then hair—but you see the person's eyes, nose, hair, and other features all at the same time, and you instantly recognize the person. Simultaneous, parallel processing of all the letters in a word enables readers to name a word as fast as they can name a letter of the alphabet. Although Cattell's observation of the amount of time for naming letters and words was correct, his interpretation of the data was not.

There are more than 800,000 words listed in modern English dictionaries. How many written words can be identified quickly by relying on rote visual memory for word patterns? The human memory is limited as to how many words can be re-

Table 2.1. Manipulation delays in word recognition

Nature of text	Average time of fixation per word	Number of regressive movements
Normal text	236 milliseconds	10.4
Transposition of letters within word	244 milliseconds	11.4
Transposition of letters at word endings	246 milliseconds	12.6
Transposition of letters at word initial position	259 milliseconds	13.0

Source: Rayner, White, Johnson, and Liversedge (2006).

membered and identified instantly. Letter knowledge provides the cues that aid in the effortless recognition of a very large number of words. The instructional implication is that a knowledge of letter–sound correspondences helps beginning readers become instant word readers.

Studies show that poor decoders are also poor instant word readers (Aaron et al., 1999). This is because letter–sound knowledge provides the basis on which skilled word recognition is built. For this reason, teachers should not assume that decoding skills can be short-circuited in reading instruction.

Short-Term Memory   According to one model of reading, the representation of the written word is moved from iconic memory into STM. The study of memory has a long history in psychology. Almost a century ago, William James, a pioneering psychologist, classified memory into two categories: temporary memory and permanent memory. Today these are called STM and LTM, respectively. Whereas it is easy to distinguish between extreme forms of STM and LTM, it is difficult to do so in the short run. For example, the name of the high school you attended is clearly in your LTM, and if you are asked to repeat the sentence you just read, you are accessing this information from your STM. But what about the lunch you had two days ago? Is that memory in LTM or STM? Notwithstanding the fuzziness of these concepts, they have played a useful role in understanding how information is processed.

STM has two components: **acoustic memories** and visual memories. Numerous studies show that readers tend to store information in STM primarily in an acoustic form, but this is not to deny the role of visual processes in reading, as visual memory can be important at the iconic stage. In one study, Liberman, Shankweiler, Liberman, Fowler, and Fischer (1977) found that in an immediate memory task that required children to recall words from a list in the same order of input, good readers surprisingly recalled correctly fewer words from a list of rhyming words (e.g., *ran, man, can*) than from a list of nonrhyming words (e.g., *pen, dog, run*). The difference in recall is attributed to the acoustic confusion caused by the rhyming words. This finding is taken as evidence that the memory mechanism in STM is primarily phonological, not visual, in nature. Several other studies using different experimental designs have confirmed the conclusion that written words are stored in STM in an acoustic form. Complementing this finding, Baddeley (1966) found that **semantic** (meaning) confusion was more prevalent in LTM than acoustic confusion when the input words were recalled several hours later. That is, words such as *king* and *bread* were recalled as *queen* and *food* after many hours. Thus, it appears that STM stores input information in the form of acoustic representations, whereas LTM stores information in the form of meaning representations. As the term implies, STM can store acoustic representations only for a brief period, perhaps a few seconds.

Another feature of STM is its limited capacity. At any given moment, STM can store only about seven items. That is, if you are orally presented digits one by one, you may be able to recall only about seven items in the same order you heard them. However, STM uses two strategies to overcome its temporal and capacity limitations. These strategies are called chunking and rehearsal. Chunking refers to the grouping of elements to help reduce cognitive load. For example, the 20 letters in the words *deoxyribonucleic acid* can be regrouped into five chunks as *de oxy ribo nucleic acid,* which is within STM's limit of seven items. Notice that chunking is accomplished by pronouncing the word, not by visually manipulating it.

Rehearsal refers to turning an item over and over in one's mind so that it can be kept in STM for almost an indefinite length of time. These two mechanisms, chunking and rehearsal, facilitate the processing of information by STM. But, what does it take to chunk and rehearse? Take another look at the word *deoxyribonucleic acid.* Can you chunk and rehearse the word if you do not know English and, therefore, cannot decode the word? In other words, can you keep the word in the STM if you cannot pronounce it? The answer is no. To illustrate further, suppose a first grader reads the sentence "Jack and Jill went up the hill to fetch a pail of water," which has 13 words in it. He starts with the first word and moves on until he comes to the ninth word, *fetch.* Not knowing what this word is, he tries vainly to decode it. All his attention is focused on the word *fetch.* During this process, he has lost track of the subjects in the sentence. Thus, if he is asked who went up the hill, he will not be able to answer correctly. Retaining these words in their acoustic format facilitates the comprehension of the entire sentence, which requires the ability to decode these words. Visual memory is not well suited for this purpose. It should come as no surprise, therefore, that poor decoders are also poor in comprehension. The ability to convert print into pronunciation (decode) is, therefore, a vital prerequisite to being able to read and comprehend.

Executive Memory   In addition to the acoustic and visual systems, the STM has another system called the executive memory. The executive memory is portrayed as a cognitive mechanism that allocates functions to the acoustic STM or the visual STM (Baddeley, 1982). For example, when an individual hears someone speak or read a sentence, the executive memory may direct the acoustic STM to attend to that information; when the individual meets a person or reads a road map, the visual STM may be directed to attend to the facial features of that person or the location of a city on the map. Thus, a major function of the executive memory is directing the memory subordinates, and therefore it can be compared to the chief executive officer of a corporation. Children who are not able to direct their attention to what they hear may not be able to process sentences in STM efficiently and, as a result, may not be able to recall what they have heard. If the difficulty in paying attention reaches a debilitating level, children are said to have attention problems. Because the acoustic, visual, and executive systems of the STM carry out a variety of functions, such as chunking, rehearsal, and attending, this cognitive complex is also referred to as working memory.

As children mature, their STM capacity increases. Children in the early elementary grades may not be able to hold more than three or four items in STM. Understandably, they can comprehend shorter sentences better than longer sentences. Children's storybooks are written with this in mind. Even adults find it difficult to process sentences and clauses that contain more than seven items.

To summarize, numerous experimental studies show that the ability to store what is read in STM depends on the ability to transform the visual input (i.e., print) into an acoustic form (i.e., pronunciation) by decoding the printed word. The ability to pronounce or decode the written word would, therefore, appear to be a fundamental skill that must be mastered by beginning readers. In the early elementary grades, instruction should be designed to help children learn to convert print into pronunciation. This can be accomplished in many ways. Strategies for developing decoding skills are described in Chapter 7.

Long-Term Memory   As previously noted, information in LTM is stored on a meaning basis. Information is not placed into LTM in a haphazard manner but is stored in a well-organized format. Cognitive psychologists call the organized information in LTM the mental lexicon. Mental lexicon is another name for mental dictionary. Cognitive psychologists have named several lexicons, the most common of which is the semantic lexicon. Information in this lexicon is organized on a conceptual basis. For instance, the names of animals might be organized in one group, names of cities in another group, and historical events in yet another group. Other lexicons relevant to reading are the phonological lexicon and the syntactic lexicon. The phonological lexicon is thought to contain rules of pronunciation, enabling individuals to pronounce even unfamiliar words. The syntactical lexicon contains rules of grammar for generating and understanding meaningful sentences.

Information in lexicons is also arranged in more than one format. The most common examples of organizational formats are conceptual, alphabetical, and chronological. Studies show that recall of information is greatly influenced by how well information is organized and stored in the mental lexicon. Information that is well organized is easy to recall. In addition to orderliness, the format of the organization is important. For example, it is relatively easy to recall the names of the months of the year in a chronological order very quickly, in a matter of seconds. However, it would take much longer to try to recall them in alphabetical order. Why? The names of the months are learned and stored in the mental lexicon in a chronological order, and recalling them in that same order is easier than recalling them in an alphabetical order. Information is best recalled if the input format corresponds to the output format. This stresses the importance of organizing input in some systematic way. For example, when children are taught new words, they will remember them better if they are aware of the fact that the words belong to a certain category. For example, the teacher may tell the students that they are going to learn words that describe the library and then introduce such words as *newspaper, magazine, journal, newsletter, storing, librarian,* and *counter.* Children are likely to remember and recall many of these words and concepts if such an organizational basis is provided and made explicit.

Metacognition   A higher order cognitive function is metacognition. In simple language, the term *metacognition* can be defined as knowing what one knows and knowing what one does not know. The implication of this definition is that if a learner knows that she is lacking in a particular area of knowledge or skill, she can take corrective steps to make up for this lack; in contrast, if the learner does not know her weakness, she invariably cannot take corrective action. For example, if a reader knows that she is a slow reader, she can double her reading time, which is likely to increase her level of comprehension. If she lacks this self-awareness, she is not likely to increase her efforts.

Yet another aspect of metacognition is the ability to monitor one's own comprehension process. When the reader realizes that what he reads does not make sense, he can reread the material. When a student reads the sentence *This is the house that Jack built* as "This is the horse that Jack built," meaning is disrupted. If the student rushes on to the next sentence, it is obvious that he has not been monitoring his own comprehension. If, however, he stops and takes another look at the word *house* and gets it right the second time, he has used metacognition to successfully understand the sentence. This going back and taking a second look at misread words involves regressive eye movement. Regressive eye movements are inferred from corrections of oral errors and tell the teacher that the reader is monitoring his comprehension process. It should be noted that it is the brain that tells the eyes where to go. Thus, regressive eye movements should not be interpreted as visual defects responsible for reading difficulties, nor should eye movement exercises be provided as a way of improving reading skills. These actions amount to ignoring the principles of the psychology of reading. Vision exercises do not improve decoding skills.

Sometimes readers substitute words and fail to correct themselves. When the substitution disrupts the meaning of the sentence, it leads to comprehension failure. In contrast, word substitution that retains the integrity of the sentence in spite of altering its meaning is indicative of a word recognition deficiency, not a comprehension problem. For instance, a child who reads the sentence *This is the house that Jack built* as "This is the horse that Jack bought" does have a word recognition problem, but her comprehension is relatively intact. Repeated failure to self-correct oral reading errors that impair the meaning of a sentence indicates a weakness in metacognition skills.

Teaching children to self-question their comprehension as they read is often suggested as one of the strategies for improving comprehension. For instance, while reading a story, children are reminded to stop after reading the first paragraph and ask themselves the question "Do I understand the story so far?" Some studies suggest that such self-monitoring does improve students' comprehension skills (Donnelly, 1999; McLaughlin & Allen, 2002).

Procognition   Procognition, or theory of mind, is a cognitive process that refers to the ability to know what goes on in another person's mind. In simple terms, it is mind reading. When a second grader reads the story *Little Red Riding Hood,* is he aware of what is going on in the mind of the wolf who is dressed like Little Red Riding Hood's grandmother? Such an awareness is necessary for an appreciation of the story. Procognition also plays an important role in day-to-day communication exchanges. Individuals often do not make explicit statements; they leave the listener to fill in the gaps because they know what goes on in the listener's mind. In everyday communication, speakers are constantly reading the mind of the listener. For example, when a restaurant waitperson asks, "Have you decided yet?" he means "Have you decided what food to order?" The waiter knows that you know what he means; in other words, he has read your mind, and he knows that you have read his, too.

Procognitive skill takes time and experience to develop, and naturally there is a wide gap between students and the teacher in the use of this skill. Many children in early elementary grades do not yet have the capacity to figure out what the teacher wants, expects, likes, or dislikes; they have to be explicitly told. In contrast, the teacher uses procognitive skills continually to infer when a child is not understanding what he hears, when he is bored, when he is frustrated, and so on. Because of this knowledge, the teacher can ask the student a question, repeat what she said, or tell an anecdote to get the child's attention—whatever her procognition has told her is the problem. Procognition helps the teacher make inferences regarding the learning that is taking place in the minds of the students and adjust her teaching accordingly.

Clinical Cognitive Psychology

One of the questions that has historically preoccupied the minds of philosophers is "How do we come to understand the world?" The branch of philosophy that deals with such questions is known as epistemology. Answers to the question of how humans come to understand the world generally conform to one of two extreme positions, although mixes of these positions also exist. The two extreme positions are known as realism and **constructivism.** Realists believe that the world is just out there and individuals understand it as it is. It is akin to picking mushrooms in the forest: The mushrooms are there, and all one has to do is to collect them. In contrast, constructivists believe that the human mind interprets the world and builds a knowledge of it according to one's own personal background. The constructivist view is expressed by the dictum "all objects are colorless," which means that objects do not have colors inherent in them; they simply reflect light in various frequencies. It is a person's visual perceptual system that interprets these frequencies as red, blue, or some other color. According to the constructivist view, an understanding or interpretation of the world can vary from person to person depending on individual experience, background, and maturation level.

Piaget, Constructivism, and Schema   Jean Piaget (1896–1980), a leading scholar of the 20th century, was a constructivist who developed a theory of children's understanding of the world and how such understanding changes as they grow. By pursuing questions of evolutionary biology, Piaget studied the evolution of human thought processes. In other words, he was interested in studying the evolution of human intelligence. Because thinking does not leave directly observable evidence, Piaget reasoned that he could draw inferences regarding the evolution of human intelligence by studying the development of thinking processes in humans, beginning with children. This approach is based on the hypothesis that the evolutionary history of organisms parallels the developmental history of individuals.

On the basis of his work with children, Piaget proposed that both maturation, which to a large extent is biologically determined, and experience, which comes from interaction with the environment, have a role in shaping children's understanding of the world. Children do not perceive the outside world as it is; rather, they develop an understanding of the external world based on their experience and their level of maturation. When reading specialists define reading as the construction of meaning from printed text, they are using a Piagetian constructive perspective. Such construction of meaning is dependent partly on the reader's mental maturity and partly on the reader's background experience, also referred to as schema (plural: schemata).

The role of experience in comprehension has been extensively studied under the topic of schema theory. In simple terms, the word *schema* means background; schema theory proposes that comprehension is greatly influenced by the schema, or background information, the reader brings to the reading task. Consider the following passage:

> Chicago hosts the LA Rams to determine the NFC's Super Bowl representative. There will be no sideshows in this one as it doesn't need any. Walter Payton running one way and Eric Dickerson the other is plenty, and add to that the Refrigerator and friends snacking on Rams quarterback Dieter Brock. (Hunt, 1986)

A group of British psychologists who listened to this statement thought it was about a country fair or picnic. They constructed a scenario based on their own background.

There are two requirements for schemata to function optimally in the reading process. First, the reader must possess schema that is relevant to the text; second, the reader must select and activate the relevant schema so that the text will be understood as the author intended. For example, when children read a passage about a hospital, they may encounter such terms as *patient, surgeon,* and *pharmaceutical*. These words will be meaningless to many young children unless they have a schema for hospital. The teacher, therefore, must first build the appropriate schema before he can expect students to read the passage and understand it. The appropriate schema can be developed in several ways. The ideal way would be to visit a hospital and let children encounter firsthand its patients, surgeons, and pharmacy. When this is not possible, the children may be shown a video of a hospital and have the terms explained. In lieu of this, the teacher might describe a hospital, show pictures of the various aspects of the hospital, and introduce the appropriate vocabulary, phrases, and concepts. The reading lesson could be introduced after this experience.

Having the schema for a topic does not itself guarantee proper comprehension of the text that is being read; the reader also needs to be able to select the appropriate schema and activate it when she reads the text. The following passage illustrates how, as each sentence is read, the reader selects a schema, rejects it if it is inappropriate, selects another schema, and so on. As you read this passage, note the images that are aroused in your mind and how they might change as you read.

> John was on his way to school. He was terribly worried about the mathematics lesson. He thought he might not be able to control the class again today. He thought it was unfair of the instructor to make him supervise the class for a second time. After all, it was not a normal part of a janitor's duties. (Sanford & Garrod, 1981, p. 132)

When you read the first sentence, it is very likely that you thought the passage was about a boy going to school. By the time you read the second sentence, you realized that you had selected the wrong schema, you discarded it, and you probably activated the schema of a teacher. But then the third sentence made you drop that schema, too, and select another one, perhaps of a student teacher or assistant. By the end, you likely realized that none of these schemata was correct!

This passage was selected for the purpose of illustration. Actual passages encountered by students, particularly in the higher grades, are not so explicit in their schema. For example, fifth-grade teachers usually consider the lesson on Columbus's voyage to be important because of the fact that the voyage opened up a new world to explore and exploit. However, when a small group of fifth-grade children taught by one of the authors of this textbook were asked what they learned from the lesson, their answers were that Columbus used three ships for sailing (and what the names of the ships were), that Columbus thought there would be monsters in the sea, and that he met with many Indians. A high school student, on the other hand, is likely to focus on Columbus's effort to find a trade route to India and the exploration of the New World. Thus, the same passage about this explorer could be understood differently by children, depending upon the schema they have or the schema they have activated. In Piagetian terms, a fifth grader and a high school student construct different views of Columbus's voyage. Preparing children for a lesson and helping them activate the appropriate schema can orient them to perceive the lesson differently. This preparation is part of the prereading exercises that play an important role in comprehension.

When applied to literacy skills, Piaget's theory—which views cognitive development as a product of biology and experience—means that until students have attained a level of cognitive maturity for a certain concept, trying to teach that concept will be unproductive. Very young children, for example, are not likely to understand the abstract meanings of statements. As a result, they may not be able to understand and appreciate proverbs and metaphors. The theory also suggests that not providing the appropriate literacy experiences to students will impede their learning. To help students learn, teachers need an accurate understanding (i.e., procognition) of students' level of cognitive maturity and understanding and must be able to provide instruction in such a way that it matches this maturity.

Vygotsky's Scaffolding Instruction   Piaget assigned much importance to the roles of biological and maturational factors in learning and viewed language as a product of children's thought processes. For him, language was a means of expressing thoughts; if the thoughts were not there, speech would be empty. In contrast, Lev Vygotsky (1896–1934), a Russian psychologist, educator, and physician, proposed that language plays an important role in children's cognitive development. Unlike Piaget, Vygotsky considered language to be a guidance system that influences children's thought processes. Young children tend to talk to themselves because, according to Vygotsky, they use this "private speech" as a guidance system for their thinking. As children mature, the language-based guidance system becomes "inner speech."

Because language is used for communicating with others, Vygotsky also believed that social interaction and cultural factors influence children's thought processes. Thus, adults can guide children's learning by providing support during the initial stages of learning through language interaction. As learning continues to unfold, the support can be gradually withdrawn. This idea has come to be referred to as instructional scaffolding, which simply means instructional support.

Vygotsky recognized three stages of skill development: learning independently, learning with help, and unable to learn even with help. Reading literature refers to the first stage as the student's independent reading level and the last one as the frustration level. Vygotsky described the level of skill between the independent learning level and the level at which a child can learn with help as the zone of proximal development. The zone of proximal development is the difference in skill between what a child can do alone and what she can do with assistance. This zone is important, because it is here that the teacher plays a crucial role by providing the necessary guidance and instructional scaffolding to help the student move forward to the independent level. When applied to reading, this scaffolding process is known as guided reading.

The concepts of zone of proximal development and scaffolding instruction can be illustrated with an example of learning to swim. At first, the instructor provides maximum help to a child who is learning to swim by supporting him in the swimming pool. As the child gains skill and confidence, the instructor gradually decreases support until the child becomes an independent swimmer. At this point, the adult's support is completely withdrawn. Providing adequate instructional support for the beginning reader and moving the student toward mastery of skills of increasing complexity is accomplished through guided reading. In their book *Effective Literacy Instruction*, Leu and Kinzer (2003) have given examples for scaffolding instruction for beginning readers. They recommended the use of predictable texts, which contain repeated phrases or rhyming words. The teacher can repeatedly read books such as *Brown Bear, Brown Bear, What Do You See?* (Carle, 1996) or nursery rhymes such as *The Little Red Hen, The House that Jack Built,* and *The Gingerbread Boy,* and the children will quickly learn the repetitive words and phrases. The teacher can then ask the children to read the books. According to these authors, even readers who struggle the most will be able to read many such books on their own when they discover the predictable patterns of the words, which make the books easy to read.

Teachers should be perceptive enough not to frustrate a child by assigning a task she cannot perform. Offering support and guidance will help the child perform the task comfortably and move her to the next level, in which she can perform successfully without assistance.

A Comparison of Piaget and Vygotsky   Although Piaget and Vygotsky differed in their pedagogical orientations, both attached much importance to the opportunities learners should experience for cognitive growth. Their theories suggest that learning is not incidental, nor does it occur through mere exposure to interesting situations; the teacher plays an integral role in the process.

The relationship between thought and language is an important issue in psychology and linguistics. There are two opposing views about this relationship. Some scholars, such as Piaget, consider thought to be the *sine qua non* of language. If there is no thought, there will be no substance to language. For instance, a child who has no concept of time cannot comprehend terms such as *past, tomorrow,* and *future.* Vygotsky held the opposite view that language helps the development of thought. The latter view receives support from studies showing that immersion of Head Start children in language experience increases their IQ scores. This issue has a long history. Benjamin Whorf, an early researcher, even went to the extent of proposing that the language we speak shapes our thought. Literally stated, this idea means that if you are a native English speaker, you will have an English mind; if you are a native French speaker, you will have a French mind. Supporters of either view have amassed much anecdotal evidence to support their respective views. Some studies show that immersing children who are in Head Start programs in language experience improves their IQ scores. Some argue that unless a child possesses the needed concepts and ideas, language will be empty; they offer examples such as the idea that a child cannot use the word *time* intelligently in his expressions unless he has grasped the concept of time.

So, what is the answer? Like many other issues, the language versus thought issue may be a false dichotomy. One difficulty with the issue lies with the definition of language. *Speech* and *language* are not synonyms. That is, language can be expressed in many forms, one of which is speech. Language is something deeper than speech. If one accepts this view of language, then language and thought may actually be one and the same mental activity. The question, therefore, of whether thought or language comes first may be a spurious one.

History of Literacy Instruction in the United States

How to teach reading to children is not agreed upon today, nor was it in the past. In spite of a substantial body of information about the psychology and **pedagogy** of reading and spelling, with very few exceptions such information has not found its way into classrooms. Often, a sensational theory is proposed and advanced, only to slowly wither away and die and be replaced by yet another sensational theory. After a period of dormancy, the old theory may resurface and be hailed as a new discovery. The history of literacy instruction confirms the dictum that history repeats itself.

A knowledge of the history of reading education in the United States will help teachers avoid being swept up by some current fad, objectively evaluate the many theoretical orientations in the field, and implement what they think is appropriate for their students. This requires a critical reading of research articles and reading textbooks.

The fund of knowledge about literacy instruction and the psychology behind it has evolved slowly over a long period of time. This part of the chapter presents a history of literacy instruction in the United States and traces the origin of the present-day controversies to their historical roots.

The 16th and 17th Centuries:
The Early Period of Reading Instruction

According to Nila Banton Smith (1965), who wrote a fascinating book on the history of reading instruction in the United States, clearly identifiable changes in teaching methods and materials have taken place in this country—changes relating to religious, cultural, and political conditions of the times. For instance, during the colonial period, Christian, Protestant, and Puritan values were prevalent, and the reading materials used at that time reflect these ideals.

The first reading material used in American schools was the hornbook (Smith, 1965). According to Mitford (1966), the hornbook resembled a tiny paddle used for table tennis with a sheet of paper pasted on one side. It contained the alphabet, some simple words, and the Lord's Prayer. The sheet of paper was protected from wet, dirty fingers by a thin, translucent sheet peeled off an animal horn, hence the name "hornbook." The material in the hornbook was used for teaching reading as well as religion. Reading instruction was simple and straightforward: the alphabetic method, in which children learned the names of the letters. Reading aloud by children and the teacher was the main tool of instruction.

Another reader, simply referred to as the ABC, went a little farther than the hornbook. As the name of this early book indicates, the first step in reading instruction was to teach the names of the letters of the alphabet. The fact that the ABC books were used almost until the middle of the 19th century indicates that for a long time very little attention was paid to methodology in teaching reading. What was taught was more important than how it was taught. Some ingenious strategies were, however, devised to teach reading through the alphabetic method. One used gingerbread shaped in the form of the letters of the alphabet. A poem in Smith (1965, p. 7) celebrates the merits of the gingerbread method.

After mastering the hornbook, a child could move on to the primer, which contained both the alphabet in addition to some religious selections. The primer was originally produced in England, and the first American edition was first published in Boston in 1655 under the name *New-England Primer* (Monaghan & Barry, 1999).

By the turn of the 18th century, the primer met with competition in the form of the speller, which was designed for teaching students how to read any passage in the Bible. The title of the book indicates that reading and spelling were taught simultaneously. The first speller was written by Noah Webster in 1783 and was produced by an American press. By the end of the 18th century the country had gone through a great political change, and the primers of the period reflected this fact. Religious and moralistic reading materials slowly were replaced by others intended to stir up patriotic fervor and promote a sense of nationalism. The portrait of King George III was renamed John Hancock on the book, although the picture itself was not changed. In 1807, Noah Webster produced the first set of readers by an American author, a series of three graded books. First in the series was the *American Spelling Book*, the next level was a treatise on grammar, and the most advanced book contained lessons on the history and geography of the United States. The content of these books, therefore, reflected students' steady progression from learning to read to reading to learn. Other readers published by different educators also became available at this time, and some of these books contained exercises and rules for correct pronunciation and articulation.

The 19th Century: Reading Instruction Gets Attention

An inspection of books used in classrooms from 1820 through 1880 indicates that the acquisition of general knowledge and principles of good citizenship were emphasized during this period. This era is also noteworthy for one other important development. The alphabetic method and the books that promoted it came under criticism when educators began to realize that recitation of the alphabet and the **rote memorization** of a handful of words were not sufficient to master the increasing amount of material that had to be read and understood. As a result, new methods of reading instruction were devised and promoted.

Alternatives to the Alphabetic Method

One method was advanced by Professor Thomas Gallaudet of Connecticut. In this program, about 50 words were first introduced, and children learned to associate each written word with its pronunciation without analyzing the names of the constituent letters. Next, children learned the letters in these words. Although this method appears to be a whole word method, it was not entirely so because at some point during the course of instruction, students were introduced to the letters of the alphabet.

By far the most ardent advocate of the whole word, look-say method during this period was Horace Mann (1796–1859). After being elected to the Massachusetts state legislature, Mann became the secretary of the board of education. Mann had personally observed German classrooms, in which reading instruction started with whole words. This appeared to make reading somewhat more meaningful to children. Mann considered this method far superior to the American alphabetic method, which he derisively called "abecedarian," in which "children blundered through sentences, spelling each word and pronouncing it before passing to the next, imitating sounds like a parrot or an idiot" (Mitford, 1966, p. 77). Mann advocated introducing a set of words first and then the names of the letters of the alphabet, because he wondered why a child should not learn to read as easily as he learns to talk, if taught in a similar manner. In spite of his power and influence, Mann failed to persuade many Massachusetts teachers to accept his way of teaching because the teachers thought that Mann did not understand the difference between teaching **letter names and letter sounds.** Furthermore, teachers who had tried his system testified that although children could successfully learn a word in one context, they were unable to recognize it later in another context. A positive outcome of this conflict was that attention was drawn to a distinction between introducing letter names first and introducing letter sounds later in teaching reading.

Although many did not agree with Mann, virtually all educators appear to have been convinced that the alphabetic method not only involved tedious drill but also confused children because the names and sounds of letters, when they appear in words, do not always match. For instance, the name of the first letter in *cat* (*c*) and its pronunciation (/k/) do not match. Subsequently, the alphabetic method of introducing the names of letters was abandoned and replaced by the phonics approach, in which letter sounds were introduced.

Even as the letter name versus letter sound controversy was raging, an approach emphasizing meaning began to emerge. In 1881 George Farnham, a superintendent of schools in New York, introduced a small manual for teachers titled *The Sentence Method of Teaching Reading.* In it he argued that pupils should develop the ability to look directly to the meaning through the written language. The sentence method worked in the following way. The teacher would read a story repeatedly until the children became thoroughly familiar with it. Then the written form of the story was presented to the children, and each sentence in the story was analyzed. In this method, analysis of words by their constituent letters was postponed indefinitely or never attempted. A strong supporter of this "meaning approach" was Francis Parker, who in his 1883 book *Talks on Teaching* observed, "Reading may be defined as the act of the mind in getting thought by means of written or printed words arranged in sentences. . . . The mere pronunciation of words however correctly and readily done, is not reading" (Mitford, 1966, p. 106). Nobody would disagree with this definition of reading. The question was, and still is, how to get meaning from the printed page.

The most widely used books during this period were the McGuffey Readers, printed from 1836 to 1907. These readers were a series of graded books. In the beginning grades, much emphasis was given to repetition and drill, and very few new words were introduced in each lesson. For example, in an early lesson, two-letter words were introduced with the aid of these sentences: "Do we go? Do we go up? We do go up." As a result, sentences were choppy and artificial, with little narrative interest. (Contemporary decodable texts follow a similar instructional approach.) The texts for upper grades, however, contained more selections from literature. The McGuffey Reader is considered to be the forerunner of the contemporary basal readers, which understandably came under heavy criticism in the 1960s for their repetitive lessons that emphasized drill.

According to Smith (1965), in the early 1880s the nation had reached a state of tranquility and security and had the time and inclination to pursue and enjoy music, art, and literature. As culture began to exert its influence, schools were blamed for not teaching children what to read and how to appreciate what they read. During the closing years of the 19th century, Charles Eliot, who at the time was the president of Harvard University, stated that he would like to see such texts as the McGuffey Reader excluded from schools, with real literature substituted in its place. To satisfy this hunger for culture, books containing selections from literature were produced for the classroom. It was also during this time that professional books about how to teach reading made their first appearance. Instructional methods of teaching, therefore, became a legitimate object of inquiry. The teaching controversy, however, was far from being settled, and in spite of a new emphasis on meaning and literature, some educators remained skeptical about the effectiveness of the whole word and sentence methods.

Spelling Reform

Convinced that the inconsistent nature of English orthography (spelling pattern) is a major impediment to reading acquisition, many reformers have, over the years, attempted to impose some regularity on English spelling. One such reformer was Shearer, who in 1894 published *The Shearer System*. This system, through extensive use of diacritical marks, set forth a "one letter–one sound" relationship. Another system called the *Scientific Alphabet* was introduced in 1902. This system, in addition to using diacritical marks, reduced the number of characters needed for representing sounds by changing spelling and omitting silent letters. *The Initial Teaching Alphabet* represented a similar effort. First introduced during the mid-19th century by Isaac Pitman in England, it received favorable reports in that country. Nevertheless, *The Shearer System, Scientific Alphabet*, and *The Initial Teaching Alphabet* all failed to capture the interest of American educators. The only changes accomplished were those suggested by Noah Webster, which eliminated some redundancies seen in British spellings, such as *favour* and *colour*. The reason for the survival of the classic spelling system is probably due to the fact that the spelling of a number of English words is *morphophonemic* in nature; that is, the spellings represent not only the pronunciation of words but also their meaning, at times giving precedence to meaning over pronunciation. The nature of English spelling is described in greater detail in Chapter 4.

The 20th Century: The Scientific Study of Reading

In addition to the ongoing controversy over reading methods, the period between 1880 and 1925 was notable for three other important events: 1) the publication of professional books on reading, such as *The Psychology and Pedagogy of Reading*, by Edmund Huey (1908/1968), *Deficiencies in Reading Ability: Their Diagnosis and Remedies*, by C.T. Gray (1922), and *The Teacher's Word Book*, by E. Thorndike (1921); 2) the beginning of research efforts comparing the effectiveness of different teaching procedures; and 3) the recognition of the existence of reading disability.

Between 1884 and 1910, 34 research studies on reading were published in the United States and England (Smith, 1965). Most of these studies examined topics such as eye movements, visual perception, and reading speed. One of the earliest "experimental" studies was conducted in 1911 by Josephine Bowden, a school-teacher who examined the effectiveness of the meaning-oriented teaching method. Because it was claimed that reading should be learned naturally, as speaking is acquired, she taught five kindergarten children using the "natural way." Under this method, children made up stories or described their experiences; the teacher wrote these on the chalkboard, and the children then read and copied the stories. After 8 weeks of instruction, children were tested and found to recognize most of the words with which they were familiar. However, they misread many words that were similar in appearance (e.g., "coat" instead of *coast*; "fed" instead of *red*). Surprisingly, they read equally well whether the test words were correctly positioned or turned upside down. Bowden concluded that children could not learn to develop a system for recognizing words on their own and that only an early introduction of phonics could help them learn this skill.

Assessment of Literacy Skills

Prior to 1900, reading assessment was primarily qualitative in nature, accomplished by listening to students' oral reading performance. Starting around 1910, tests designed to assess comprehension and other reading-related skills, such as spelling, were developed. These instruments not only were useful in evaluating children's reading ability but also were helpful in facilitating reading research by making possible a comparison of the effectiveness of different methods of reading instruction. In the 1920s, statistical procedures were applied and most of the tests were standardized, making them quite reliable. The speed with which reading achievement tests were developed and utilized during this period can be appreciated by noting the different tests used by Arthur Gates in his 1922 study of the relationship between intelligence and reading and spelling achievement. The list of tests includes Holley's Sentence Vocabulary Test, Burgess Reading Test, Brown's Reading Test, Curtis Silent Reading Test, Monroe's Silent Reading Test, Thorndike-McCall Reading Test, Gray's Reading Test, and Stanford-Binet Intelligence Test. Assessment of reading ability made educators realize that some children experienced a considerable amount of difficulty in learning to read. The publication of *Deficiencies in Reading Ability: Their Diagnosis and Remedies* by C.T. Gray (1922) is an outcome of this realization.

The term *remedial reading* was first used by Uhl in 1916 and came to be widely used in the early 1920s. Three different kinds of remedial methods were used. The alphabet-spelling method was used very early primarily by those in the medical profession; phonics and kinesthetic methods were used primarily by clinicians in educational settings; and exercises to improve oral reading, silent reading, and word recognition were used primarily by teachers in classrooms. Innovative classroom instructional techniques such as experience charts, which were a forerunner of the language experience approach, were also developed. The phonics-kinesthetic method used primarily in clinics is referred to as the **multisensory approach** at present. The origins of this approach can be traced to Grace Fernald, whose work influenced physician Samuel Orton. In addition to proposing a theory about the cause of reading disability, Orton collaborated with the educators Anna Gillingham and Bessie Stillman to develop an instructional method that utilizes auditory, visual, and kinesthetic elements for teaching reading. Chapter 9 presents more information about Orton and the multisensory method of teaching reading.

Textbooks of this period began to make use of highly controlled lists of vocabulary. Because the major goal of these books was to introduce basic vocabulary, they came to be referred to as basal readers. Basal readers have had a tremendous influence on reading instruction since this time. Over the years, the content of basal readers has changed to reflect shifts in educational philosophy and in the understanding of reading psychology. Basal readers are discussed in greater detail in Appendix B.

The Skills Versus Meaning Approach to Literacy Instruction

The three decades following the 1930s witnessed the Second World War and the flight of the Russian *Sputnik.* Both events drew attention to the need for an educated populace and a high-quality education in general. Criticism of reading instruction reached a feverous pitch with the publication of the book *Why Johnny Can't Read* by Rudolph Flesch (1955). Flesch asserted that children were not learning to read because they were not being taught phonics skills. Naturally, the solution to this problem was to teach beginning reading through systematic phonics instruction. Although this book was considered in academic circles to be polemic and an oversimplification of the issue, it was instrumental in drawing public attention to both the importance of reading and to how it was being taught in the schools. An important publication that followed Flesch's book was Jean Chall's *Learning to Read: The Great Debate*, published in 1967. Chall evaluated nearly 50 years of research in reading instruction and compared the effectiveness of methods that emphasized code (i.e., phonics) with those that focused on meaning. She cautiously concluded that

> It would seem, at our present state of knowledge, that a code emphasis—one that combines control of words on spelling regularity, some direct teaching of letter-sound correspondences, as well as the use of writing, tracing, or typing—produces better results with unselected groups of beginners than a meaning emphasis. (p. 178)

In a newer edition of this book in 1996, the conclusions reached in the previous edition remained essentially unchanged. Chall did warn educators not to overemphasize decoding drill at the expense of meaning and interest and advised moderation in the use of different methods of teaching.

During the 1964–1965 academic year, the U.S. Office of Education supported 27 studies that assessed the effectiveness of instructional techniques in the first grade and followed the children through the second year. Bond and Dykstra (1967) summarized the results of the first-year studies and concluded that word study skills must be emphasized and taught systematically regardless of which approach to initial reading instruction was utilized. Reflecting on the results of the first year and the follow-up studies, Dykstra later wrote,

> We can summarize the results of 60 years of research dealing with beginning reading instruction by stating that early systematic instruction in phonics provides the child with the skills necessary to become an independent reader at an earlier age than is likely if phonics instruction is delayed and less systematic. (1974, p. 97)

In spite of these publications, the 1980s saw a resurgence of interest in the meaning-based approach to reading instruction. Based on the writings of educators such as Kenneth Goodman, meaning-based instruction was promoted under the name of

whole language. The whole language philosophy downplayed the importance of skills instruction as well as the use of basal readers and stressed the use of literature and trade books. It was believed that this approach would give freedom to teachers and empower them and at the same time make reading more interesting and authentic for children than the skills approach. The whole language approach (WLA) enjoyed a great deal of popularity and support; many school systems across the nation urged their teachers to implement whole language instruction and not to stress phonics, drill, and worksheets in their instruction. A few years later, however, states such as California and Texas realized that the overall reading scores of students had declined, possibly because of the adoption of the whole language philosophy, and they passed legislation requiring schools to go back to skills instruction.

The Current Scene: Concerns About Children's Reading Performance

It is in this milieu that reports such as *Becoming a Nation of Readers* (Anderson, Hiebert, Scott, & Wilkinson, 1985), *Preventing Reading Difficulties in Young Children* (Snow, Burns, & Griffin, 1998), and the NRP's report (2000) had their genesis. This brief history of American literacy instruction shows that both materials and methods were influenced by cultural, political, and religious forces prevalent at different periods of history. The contemporary scene could be viewed to be more influenced by science and technology than any other period in history. Science and research go hand in hand. Consequently, research in reading and reading instruction is expected to determine which method of instruction is the most effective in teaching young children how to read and write. This is evident in the frequent occurrence of phrases such as *research based* and *evidence based* in federal initiatives such as the No Child Left Behind Act and descriptors such as *scientifically based reading research* and *scientifically proven information* in reading research literature. (See Box 2.3.) Not all educators, however, agree that research-based findings are reliable and trustworthy.

Throughout the 20th century, grave concern was expressed time and again about children's reading performance. One report that addressed the issue of illiteracy among schoolchildren was the National Academy of Education's *Becoming a Nation of Readers* (Anderson et al., 1985). The report summarized available research findings and concluded that "the issue is no longer, as it was several

---

Box 2.3. The National Reading Panel report and the No Child Left Behind Act of 2001 (PL 107-110)

The National Reading Panel (NRP) report has served as the foundation for the No Child Left Behind Act of 2001 (PL 107-110), which is guided by four principles: accountability, flexibility and local control, parental choice, and scientifically based research (what works). Of these four guiding principles, the phrase *scientifically based research* captures the essence of the NRP report. Because No Child Left Behind has been implemented on a nationwide scale, it is important that teachers have an accurate perception of the NRP report. A copy of the report can be obtained free of cost through http://www.nationalreadingpanel.org/Publications/subgroups.htm.

decades ago, whether children should be taught phonics; the issue is . . . how it should be done" (p. 36). In 1998, the National Research Council sponsored the publication of its committee's report, *Preventing Reading Difficulties in Young Children* (Snow et al., 1998). The committee stated that adequate progress in learning to read beyond the initial level depends on 1) having established a working understanding of how sounds are represented alphabetically; 2) having sufficient practice in reading to achieve fluency; and 3) having control over procedures for monitoring comprehension. Another recent national effort was the establishment of the National Reading Panel, which was mentioned in Chapter 1. The NRP was charged by the U.S. Congress in 1997 to conduct a thorough study of the research and knowledge relevant to reading development and instruction in early reading and to determine the research findings and knowledge available in the nation's classrooms. The findings of the NRP were released in 2000. These included research findings that teaching children to manipulate phonemes in words is highly effective across all the literacy domains and that phonics instruction has a strong impact on typically developing first graders as well as on kindergartners and first graders who are at risk. Other findings are as follows:

- Well-defined instruction that encourages repeated guided oral reading results in increased reading proficiency.
- Vocabulary can be learned incidentally in the context of storybook reading.
- Vocabulary instruction leads to gains in comprehension; instruction in cognitive strategies such as comprehension monitoring, use of semantic organizers and story maps, use of question and answer techniques, and summarization improves reading comprehension in readers with a range of abilities.

The NRP's recommendations, as well as the recommendations made by other committees that have relied on published research, did not go unchallenged. Allington (2002), for instance, observed that the initiative for a national reading curriculum is simply part of an attempt to shift control of public education from local taxpayers and teachers to those who sit in bureaucratic offices far from classrooms. Yatvin (2000), who was a member of the NRP, was more specific in her criticisms of the NRP. She noted that the NRP used only one model of reading for all of its investigations and excluded lines of research on children's knowledge of oral language and literature; it also neglected the interdependence between reading and writing as well as the type, quality, and amount of material children read. In addition, all the scientist members of the NRP held the same general view of the reading process; the panel adopted a sequential model of decoding, fluency, and comprehension; and there was only one classroom teacher on the panel and no reading teacher. Another critic, Coles (2000), after raising the question of whether it is true that one of the most well-established conclusions in behavioral science is that direct instruction in the alphabetic code facilitates early reading acquisition, concluded that a close examination of research does not support this view.

Is the NRP report flawed? Shanahan (2003), who also was a member of the NRP, tried to answer most of the criticisms by clarifying a number of the misconceptions people seem to have about the NRP report. According to Shanahan, the NRP report is not merely a phonics report because it also deals with other aspects of language; it addresses classroom reading instruction for all students at all age levels; it is not biased against qualitative research even though it examined only experimental studies that could answer the type of questions the panel was asked to address; and, finally, it does not recommend phoneme awareness training or any other single method as a cure-all.

Has any good come out of these arguments? Although none of the sides has a monopoly on the truth, the controversy has made an entire educational community more aware of reading and reading instruction. But this is not the first time this has happened. Disagreement about reading instruction has such a long history that an article in *Newsweek* described it as the "reading wars" (Kantrowitz & Underwood, 1999). A review of the history of literacy education in the United States provides a backdrop that is useful in understanding the contemporary controversies over literacy.

Approaches to Literacy Instruction: Today's Major Players

This brief history of literacy instruction shows that controversies about reading methods and materials have a checkered past. If the 200-year history of reading instruction were distilled, it would be clear that although a variety of instructional methods were used in the past, today the code or skills emphasis and meaning emphasis are the major contenders, representing the two extremes of the philosophy of reading instruction. These are represented by the phonics instruction and the WLA, respectively.

Phonics instruction is teaching reading in a way that helps children learn how speech sounds are represented by the letters of the alphabet. In technical terms, it refers to a knowledge of the correspondence between phonemes and graphemes. This knowledge is the basis of the ability to decode written words. In recent years, **phonemic awareness** (the understanding that speech is made up of units of sounds) has been discovered to be positively correlated with reading achievement, and phonemic awareness training is recommended as the starting point for phonics-based instruction. Those who advocate phonics instruction for beginning readers believe that the relationship between the English alphabet and the sounds represented by the letters is reasonably predictable and that teaching children about such relationships makes learning to read and write easier. The skills approach is recommended for beginning readers only; an emphasis on meaning is inferred for children in grades 4 and above when they use reading to learn.

The WLA, in contrast, is more of a philosophy than a method of instruction. It is also described as an approach, a belief, a theory, a movement, and an orientation. There is no universally accepted definition of WLA. According to Bergeron (1990), any approach or program that supports literature-based instruction, that integrates reading, writing, and literature, is described under the WLA umbrella. In spite of not having a clearly discernible set of characteristics, the roots of WLA can be traced to certain philosophical foundations. These are collectively described as humanistic education, which emphasizes meaning so that reading becomes authentic, purposeful, and interesting, and promotes the integration of reading and writing into a unified learning experience. The distinction between WLA and other meaning-based instructional approaches is so blurred that sometimes exclusionary criteria are used to describe WLA. For instance, Newman and Church (1990), in an attempt to clarify misunderstandings about WLA, listed the following myths about WLA: Phonics is not taught in WLA; WLA is limited to a literature-based curriculum; it is a way of teaching language arts only; students are not evaluated in WLA; WLA classrooms have no standards; WLA teachers deal only with the teaching process and not the outcome; and there is one set of prescribed principles for teaching WLA.

In spite of its lack of specificity, WLA differs from methods that emphasize the code approach in certain important ways. WLA is based on the premise that learning to read is as natural as learning to speak (e.g., Goodman, 1986) and, therefore, any prescribed form of reading instruction makes reading acquisition unnatural. It assumes that because the goal of teaching reading is comprehension, explicit and systematic teaching of phonics is unnecessary and can even be counterproductive. WLA holds the distinction between learning to read and reading to learn to be artificial and, therefore, does not make such a distinction. In contrast to the code approach, WLA allows risk taking and guessing for recognizing written words. Consequently, word-recognition skill development is not vigorously promoted by WLA proponents. WLA recommends the use of literature, not basal readers. WLA also discourages the use of practice exercises and worksheets because these are uninteresting for children (see Table 2.2).

Another argument often presented in the WLA literature undermining the importance of phonics in reading is an allegation that children in China are able to learn to read their language, which is logographic (icon-like) and not alphabetic in nature. It is argued that because logographs are nonalphabetic, they can be learned as wholes without the reader's resorting to phonological analysis. Decoding skill, therefore, is not essential for learning to read English either. As noted in Box 2.4, however, the size of an average Chinese speaker's sight vocabulary is limited to approximately 4,000 logographs. Even a Chinese scholar may not be able to read more than 8,000 logographs (Goody, 1968).

In contrast, an English-speaking high school student can read more than 20,000 words easily and can decode words he or she has never encountered before. Furthermore, Chinese characters are not purely logographic in nature; nearly 70%–80% of Chinese characters contain phonetic compounds that provide information about the pronunciation of the character even though the phonetic elements do not map directly onto phonetic units (Leong & Tamaoka, 1998). According to Tan and Perfetti (1998), while one reads Chinese characters, phonology is rapidly activated even though visual recognition of the characters may also take place at the same time (see Box 2.4).

Table 2.2. Major differences between the whole language approach and methods with a code emphasis

Whole language approach	Methods with a code emphasis
Learning to read is as natural as learning to speak.	Learning to read does not come naturally for most children; explicit instruction is needed.
Comprehension of meaning is the goal of instruction, even in beginning reading.	Word recognition is necessary for comprehension; therefore, skills instruction is necessary.
No distinction is maintained between learning to read and reading to learn.	Learning to read precedes reading to learn.
Risk taking and guessing the pronunciation of words are to be encouraged.	Reading is a precise act; guessing the word from context is risky.
Literature is the main material for instruction.	Basal readers are used for instruction.
Practice exercises, drills, and the use of worksheets are to be discouraged.	Exercises, drills, and worksheets are among the aids to learning to read.
Phonics skills are to be taught incidentally.	Phonics is taught systematically and explicitly.

> **Box 2.4.   Does learning to read Chinese involve no phonetic elements at all?**
>
> An argument often presented in the whole language approach literature negating the importance of phonics in reading is an allegation that children in China are able to learn to read their language, which is logographic (icon-like) and not alphabetic in nature. Logographs, it is argued, can be learned as wholes without resorting to phonological analysis. Decoding skill, therefore, is not essential for learning to read English either. However, Chinese characters are not purely logographic in nature; nearly 70%–80% contain phonetic compounds that provide information about the pronunciation of the character even though the phonetic elements do not map directly onto phonetic units (Leong & Tamaoka, 1998). According to Tan and Perfetti (1998), as one reads Chinese characters, phonology is rapidly activated even though visual recognition of the characters may also take place at the same time. The size of an average Chinese speaker's reading vocabulary is limited to about 4,000 logographs. Even a Chinese scholar may not be able to read more than 8,000 logographs (Goody, 1968). In contrast, an English-speaking high school student can read more than 20,000 words easily and can decode words she has never encountered before. Apparently, phonics serves as a key to decode unfamiliar words.
>
> Realizing the difficulty encountered by children in learning to read Chinese, the People's Republic of China has introduced the Pinyin alphabetic system, which draws on alphabetic principles to represent the different sounds in Putonghua, the official language of China. Similarly, the Taiwanese government has introduced Zhuyin Fuhao, which consists of a set of phonetic symbols based on the International Phonetic Alphabet.

One advantage of the Chinese logographic orthography is worth mentioning. Several languages are spoken in mainland China, which are mutually incomprehensible to the speakers. Nevertheless, all these languages are represented by a single writing system. This is possible because the Chinese logographic orthography enables the identification of the concept represented by the character with minimal reliance on phonology, which of course, varies from language to language. Thus, Chinese orthography is a factor that binds the nation together.

A study by Stahl and Miller (1989) carried out a meta-analysis of studies that compared the effectiveness of basal readers, which emphasize the code approach, with that of WLA and language experience methods. After analyzing the results of 15 studies, these investigators concluded that "the studies that met more of our rigorous criteria for inclusion tended to favor basal reading programs over whole-language/language experience programs" (p. 107). These researchers, however suggested that whole language programs may be more effective when used with preschool children, prior to starting a formal reading program. It should also be noted that no single instructional method is representative of WLA, which makes comparison between WLA and code approaches difficult.

There is no single answer to the question of how to develop literacy skills in children. It depends on children's age, potential skills, and the psychological and environmental factors presented in Chapter 1. Children vary a great deal in literacy skills and in their ability to acquire these skills. Instruction in the elementary grades, therefore, must be individualized. Some children who are in the first grade may already have mastered basic reading skills; phonics instruction for such children may overburden them with exercises they may not need. These children can be introduced to literary materials and creative writing. Other children may not have mastered decoding skills even by the time they reach fifth grade. It is unrealistic to expect them to read stories, enjoy literature, or read for information when they cannot recognize most of the printed words in the text. These children will have to master basic word recognition skills before they can read and appreciate even the simplest of stories.

To be effective, phonics instruction for beginning readers must be explicit and systematic. Once children have mastered decoding skills, teaching can focus more heavily on meaning. The nature and amount of phonics instruction and the extent to which literature should be integrated with instruction should be determined by the teacher. Judging each child's reading level, selecting the appropriate instructional procedures, and implementing them in a way that is most helpful for each child are the challenging tasks facing the professional reading teacher. Ultimately, it is the teacher who emerges as the most important factor in literacy instruction, because instructional decisions must be made on an individual basis. The teacher must also be careful not to be swayed by any one philosophy that is popular at any given time.

Assignments for the Student Teacher

1. Observe the use of reinforcers in a first- or second-grade classroom.
   What reinforcers does the teacher use?
   Which reinforcers are used most often?

2. Observe children in grades 1, 2, and 3.
   Do they seem to use private speech to guide their own behavior?
   What are the differences in the use of private speech between children in grade 1 and children in grade 3?

3. Observe several children as they read a story or text aloud.
   How many of these children self-correct their own reading errors?
   What does this suggest about their self-monitoring and metacognitive skills?

4. In your observations, have you noticed some children who are reluctant to read aloud? Observe these children and try to determine why they might be reluctant. Could it be due to any psychological factors? Could it be due to lack of family support?

5. Observe several instructional sessions of one first- or second-grade teacher.
   What instructional approach does the teacher seem to stress, a skills approach or a meaning approach?
   Does the teacher rely heavily on a basal reader? What other materials, if any, are used?
   Is there evidence of individualized instruction? What are some examples?
   Is time a constraint for individualizing instruction? Explain. As a teacher, what steps might you adopt to overcome such restraints?

6. Examine the spelling of a few children in grade 5. Are they able to correctly spell words with morphophonemic spellings?

Reading Assignment

Read one of the following articles, discuss it, and write a one-page summary. These articles can be obtained at your college library or downloaded by accessing the library's electronic holdings.

Dorr, R.E. (2006). Something old is new again: Revisiting language experience. *The Reading Teacher, 60*(2), 138–146.

Fisher, D., & Frey, N. (2007). Implementing a school-wide literacy framework: Improving achievement in an urban elementary school. *The Reading Teacher, 61*(1), 32–43.

CHAPTER 3

The Psycholinguistics of Spoken Language

Summary

This chapter provides a brief background in linguistics that will be helpful in understanding the reading process. Topics include the sound systems, meaning systems, and grammar of the English language. This knowledge will help readers appreciate the rationale for the instructional procedures, presented in the following chapters, for teaching and assessing reading, writing, and spelling.

Main ideas presented in this chapter

1. An understanding of language and linguistics is helpful to the teacher of literacy skills.
2. The reading teacher benefits from an understanding of the difference between two terms often encountered in the literature: *linguistics* and **psycholinguistics**.
3. Inner language is an abstract cognitive skill that can be expressed in more than one form, such as spoken language, written language, and sign language.
4. Language has three major components: phonology (sound), semantics (meaning), and structure (word structure and sentence structure).
5. The term **morphology** refers to word structure, and *syntax* refers to sentence structure.
6. The concept that language is influenced by contextual, social, and cultural factors is referred to as the **pragmatics of language.**
7. Language is the foundation on which reading and writing skills are built.

**After reading this chapter,
you will be able to answer the following questions:**

1. What is psycholinguistics?
2. What are phonology, semantics, morphology, and syntax? How do they influence reading?
3. What are paralinguistic features of spoken language, and what specific information do these provide to teachers?
4. What is pragmatics?
5. What are the differences between spoken language and written language?
6. What is a phoneme? How many phonemes are there in the English language?
7. What is **phonological awareness**? What is phonemic awareness? What is the difference between the two?
8. What is the relationship between phonemic awareness and reading? Is there a cause-and-effect relationship between phonemic awareness training and reading improvement?
9. What is the difference between content words and function words?
10. Why do some children find it difficult to read and write function words?
11. What is morphology? What is morphemic awareness?
12. What is a clause? What is a phrase?

The Importance of a Knowledge of Linguistics

Written language and spoken language are not separate entities but manifestations of an inner language expressed through different modalities; they are two sides of the same coin. Therefore, it should not be surprising that children who have difficulty with spoken language also, more often than not, have difficulty with written language. For instance, children who have not developed a sensitivity to the sounds of language because of ear infection or hearing impairment have difficulty in pronouncing and spelling words. Some children, because of the dialectal nature of the language they speak, fail to perceive subtle differences in speech sounds. Because of this, they are likely to have difficulty in decoding written language with ease and may make spelling errors that reflect a dialect effect. Children with limited vocabulary knowledge have difficulty in understanding the meaning of words, which in turn affects their comprehension. Professional reading teachers, therefore, need to be sensitive to each child's phonological skills as well as the child's vocabulary and related comprehension skills.

Linguistics and Psycholinguistics

Linguistics is a branch of knowledge that deals with the study of the nature and structure of language. The major branches of linguistics are structural linguistics, functional linguistics, **sociolinguistics,** and psycholinguistics. More than 6,000 languages are spoken in the present-day world, and there are at least 5,000 written languages in use. However, some linguists would argue that there is only one "language" with a uniform underlying structure, shared by all human beings and expressed in 6,000 different ways. For present purposes, the term *language* will represent the spoken form of language.

American linguist Leonard Bloomfield (1887–1949) examined languages from a scientific perspective by looking for their similarities and differences. This form of linguistics, which examines similarities and differences among languages, is referred to as structural linguistics. Those who are interested in structural linguistics classify languages into families and subfamilies and pursue the question of whether all languages are equal or some are more advanced than others. In contrast, functional linguistics examines languages as tools that facilitate social interaction. For example, functional linguists tend to view grammar not as a fixed entity with features common to all languages but as a flexible cognitive tool that is shaped by the needs of the society in which a language is spoken. In English, for example, the order in which words are embedded in a sentence is so important that word order determines the sentence's subject and object. In the sentence "The knight killed the dragon," *knight* is the subject, or the actor, and *dragon* is the object, or the victim. *Dragon* can become the subject of the sentence by being placed in the initial position. In contrast, in some Australian languages word order is relatively unimportant. The sentences "The dingo killed the kangaroo" and "The kangaroo killed the dingo" are understood to mean the same thing: It is the dingo that killed the kangaroo. This is because the speakers of this particular Australian language know from experience that a dingo (dog) can kill a kangaroo but a kangaroo cannot kill a dingo. Thus, context and not word order is important in this language. In this respect, functional linguistics is close to sociolinguistics.

In addition to being marked by word order and context, in some languages (e.g., Latin, Spanish) the case, number, and gender are marked mainly by inflections. For example, in Spanish *gat* means "cat," *gato* means "male cat," *gata* means "female cat," and *gatos* means "male cats." Even though the English language does not rely on inflections to indicate the subject and object, it does use a limited number of inflections to mark tense and number. For instance, the *ed* inflection in *played* and *worked* is a marker for tense; the *s* inflection in *boys* and *girls* is a marker for number.

During the 1960s and up to the present, the focus of linguistic investigation shifted from structure-related questions to theoretical issues, such as language change and language evolution. More specifically, researchers became interested in how language has evolved and under what conditions languages change. Related issues of interest were the question of whether human language is species specific or represents one end of the evolutionary continuum, the relationship between thought and language, and how a complex cognitive skill such as language can be learned so quickly and effortlessly by children within a few years. Knowledge accrued by raising such questions came to make up another branch of linguistics called psycholinguistics. These linguistic orientations (structural, functional, socio, and psycholinguistic), however, do not exhaust the field of linguistics. There are other varieties of linguistics, such as historical linguistics, anthropological linguistics, clinical linguistics, and neurolinguistics. One other area of interest is **biolinguistics,** which explores the biological aspects of language, especially from an

Although the view that language in the spoken form is natural but written language is an invention has been propounded by such authorities as Darwin (1871) and Bloomfield (1933) and accepted by many scholars since, this view is beginning to be challenged. Writers such as Pontecorvo and Orsolini (1996) and Olson (1991) have noted that the view about the divide between spoken and written language is beginning to disappear slowly.

evolutionary perspective. Spoken language is considered by many linguists to be an aspect of biology and, therefore, is believed to have evolved along Darwinian lines similar to biological characteristics of organisms (Pinker & Bloom, 1990). In contrast, written language is considered to be an invention and a cultural artifact. This view, as can be seen, does not fit the statement made earlier in this chapter that spoken language and written language are manifestations of the same inner language. It should be obvious by now that a knowledge of linguistics, particularly psycholinguistics, is important to teachers of literacy in more than one respect. For instance, an understanding of terms such as *phonology, phonemic awareness,* and *morphological awareness,* which are encountered often in reading instruction, requires a knowledge of linguistics.

The Different Expressions of Inner Language

Linguists who are purists use the term *language* to refer to an innate abstract construct. However, the nature of language can be studied only from the different forms of its manifestation, such as spoken language, written language, and sign language. These two perspectives on language are also referred to as language competence and language performance, respectively. Many linguists (e.g., Pinker & Bloom, 1990) consider spoken language to be innate, natural, and part of the biological system for the following reasons:

1. All human societies have spoken language.

2. Children learn spoken language without formal instruction.

3. The history of spoken language is as old as human history itself.

In contrast, written language is considered to be an invention and an artifact (Bloomfield, 1933; Darwin, 1871; Pinker & Bloom, 1990) because it does not fulfill these requirements. An argument, however, can be made in favor of considering written language to be as natural as spoken language. The proposition argues that language is a product of societal demands and, given the existence of the right kind of social needs—such as commerce and empire building—written language also emerges naturally. Both spoken language and written language are the results of such functional needs but have emerged at different times because the needs emerged at different times. For example, until the techniques of agriculture were mastered and resulted in an increase in crop production which, in turn, triggered substantial commercial transaction, there was no need for recording such transactions in some form of writing. Written language, not spoken language, is suitable for record keeping.

Another argument questions the premise that spoken language is learned without some instruction from adults. Observations of mother–child interactions show that parents do restructure their speech by simplifying their sentences and slowing down when they talk to young children, which promotes the acquisition of language. It is also claimed that spoken language, unlike written language, is as old as humanity. From an evolutionary perspective, however, spoken language may not be old in the sense that it may be only a few thousand, rather than million, years old. When the history of written language is said to be short, this means that it is only relatively short when compared with spoken language (see Aaron & Joshi, 2006, for an elaboration of these arguments).

If written language is as natural as spoken language, formal literacy instruction need not wait until kindergarten. This makes creating opportunities for written language to emerge at an early age and nurturing it important undertakings. When whole language proponents claim that reading is as natural as speaking, they are relating to this perception of written language.

Components of Spoken Language

So far, this discussion of language has been in very general terms. A deeper understanding of language requires an acquaintance with some basic linguistic concepts and the terms used for describing them. Every known spoken language has three features marking it as a human language: a sound system, a meaning system, and a structural system. Linguists refer to these as phonology, semantics, and structure (or **grammar**), respectively. The field of linguistics defines the term *grammar* broadly as the set of rules that governs the use of language. In the present context, however, the word is used in a narrow sense to describe the rules used for describing the structure of words and sentences. Word structure is also referred to as morphology, and sentence structure is known as syntax. Thus, grammar includes morphology and syntax. Some linguists claim that these three features, phonology, grammar, and semantics, are unique to human language and set it apart from animal communication. In the following sections, these three components of language are examined with particular reference to their role in the reading process.

Phonology

Humans are capable of perceiving and producing a variety of fine-tuned sounds. Languages differ in the sounds they use, though many sounds are shared by many languages. A phoneme is the smallest unit of speech sound that can change a word. For example, when the phoneme /k/ in the word *cat* is changed to the phonemes /r/ or /m/, the word becomes *rat* or *mat*. In this textbook, phonemes are indicated by slash marks; for instance, the three phonemes of the word *cat* would be marked /c/ /a/ /t/. International phonetic symbols offer a more precise way of representing phonemes. The three phonemes of the word *cat* would be indicated in international phonetic symbols as kæt.

An important characteristic of a phoneme is that when a phoneme in a word is changed, the word itself is changed. For example, /c/ /a/ /r/ becomes /f/ /a/ /r/ when the initial phoneme is changed; it becomes /c/ /a/ /p/ when the final phoneme is replaced by another phoneme. Many phonemes in the English language do not relate to the letters of the alphabet in a one-to-one manner. For instance, though the three-letter word *cat* has three phonemes, the six-letter word *though* has only two phonemes, /th/ and /o/.

The Alphabetic Principle

As these examples show, each phoneme can be represented by a single letter of the alphabet or a group of letters. A letter of the alphabet or a group of letters that represents a phoneme is called a **grapheme.** The relationship between phonemes and graphemes is referred to as grapheme–phoneme correspondence (GPC). A knowledge of this relationship is referred to as the alphabetic principle. This knowledge is important for beginning readers, as they must learn that written letters represent sounds in speech. Difficulty in the acquisition of the alphabetic principle and the skill to relate graphemes to phonemes presents an obstacle for learning to read.

Though phonemes can be described, classified, and discussed, individual phonemes are not readily recognizable in speech. For the most part, people speak and listen without being aware of the phonemes in words. Even educated adults may have difficulty identifying the number of phonemes in some spoken words. (Try asking a friend how many phonemes are in the words *though, blue, auto,* and *box.*) This difficulty arises because words are not uttered by sounding out the phonemes one by one. In the word *cat,* for example, the three phonemes flow into one another to produce a continuous stream of sound. Phonologists refer to this feature as the shingling effect, or co-articulation, as each phoneme overlaps the following one, much like the shingles on a roof. Words, too, tend to be strung together in speech, although speakers generally pause between clauses and units of ideas. It is truly a marvel that the human perceptual system is able to sort out phonemes and words and make sense of what is heard. Continuous exposure to spoken language helps the development of this skill. Children must learn all this from step one, so it is no wonder children who are not sensitive to phonemes experience difficulty in learning to read.

Phonemic Awareness

Sensitivity to phonemes is referred to as phonemic awareness. It is important to keep in mind that phonemic awareness refers only to spoken language and not to written language. To make progress in reading acquisition, beginning readers must become sensitive to phonemes and relate them to graphemes. As noted earlier, in the beginning stages of learning to read, written word recognition requires associating graphemes to phonemes. Skilled readers may be able to circumvent this route and directly access the meaning of many words without converting each grapheme in a word into the corresponding sound. Nevertheless, to comprehend a sentence readers must store the words in the sentence in short-term mem-

> If the words in a sentence cannot be understood, the sentence also cannot be understood. Therefore, a weakness in decoding skill will impede comprehension of written language. Consequently, reading comprehension cannot be expected to improve unless decoding skills improve.

ory (STM). Decoding written words into their sound representation appears to be the most efficient way of storing them in the STM.

A number of research studies show that enhancing phonemic awareness in children who are having difficultly learning to read improves their reading performance (Ball & Blachman, 1991; Bradley & Bryant, 1985; Lundberg, Frost, & Peterson, 1988). The positive relationship between phonemic awareness and reading performance has been confirmed over and over again by so many studies that some psychologists consider it to be a major achievement of applied cognitive psychology. While awareness of phonemes may help the beginning reader, reading experience is also known to enhance phonemic awareness. In one study, Morais, Cary, Alegria, and Bertelson (1979) found that the phonemic awareness of a group of Portuguese adults who did not read and who received adult literacy training exceeded that of another group of adults who also did not read but who did not receive such training in reading. Thus, the relationship between phonemic awareness and reading is reciprocal. An awareness of phonemes develops relatively late, partly because **print awareness** contributes its development (Goswami, 1998). That is, exposure to written language also increases sensitivity to phonemes.

Psycholinguists who have studied infants report that even newborns have the capacity to discriminate among different phonemes. However, like many other abilities, it gradually develops and is refined over the years. Further, if an individual is not exposed to a particular phoneme until about adolescence, it is difficult for him or her to perceive and produce that phoneme. The Japanese language, for example, does not have the separate phonemes /l/ and /r/. Japanese adults not accustomed to English experience difficulty distinguishing between spoken /l/ and /r/ (*Robert* may be perceived as *Lobelt*). Similarly, the difficulties experienced in learning to read by students who are hearing impaired is partly attributable to not being able to hear the phonemes of the language. The question of whether a child in kindergarten should be promoted to first grade can be partially answered by assessing the child's level of phonemic awareness. Another good predictor of the child's reading skill is letter knowledge.

The phoneme is one of the many units that make up spoken words. Words can also be broken into syllables, onsets, and rimes. Words that rhyme can be placed in groups known as word families.

A syllable is a speech sound consisting of a vowel or a combination of a vowel and consonant that can be produced as an uninterrupted unit. Words can be classified as monosyllabic or multisyllabic depending on the number of syllables. Syllables are readily identifiable in speech but not in written language. Though many multisyllabic words are easily divided into their constituent syllables, others are more difficult, such as *horses* (hors/es or hor/ses?). Research studies show that syllabic awareness is present at the age of 4 years or even earlier, before children begin to learn to read.

A knowledge of syllables helps with vowel pronunciation, as vowels tend to have more than one sound in English. Syllables in the English language are classified into six types, as shown in Table 3.1.

Other units of speech that are helpful in decoding written language are **onset and rime.** Onset is the **consonant** or consonants that precede a vowel in a syllable; rime is the vowel and all letters (or sounds) that follow it. For example, in the word *strong*, [str] is the onset and [ong] is the rime. In the word *string*, again [str] is the onset, but [ing] is the rime. Multisyllabic words can have more than one

Table 3.1. The six syllable types occurring in English

Syllable type	Examples
Closed	*it, bed, and, lost*
Open	*be, no, me, she*
Vowel-consonant-e	*name, five, slope, these*
Vowel pair (vowel team)	*each, boil, sweet, tray*
Vowel-*r*	*fern, burn, thirst, star*
Final stable syllable (/ge/, /tion/)	*page, motion*

From Carreker, S. (2005). Teaching reading: Accurate decoding and fluency. In J.R. Birsh (Ed.), *Multisensory teaching of basic language skills* (2nd ed, p. 230). Baltimore: Paul H. Brookes Publishing Co.; adapted by permission.

onset and more than one rime. For instance, the word *pumpkin* has two onsets, [p] and [k], and two rimes, [ump] and [in]. The words *eat* and *ear* have no onsets but have one rime each. As a rule, every word has a rime, but not all words have an onset.

Word families may help children learn word recognition skills. Word families may consist of words that have the same onset but different rimes, such as *brother, broom, break,* and *bread.* Word families may also consist of words with the same rime but different onsets. Examples of the word families [ack] and [all] are *back, jack, rack,* and *stack* and *hall, mall, fall,* and *ball.* The ability to identify and generate onsets and rimes develops later than the ability to perceive syllables.

The ability to identify syllables, onset, rimes, phonemes, and rhyming words is collectively referred to as phonological awareness. Thus, *phonological awareness* is an umbrella term that includes knowledge of syllables, onsets and rimes, and phonemes. Experienced teachers use all these features of words and sounds to teach children word recognition skills. Games involving rhyming and syllabication are useful in developing an awareness about the print–speech relationship. Even at the preschool level, teachers can make liberal use of such activities.

The branch of linguistics that studies the sound systems of languages is called phonology. The description, classification, transcription, and naming of phonemes in a language is referred to as **phonetics.** Thus, phonetics is a science of the study of sounds, not an instructional method. Teachers usually do not instruct children in phonology as an isolated skill but introduce phonology in association with the letters of the alphabet or in the context of reading. When phonology is combined with the written letters of the alphabet, it becomes the phonics method of instruction.

It is important for professional reading teachers to be able to identify children who are not sensitive to phonemes and to further identify which phonemes are the most troublesome ones for each child to perceive and produce. This would naturally lead to efforts to develop an awareness for these phonemes in each child. (Tests for assessing and developing phonemic awareness are described in Chapter 10.) It has to be remembered that since many children in kindergarten and even first grade may not have an awareness of all the phonemes, the diagnostic and instructional techniques described in this book apply to a substantial number of children in the beginning grades. For these reasons, a knowledge of the different kinds of phonemes and how they are classified is helpful for teachers of beginning reading.

Speech Production

Speech is produced when air is expelled from the lungs and travels through the windpipe, the larynx, and ultimately the oral cavity (see Figure 3.1). The voice is produced by vocal folds, which are located in the topmost part of the larynx and constitute the voice box, located behind the Adam's apple. Voice is produced as the air escapes through the vocal folds and makes them vibrate, creating a buzz. If you hold your hand against your Adam's apple and say "zzzzzz," you can feel the voice box resonating. Phonemes accompanied by a buzz sound are said to be voiced.

From the larynx, air passes as a single stream through the throat, behind the tongue, behind the mouth, between the tongue, between the palate (roof of the mouth), and between the teeth and lips. When sound is produced without any major obstruction or blockage by any of these anatomical parts, vowel sounds are generated. Consonants are produced by obstructing the flow of air with either the tongue or the lips. Speech sounds, therefore, can be classified into vowels and consonants.

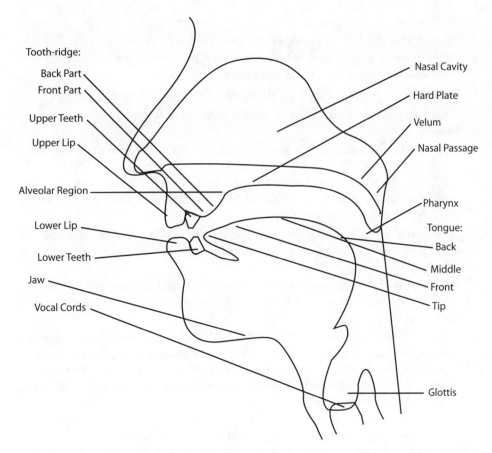

Figure 3.1. Diagram of the human articulatory structure. (From FOSS & HAKES, PSYCHOLINGUISTICS: AN INTRODUCTION TO THE PSYCHOLOGY OF LANGUAGE, 1st Edition, © 1978, p. 204. Reprinted by permission of Pearson Education, Inc., Upper Saddle River, NJ.)

Consonants Consonants are further described in terms of the manner in which they are obstructed—either completely or partially. The place of obstruction is described using the following terms:

- Bilabial = both lips (/b/, /p/) (e.g., *boy*)
- Labiodental = between teeth and lower lip (/f/, /v/) (e.g., *far*)
- Linguodental = tongue between the teeth (/th/) (e.g., *through*)
- Alveolar = ridge behind the upper teeth in the anterior part of the roof of the mouth (/t/, /d/) (e.g., *true*)
- Velar = soft palate at the back of the mouth (/k/,/g/) (e.g., *king*)
- Glottis = space between vocal folds and larynx (/h/) (e.g., *ghost*)

Consonants are also classified according to how they are articulated. The following terms are used to describe the various forms of obstruction and articulation:

- Stops: Sounds produced with a maximum obstruction. The following six phonemes are consonantal stops in the English language: /b/, /p,/ /d,/ /t,/ /g,/ and /k/.
- Fricatives: Articulators coming close together, but not completely closing, so that air passes between them and produces friction that is audible. The initial phonemes in the following words are examples of fricatives: *thin, fin,* and *zoo*.
- Affricatives: A stop consonant starting like a fricative and then released. The /ch/ sound in the word *chip* is an example.
- Obstruents: Nonnasal stops, fricatives, and affricates.
- Voiced consonant: Consonant produced with vocal folds vibrating (/z/, /g/) *(zoo)*.
- Unvoiced consonant: Consonant produced with vocal folds not vibrating. Place your hands on your larynx and pronounce the consonants /b/, /d/, /g/, /v/, /j/, and /z/ and compare the vibrations with the ones produced by the consonants /p/, /t/, /k/, /f/, and /s/. The first set of consonants is voiced and the second set is unvoiced.

Some consonants sound more or less like vowels because of the minimal obstruction they meet during their production. Glides, liquids, and nasals belong to this category.

- Glides: Sounds appearing to change from one sound to another (e.g., /w/ in *woe;* /y/ in *you*). Because of their vowel-like qualities, glides are also called semivowels.
- Liquids: The consonants /r/ and /l/, articulated at the alveolar ridge. In this respect, liquids differ from glides. According to Moats (2000), these sounds are learned later than others and are the most difficult to teach. The consonant /r/ is also articulated differently depending on whether it occurs at the beginning of a word or follows a vowel.
- Nasals: Consonant produced when some of the air passes through the nasal cavity (/m/ and /n/ in *man*). Nasals, along with glides and liquids, are also included in the group of semivowels. The consonants and consonant clusters of American English are shown in Table 3.2. Classification of American English consonants by place and manner of articulation are shown in Table 3.3.

Table 3.2. Consonants and consonant clusters of American English

Consonants with one sound				
b = /b/ (*bat*)	d = /d/ (*dog*)	f = /f/ (*fat*)	h = /h/ (*hat*)	j = /j/ (*jam*)
k = /k/ (*kite*)	l = /l/ (*leaf*)	m = /m/ (*man*)	p = /p/ (*pig*)	r = /r/ (*rabbit*)
t = /t/ (*table*)	v = /v/ (*valentine*)			

Consonants with more than one sound		
c = /k/ (*kite*); /s/ (*city*)	g = /g/ (*goat*); /j/ (*gem*)	s = /s/ (*sock*); /z/ (*dogs*)
x = /z/ (*xylophone*); /ks/ (*excite*)	n = /n/ (*nest*); /ng/ (*finger*)	

Consonant digraphs with one frequent sound			
ck = /ck/ (*truck*)	ng = /ng/ (*king*)	sh = /sh/ (*ship*)	wh = /wh/ (*when*)

Consonant digraphs with more than one sound	
ch = /ch/ (*chair*); /k/ (*school*); /sh/ (*chef*)	th = /th/ (*mother*); /th/ (*Thursday*)

Trigraphs with one sound	
dge = /j/ (*badge*)	tch = /ch/ (*witch*)

From Carreker, S. (2005). Teaching reading: Accurate decoding and fluency. In J.R. Birsh (Ed.), *Multisensory teaching of basic language skills* (2nd ed., p. 218). Baltimore: Paul H. Brookes Publishing Co; adapted by permission.

In general, children often fail to perceive and produce many glide, liquid, and nasal sounds correctly. Their spelling reflects such errors (e.g., *witch* for *which, tain* for *train, goin* for *going*). Children who speak African American English (AAE) experience particular difficulties with these sounds. A knowledge of phonemes will be helpful to teachers in identifying the source of reading and spelling errors and drawing children's attention to such errors.

Consonant sounds in the English language are generally represented by a single letter of the alphabet. Exceptions are sounds represented by the letters *c, g, n, s, x,* and *y*. All of these letters can represent more than one sound. In addition, a single sound can be made by a consonant in combination with another consonant, as the ending sound /k/ in *clock*. In contrast, more than one vowel sound can be produced by each letter. For example, the letter *a* stands for different sounds in the words *America, alien,* and *all*.

Table 3.3. Places of articulation of consonant sounds

Both lips	Teeth and lower lip	Between the teeth	Ridge behind teeth	Roof of mouth	Back of mouth	From the throat
/b/	/f/	/th/	/d/	/ch/	/g/	/h/
/m/	/v/	/th/	/l/	/j/	/k/	/tw/
/p/			/n/	/sh/	/ks/*	
			/r/	/y/	/kw/*	
			/s/	/zh/	/ng/	
			/t/	/w/		
			/z/			

From Carreker, S. (2005). Teaching spelling. In J.R. Birsh (Ed.), *Multisensory teaching of basic language skills* (2nd ed., p. 264). Baltimore: Paul H. Brookes Publishing Co.; reprinted by permission.

*These combination sounds represent the most frequent sound of *x* (/ks/) and *q* (/kw/), which is usually followed by a *u*.

Vowels   The vowels *a, e, i, o,* and *u* represent more than one sound. Furthermore, a single vowel sound can be represented by more than one letter. Consider the vowel sounds /e/ and /a/. The *e* in the words *else* and *eight* is often not pronounced as /e/ and the *i* in *if* is not pronounced as /i/. Vowels are described in terms of three parameters: tongue height (high, medium, or low), tongue position (front or back), and lip shape (rounded or not rounded). Examples of vowel sounds in these categories include the following:

- Tongue height: high *(he)*, mid position *(hay)*, and low *(ate)*

- Tongue position: front *(he)*, mid *(pot)*, and back *(who)*

- Lip shape: rounded *(hoe)* and not rounded *(hay)*

When introducing vowel sounds, draw children's attention to the height and position of their tongue and to the shape of their lips when they say certain words. Encourage them to notice whether the tongue is high or low when saying these words: *he* versus *ate*; the position of the tongue (front or back) when they say *he* and *eat* versus *who* and *hood*; the shape of the lips (rounded or not rounded) when they say *hold* versus *hay*.

In addition to these vowel categories, there are diphthong and **schwa sounds.** In diphthongs, the pronunciation of the first vowel glides into the sound of the second vowel. Examples of diphthongs are *boil, toy,* and *out.* Schwa is a neutral or reduced short vowel sound that is almost imperceptible and occurs in unstressed syllables, such as the first syllable in *ago* or the second syllable in *linen.* Other examples of schwa in American English are /a/ in *about,* /e/ in *taken,* /i/ in *pencil,* and /u/ in *circus.* The /o/ sound in the word *commercial* is a schwa, whereas the /o/ sound in *commerce* is not.

The schwa sound is barely perceptible and is a source of difficulty for children. Teachers will have to make a special effort to draw children's attention to the sound, especially when they are trying to spell words. Because the schwa vowel is barely noticeable, children tend to omit it in their spelling. For instance, they may spell *about* as *bout, pencil* as *pencl,* and *every* as *evry.*

Vowels are also classified as long and short. Examples of long vowels are the /a/ sound in *mate* and the /o/ in *go*; examples of short vowels are /a/ in *mat* and /o/ in *cook.* Long and short vowels are also referred to as tense and lax vowels, respectively. Some vowels in the English language are described as **r-controlled.** Compare the pronunciation of the following words: *can, bad,* and *fat* with the pronunciation of these words *car, bar,* and *far.* Did you notice the pronunciation of the vowel sound /a/ in the last three words? The change in pronunciation of the vowel *a* is attributed to the presence of the letter *r* in these words.

Children have a tendency to spell the words *else* and *eight* as *alse* and *aight.* Examples of other spelling errors in which children tend to spell words the way they sound are *my* as *mi, if* as *ef,* and *happy* as *hape* (Treiman, 1993). In contrast to most consonants, each vowel sound is represented by more than one letter, and some letters can stand for more than one vowel sound. Except for the letters *c, k, g,* and *j,* the relationship between consonants and phonemes is almost one-to-one. For this reason, children's spelling errors involve vowels more often than consonants. Children also tend to misspell words with diphthong and schwa sounds more often than words with other vowel sounds.

Prosodic Features

In addition to phonemes, spoken language contains other elements that affect word meaning. Collectively known as prosodic features (see Chapter 2 for further description), these include stress, elongation of phonemes, and pause between words. Linguists call these paralinguistic features or supra-segmental features. The term *intonation* is also a prosodic feature. Read aloud the following two sentences at normal speed, and notice the difference in the way the two sentences are read.

1.   Mary's parents were very poor; they fed her dog biscuits.

2.   Jane's parents were very rich; they fed her dog biscuits.

Notice that the word *her* in sentence 1 is more stressed and elongated than the same word in sentence 2. Also, there is a longer pause between the words *her* and *dog* in sentence 1, but in sentence 2 the pause is inserted between *dog* and *biscuits*. These differences are not random but are determined by the meanings of the sentences.

Grammar: Morphology and Syntax

In general, the term *grammar* refers to the pattern or structure that emerges as a result of the systematic relationship among units within words and sentences. Such relationships can be found among morphemic units such as root words, suffixes, and prefixes as well as among words in sentences (see Box 3.1).

Grammar has two components, morphology and syntax. Morphology is the study of the structural feature of morphemes. To be meaningful, words within an English sentence should also be arranged in a prescribed order, a linguistic feature known as syntax. A group of linguists has asserted that human beings have an internalized set of rules that governs morphology and syntax. They use the word *grammar* to refer to this set of internal rules. Some linguists (e.g., Chomsky, 1965) consider grammar to be the quintessence of language. Others, however, believe that meaning is also an important element of language.

Box 3.1.   The nature of morphemes

- A root word is a word that can stand by itself, such as *run* in the word *running*. Root words are also called free morphemes.

- A prefix is a letter or group of letters added to the beginning of a root word, such as *dis* in *dislike*.

- A suffix is a letter or group of letters added to the end of a root word, such as *ful* in the word *unlawful*.

- Collectively, prefixes and suffixes are called affixes. They are also called bound morphemes. One category of suffixes is inflection. Inflections are markers that reflect information about tense (*play/played*), number (*boy/boys*), and grammatical categories (*show/showing, love/lovable*).

- Compound words are made up of two morphemes, neither of which is an affix. *Textbook* and *classroom* are examples of compound words.

Morphology

The term *morphology* comes from the word *morpheme,* which refers to the basic linguistic unit of meaning. *Morpheme* is not a synonym for *word.* Whereas the word *boy* is a single morpheme, the word *boys* contains two morphemes, the root referring to gender and the suffix referring to number. The single word *distasteful* has three morphemes, or three meaning units, *dis, taste,* and *ful.* In these examples, the words *boy* and *taste* have inherent meaning and can stand by themselves. They are, therefore, called free or root morphemes. The suffixes *s* in *boys* and *ful* in *distasteful,* as well as the prefix *dis,* cannot stand by themselves. They are, therefore, called bound morphemes (see Box 3.1 for a summary of terms relating to morphemes). Children in the early grades tend to omit bound morphemes when they read aloud and write because these elements are abstract and have no inherent meaning.

When word structure is altered, word meaning is also altered. Such changes are particularly useful in indicating tense (e.g., *cook, cooked; run, ran*) and number (e.g., *pen, pens; dog, dogs*). Consider the following sentences:

- We *play* soccer.

- We *played* soccer.

- The play was very *realistic.*

- The play was *unrealistic.*

As these examples show, the meaning of a sentence can be changed by altering the structure (or morphology) of a word by adding something to the end (suffix) or the beginning (prefix) of the word. In some languages, meaning can be altered by making changes within the word itself (infix). Suffixes and prefixes are common in Indo-European languages such as English and German, but infixes are uncommon. One rare example is the Latin word *rup* ("break"), which becomes *rumpo* ("I break") by inserting the infix *m* and the suffix *o.* Collectively, prefixes, suffixes, and infixes are referred to as affixes.

Now consider the following sentences:

- The student lives in a *house.*

- The students were *housed* in a dormitory.

Note the words *house* in the first sentence and *housed* in the second sentence. Adding *ed* changes not only the meaning of the sentence but also the grammatical nature of the morpheme. The word *house* in the first sentence is a noun, whereas *housed* is a verb. This type of change in word structure that alters the grammatical nature of the morpheme is an example of derivational morphology.

Morphemes are also classified as lexical morphemes and grammatical morphemes. Nouns, verbs, and adjectives are lexical morphemes, whereas prepositions (e.g., *on, to*), conjunctions (e.g., *and, but*), and articles (e.g., *a, the*) constitute grammatical morphemes. Lexical morphemes are also referred to as **content words,** and grammar words are known as **function words.** Lexical morphemes number in the thousands, and their number continually increases as new words enter the language. For example, words such as *kerning* and *modem* are words from the computer field that have recently been added to the English lexicon. Furthermore, existing words can take on new meanings. With the advent of computers, words such as *or-*

phan and *floppy* have taken on meanings different from those they once represented. Consequently, lexical morphemes are also classified as open class because this category of morphemes is open to addition (see Box 3.2). Grammatical morphemes, in contrast, are considered closed because no new grammar word can easily enter a language. Even though grammar words number only about one hundred, children find these words more difficult to read and write than lexical morphemes. This is because unlike most nouns and verbs, grammar words and bound morphemes are abstractions and do not represent observable properties. The *Dictionary of American Regional English* (see http://polyglot.lss.wisc.edu/dare/dare.html for more information) lists several words that have crept into local dialects in some places but are not known elsewhere. Some of these words appear in Box 3.2.

A knowledge of the nature of morphemes and their structure is referred to as morphological awareness. Recent studies show that just as phonemic awareness plays an important role in the acquisition of literacy skills, morphological awareness plays an important role in reading comprehension.

Syntax

Whereas morphology operates at the word level, syntax operates at the sentence level. Just as a change in word structure can affect meaning, a change in the order of words in a sentence can also affect meaning. The meaning of sentences in English is largely dictated by the way the words are arranged within the sentence. As a result, English requires that words in a sentence follow a prescribed order to make the sentence meaningful. If a strict word order is not followed, the meaning of the sentence may be altered or even completely lost. For example, the sentences "Dog bites man" and "Man bites dog" contain the same words; only the word order is changed. English is described as an SVO language, the acronym standing

---

Box 3.2. **Open class of words**

What do the following open class of words mean: "paddybass", "quituate", "puckersnatch", "pinkletink", "scaper"?

- "Paddybass" is to walk back and forth (North Carolina).
- "Quituate" is to drop out of school (Midwest).
- "Puckersnatch" is a difficult or muddled situation (New England).
- "Pinkletink" is a spring peeper, a small frog (Nantucket).
- "Scaper" is a rascal (parts of Florida and Georgia).

Describing a rodent that ruined his garden, the poet Galway Kinnell wrote that he had trapped and killed the vole that had slorped too often at the flowers. Now a beetle is moiling across the body, spewing at both ends, drooking him in chemical juices. A larger beetle noggles into view and plouters past the barrier teeth."

From Kilpatrick, J.J., (2002, October 20). Growing the language with new uses. *Tribune Star*; reprinted by permission.

for subject–verb–object. An example of SVO construction is the sentence "I write this letter." For stylistic purposes, sometimes the conventional SVO order is changed. For example, the sentence "With this ring I thee wed" follows an SOV structure and sounds rather quaint. However, such sentences are exceptions.

Word order is not the only device languages use to express meaning. Subjects and objects in a sentence can be marked by other means also. Languages such as Latin, Greek, and Arabic do not rely on word order as much as English does. These languages use inflections to indicate subject and object. In some languages, such as Latin, words use different inflections to show their grammatical function as subject and object. The sentences "Marcus amat Juliam" and "Juliam amat Marcus" mean the same thing ("Marcus loves Julia"). In these two sentences, the object is *Julia*. This is indicated by adding *m* to *Julia*. Latin, therefore, is less dependent on word order than English. In fact, Old English that was spoken a thousand years ago was a highly inflected language; modern English retains only about 12 of these inflections. Because Old English was an inflected language, word order within the sentence was less important at that time than it is today. Compare the Old English (ninth century) passage in Box 3.3 with its translation into Modern English. Also note how the English language has changed over the centuries.

In a classic study, Berko (1958) made up a mythical creature and named it a wug. She showed a picture of the wug to very young children and told them, "This is a wug." Then she showed them a picture of two of these creatures and told them, "Now there are two of them," and asked the children to complete the sentence "Now we have two _____. " A majority of the children had no difficulty in saying "wugs," indicating that they had generalized a morphological rule for indicating plurals. General observation also shows that children generalize morphological rules; they are often heard to say such things as "I drinked," "I sleeped," and "I runned." It should be remembered, however, that the view of language as innate applies to syntax and not necessarily to phonology or vocabulary learning. This means that learning and imitation cannot be completely ruled out as explanations of the acquisition of all the components of language.

Box 3.3.   Comparison of Old English and Modern English text

He aerest He first	*sceop* made	*eordan* on earth	*bearnum* for men
Heofon Heaven	*to hrofe* as a roof	*halig* of mankind	*Scyppend* the Guardian
pa middangeard everlasting Lord	*monncynnes* afterwards	*Weard* adorned	
ece for men	*Drihten* the earth	*aefter* afterwards	*teode* adorned
firum for men	*foldan* the earth	*Frea* God	*aelmihtig* almighty

From Leith, D. (1996). The origins of English. In D. Graddol, D. Leith, & J. Swann (Eds.), *English: History, diversity, and change* (p. 12). London: The Open University.

Children's syntactic skills can be improved by telling them stories and then asking them questions. This encourages them to create their own sentences. This is a more effective way of improving language skills than using repetition and drill.

Semantics

Though messages are communicated through sentences, words are the basic units that carry meaning. In fact, early linguists used the term *semantics* almost exclusively to refer to the study of words. In recent years, however, the concept of comprehension processes has been expanded to include sentence and text processing. Moats (2000) identified three categories of semantics: lexical semantics, dealing with word meaning; sentential semantics, the study of sentence meaning; and pragmatics, the study of meaning within a context.

Lexical Semantics

The study of the mental lexicon, or mental dictionary, for words is referred to as lexical semantics. The English language is said to have the largest vocabulary of any language, with nearly 800,000 words. The most recent *Oxford English Dictionary* lists around 825,000 words. This is because the English language has absorbed words from many other languages. As King (2000) put it, when you teach English to children in your classroom, you teach at least four languages: Anglo-Saxon (Germanic), French, Latin, and Greek.

Words of Anglo-Saxon origin are those most commonly used in English and, therefore, make up the core of spoken English even though they constitute only a small portion of the total number of words. Examples of Anglo-Saxon words are *mother, father, friend, eats, earth, fire,* and *water*. Words of Anglo-Saxon origin can be identified by noting their similarity to the respective German words; *mutter, vater, freund, essen, erde, feuer,* and *wasser*. Anglo-Saxon words also refer to day-to-day common occupations, such as farmer, carpenter, barber, and baker, for these are the types of work in which most early Anglo-Saxons were engaged. Most of these words have an *er* ending. Many of the grammar words (e.g., *the, and, but*) are also Anglo-Saxon in origin. Anglo-Saxon words are short but often irregular in the sense that their spelling pattern and pronunciation do not match.

Latin was the court language in Europe during the 14th and 15th centuries. Crossing geographic and political boundaries, it left its influence on English. Many Latin words are marked by prefixes and suffixes. Examples of such words are *adjacent, prosecution,* and *rationality* (Henry, 1999).

Greek words account for about 10% of the words in the English language. They are, according to King (2000), the most abstract and scientific sounding. Words such as *geography, hydrogen, astronomy,* and *anthropology* are Greek in origin.

After the Norman conquest in 1066, England came under French influence and remained so for nearly 400 years. French became the court language in England, even though English remained as the spoken language of the common people. During this period of language hybridization, English spelling had to accommodate two languages, English and French. Over the centuries, the spelling that was compromised in this way remained relatively unchanged because of printing while pronunciation changed, creating an ever-widening discordance between spelling and pronunciation. King (2000) noted that the pronunciation of French words introduced at an earlier period has been Anglicized, whereas recently introduced words have retained their French pronunciations. The /ch/ digraph in words such as *avalanche, bachelor, chamber, champion,* and *change* have been anglicized to /ch/ pronunciation; however, recently introduced words such as *brochure, champagne, chef, chivalry, machine, nonchalant,* and *parachute* have retained the /sh/ pronunciation as in modern-day French. The digraph /ou/ is pronounced /oo/ in words such as *acoustic, cougar, route,* and *coupon,* as in modern French. Examples of other modern French pronunciation are /et/ as /a/, as in *buffet, filet, and passé;* /ge/ as /j/ as in *camouflage, collage, fuselage,* and *garage;* /qu/ as /k/ as in *antique, cheque, clique, etiquette,* and *mosquito.* French /i/ is pronounced as long /e/, as in *cliché, elite, machine,* and *marine.* In addition to these four languages, Danish also left its stamp on the English language. English words of Danish origin include *book* (*bog*), *cold* (*kold*), *come* (*kom*), *ice* (*is*), *know* (*kende*), and *snow* (*sne*). Native American languages have also contributed to the vocabulary of American English names. Names such as *Mississippi, Minnesota, Nebraska, Oklahoma,* and *Tennessee* are derived from Native American names.

Exploring the historical roots of English words may make upper elementary students more sensitive to the different spelling patterns in English. It can also make many of the words more meaningful and, therefore, easier to learn. Teachers can ask students to do some research to create a list of English words that came from other languages, including Native American languages (see Box 3.4).

Word meanings are influenced not only by historical events but also by contemporary events. What does the word *black* bring to mind? A dictionary definition of the word is "of achromatic value; reflecting no light." However, the word is also associated with such terms as black Friday (stock market), Black Americans, and the budget being in the black. Associations of this kind, learned because of social and historical changes, are said to have connotative meaning. In contrast, denotative meaning is primarily a word's definition as given in the dictionary. Some children may be only vaguely aware of the differences between connotative and denotative meanings of words and may need the teacher's direction and guidance to fully comprehend the meaning of sentences when words are used for their connotative, or implied, meaning.

The knowledge of word parts, the ways in which words are combined, and how inflectional and derivational changes alter the meaning of words is referred to as morphological awareness. Phonological awareness is reported to facilitate morphological awareness in young children (Carlisle & Nomanbhoy, 1993); both

---

Box 3.4. English words borrowed from Native American languages

Algonquian: *caribou, chipmunk, hickory, hominy, moccasin, moose, opossum, persimmon, powwow, raccoon, skunk, squash, toboggan, tomahawk, totem*

Nahuatl (Middle America): *avocado, cocoa, chilli, chocolate, coyote, tamale, tomato*

Tupinamba (South America): *jaguar, cashew, tapioca*

Quechua (South America): *alpaca, condor, jerky, puma, quinine*

Arawakan (South America): *barbecue, canoe, hammock, maize, papaya, potato*

of these are believed to play a role in the acquisition of reading skills (Snow, 1990). It is also known that children with reading and spelling difficulties tend to misuse, substitute, or omit inflected endings more than average readers do (Bailet, 1990).

Sentential Semantics

A sentence is a unit of meaning that conforms to grammatical rules. It can be made up of a single clause, many clauses, and additional phrases (see Box 3.5). A simple sentence contains one finite verb (a verb that is limited by person and number, as the verb in the sentence "My students *like* me"). A simple sentence can be combined with another simple sentence or with a clause using a conjunction. In these cases, the sentence becomes a compound sentence. An example of a compound sentence is "John loves Jane, but Jane does not love him." A large number of sentences encountered in textbooks are combinations of more than a main clause and subordinate clauses. A subordinate clause cannot stand by itself but depends on the main clause. It also describes the main clause. For example, in the sentence "When evening came, they danced," "when evening came" is a clause that cannot stand by itself but qualifies the main clause, "they danced." In these constructions, the two clauses are not equal; the subordinate clause qualifies the main clause with a relative term, such as *which, what, when* or *that*.

Compound sentences can also be created by embedding one clause within the main sentence. An example of a sentence containing an embedded clause is "The boy who is sitting at the back row is one of my best students." In this sentence, the clause "who is sitting at the back row" is embedded within the main sentence "The boy . . . is one of my best students." It is thought by linguists that human language might have evolved in this way from one-word utterances to more syntactically complex sentences. The presence of clause subordination and embeddings is, therefore, considered one of the advanced evolutionary features of languages. A language that is less advanced may express the same message by stringing together the clauses in this way: "The boy is sitting at the back, and he is one of my best students." In upper elementary grades, the teacher may draw children's attention to these characteristics of sentences and encourage them to use such constructions in their writing. The number of embeddings in students' written sentences can indicate the quality of their written work.

Box 3.5. Phrases and clauses

A **phrase** is a group of words that has either no subject or no predicate. The subject is an action word in a sentence and answers *who* and *what*. Predicate denotes action (e.g., "reading") or description (e.g., "reading quietly"). Examples of phrases include "reading a book" (no subject) and "the boy in the classroom" (no predicate).

A **clause** is a group of words containing both a subject and a predicate. There are two kinds of clauses: dependent and independent. A dependent clause cannot stand alone as a sentence (e.g., "although the girl was beautiful"). Independent clauses can stand alone (e.g., "he did not want to go to school").

Creating an awareness about the nature of clauses and phrases can facilitate reading comprehension in upper elementary students.

Inferential Comprehension   In addition to using grammatical clues to obtain meaning from text, readers are expected to make inferences about the text using their own prior knowledge. For example, a second grader is asked to read the following sentence and answer the accompanying question:

- Sentence: *We went to a restaurant and had a good time.*

- Question: *What did we do at the restaurant?*

The information "We ate breakfast" is not given in the text; it has to be inferred. Such inference making requires that readers possess the appropriate schema, or background knowledge. Comprehension that depends on making inferences is referred to as inferential comprehension; comprehension that does not require making inferences is referred to as literal comprehension. With regard to the statement about the restaurant, the question "Where did we go?" taps literal comprehension, whereas the question "What did we do at the restaurant?" taps inferential comprehension. It is apparent, then, that inferential comprehension depends on background knowledge, which comes from experience.

Idioms and Metaphors   Language is enriched by the use of idioms and metaphors. An understanding of these devices is necessary to grasp and appreciate literary writings. These figures of speech add a literary quality to stories or to reports of an event and, as such, play a role in the literacy education of children in the higher elementary grades.

According to Moats (2000), **idioms** are word combinations or phrases that do not mean literally the sum of what their individual words mean. Idioms are also described as ready-made utterances. Some examples of idioms are "He escaped by the skin of his teeth," "He spilled the beans," and "Stop pulling my leg." Words in an idiom function syntactically and semantically as a single unit and lose their intended meaning if broken up. For example, "It is raining cats and dogs" cannot be broken into "It is raining cats" and "It is raining dogs." Readers must already have a knowledge of the idiom or be able to interpret it from context in order to understand it in text. Idioms can be misleading to younger readers because a literal interpretation of the idiom does not reveal its meaning. Although idioms can be challenging to younger children, they may be introduced in the upper grades as a means of embellishing written language and enhancing its quality.

Idioms can also be used as a means of increasing students' sensitivity to social diversity because idioms grow out of cultural history and practices; therefore, they constitute an element of the pragmatics of language. Examples of culturally derived idioms are "He lives on Skid Row" (American), "She quit cold turkey" (American), "The young man made ducks and drakes of his wealth" (British), "He will never set the Thames on fire" (British), "The notes were sour because the seams were split" (Scottish, referring to a bagpipe), and "She is currying favour with her boss" (British, Indian). Direct instruction is necessary for students to interpret and use idioms properly.

Another type of figure of speech is the **metaphor.** A metaphor is a phrase or statement whose meaning is extended to mean something other than for what it was originally intended. Consider the following statement: "She did a lousy job in writing this paper." The term *lousy* is a metaphorical extension of the phrase "full of lice." When used as a metaphor, it refers not to lice but to a poorly done job. The words that make up metaphors have a literal meaning, but as metaphors they are used to mean something different. In addition, the metaphor can be used to express higher level concepts in terms of lower level facts. Examples are "We will leave no stone unturned until we find the culprit" and "Wooden legs are not inherited; wooden heads are."

A metaphor is a figure of speech that expresses an idea succinctly by juxtaposing one thing with another. It accomplishes this function without using comparative words such as *like* and *as*. In this respect, a metaphor differs from a simile. Examples of some metaphors used in the American language are "Her bark is worse than her bite," "Two captains will sink a ship," "His new car turned out to be a lemon," "She is a top banana in the firm where she works," and "His stomach is a bottomless pit." Compare these metaphors with the following *similes*: "She is as lovely as a rose," "He is as tough as a rock," "He drinks like a fish," "The ideas in this book are packed like sardines in a can," and "The ideas expressed in the student's paper are as clear as a chocolate milkshake." Though they employ different techniques, both metaphors and similes enrich written and spoken language. Similes evoke visual images of sentences that would otherwise be vague. Metaphors embellish language and spark life into sentences.

Because understanding metaphors requires extracting their abstract meaning, metaphoric language is difficult for children in the early elementary grades to understand and use. A metaphoric expression such as "If you lay down with dogs, you will get up with fleas" is likely to be literally interpreted by children. Children should be made aware that metaphors and idioms are not to be literally interpreted.

Etymology and Vocabulary   **Etymology** is the study of the historical origin of words and is, therefore, a branch of historic linguistics. The word *sheep*, for instance, can be traced to the German word *Schaf*, and the word *street* can be traced to the Latin word *strata*. The word *receipt* comes from the Latin word *recipere* and the word *hour* from the word *ora*. The spelling of some English words retain elements of their origin, as with the silent *p* in the word *receipt*. Knowledge of etymology can be helpful in building children's vocabulary and spelling skills. Interestingly, the order in which words are introduced in the elementary curriculum follows, to a certain degree, the etymology of English words. For instance, material in the early grade levels includes many Anglo-Saxon monosyllabic words, such as *book*, *play*, *run*, *hand*, *head*, and *cup*. This is followed by Latin words, such as *important*, *illegal*, *direction*, and *excellent*, which are frequently encountered in literary writings. Words used in science literature that are of Greek origin are introduced in the higher grades. Examples include *microscope*, *hemisphere*, and *biochemistry*.

Pragmatics of Language

Pragmatics is a branch of semantics that studies language usage with reference to the context in which sentences are uttered. Context and previous experience helps language users go beyond a literal interpretation of utterances to understand the underlying practical meaning. More specifically, pragmatics refers to language used as a tool for social interaction and can, therefore, be considered to be an aspect of sociolinguistics.

Use of the pragmatics of language leads an individual to interpret and use language properly under two circumstances: the immediate context and the cultural context. For example, the question "Can you pass the salt?" is not a question that requires a yes or no answer but is a request to pass the salt. This form of communication is context bound; it is not unique to any given culture. On the other hand, when a boy asks a girl, "Are you free this weekend?" the question can be interpreted in more than one way, depending on the culture. In cultures in which dating is not prevalent, the question bears information that is different from those in which dating is a part of life. Whereas semantics and syntax deal with the internal structure of language, pragmatics deals with its usage with reference to a particular context and culture.

Summary of the Components of Language

It is apparent that reading comprehension involves more than knowing words, word meanings, and the literal meaning of sentences. Several higher order language and cognitive skills are necessary for text comprehension. Included in this list of skills are understanding the relationship between words and word parts, grasping the relationship between two sentences, determining multiple meaning of words and figurative language, identifying main ideas, determining the communicative intent of the author, disregarding irrelevant information, and drawing inferences. In addition, comprehension is constructed with reference to the culture and context in which language occurs. Many of these skills play a more important role as children move to higher grades. Reading comprehension depends a great deal on readers' facility in understanding the connotative meaning of words, their multiple meanings, figurative use of language, the intention of the writer, implicit meaning of sentences, idioms, and metaphors. Children whose first language is not English often find these elements of language particularly difficult.

The Influence of Language on Reading and Writing Skills

As syntax and morphology affect the meaning of sentences, grammatical competence is necessary for comprehension. In general, most children acquire grammatical competency in spoken language fairly quickly and without any apparent effort. Such a statement cannot, however, be made when it comes to written language. Grammatical errors in children's writing are fairly common. Why is this so? Spoken language is informal, often uttered with little thought beforehand, and fleeting. Spoken communication is filled with stops, hesitations, repetitions, and omission of words. The listener fills in the missing words, recasts the message in his own vocabulary, and thus perceives meaning. Spoken language is colloquial, error tolerant, and forgiving. In addition, spoken language is bolstered by gestures and facial expressions. Written language, in contrast, is formal and durable. It lacks the additional informational input from gestures and context. The reader has to rely solely on the message because the messenger is not present. Whereas spoken language is often informal and colloquial, written language follows a standard format. It is not surprising, then, to find a large difference in the quality of children's language in its spoken and written forms. Many children and adolescents tend to use the spoken, colloquial form of English when they write.

As noted in the previous section, spoken language has three main constituents: sound, structure, and meaning. These features are also referred to as phonology, grammar, and semantics. Research shows that deficiency in any one of these three aspects of language can adversely affect reading performance.

Phonology

Take, for instance, phonology. When children pronounce a written word, they are converting the written word into its sound equivalent. This process is referred to as decoding. During the beginning stages of learning to read, readers convert most of the printed words in sentences into their pronunciations either covertly or overtly to keep the words in STM until the end of the sentence is reached. At this point, they are able to comprehend the meaning of the entire sentence. In skilled readers, the process of conversion *may* take place after the meaning of the words is realized. Some researchers suggest that readers first make a phonological rendering of the written word and then comprehend meaning. Other researchers propose that skilled readers comprehend the meaning of words and clauses and then recognize their pronunciation. Regardless of the point at which meaning is realized, phonological conversion of the written word aids comprehension immensely. In fact, it can be said that phonological conversion of the written word is a requirement for reading comprehension. A precursor for such a phonological conversion is thought to be an awareness that speech contains units of sounds, the phonemes. As noted earlier, sensitivity to phonemes is referred to as phonemic awareness. Impairment in phonology is said to be a main reason a majority of individuals who are hearing impaired remain poor readers. In addition, a number of studies have shown that even some children with average hearing have difficulty in recognizing discrete sounds in the spoken language and that these children experience difficulties in learning to read. A review of 24 studies by Snow et al. (1998) showed that phonemic awareness and phonological awareness scores obtained in kindergarten and reading scores obtained in first grade have a correlation of 0.42, making these awareness tasks moderate predictors of later reading skill.

Furthermore, research studies have shown that when children's sensitivity to phonemes is increased by training in phonemic awareness, their reading skill also improves (Ball & Blachman, 1991; Bradley & Bryant, 1985; Foorman, Francis, Fletcher, Schatschneider, & Mehta, 1998; Torgesen, Wagner, & Rashotte, 1997). Current research also shows that the best reading achievement scores are obtained when phonemic awareness training is carried out in the context of written language.

Grammar

As noted earlier, grammar refers to the structure of language. There are two types of structures, word structure and sentence structure. Word structure has a bearing on word meaning. Changes in word structure are particularly useful in indicating tense (past, present, future), number (singular, plural), and negation. In the English language, such alterations are accomplished in one of three ways: by altering the internal structure of the word (e.g., *run → ran; begin → began*), by inflecting the word using a suffix (e.g., *ball* → *balls; walk* → *walked*), or by adding a prefix (e.g., *changed* → *unchanged; possible* → *impossible*). Knowledge about the structure of words and an understanding of how changes in the structure of the word affect meaning is referred to as morphological awareness. Morphological awareness is a contributor to reading skills, especially in the higher grades (Carlisle & Noman-bhoy, 1993). Students of literacy classify sentences into four classes depending on their complexity: simple, compound, complex, and compound-complex. A simple sentence consists of a subject and a verb with no subordinate clauses (e.g., "John reads books"). In a compound sentence, two independent clauses are joined by a conjunction (e.g., "John reads books, but Jack loves to play"). A complex sentence has one independent clause joined to a dependent clause (e.g., "John reads books that contain stories"). When two independent clauses are joined by one or more dependent clauses, a compound-complex sentence is created (e.g., "John reads books, but Jack loves to play because books are uninteresting"). In the lower elementary grades, children cannot be expected to write compound-complex sentences, but children in the upper grades can be taught the nature of these types of sentences and encouraged to use them in their writing.

Semantics

The meaning aspect of language, or semantics, can also be approached from two levels, the vocabulary level and the sentence level. It stands to reason that a limited vocabulary can impede comprehension, and indeed the relationship between vocabulary size and reading comprehension is quite strong. The **correlation coefficients** obtained between vocabulary knowledge and reading comprehension range from .41 to .93 (Anderson & Freebody, 1981; Mezynski, 1983). This means that 16.8%–86.5% of the difference in reading comprehension test scores of readers can be explained by differences in vocabulary knowledge. Much stronger evidence for the belief that vocabulary knowledge plays an important role in reading comprehension comes from studies showing that improvement in vocabulary knowledge also improves reading comprehension (Beck, Perfetti, & McKeown, 1982).

Comprehending the meaning of a sentence, of course, involves more than vocabulary knowledge. Most sentences are not merely a string of nouns and verbs but are an elaboration of these elements. Usually, they contain noun clauses, relational clauses, adverbial clauses, and a combination of these. Higher level literature is also liberally sprinkled with metaphors and idioms. As sentences become more and more complex, higher level comprehension skills are required to understand these sentences. Elementary classroom textbook writers have taken this fact into account and include simple sentences in beginning grades and more complex sentences in later grades. In upper elementary grades, professional reading teachers can enhance students' literacy skills by drawing their attention to the use of pragmatics, idioms, and metaphors.

Assignments for the Student Teacher

1. Prepare a list of rhyming words. Identify the onsets and rimes in each of these words.

2. Consider the sound /t/ in these two words: *water* and *patron*. The *t* in the first word is not fully articulated, whereas the second *t* is articulated. For this reason, young children tend to spell *water* as *wader* but not *patron* as *padron*. The *t* in *water* is called a tongue flap. When *t* is not flanked by two vowels, it is fully articulated. Make a list of words that have a flap *t* in them.

3. Consider the following words: *furniture* and *cordial*. In these words, the *t* and *d* are articulated like a /c/ and a /j/. In words such as *petrol* and *adder,* these letters are fully stressed. Do you think these differences in pronunciation have an effect on children's spelling? If so, what types of spelling errors are likely to be seen in children's writings?

4. Make a list of idioms and metaphors. Read a few idioms and metaphors to children from different elementary grades and ask them what the sentences mean. Note at what age an appreciation of simple idioms and metaphors appears to emerge.

5. Turn-taking during conversation is thought to be an aspect of pragmatics. Observe children from early elementary grades and note whether all the children from these grades understand and use this aspect of language.

6. Make a short list of words such as *blue* and *though*. After explaining to some of your friends what a phoneme is, ask them how many phonemes there are in each word on your list. How many of them confuse letter names with phonemes?

7. Make a list of 10 short sentences in English. What is the order of syntax in the sentences: SVO, SOV, or OSV?

Reading Assignment

Read one of the following articles, discuss it, and write a one-page summary. These articles can be obtained at your college library or downloaded by accessing the library's electronic holdings.

Paratore, J.R., & Jordan, G. (2007). Starting out together: A home–school partnership for preschool and beyond. *The Reading Teacher, 60*(7), 694–696.

Schwartz, R.M. (2005). Responding to primary students during guided reading. *The Reading Teacher, 58*(5), 436–443.

CHAPTER 4

The Psycholinguistics of Written Language

Summary

This chapter introduces basic concepts used in the description of written language and provides background information about the origins of writing systems and the history of English spelling. Although English spelling is often characterized as irregular and chaotic, the chapter presents the argument that English is more regular than it is thought to be. Evidence shows that apparent inconsistencies are due to the facts that written English is a product of many languages and English orthography at times gives precedence to meaning rather than to pronunciation. For this reason, many English words, although phonologically irregular, are regular from a morphological perspective. The goal of this presentation is to have students (and the teacher) to consider spelling as a product of several factors, such as the history of the English language and its linguistic basis. The final section of the chapter addresses the question of whether the "irregular" nature of English spelling is a source of reading and spelling problems.

Main ideas presented in this chapter

1. Understanding the basic concepts involved in the study of written language forms a foundation for grasping the subject's more complicated concepts.

2. It is helpful for the reading teacher to know the origins and history of writing systems.

3. Written language is as natural as spoken language and is not mere speech written down.

4. The term *orthography* refers to the way written language is represented. In alphabetic systems such as English, orthography means spelling. In nonalphabetic writing systems such as Chinese, orthography refers to characters.

5. Comprehension of the nature and history of English orthography will be useful to the reading teacher.

6. English spelling is not as chaotic as it is sometimes thought to be.

7. The nature of English orthography is not the major cause of reading and spelling difficulties of children.

1. What is spelling, and what is orthography? What is **transparent orthography**? What is **opaque orthography**?

2. What is a writing system? How many writing systems are there? When and where did writing originate, and what was its original purpose?

3. Why is written language considered an invention and an artifact? Do you agree with this view?

4. What is the difference between English orthography and Chinese orthography? Does phonology play a role in the reading of Chinese characters?

5. What is meant by the statement "English spelling is morphophonemic in nature"?

6. Words such as *health* and *heal* are pronounced differently even though they have the same root word. Does this inconsistency of English spelling have any advantage?

7. Is English spelling really as chaotic as some people assert? Is it is governed by any rules?

8. Are some written languages easier to learn to read and spell than others?

9. Is the nature of English orthography a source of reading difficulty for children?

Basic Concepts Involved in the Study of Writing Systems

An understanding of some basic terminology frequently used in the discussion of written language will assist in the comprehension of the concepts presented in this chapter. Definitions and descriptions of these terms are given next.

Orthography

Orthography is defined as the visual representation of language that is influenced by phonological, syntactic, morphological, and semantic features of the language. The term *spelling* is similar to the term *orthography*, but these two terms are not synonyms. *Orthography* is an umbrella term that includes all writing systems, alphabetic as well as nonalphabetic. In English, orthography refers to the spelling of words, whereas in Chinese, which is a nonalphabetic writing system, orthography refers to the characters used for writing. Some writing systems, such as Korean and Japanese Kana, are syllabic in nature. In these languages, orthography refers to syllables. The definition of orthography also implies that spelling is influenced not only by pronunciation but also by syntactical and semantic features of the language.

Transparent Orthography

An orthography in which the names of the letters and their pronunciation in words are closely aligned is described as *transparent* or *shallow*. In other words, letters and their pronunciation have almost a one-to-one relationship. In transparent orthographies, readers who know the names of the letters can correctly pronounce most written words. Finnish and Italian are examples of transparent orthographies.

Opaque Orthography

If words cannot be pronounced correctly simply by knowing the names of the letters of the alphabet, the orthography is described as *opaque* or *deep*. English is often described as an opaque orthography. For example, the word *although* cannot be pronounced by sounding out the individual letters in it. French orthography is also opaque, and German orthography falls somewhere between Finnish and English. As orthographic depth is a relative phenomenon, it is appropriate to describe English orthography as relatively more opaque than Italian. One other fact worth noting is that pronouncing written words and spelling these words do not always present the same degree of difficulty, especially in opaque orthographies. When spelling is more difficult than pronunciation, as it is in French, the reading–spelling relationship is described as *asymmetric*.

Graphemes

A *grapheme* is a letter or group of letters that represents a phoneme. For example, the letter *c* in the word *cat* is a grapheme; the four letters *ough* in the word *although* are also a grapheme. In the initial phases of learning to read, children gain the ability to relate graphemes to their corresponding phonemes. This relationship is referred to as grapheme–phoneme correspondence, or GPC.

Scripts

The graphic format in which writing is represented is referred to as the *script*. Examples of different scripts are Roman script, Arabic script, and Brahmi script.

Writing Systems

The term *writing systems* refers to the nature of the linguistic units in which orthography is represented. Examples of writing systems are alphabetic writing, **syllabic writing,** and morphemic writing. English orthography is an alphabetic writing system because the alphabet letter is the basic unit of writing. A writing system that uses a single sign to represent one or more phonemes is syllabic in nature. For example, signs such as @ and & and digits such as *1, 2,* and *3* can be considered syllabic signs that represent phonemes. Korean and Japanese Kana writing systems are syllabic. If English orthography were a syllabic system, the word *cat* would be represented by a single symbol, instead of three letters, and *cater* would be represented by two symbols, instead of five letters. It might seem as if a syllabic system of writing would be easier to learn than an alphabetic system; however, a syllabic system requires the memorization of many syllables and puts a great burden on memory. It may be for this reason that the syllabic form of writing did not come to be widely used (Mair, 1996). Chinese orthography is described as morphemic. In Chinese writing, each logogram, or character, represents a morpheme, or meaning unit. Logograms are similar to the icons seen on a computer screen. The difference between syllabic and logographic writing is that in a syllabic system, each sign can represent a syllable (which can be part of a word), whereas in a logographic system, each sign represents a whole word.

It is sometimes argued that phonics instruction is irrelevant for learning to read English because readers of Chinese do not use phonology in learning to read; they learn to read logograms by using the whole word strategy. This is not a valid argument because Chinese orthography is not purely morphemic; a more accurate description is that it is morphophonemic. About 2,400 logograms cover 99% of all occurrences of morphemes in typical Chinese texts (Mair, 1996). The logographic system of Chinese writing, however, places a strain on memory, as rote learning of the nearly 4,000 logograms required for reading is a formidable task (see Chapter 2 for more information). This situation is somewhat eased by adding phonetic elements to the characters, which provides clues to the pronunciation of the characters. From 70% to 80% of the Chinese characters have a phonetic element embedded in them. Like Chinese, English orthography can be described as morphophonemic, although it is less so than Chinese. For instance, the root morpheme *sign* is pronounced differently when it appears in the word *signature*. Here, meaning is given precedence over pronunciation. Other examples of such word pairs are *nation/national, combine/combination, magic/magician,* and *hear/rehearsal.*

Origins and History of Writing Systems

Compared with spoken language, the history of written language is relatively brief. Archaeological findings indicate that the first known writing system was in use at about 3500 BC in Sumer in Mesopotamia, a region in present-day southern Iraq. Recent excavations in widespread areas such as Uruk and Nineveh in Iraq, Susa in Iran, and Tell Brak and Habuba Kabira in Syria have unearthed tablets with early inscriptions. The existence of these inscriptions indicates that writing might have originated over widely separated areas rather than from a single Sumerian source in Mesopotamia (Walker, 1987). There is also a belief among scholars that writing systems emerged, independent of Mesopotamian influence, in China and among the Mayans anywhere from 2,000–4,000 years ago (Coe, 1999; Gelb, 1974; Sampson, 1985).

Evidence shows that early writing systems were not developed to represent spoken language. The early Mesopotamian writings from Sumer, for instance, were used as a counting device (Jean, 1992; Robinson, 1995; Schmandt-Besserat, 1992). In Mesopotamia, records of commercial transactions were maintained in the form of solid clay tokens molded in the shape of cones, spheres, and disks, with each token representing a certain type of commodity. Soon, these tokens gave way to pictorial representations that were scratched on the surface of wet clay tablets. Subsequently these drawings were stylized, bearing only vague resemblance to the objects they represented, and became what is known as cuneiform writing (see Coulmas, 1996, and Figure 4.1). This suggests that writing had an origin independent of spoken language.

These early iconic writings were used as meaning symbols and, therefore, could not represent grammatical elements. This limitation was eventually overcome by making these icons stand for the sounds in the language. For instance, the Sumerian word for barley is *se*, and thus the drawing of a stalk of barley came

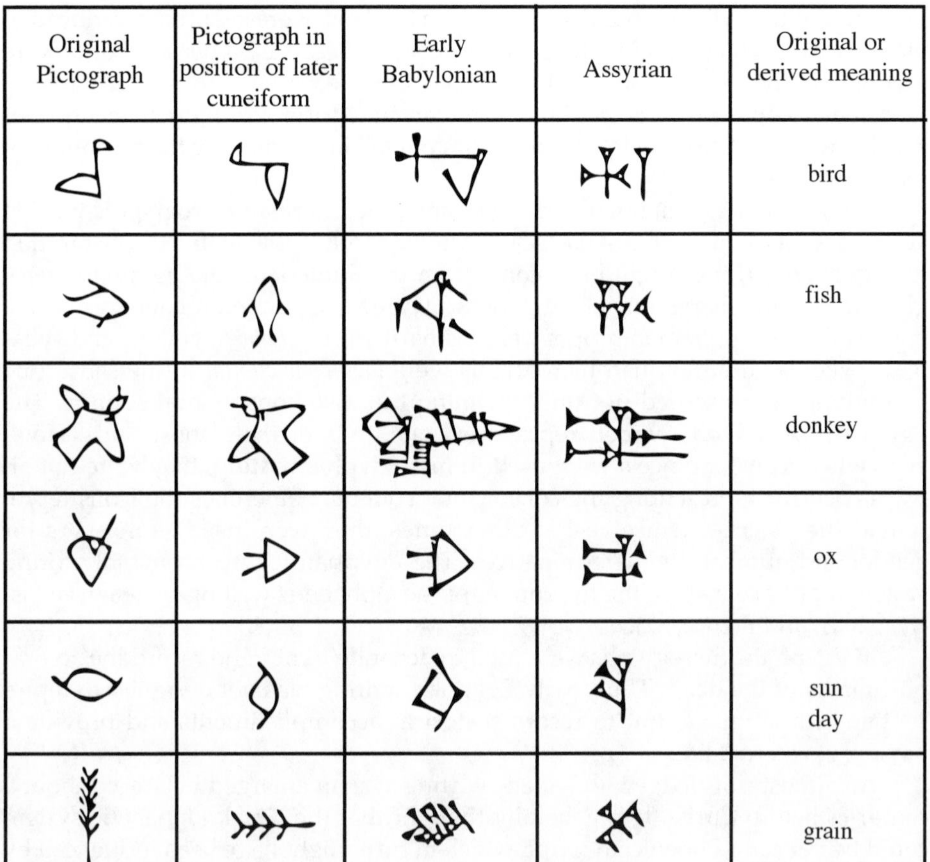

Original Pictograph	Pictograph in position of later cuneiform	Early Babylonian	Assyrian	Original or derived meaning
				bird
				fish
				donkey
				ox
				sun day
				grain
				orchard
				to plough to till
				boomerang to throw to throw down
				to stand to go

Figure 4.1. The evolution of cuneiform writing. (From Coulmas, F. [1996]. *The Blackwell encyclopedia of writing systems* [p. 100]. Malden, MA: Blackwell Publishing; reprinted by permission.)

to represent the syllabic sound *se*. Icons such as *barley* were eventually reduced to mere strokes, which became the cuneiform signs. Because Sumerian words were predominantly monosyllabic (Michalowski, 1996), each cuneiform sign came to represent a single morpheme. Thus, Sumerian cuneiform writing is an example of syllabic writing. The cuneiform writing system fell into disuse by the beginning of the Christian era.

Unlike the Mesopotamian writing system, the Egyptian hieroglyphic writing system lasted for more than 4,000 years. Although it is possible that the inspiration for Egyptian writing might have come from the Sumerians, the Egyptian hieroglyphic writing shares few characteristics with Mesopotamian cuneiform writings. Early Mesopotamian scripts were primarily *logo-syllabic* (symbols and syllables), whereas the Egyptian hieroglyphs were *logo-consonantal* in the sense that hieroglyphs represented not only meaning but also consonantal sounds. The Egyptian hieroglyph symbols represented one, two, or three consonants. However, when icons of objects were used in hieroglyphic writing, they were not always used for representing the consonantal sounds. Sometimes the icons represented the objects themselves; at other times, they were used as markers for gender and number, the determinatives. The Egyptian logo-consonantal writing system may very well be the forerunner of the alphabetic writing system (see Fischer, 2001, and Figure 4.2).

In Egypt, the hieroglyphs were used to decorate tombs and record the accomplishments of the dead. Thus, early Egyptian writing was not designed to represent spoken language but to record historical accomplishments and provide a passport to eternal life.

An almost full-fledged alphabetic writing system emerged in Greece about 5 centuries before Christ. It is generally thought that the Greek alphabetic system could be traced to Phoenician script, which in turn might have been influenced by Aramaic, Canaanite–Semitic, and Egyptian consonantal writing. The very term *alphabet* is a combination of the Greek words *alpha* and *beta,* (which came from the Phoenician words *aleph* ["ox"] and *beth* ["house"]) and was used by the Greeks to refer to all letters. Nevertheless, the Greeks took the Egyptian consonantal script and added a set of vowels, turning it into a complete alphabetic system.

As this brief discussion indicates, sociocultural factors such as economic necessities, religious beliefs, and proclamations of war exploits, along with the availability of materials such as clay or papyrus, played an important role in the evolution of writing systems.

Written Language Is as Natural as Spoken Language

An argument can be made in support of the proposition that written language is as natural as spoken language. There are several reasons this is an important issue. In addition to clarifying our understanding of the nature of written language, this viewpoint can also have an impact on teachers' instructional philosophy. For instance, advocates of the whole language approach to reading recommend that very young children be immersed in a print-rich environment to help them learn to read. Although this view should not be interpreted to mean that phonics instruction is irrelevant, exposure to print can be an effective means of promoting reading and writing skills if written language is also a natural way of expressing oneself.

Egyptian	Proto-Sinaitic	Phoenician	Early Greek	Greek	Latin
𐃆	𐤀	𐤊	𐌀	Α	A
⊐	☐	₇	⊴	Β	B
〉	∟	↑	↑	Γ	G
𓀠	𓀠	∃	∃	E	E
⊂	𝗪	Υ	Ж	Κ	K
∿∿∿	∼∼∼	ϻ	ϻ	Λ	M
∿	∿	↑	↑	N	N
◠	◠	⊙	⊙	Ο	O
◉	◉	↑	ϙ	Ρ	R
✝	✝	Χ	Τ	Τ	T
⚬⚬⚬	∪	W	ϟ	Ϟ	S

Figure 4.2. The evolution of the alphabetic writing system. (From Fischer, S.R. [2001]. *A history of writing* [p. 48]. London: Reaktion Books; adapted by permission.)

Universal Grammar

This issue also brings to teachers' attention the importance of the practice of writing for acquiring reading skills. In the description of syntax in the previous chapter, it was noted that syntax is an essential feature of language and that rules of syntax enable people to generate an infinite number of intelligible sentences. Although syntactical rules may differ from one language to another, all human languages have a system of rules. Because of this, some linguists (e.g., Chomsky, 1975; Pinker & Bloom, 1990) believe that human beings are endowed with an innate *universal grammar*. In Chapter 3, grammar was described as the pattern or structure that emerges as a result of the relationship among linguistic units. If an orderly structure or a consistent pattern of arrangement of words within a sentence or letters within a word is taken to be the essence of grammar, in a similar manner, the orthography of a language also has its own grammar. The spelling of words is not a mere stringing of letters in a random sequence but is based on a system of phoneme–grapheme mapping, particularly in transparent orthographies. In less transparent orthographies, such as English, the sound–letter relationship is complex because word spellings, in addition to having been influenced by the history of the language, are also determined by meaning.

Universality of Spoken Versus Written Language

A common argument *against* written language as a natural phenomenon is that only spoken language is universal. That is, all societies have an oral language system, but many societies do not have a written language. However, a combination of biological predisposition and sociocultural incentives in the form of economic and commercial needs and rituals could provide a reasonable explanation of the emergence of written language in geographically diverse areas such as China and the Mayan society. Had commerce been widespread throughout the world and a global economy in place 5,000 years ago, societies would have been obligated to record transactions, and writing also might have become a global phenomenon.

Another explanation of why writing is not universal could be that historically, there were deliberate efforts to keep reading and writing a monopoly. Attempts by average people in a society to acquire these skills were frequently thwarted by the privileged. This was the case with the Egyptian scribes, the Vedic Brahmins of India, and slave owners in the plantation states in the United States. Taylor and Taylor (1995) reported that at the beginning of the feudal Edo period (1600–1868) in Japan, only a small group of privileged people, such as priests and members of noble families, were literate. However, a survey conducted in 1947, 2 years after the second world war, indicated that more than 90% of the Japanese population could be considered literate. This indicates that there is a strong likelihood that literacy eventually would become universal.

The Acquisition of Written Language Without Formal Instruction

Another argument used against the claim that spoken language is natural but writing is not is that children seem to acquire language spontaneously without formal instruction, whereas they have to be taught to read and write. However, though parents and caregivers may not provide *formal* oral language instruction to their very young children, there is evidence that they do provide informal instruction. For instance, Snow (1977) found that mothers spoke in short, simple sentences, attempted to elicit responses from their infants, and provided pauses to give the infants opportunities to respond. This form of informal conversation between adults and infants is described as **motherese** (Karmiloff & Karmiloff-Smith, 2001) or "caretaker language." After reviewing research in this area, Bohannon and Bonvillian (2001) concluded that "adults do respond differentially to well-formed versus ill-formed child utterances, and children, in turn, respond to adults' feedback" (p. 273). Thus, spoken language cannot be said to develop without any instruction at all.

Is there any evidence that elements of written language, or at least its rudiments, are acquired without formal instruction? Studies examining the writings of preschoolers as young as 3 years old indicate that children do develop an awareness about writing without having received deliberate instruction. Developmental studies indicate that written language and spoken language complement each other because "both oral and written languages said to be being acquired simultaneously, and that the two together comprise language" (Sulzby, 1996, p. 28; Sulzby, Barnhart, & Hieshima, 1989). Investigations of children led Pontecorvo and Orsolini (1996) to conclude that children process written marks first by assigning a meaning to their writing and only later by relating them to phonological forms.

The strongest evidence for the acquisition of writing skills without formal schooling comes from studies of the Cree Indian Nation in the northern tip of Lake Winnipeg in Canada. The Cree use a Cree syllabary for writing (McCarthy, 1995), introduced in 1840 by the Methodist minister James Evans. By 1851, after just 10 years of using this system, the Cree nation had become almost fully literate (Berry & Bennett, 1989). According to McCarthy, "monolingual men, women, and children were able to become literate in their own language without formal education" (p. 59). Bennett and Berry (1991) commented that literacy spread almost uncontrollably through the Cree population, like an epidemic.

The puzzle is how a predominantly oral culture could become a culture of mass literacy within one generation. McCarthy's answer to this question is that written language emerged to satisfy a need. The Cree settlements were widely scattered in the snowy plains of Canada and, before the days of the telephone, writing was the only means of communication. This explanation gains strength from the observation that when the telephone was introduced, reading and writing in Cree syllabary lost ground (Bennett & Berry, 1987). This history of Cree literacy, therefore, indicates that sociocultural and other environmental factors play an important role in the acquisition and maintenance of written language skills, just as they affected the historic development of spoken language.

Despite evidence that written language is as natural as spoken language, the question of why all children do not automatically learn to write and spell without formal instruction still persists. A tentative answer to this question is that as long as a single means of expression and communication—in most instances, speech—is available, cognitive economy prevails and there is no need for learning to communicate through another medium. Preliminary reports of a study by Joshi, Aaron, Dean, and Rupley (in press) indicate that letting elementary school children communicate with one another only in writing for about 30 minutes during every school day improved their writing *and* reading skills considerably. Creating a need for communication through writing in the classroom seems an effective way to promote children's literacy.

Written Language Is Not Merely Speech Written Down

As noted previously in this chapter, writing began not as a means of recording spoken language but for other purposes. The early Mesopotamian writings were records of transactions of agricultural commodities (Schmandt-Besserat, 1992). Coulmas (1997) described early Sumerian as "word writing," and Falkenstein (1964) called it "sentenceless language." Early Egyptian writing (3,000 BC) consisted mainly of "king lists" (Waterson, 1997) and recordings of accomplishments of the Pharaohs. In China, the oldest writings were used for keeping track of offerings to gods; in Mesoamerica, writing was initially used for recording astronomical and calendrical information (Daniels, 1996). A documentary form of list writing can be seen even in the Old Testament (e.g., "Irad begat Mehajael; Mehajael begat Methusael," Ong, 1982).

Another piece of evidence to support the supposition that written language was not intended for representing speech comes from China. In that country several distinct languages are spoken, but there is only one major writing system. If written language was intended to represent speech, one would expect as many writing systems in China as there are spoken languages.

The Influence of Written Language on Spoken Language

Researchers who have compared written language and spoken language have noted that written texts are rich in integrated linguistic units, containing noun or verb phrases often expanded with embedded clauses. In contrast, informal oral discourse is of a rather fragmented nature, with limited use of formal syntax and intonation providing a major clue for linking utterances (Chafe, 1985; Olson, 1977). After noting that the terms *spoken language* and *written language* do not refer merely to different media, Miller and Weinert (1998) showed that "the syntactic structure of phrases and clauses in spontaneous spoken language is different from the structure of phrases and clauses in written language" (p. 1). Written language also contains longer clause and phrase structures and more embeddings than spoken language and, therefore, can influence speech. Because of this, children and adults who have become literate are exposed to a system of communication that is more enriched than oral language. Consequently, they tend to use in their oral communication formal syntactic structures, integrated linguistic units, and compound sentences with embedded clauses—features they have acquired through exposure to written language. Individuals who are not literate do not have this privilege.

Support for the view that written language can influence spoken language comes from an investigation of Vai language speakers by Scribner and Cole (1981). These researchers tested participants who were either literate or nonliterate in the Vai language for their ability to produce sentences. They found that those who were literate produced speech forms derived mostly from written models, which indicated that writing has a general influence on speech. Michaels and Collins (1984) analyzed spoken narratives produced by English-speaking children and found that familiarity with written language greatly affected the children's use of cohesive devices in speech. Scholes and Willis (1991) tested knowledge of morphemes in adults who were literate and adults who were not literate and their ability to comprehend syntactically complex sentences. The investigators concluded that literacy contributes to a knowledge of morphemic analysis and that many of the complex syntactic rules employed by literate adult native speakers of English are not found in those who have not acquired literacy.

An example of a spoken language having been influenced by written language is Japanese, whose Kanji characters were borrowed from the Chinese language. Eventually, these borrowed characters entered spoken language in the form of Sino-Japanese loanwords, which constitute as much as 50% of the vocabulary of contemporary spoken Japanese (Taylor, 1976).

The phenomenon of diglossia demonstrates yet another instance of the influence of written language on spoken language. *Diglossia* refers to a relatively stable language situation in which there is a highly codified and grammatically complex "high" variety of the language, which is used for most written purposes and formal oral presentations but not for ordinary conversation (Ferguson, 1959; Hudson, 1999). Diglossia is seen in several languages, such as Tamil and Bengali (India) and Sinhalese (Sri Lanka). According to De Silva (1982), high Sinhalese is not a spoken language at all; it is the language of written Sinhalese.

The influence of written language on spoken language demonstrates that teachers should provide an abundance of writing exercises for students, which can promote reading and other literacy skills.

The Matthew Effect

Developmental studies also indicate that even very young children's oral language reflects the influence of written language. Sulzby (1996), who studied children's acts of reading and writing and also collected children's speech samples, concluded that the conversational level of children who read is more complex than that of children who do not read.

It has also been documented that vocabulary growth depends heavily on reading experience. Children who do not have much exposure to reading are limited in their vocabulary knowledge; over a period of time, these children fail to keep up in vocabulary knowledge with their peers who are reading. Stanovich (1986) described this phenomenon as "the **Matthew effect**," after a verse in the Gospel of St. Matthew: "For to everyone who has, more will be given, and he will have abundance; but from him who does not have, even what he has will be taken away" (Matt. 25:29, New King James Version).

The concept of the Matthew effect, first used in the field of economics, can be described in everyday language as "the rich get richer and the poor get poorer." There is ample evidence to show that this notion applies to the field of reading as well. Although estimates of children's vocabulary vary considerably, a figure of 40,000 words appears reasonable for an average high school student. However, there is wide variation in vocabulary size among high school students. This difference is largely due to reading experience, because spoken language is limited both in variety and quality of words. As oral vocabulary level is approximately at the 7th grade level, development of oral vocabulary beyond the seventh grade level depends on reading experience. According to Nagy and Anderson (1984), the least motivated students in the middle school grades might read 100,000 words a year, whereas average readers encounter 10 times more, or about 1,000,000 words. Avid middle-school readers might read as many as 10,000,000 words a year. Consequently, good readers build a large vocabulary knowledge and are, therefore, able to comprehend and enjoy much of what they read. Poor readers, on the other hand, often avoid reading and have a more limited vocabulary. This further affects their reading comprehension. The gap in the reading skills of good readers and poor readers widens as children age, confirming the Matthew effect.

One of the most durable findings of recent research in the area of reading instruction is the relationship between phonemic awareness and reading skill. A number of studies have shown that training in phonemic awareness facilitates reading achievement (Bradley & Bryant, 1985; Lundberg et al., 1988). These results are generally understood to imply a cause-and-effect relationship between phonemic awareness and reading; that is, an awareness of phonemes has a positive effect on reading skill. However, some investigators are reluctant to attribute a causal role to phonemic awareness. Hewes (1983), for instance, noted that it is unlikely that linguists would have hit upon the notion of phonemes had they not been familiar with alphabetic systems. This means that exposure to written language is also responsible for creating an awareness of phonemes. Support for this position comes from a study by Morais, Bertelson, Cary, and Alegria (1986), who found that Portuguese peasants who had received only a minimal amount of schooling and instruction in reading were, years later, superior in tasks that tested phoneme awareness compared with those who had no experience with reading. Scholes and Willis (1991) reported a similar finding with adults who were illiterate and enrolled in an adult literacy program in the United States. A review study by Bertelson and de Gelder (1988) indicated that phoneme awareness is present only if a person can read an alphabetic representation of that language. Pontecorvo and Orsolini (1996) even asserted that awareness of phonemes is acquired only through the mastery of an alphabetic system of writing.

These findings indicate that writing need not be a mere phonetic transcription of spoken language; neither is a text simply speech written down (Coulmas, 1997). Literacy experience also has a positive influence on spoken language.

What does all of this information have to do with classroom instruction? Making writing a necessary avenue of communication in the classroom in addition to an instructional activity has positive effects on literacy acquisition. Students can be asked to communicate with one another only through written messages for about 20 minutes every day, using sheets of paper or computers. Spelling should not be a major concern during writing time; rather, teachers should encourage children to focus on communicating their message.

The Nature and History of English Orthography

A study of the history of any language has to rely on documents and written manuscripts from the past. Graddol (1996) provided a bird's eye view of the developmental history of the English language gleaned from written documents (see Box 4.1). According to Graddol, during the Roman occupation of Britain (AD 43–410) Latin was the official language, but Celtic may have been the spoken language. When the Romans withdrew from England, the country was under pressure of invasion from various groups from neighboring European countries. During the next 200 years, a language roughly identifiable as English emerged. This language is identified as Old English, and speakers are described as Anglo-Saxons. By the end of the 9th century, King Alfred issued a document appealing to his bishops for their assistance in the renewal of scholarship and literacy. The subsequent period witnessed an increase in manuscript and book production in Old English, written mainly by monks working in monasteries.

According to Graddol, the 11th century was an important period in the history of the English language because it marked the transition between Old English and **Middle English.** During this period the Norman Conquest took place, which introduced French into English society. Although French became the court language, Latin continued to be used for recording documents, and a person unfamiliar with Latin was considered illiterate. As a result, English spelling was based on

---

Box 4.1. **The seven ages of English**

1. Pre-English period (450 AD and earlier)
   Local languages in Britain belonged to the Celtic family. Following the Roman invasion (about 55 BC), Latin becomes the language of culture and government.

2. Early Old English (450 AD–850)
   Anglo-Saxons invade and Romans leave. Angles, Jutes, and Saxons bring a variety of Germanic dialects from mainland Europe.

3. Later Old English (850 AD–1100)
   Extensive invasion and settlement by Scandinavians occur. In southern England, King Alfred arranges for many Latin texts to be translated.

4. Middle English (1100 AD–1450)
   Normans conquer and rule England. English vocabulary and spelling are affected by French, which becomes the court language of England.

5. Early Modern English (1450 AD–1750), Elizabethan and Shakespearean era
   Influence of Latin and French declines, and English becomes the language of government and science. Printing brings a typographical identity to English. Publication of dictionaries and grammar books introduces some measure of standardization. Colonial rule takes English language to America, Australia, and India. Black speakers from Africa and the Caribbean give rise to English Creole.

6. Modern English (1750 AD–1950)
   English as a medium of instruction is introduced in many parts of the world. English becomes an international language.

7. Late Modern English (1950–present)
   The British retreat from empire. New varieties of spoken English emerge in newly independent countries. English becomes the medium of communication and technology.

From Graddol, D. (1996). English manuscripts: The emergence of a visual identity. In D. Graddol, D. Leith, & J. Swann (Eds.), *English: History, diversity, and change* (pp. 41–94). London: Routledge.

the Latin format. Although there were differences in spelling mainly due to dialectal variations, from the time of King Alfred spelling was becoming standardized. The Norman invasion in 1066 ended this consistency in spellings, and dialectal differences exerted a greater influence, resulting in regional spellings. As a result, Middle English shows greater variation in spelling than Old English. For instance, in Middle English the word *such* was spelled as *swilk, swich,* and *swech* in one part of England and as *soch, sech,* and *sich* in another part, probably reflecting dialectal differences (Samuels, 1969).

The end of the 15th century can be viewed as the beginning of Modern English. In 1473, William Caxton published the first printed book in English, *History of Troy.* Publication of the King James Version of the Holy Bible in 1611 and *A Dictionary of the English Language* by Samuel Johnson in 1755 were major milestones in the development of English spelling and writing. Work on the publication of the *Oxford English Dictionary* was started in 1878 and completed five decades later, in 1927. These projects standardized spelling and preserved spelling patterns to a large extent. Although printing accelerated the standardization of spelling, it had little or no influence on dialect, and the discrepancy between spelling and speech continued to widen. However, printing made it possible to mass-produce printed material and distribute such material among the general population. As a result, literacy became widespread, and schools paid a great deal of attention to reading and writing instruction.

In general, words have fixed meanings, but their spellings have varied a great deal over the centuries. For instance, as described previously, during the Middle English period many dialects were spoken in different parts of England and words were spelled the way they were spoken. A reader who could sound the letters out in a word could pronounce the word successfully and recognize the meaning of the word. There was no such thing as a spelling error because words were spelled as they were spoken. Thus, a word such as *knife* was pronounced with a /k/ at one time but later came to be pronounced without the /k/. The introduction of the printing press changed this situation by solidifying spelling, leaving spoken language to vary with time. The ever-increasing discrepancy between spelling and pronunciation resulted in many Modern English words having spellings that cannot be explained in terms of phonetics. The spelling of many English words is, therefore, a product of tradition and history in addition to *etymology* (word origin). Nevertheless, "chaotic" is too strong a term to describe English spelling. As noted earlier, many words that appear to have an illogical spelling will be found on closer inspection to be the product of history. As Vallins (1954) noted, English spelling is often etymological rather than phonetic.

The inconsistencies in English spelling have spurred many writers and literary individuals to try to impose some orthographic regularity. The reform movement is said to have started with Sir Thomas Smith, a Cambridge don, who argued for orthographic consistency in his book published in 1568 (Scragg, 1975). John Hart, author of several books on English spelling, proposed in 1569 that English orthography should contain as many letters as there were sounds (Graddol, 1996). As previously noted, there are about 45 phonemes in the English language but only 26 letters. Would the introduction of an additional 20 letters or signs solve the spelling problem? Probably not. For one thing, contemporary English has become a global language, and those who learn it as a second language speak it with the nuances of their native language. Thus, there is British English, American English, Indian English, Japanese English, and so on. Even among English-speaking nations, there are marked differences in pronunciation. For instance, the rhotic /r/ (which may be pronounced or not) in *farther* is enunciated by many American speakers but not by many British speakers, who pronounce the word almost like "fatha."

In the United States, Benjamin Franklin urged a reformation of English spelling. Noah Webster, who compiled the first American dictionary, argued that English spelling should be Americanized to create American English, a language independent of colonial ties. Webster's efforts, although not carried to the degree he envisioned, can be seen in the American spelling of words such as *center, color,* and *favor,* which differ from the British spelling of these words (*centre, colour,* and *favour*).

It was noted previously that the precursor to the English language was brought to England by Anglo-Saxon tribes from continental Europe during the Old English period. Society at that time might have been quite simple, and people for the most part were farmers, hunters, bakers, brewers, carpenters, weavers, shop-keepers, and barbers. Notice that all of these Anglo-Saxon words have an *er* ending. Later, Roman rule introduced a class system with a diversification of professions, and England came to have doctors, professors, sailors, administrators, senators, and actors. Many Old English words, such as *workable, readable,* and *breakable,* had an *able* ending, whereas many words of Latin origin ended with *ible,* as in *visible, audible,* and *convertible.* Many of the Old English words used *es* as a marker for plural, as in *potatoes* and *vegetables,* whereas some words of Latin origin generally added an *s,* as in *sopranos, actors,* and *soldiers.* English spelling is also constrained by certain conventions. For instance, very few English words end with the letter *v.* Invariably, an *e* is added to words with a final *v,* as in *give, love,* and *prove.*

In addition to Latin, the French language also influenced English spelling. Words such as *chagrin, machine* (where /ch/ pronounced as /sh/), *genre, prestige, rouge* (where /g/ has a value of /zh/), *cognac, champagne* (where /gn/ has a value of /n/), *coup, gourmet* (where /ou/ has a value of /oo/), and many words with silent letters, such as *chassis, debris, ballet, bouquet, depot, gourmet, corps, coup, centre,* and *metre,* are French in origin.

Role of Punctuation Marks in Written Language

Old English—indeed, almost all early writing systems—had no punctuation marks. These were introduced much later into written language. Punctuation marks serve two purposes. They help the reader identify grammatical units, such as clauses, embedded sentences, and sentences. Punctuation marks also cue the reader when to pause and breathe. This function, however, applies only to oral reading. It takes a few years and a great deal of experience with written language for children to learn to use punctuation marks correctly.

The Role of Phonology in Spelling

The belief that English spelling is chaotic can be unconsciously transmitted to students. In contrast, presenting the conventions that govern English spelling can inspire children to look for regularities and instill a feeling of confidence in spelling words. That children are avid pattern learners is seen in the errors committed by many beginning spellers. Such errors reflect children's efforts to regularize English spelling (Read, 1971) and to align the spelling of words with their pronunciation (e.g., "thay" for *they*, "sed" for *said*). In these instances of misspellings, the pronunciation of the words being spelled are represented (Ehri, 1986, 1992; Gentry, 1982; Treiman, 1993). Efforts to regularize spelling are seen not only among beginning readers but also among college students (see Table 4.1). This indicates that the tendency to generate rule-based spelling is independent of age.

Teachers need not despair over the nature of English spelling. Drawing children's attention to the patterns of English spelling and its stochastic conventions (discussed in a later section) can assist them in learning to spell. The spontaneous writings of preschool children indicate that they have acquired some ideas about the nature of spelling. Treiman's 1993 study of first-grade children showed that most of the children's spellings were approximations of their pronunciations (e.g., *gowng* for "going," *saied* for "said," and *buks* for "books") and not the result of rote visual memorization.

Based on their spelling patterns and pronunciation, words can be classified as regular or irregular. Words in which the letter names and pronunciation correspond at least roughly with each other are called *regular* or *consistent* words. Words that cannot be pronounced correctly on the basis of the sounds of the constituent letters are described as *irregular* or *inconsistent* words. An additional feature that distinguishes regular/consistent words from irregular/inconsistent words is that consistent words have many rhyming cohorts, whereas inconsistent words do not have rhyming cohorts. For example, the pronunciation of words such as *gave*, *pave*, and *rave* are consistent with one another, whereas the pronunciation of the word *have* is inconsistent with these words.

If spelling were mainly an effort to visually memorize the string of letters that make up a word, then there should be no difference in children's spelling of regu-

Table 4.1. Common spelling errors of children and college students

Phonetic	Letter omission	Syllable omission
Children		
cub $\rightarrow$ *cube*	napkin $\rightarrow$ *nakin*	distance $\rightarrow$ *dinste*
guard $\rightarrow$ *gard*	bandit $\rightarrow$ *banet*	thorough $\rightarrow$ *thorgh*
bomb $\rightarrow$ *bom*	picnic $\rightarrow$ *pinic*	gender $\rightarrow$ *gend*
thief $\rightarrow$ *thef*	prove $\rightarrow$ *prue*	believe $\rightarrow$ *belve*
picnic $\rightarrow$ *piknik*	health $\rightarrow$ *heath*	father $\rightarrow$ *fathr*
said $\rightarrow$ *sed*		
they $\rightarrow$ *thay*		
College students		
separate $\rightarrow$ *seperate*	doubt $\rightarrow$ *dout*	necessary $\rightarrow$ *nessary*
negative $\rightarrow$ *negitive*	receipt $\rightarrow$ *receit*	thorough $\rightarrow$ *through*
distance $\rightarrow$ *distence*		
grammar $\rightarrow$ *grammer*		
rehearsal $\rightarrow$ *rehersal*		
height $\rightarrow$ *hight*	height $\rightarrow$ *hight*	
island $\rightarrow$ *iland*	island $\rightarrow$ *iland*	
tomb $\rightarrow$ *toomb*		
prove $\rightarrow$ *proove*		

From Aaron, P.G., & Joshi, R.M. (1992). *Reading problems: Consultation and remediation* (p. 93). New York: Guilford Press.

lar and irregular words. After all, the notion of regularity and irregularity in English words arises from their pronunciation. But several studies show that more irregular words are misspelled than regular words, regardless of the speller's age (Ehri, 1986). Children, therefore, need more practice spelling irregular words than regular words.

Although phonology plays a major role in spelling, the role of visual memory cannot be ignored altogether. For instance, phonology will not be helpful in spelling words that are pronounced the same way but spelled differently (heterographic homophones). Examples of such words are *to/two/too, week/weak*, and *reed/read*. In these instances, visual memory must override pronunciation to correctly spell a word. In addition, there are words with similar spellings but different pronunciation (homographic heterophones). Examples are *minute, lead, wound, produce*, and *dove*. Exclusive reliance on phonology will lead to such spellings of these words as *mynute, ledd*, and *woond*, and so on.

The Morphophonemic Nature of English Spelling

Throughout this chapter the argument has been made that written language is not merely speech written down. The major goal of the English writing system, and for that matter the goal of any writing system, is to convey meaning and not merely to ensure the accurate pronunciation of the written word. Viewed from this perspective, written language must be considered an independent system and not a proxy for speech. For readers to comprehend written sentences, each printed word must be easily and readily distinguishable from other, similar-looking words. The more words tend to look similar, the more difficult it is to distinguish their meanings. It follows, then, that if words that sound the same (homophones such as *weak/week* and *rain/rein/reign*) are regularized and spelled the same way, the distinctiveness of these words would be lost. The absence of distinctiveness caused by regularizing spelling can interfere with the word identification process and impede comprehension. Under such circumstances, comprehension would be dependent entirely on context. Consider the following sentence, which has been "improved" by regularizing the spelling of some of the words:

They rode along the rode and when they reached the lake, rode across it.

Now, consider the sentence using conventional spelling:

They rode along the road and when they reached the lake, rowed across it.

Which of these two sentences is easier to understand? The fact that the spelling of the homophones does not match their pronunciation improves the clarity of these words and actually facilitates comprehension.

An additional aid to meaning is the alteration of the size of a word by adding a letter. Kessler and Treiman (2003) pointed out that most grammar words are short, whereas content words with similar pronunciations are generally longer. Thus, differences in the spelling of word pairs, such as in/inn, by/bye, be/bee, and to/too, may facilitate easy recognition of the word, whether it is a grammar word or a content word. There are several other examples that illustrate that the structure of English spelling is helpful in avoiding ambiguity of meaning. Compare the words *ox, box*, and *fox* with *rocks, socks*, and *locks*. All these words end with an /s/ sound, but the sound is indicated differently, either by *x* or by *s*. In these words, the presence of *s* indicates plurality, whereas *x* indicates that the word refers to the singular. Words that indicate the singular but end in *s* take on an *e* at the end to indicate that they represent the singular rather than the plural. Examples are *horse, curse,* and *purse.* Furthermore, having a final *e* or not having it can alter a word's meaning (e.g., tense/tens, tease/teas, dens/dense). When the spelling of these words is examined in light of this rationale, the final *e* ceases to be seen as a frivolous addition.

The spelling of the root morpheme of a word is sometimes preserved to emphasize meaning over pronunciation. In the following examples, for instance, the root words in each pair are not pronounced the same: *heal, health; hear, rehearsal; know, knowledge; wise, wisdom;* and *sign, signature.* The pronunciation of these pairs of words differs, but the spelling is preserved. These are examples of morphophonemic spelling, in which meaning influences spelling. The seemingly capricious spellings of these words function as cues that enable quick accessing of the words' meaning and grammatical status.

Is English Spelling Really that Haphazard?

The *American College Dictionary* (Barnhart, 1956) describes the word *chaos* as "utter confusion or disorder, wholly without organization or order." According to Finegan (1987), modern English orthography is more out of harmony with spoken English compared with many other languages whose orthography and pronunciation are in line with each other. However, fond sentiments about the advantages of contemporary English spelling have been expressed throughout history; for instance, Chomsky and Halle (1968) claimed that English orthography comes remarkably close to being an optimal system. Some scholars, however, have remarked that this claim is overstated (Rogers, 1994; Sampson, 1985). Nevertheless, it is important to note that only about 20% of English words have idiosyncratic spelling, conforming neither to phonological nor morphological rules.

Arguments refuting the allegation that English spelling is chaotic and irrational draw support from three sources:

1. Evolutionary history of English spelling (etymology)
2. Morphophonemic nature of English spelling
3. Effect on spelling of the position of letters within words and the influence of neighboring letters

The evolutionary history of English spelling and its morphophonemic nature were presented previously in this chapter. This section discusses the effects on spelling of neighboring letters within words.

The claim that the made-up word *ghoti* could be pronounced as "fish" is often attributed to Bernard Shaw. According to Kessler and Treiman (2003), this is an ironic statement because the phoneme /f/ is never spelled *gh* at the beginning of a word, nor is /sh/ spelled *ti* at the end of a word. This indicates that the spelling and pronunciation of words are constrained by the position in which a letter or letter groups appear within a word. Not all letters can occur in all positions in a word; they follow certain conventions. For example, English words do not begin with digraphs such as *ck, sr,* and *zt,* nor do they end with *v* or *q;* the letter *q* is always followed by the letter *u* unless the word happens to be a non-English name, such as *Qatar.* The letter *t* is more often followed by the letter *h* than, say, the letter *a.* The aphorism *"i before e except after c"* also indicates the influence of the letter environment. Whether *c* has an /s/ sound or a /k/ sound is determined by the environment in which the letter *c* occurs. For instance, *c* is pronounced as /k/ when followed by *a, o,* or *u* as, in *cat, cot,* and *cut;* it is pronounced as /s/ when followed by *e, i,* or *y* as in *cent, city,* and *cyanide.*

These conventions are governed by statistical probabilities and constitute the stochastic rules of spelling. That is, some letters in words are more likely to be followed by certain letters than others. Thus, laws of probability rather than randomness govern the spelling patterns of English words. These "rules" can be thought of as the grammar of orthography. These rules are not, of course, consciously used by English writers any more than speakers of English are aware of the rules of syntax, but teachers can draw children's attention to these recurring patterns in English spelling.

Kessler and Treiman (2003) analyzed the spellings of words commonly found in kindergarten and first-grade books for letter position and letter environment. They examined the extent of statistical probabilities that govern the spellings of these words. If a sound was represented by only one letter in all the words studied, it would yield a measure of 1.0; if a sound could be spelled in two different ways, the measure would be 0.50; if a sound was represented by letters in a totally unpredictable way, the consistency measure would approach 0.0. Their analysis yielded a consistency measure of more than 0.5 for vowels and a consistency measure of .92 for onsets. Kessler and Treiman concluded that spelling consistency increases significantly if one takes into account the position of a phoneme within words and the identity of adjacent phonemes.

In summary, upon close scrutiny, English spelling turns out to be more systematic and rule based than is often thought.

Is the Nature of English Orthography a Source of Reading Difficulties?

A notion that has attracted the attention of researchers is whether the nature of an orthography is related to the ease with which children learn to read that orthography. This idea, known as the **orthographic depth hypothesis,** proposes that deep orthographies, such as English, are harder to learn to read and write than shallow orthographies, such as Italian and Finnish. Research shows that the nature of orthography is not a major impediment to learning to read but that deep orthographies can slow down the initial acquisition of reading skills by almost 1 year (Seymour, 2006).

The belief that reading problems may be caused by deep orthographies was first suggested by Makita (1968), who reported that reading disability was extremely rare (0.98%) among Japanese children. Because Japanese orthography maps more directly to pronunciation and meaning than English orthography, it was reasoned that the reported higher percentage of children who experience difficulty learning to read English (10% to 20%) could be traced to the nature of English orthography. However, a more carefully conducted study by Hatta and Hirose (1995) using standardized reading tests reported that the incidence of reading difficulties in Japan was no lower than reported for children in other countries. A similar conclusion was reached by Stevenson and his associates (1982), who studied the reading and math skills of Chinese and Japanese children.

A more direct test of the orthographic depth hypothesis was conducted by Geva and Siegel (1991) and involved 245 English/Hebrew bilingual children. Unlike English, Hebrew orthography is shallow, and this research provided a good opportunity to see if children who had difficulty learning to read English also had difficulty learning Hebrew. In a subsequent study, Geva (1995) examined the reading performance on different tests of cognitive skills of 91 typically achieving children and 16 who were underachieving. All these children were attending an English/Hebrew bilingual school. Geva found that children with impaired reading skills in English experienced similar difficulties in Hebrew; those who made few decoding errors in English likewise made few errors in Hebrew. Taking the findings of these two studies together, Geva (1995) concluded that the nature of orthography alone does not lead to reading difficulties, although English orthography can exacerbate the difficulties of children who have weak decoding skills.

Additional evidence for the relatively small contribution of orthographic differences to reading and spelling comes from studies of German children. The relationship between orthography and pronunciation is more regular in German than in English. In one such study, Seymour (2006) found that in general, German children may be able to acquire decoding skills much sooner than English-speaking children, but nevertheless some are less fluent at reading than others. Similar observations have been made about children who speak languages such as Italian and Hindi. In fact, there are children with reading disabilities in every language. They may be able to sound out written words, but they are slow in doing so. These children are described as having dyslexia by researchers in their respective countries. In addition to reading slowly, poor readers of even regular orthographies tend to make errors of segmentation and letter substitutions. These observations confirm the minimal contribution of orthography to reading difficulties and suggest a central processing weakness as the major source of reading difficulties.

A collection of papers on orthography and the reading and writing difficulties experienced by children who speak different languages is published in the *Handbook of Orthography and Literacy*, edited by Joshi and Aaron (2006). The consensus that emerges from the many papers in this book is that orthography may not be the main reason why some children find it difficult to learn to read and spell.

Assignments for the Student Teacher

1. Collect samples of spelling from students in grades 1 through 5. Are there noticeable changes in the spellings of older children compared with younger children?

2. Count the number of embedded clauses in the writings of four or five children from different grades. Using these figures as indices, evaluate the quality of the children's writings.

3. What age-related errors can be seen in the spellings of students in grades 1 through 5?

4. Do some of the spelling errors reflect children's local dialect? If so, offer examples.

5. Observe and collect writing samples from a group of kindergarten children, then answer the questions below.

   What general conclusions can you draw from these writings?

   Are some children more advanced than other children in their writing?
      Give examples.

   How many children are able to print the letters of the alphabet?

   Can children's writing skills in kindergarten predict how well these children will read when they are in first grade? Explain your answer.

6. Examine the spontaneous writing productions of children in grade 5. Note their spelling errors. Are more irregular words misspelled than regular words? What is the ratio of spelling errors involving vowels to those involving consonants?

Reading Assignment

Read one of the following articles, discuss it, and write a one-page summary. These articles can be obtained at your college library or downloaded by accessing the library's electronic holdings.

Perez, C. (2005). English and Spanish spelling: Are they really different? *The Reading Teacher, 58*(6), 522–530.

Robin, R., & Carlan, V. (2005). Using writing to understand bilingual children's literacy development. *The Reading Teacher, 58*(8), 728–739.

CHAPTER 5

Development of Spoken and Written Language Skills

Summary

This chapter provides background information about the linguistic concepts related to the acquisition and development of reading, spelling, and writing skills. It describes the developmental sequences of phonological, syntactic, and semantic skills as well as of vocabulary knowledge. Developmental milestones for these aspects of reading and spelling skills are provided, which can help teachers informally assess children's level of attainment in these areas. The question of whether spelling development occurs in stages is also raised and answered.

Main ideas presented in this chapter

1. Development of literacy skills progresses in a systematic fashion.

2. Noticeable individual differences in literacy skills exist among children in preschool and the primary grades.

3. The concept of emergent literacy states that literacy acquisition in preschoolers does not wait for formal instruction to begin.

4. Prereading skills and print awareness develop during preschool years.

5. Development of the following elements of spoken language follows a predictable sequence: phonological skills, syntactical skills, morphological skills, and vocabulary knowledge.

6. Increased attention is to be given to vocabulary instruction if enhancing children's reading comprehension is a target of teaching.

7. Spelling skill follows a developmental sequence.

8. The reading teacher should understand the concepts of Standard English and dialectical English, as dialect has an influence on spelling.

9. Expected reading-related skills appear at different age levels.

After reading this chapter, you will be able to answer the following questions:

1. What is phonemic awareness and its relationship to reading? Are all phonemes learned at the same time? How can you assess students' level of phonemic awareness?

2. What is the developmental sequence of children's syntactical skills? How can children's syntactical ability be evaluated?

3. What information does **mean length of utterance (MLU)** give?

4. How do morphological skills affect reading comprehension?

5. How many words does an average child in the early elementary grades have in his or her vocabulary?

6. Does spelling acquisition occur in stages?

7. What is the relationship between spelling and decoding skills?

8. What is Standard English? What is dialectal English? In what ways could dialect affect spelling?

9. How can you help students become better writers?

Prereading Skills: Print Awareness, Emergent Literacy, and Invented Spelling

Exposure to the world of written language is a gateway to the world of literacy. Beyond that entry point, successful reading depends on possessing basic, age-appropriate language skills. A knowledge of the requisite skills for reading will help preschool and kindergarten teachers identify children who might face later reading difficulties. Early attention to these children's language skills can help minimize future problems.

Print Awareness

Print awareness is an understanding and appreciation of the nature and purposes of written language (Birsh, 2005). Children are exposed to printed materials both at home and outside the home. At home parents might read to children, or children might observe parents and siblings reading. Such exposure is believed to lead to a knowledge about the nature of written language. This knowledge includes understanding about the following:

- Books contain stories and other information.

- Books are written by someone.

- Every book has a beginning and an end.

- Books have titles.

- The reader starts reading at the beginning of the book and proceeds to the end of the book.

- Books contain stories, and stories are made up of sentences.
- In English, sentences are read from left to right.
- Sentences contain words, which are separated from each other.
- Words are made up of letters, and each letter has a name.

Once this basic knowledge has developed, children are ready to understand that letters are associated with certain sounds and that getting to know the letters and their sounds is important for learning to read. Repeated exposure to literary material can help children learn the letters and develop an appreciation for the sounds in language—that is, develop an awareness of phonemes. Eventually, this leads children to associate the sounds of the language with the letters of the alphabet. This achievement is referred to as gaining a knowledge about the written letters, or alphabetic knowledge.

It is difficult for adults whose daily lives are immersed in written language to realize what their world would be like without it. Members of oral cultures, who live without written language, are limited in their communication and interaction with the world. Prereaders live in similar conditions. It should come as no surprise that young children's experiences with written language lead to print awareness and empower them as learners. Researchers have used the number of books available in a home as an index of the family's literacy richness because such a measure is associated with the development of print knowledge; it can also be used as a rough predictor of children's reading skill.

Emergent Literacy

Chapter 1 noted that the old notion that reading instruction should not be provided for children until the age of 6 was shown to be pedagogically unsound (Chomsky, 1970; Read, 1971). These studies and subsequent observations by many educators have shown that many preschool children are strongly interested in trying to produce the words in their vocabulary by "writing" them down. Of course, many of their efforts look far different than conventional writing. Nevertheless, this indicates that children as young as 3 and 4 years of age do have some conceptions about writing and written language.

In American schools, reading was traditionally introduced first and writing was undertaken after reading. However, it was observed that even before formal schooling starts, children are exposed to print from sources other than books. This leads them to try to produce written "language." Thus, reading and writing are not mutually exclusive but should complement each other. Children's knowledge of written language, however unrefined it might be, is described by the term *emergent literacy* (Teale & Sulzby, 1986). The term *emergent* suggests that the desire to read and write emanate naturally and spontaneously at a very early age in the absence of formal instruction. The educational implication of this is that parents and teachers should take advantage of children's natural desire to explore literacy and create opportunities at home and at school for it to blossom.

Invented Spelling

Children's early "writings" do not contain letters of the alphabet but consist of lines of different shapes and squiggles of different length. Researchers describe this as *preliterate writing*. As children grow older, some of their scribbles begin to resemble letters of the alphabet and occasionally do contain a few letters. At later stages, these productions can contain the skeletal elements of real words. As noted in Chapter 1, these first writings are described as *invented spelling* (Chomsky, 1970; Read, 1971). By the time they are midway through the first grade, many children are able to correctly spell many words they have encountered in their textbooks.

Developmental Sequence of the Components of Spoken Language

In the following pages, the developmental sequence of phonological, syntactic, and morphological skills is described. Sequences in the acquisition of vocabulary knowledge and spelling skills are also presented. Informal assessment of these skills is briefly noted.

Phonological Skills

Phonological skills is an umbrella term that includes the ability to produce rhyming words, segment words into syllables, and possess an awareness of phonemes. These elements generally develop in sequence, with rhyming skills developing first, then syllabication skills, and then phonemic awareness. Of course, depending on the material used for testing these skills, some degree of overlapping in acquisition can be expected.

Children's acquisition of phonological skills has interested several researchers, who have collected data from carefully conducted studies (Cooper, Roth, Speece, & Schatschneider, 2002; Lonigan, 2006). Such studies have two motivations. One, of course, is that this knowledge can lead to an understanding of delayed or disordered phonological development, which allows practitioners to take corrective action to remediate such difficulties. The second reason, less obvious, is that such studies can illuminate the nature of phonology and lead to comprehensive theories of early reading and language acquisition.

Developmental Sequence of Phonological Skills

Studies of phonological development date to the 1880s, when many investigators followed their own children's development and recorded their observations in diaries. Such documents are called diary studies. Although early diary studies are somewhat rudimentary by current standards, more recent diaries are detailed and elaborate. Early in 1947, Leopold studied the production of English and German sounds by his daughter Hildegard from birth until her third year and published the results in a book. He published details of her vocabulary development in another volume.

Large group studies that produced normative data were carried out around the same time. Table 5.1 summarizes the results of three such studies. As can be seen from the table, there is some variation among these studies regarding the age of acquisition of different phonemes. This is due partly to the differences in the criteria used. One investigator may have required that 75% of the children in the sample produce a certain phoneme for an age level to be considered the norm, whereas another may have required that 90% of the sample produce the phoneme.

Table 5.1. Age norms for English consonant sounds from three studies

Sound	Age of acquisition in years and months		
	Wellman et al. (1931)	Poole (1934)	Templin (1957)
/m/ [man]	3	3,6	3
/n/ [no]	3	4,6	3
/p/ [papa]	4	3,6	3
/f/ [fill]	3	5,6	3
/h/ [hot]	3	3,6	3
/w/ [wet]	3	3,6	3
/j/ [jump]	4	4,6	3,6
/k/ [cat]	4	4,6	4
/b/ [ball]	3	3,6	4
/d/ [dog]	5	4,6	4
/g/ [go]	4	4,6	4
/t/ [two]	5	4,6	6
/θ/ [that]	. . .	7,6	6
/v/ [very]	5	6,6	6
/l/ [like]	4	6,6	6
/r/ [run]	5	7,6	4
/s/ [sit]	5	7,6	4,6
/z/ [zoo]	5	7,6	7
/dz/ [George]	6	. . .	7
/hw/ [who]	. . .	7,6	4,6

From Wellman, B., Case, I.M., Mengert, I.G., & Bradbury, D.E. (1931). Speech sounds of young children. *University of Iowa Studies in Child Welfare, 5*(2); adapted by permission; from Poole, I. (1934). Genetic development of articulation of consonant sounds in speech. *Elementary English Review, 11,* 159–161; originally published by the National Council of Teachers of English; adapted by permission; and from Templin, M.C. (1957). Certain language skills in children, their development and interrelationships. *Institute of Child Welfare Monograph Series.* Minneapolis: University of Minnesota Press; adapted by permission.

Key: . . . = no age provided by the researcher.

Nevertheless, there is agreement that all phonemes are not mastered at the same time. The information presented in the table can help teachers understand which phonemic skills to expect at what ages. They can identify children who are behind by closely observing their articulation of speech sounds. Of course, using observation to assess children's phoneme development is an informal procedure. Formal assessment procedures and standardized tests used for the production of phonemic awareness are described in Chapter 10.

Informal Assessment of Phonological Skills

Rhyming skills can be assessed by asking a child to produce a rhyming word for a target word. For instance, the teacher might say the word *cat* and ask the child to produce words that rhyme with it. Syllabication skill can be tested by saying a word and asking the child to indicate how many parts the word has by tapping on the table or clapping the hands. The child would tap the table or clap his or her hands twice in response to both of the words *doggy* and *Christmas*.

A rough assessment of children's phonemic awareness can be carried out in the classroom. The teacher selects a set of simple pictures whose names include the consonant sounds to be tested, for example, *cap, cat, car, dog, doll, drum, pen,* and *pail*. The child is then asked to put the pictures that start with the /k/ sound in one pile, those that start with the /d/ sound in another pile, and so on.

An advanced form of testing is to ask the child to sound out the phoneme at the beginning of words spoken by the teacher. A still higher level of testing is to ask the child to say the word without the first sound (phoneme deletion task). Pictures could also be used to test knowledge of phonemes in the final position. Standardized tests for assessing phonemic awareness are described in Chapter 10.

The information in Table 5.1 indicates that the ability to produce all of the phonemes is not mastered at once. Phonemes such as /m/ and /p/ are learned relatively early, by about 3 years of age, whereas phonemes such as /r/ and /z/ take several more months or even years to learn. In general, sounds produced in the front of the mouth are mastered earlier than those produced in the back. It is important to note two factors regarding phoneme awareness and phoneme production. One is that lack of mastery of some phonemes indicates an articulation difficulty and not necessarily a syntactic or semantic language difficulty. Significant variation in phoneme mastery can be seen among children who are otherwise developing typically. Second, girls acquire phonological skills faster than boys, and fewer girls exhibit articulation difficulties than boys (Dodd, Holm, Hua, & Crosbie, 2003).

Research shows that, in general, children who have difficulty in acquiring phonemes also are likely to encounter reading difficulties, especially in the area of decoding. In some children, a delay in acquisition might be due to maturational factors; in others it might be due to hearing difficulties. Ear infections are a common cause of hearing difficulties in children, and hearing should be evaluated before diagnosing a phonological problem.

Syntactical Skills

As noted in Chapter 3, *syntax* refers to the structure of sentences. In English and many other languages, syntax enables speakers to generate meaningful sentences. Sentences in these languages are made intelligible by having the words in the sentences follow a specific order. In some languages, word order is not as important for conveying meaning. These languages mark the subject and object of sentences with affixes (prefixes and suffixes). In these languages, therefore, meaning is more dependent on the structure of words (morphology) than on the structure of sentences.

Some linguists believe that syntax is hard-wired in the human brain, as individuals whose IQ is below the average can produce syntactically acceptable sentences. Others believe that syntactical skills are acquired by learning repetitive patterns of utterances and that, therefore, syntax is acquired, just like any other cognitive skill. The latter position would imply that the more children interact with adult speakers, the more competent their syntactical skills would become.

Developmental Sequence of Syntactic Skills

By the time children are about 18 months old, they begin to express themselves using single words. These are generally names of items, such as *mommy, cookie,* and *doggie.* Some children start off with words such as *no* and *bye-bye.* These utterances are actually single-word sentences known as *holophrases.* During the next stage of syntax development, children add another word to the holophrase. The addition of the second word is not random but follows a systematic pattern, so that the two-word utterance is meaningful. Thus, children at this stage produce utterances such as *bye-bye mommy* and *mommy cookie* but not meaningless sentences such as *catty-doggy* or *mommy daddy*. In other words, children's utterances are "rule based" even though they may not resemble adult language. This also shows that children do not simply imitate adults' speech; imitation, therefore, is not an adequate explanation of the learning of syntax. At the two-word stage, most of children's utterances do not contain morphemic units such as articles, conjunctions, pronouns, and prepositions. These are slowly added to speech as children grow older.

Another important milestone in syntactic development is the meaningful use of *wh-* **words** in sentences, such as *what, where,* and *when*. Use of such words indicates that children are actively seeking information, a good indicator of cognitive development. Not all *wh-* words emerge at the same time; they parallel children's cognitive maturity. The following sequence is generally seen: *what, where,* and *when*. The last word in this sequence, *when,* involves the abstract concept of time and is therefore learned much later than the other two.

Just as children combine two words to form simple sentences, they later combine two sentences using conjunctions. At first they employ simple conjunctions, such as *and* and *but*, to string sentences together. Later they use more sophisticated conjunctions, such as *because, however,* and *nevertheless*. The use of such conjunctions in writing may not appear until children reach middle school. Modals (*would, could*) and the passive voice are also generally not seen in children's writing until the higher elementary grades and even middle school. In spite of the slowness in acquisition of complex syntactic structures, by the age of 4 years children have mastered the basics of syntax to the extent that they can carry on simple conversations with teachers and peers.

The ability to produce utterances with complex syntactic constructions continues to develop until adolescence. Table 5.2 displays some syntactical elements typically seen in older students. The ability to produce sentences with sophisticated syntactic structures is accompanied by the ability to understand sentences and texts with complex syntactic structures. Thus, syntactic ability is positively correlated with comprehension.

Informal Assessment of Syntactic Skills

One way of evaluating children's syntactic development is to note the length of sentences produced in spontaneous speech. This measure of syntactic ability, known as the mean length of utterance (MLU), calculates the number of morphemes, rather than words, in a sentence. Each new syntactic element adds length to the speaker's utterance (Gleason, 2001). Brown (1973) described a procedure for

Table 5.2. Syntactical elements of older students' speech

Syntactical element	Example
Embedded clause: two sentences combined into one	It was raining. I did not go out.
	→ *Because* it was raining, I did not go out.
Passive voice	I *was warned* by my teacher.
Passive, negative interrogation	Have you *not been told not to waste* your time?
Relative clause: gives information about the identity of the person or thing being talking about	A teacher is a person *who teaches you* to read.

calculating MLU. A child's informal speech of about half an hour is recorded on tape. Then the transcript is analyzed for number of morphemes. The total number of morphemes is divided by the number of sentences in the transcription, which yields the child's MLU. For instance, in the sentence "She walked to school on her birthday," the word *walked* is counted as two morphemes and the word *birthday* is counted as one morpheme, making the MLU of the sentence 8.

Many children are reluctant to produce utterances, especially when their responses are recorded. It is also common for children to adjust their level of conversation depending on their conversational partner. A simple way to collect speech samples is to show a story picture or pictures to the child and ask the child to describe the picture(s). The number of pictures could be increased until a critical mass of sentences is collected.

Consider the following sentences produced by two children:

- Child A: "I want to play. I am not hungry. See you 'morrow, 'bye." (MLU 4.0)

- Child B: "I wanted to play because I am not hungry. I'll see you tomorrow." (MLU 7.5)

The quantative difference between the language of the two children is obvious. The sentences spoken by Child A are shorter than the ones spoken by Child B. In addition, Child B uses a conjunction, which increases the syntactical complexity of the utterances and boosts the MLU. Child B is clearly more sophisticated than Child A in syntactical development.

Although classroom teachers may not have the time to calculate MLUs for all students, they can obtain a rough indication of children's syntactic skills by paying attention to children's informal conversation. Normative studies show that the mean MLU of a typical 4-year-old is about 4.0; that of a 5-year-old is about 5.0 (Miller & Chapman, 1981). The Northwestern Syntax Screening Test (Lee, 1971) is an informal screening measure of syntactical development, although it does not provide a measure of MLU.

Morphological Skills

Morphological skills include the ability to use suffixes and prefixes in words to do the following:

- Mark tense and number *(walk → walked; boy → boys)*

- Formulate relative nouns *(tall → taller; short → shortest)*

- Indicate negation *(wanted → unwanted)*

- Change grammatical category *(house* [noun] *→ housed* [verb])

Like syntax, morphology plays a role in sentence meaning. For example, the word *bitten,* a derivative of the root word *bite,* indicates that the word is referring to the object of the sentence (as in "John was bitten"). This is marked by the suffix *en* in the word *bitten.* Another example is the word *played;* the suffix *ed* indicates that the action referred to took place in the past. In this case, the word functions as a tense marker and conveys the information by inflecting the morpheme *play.* Thus, the word *played* is an example of an inflectional morpheme. Inflectional morphemes indicate tense *(play → played),* possession *(John → John's),* or number *(book → books).* A root morpheme can also be changed from one part of speech into another, as in the previous example of the noun *house* being changed to the verb *housed* by adding a suffix. Such morphemes are referred to as derivational morphemes. (See Chapter 3 for more information on morphemes.)

Developmental Sequence of Morphological Skills

The development of morphological skills has been studied extensively by linguists. These researchers have concluded that morphological development takes place in a prescribed *order*, although there is a great deal of variation in the *rate* at which morphemes are learned by children. Table 5.3 shows the sequence of morphological development to the age of 5.

The sequence of acquisition of syntactical structures by Gleason (2001) is shown in Table 5.4. Most of the structures shown are acquired by 4 years of age, but there is wide variation among children even though the sequence of acquisition is stable. Notice the similarity between the data shown in Table 5.3 and in Table 5.4.

Morphology obviously plays an important role in literacy acquisition. If children do not use appropriate morphological structures in speech, they are not likely to use them in their writing. Reading comprehension might also be affected because children would not be likely to grasp the nuances of written language expressed through morphemic variations. For these reasons, the concept of morphological awareness, also referred to as morphemic awareness, and its relationship to reading achievement have received much research attention (Carlisle, 1988; Kuo & Anderson, 2006).

Informal Assessment of Morphological Skills

Teachers can observe or record and analyze children's informal conversations for morphological structures. The information provided in Tables 5.3 and 5.4 could be used for such an analysis. Features to note are whether children have ceased applying regular endings to all past tense verbs (e.g., "drinked" for *drank*), to what extent they use affixes, and whether they use articles, conjunctions, and prepositions appropriately.

Vocabulary Knowledge

In everyday language, *vocabulary* generally refers to words. Linguists recognize two kinds of vocabulary: receptive and expressive. *Receptive vocabulary* refers to

Table 5.3. Order of acquisition of morphemes by preschool children

Morphemic structure	Example
Possessive inflection	baby's toy; cat's box
Uncontractible copula: Use of the verb *to be* without contraction	The books are on the floor.
Past regular: Addition of *-ed* to the end of verbs	I played. I walked.
Third person regular: Inflection *-s* or *-es* added to noun	He walks. She kisses.
Third person irregular	He ran. He drank.
Uncontractible progressive auxiliary: Use of the verb *to be* + *ing*	I was walking. He was running.
Contractible copula	I'm going. It's raining.
Passive	He is punished. The rat was killed.
Past progressive: Use of the verb *to be*	He was running.
Gerund (*-ing*) as a noun	Walking is good exercise.

From Potts, M., Carlson, P., Cocking, R., & Copple, C. (1979). *Structure and development in child language: The preschool years.* Ithaca, NY: Cornell University Press; adapted by permission.

See also Anisfeld (1984).

Table 5.4. Order of acquisition of morphological structures

Syntactical structure	Example
Present progressive	eat*ing*; play*ing*
Prepositions	*in* the cup; *on* the table
Plural	book*s*; doll*s*
Irregular past tense	broke; went
Possessive	mommy*'s*; daddy*'s*
Copula uncontractible	This *is* my book.
Articles	*the* book; *the* doll
Regular past tense	walk*ed*; play*ed*
Third-person present tense regular	plays; drinks
Third-person present tense irregular	Mommy *has*
Auxiliary uncontractible	She *was* playing. *Do* you like me?
Copula contractible	I*'m* happy. You*'re* big.
Auxiliary contractible	Mommy*'s* going shopping.

From Berko Gleason, Jean *Development Of Language, The*, 6e; Published by Allyn and Bacon, Boston, MA. Copyright © 2005 by Pearson Education. Reprinted by permission of the publisher.

words that are understood; *expressive vocabulary* refers to words actually used in day-to-day conversation. Generally, receptive vocabulary is larger than expressive vocabulary. Vocabulary includes not only root words but also derived words (e.g., *play, played, playing*). Educators prefer the phrase *vocabulary knowledge* to *vocabulary size*. Growth in vocabulary is marked by two kinds of changes, quantitative and qualitative.

Quantitative Changes in Vocabulary

Estimates of children's vocabulary vary considerably. There are at least three reasons for this variation. One is the type of words sampled in different vocabulary studies. Some investigators include only root words in their count, whereas others include derivatives of the root words as well. Thus, in one study the words *play, played, plays,* and *playing* would all be considered one word; in another they would be counted as four separate words. A second reason for the variation in vocabulary estimation is the method used for assessment. Children might be tested for receptive vocabulary or for expressive vocabulary. A third reason is sample differences. In one study, Hart and Risley (1995) found that children from advantaged homes had receptive vocabularies as much as five times larger than children from disadvantaged homes. This gap widens as children progress through school. Therefore, sample variation can account for significant differences in vocabulary estimates.

In spite of inconsistencies among vocabulary study findings, certain broad conclusions can be drawn from these studies. Owens (1988) estimated the vocabulary of children at different ages:

- 2 years: about 200–300 words
- 3 years: 900–1,000 words
- 4 years: 1,500–1,600 words
- 5 years: expressive vocabulary of 2,100–2,200 words
- 6 years: expressive vocabulary of 2,600 words and receptive vocabulary of 20,200–24,000 words

Nagy and Anderson (1984), however, estimated that an average graduating high school senior knows about 45,000 different words. Extrapolating from this figure, one comes to the conclusion that children learn about 3,000 words per year, or about 10 words per day. Although this would appear to be an inflated number, it has been argued that it is possible for some children (White, Graves, & Slater, 1990). A more modest set of figures, provided by Diamond and Gutlohn (2007), is shown in Table 5.5.

Qualitative Changes in Vocabulary

Equally important as net gains in vocabulary are the qualitative differences that emerge during the course of vocabulary acquisition. Of course, quantitative and qualitative differences in vocabulary are not mutually exclusive. Child A, who knows more words than Child B, is also likely to know more low-frequency and unusual words than Child B. But a child can obtain a higher score on a vocabulary test simply because she knows more words, not necessarily because she knows more uncommon words.

The variability in the qualitative nature of vocabulary knowledge is evident from a study by Biemiller (2005). He selected a sample of 17,500 root words, known by children, from *The Living Word Vocabulary* by Dale and O'Rourke (1981). From this sample, Biemiller ordered the words in deciles (i.e., a 10-point scale); words best known by most children were placed in lower deciles, and words less known by children were placed in higher deciles. Administering these words as a vocabulary test, he found that children who knew only about 3% to 20% of the words on the list knew only words in the lowest deciles (i.e., the most common words), whereas children who knew about 45% of the words knew words from the 5th and 6th deciles. Biemiller concluded that children acquire word knowledge in a predictable manner and that children who have reached an optimal level of vocabulary size are likely to also know more word meanings. This decile classification of words, based on the developmental history of vocabulary acquisition, shows that it is important to identify not only how many words children know but also *which* words they know. This means that teachers should attend to the quality of the words they teach as well as to the number of words.

Table 5.5. Estimates of cumulative root-word knowledge of children

Age or grade	Average number of root words
End of age 1	860
End of age 2	1,720
End of age 3	2,580
End of age 4 (Pre-K)	3,440
End of age 5 (K)	4,300
End of grade 1	5,160
End of grade 2	6,020
End of grade 3	7,020
End of grade 4	8,020
End of grade 5	9,020

Based on Biemiller (2005a).

From Diamond, L., & Gutlohn, L. (2006). *Vocabulary handbook* (p. 7). Baltimore: Paul H. Brookes Publishing Co.; reprinted by permission.

Spelling: A Component of Written Language

As noted in Chapter 2, during America's Colonial days, schools considered spelling an integral part of reading and therefore gave much attention to spelling. During the 20th century, an attitude of indifference came to prevail and spelling instruction was neglected. This was partly because spelling was considered a product of rote learning and visual memory for a sequence of letters. Recently, however, there has been a resurgence of interest in the cognitive processes that underlie spelling and their development. Some of the research in these areas is discussed next.

Developmental Sequence of Spelling Skills

The progression of spelling from preschool through the primary grades gives the impression that systematic changes take place during the course of children's spelling acquisition. Indeed, researchers note that children's spelling develops in stages. However, these stages are not well defined, and one stage often overlaps with the next. In addition, a great deal of variability is seen in children's spelling skills. Following the lead provided by Henderson (1981), Bear, Invernizzi, Templeton, and Johnston (1996) closely examined children's spelling and identified six stages, describing each in some detail. Box 5.1 shows these stages collapsed into four stages: 1) preliterate, 2) prephonetic, 3) phonetic, and 4) morphophonemic.

Informal Assessment of Spelling Skills

Spelling is a recall task in which all the letters in a word must be retrieved in the correct order. This makes spelling a more demanding task than reading words, which is a recognition task. However, slow, hesitant oral reading and poor decoding performance can suggest spelling difficulties. The spelling level of children in kindergarten can be informally surmised by using invented spelling productions. In early elementary grades, curriculum-based assessment can be used (Invernizzi, Abouzeid, & Gill, 1994; Jones, 2001). Spelling and decoding are considered skills rather than higher order cognitive functions and are independent of general intelligence. Therefore, spelling performance cannot be taken as an indication of a speller's intelligence.

Children's experience with reading and writing and their dialect are among the factors that affect spelling. As noted in Chapter 1, children who use AAE may not perceive some sounds in speech and may not use them in their own speech. These children are likely to omit graphemes that represent these phonemes in their spellings. Dialectal effects are also seen in the spellings of children who speak SE. For instance, Treiman (1993) found that children from Indiana spelled *water* as *wader*, reflecting their pronunciation of the word. It is worthy of note that the quality of children's spelling at the end of kindergarten is a reliable predictor of their reading performance in grade 1 (Morris, Bloodgood, & Perney, 2003; Smith, 1990).

Writing Skills

Composing and writing sentences and text is a complex cognitive act. It involves understanding and using phonology, morphology, vocabulary, and syntax as well

---

Box 5.1. Stages of prephonetic and phonetic spelling

1. *Preliterate stage:* Simplistic drawings by children 3–4 years old that bear a vague resemblance to real objects or animals may be present.

2. *Prephonetic stage:* By about 4 years of age, children's spontaneous writing contains a few letters of the alphabet, although they are not in the correct sequence and some letters may be missing altogether. Examples of prephonetic writings are *bko* for *book* and *shol* for *school.* Many spellings are *invented spellings.* However, prephonetic spellings reveal that children are beginning to grasp the essence of the alphabetic principle.

3. *Phonetic stage:* By the end of kindergarten, children's writings display evidence of their attempts to spell words the way they sound. Common words with phonetic spellings, such as *mom* and *dog,* are generally spelled correctly. Words that have irregular spellings (e.g., *said*) may be spelled incorrectly (e.g., *sed*). Some children's writing may not reach the phonetic stage even by the end of first grade. Invariably, these children experience difficulty in decoding words, and the obvious misspellings of these children may alert the teacher to their difficulty in learning to read.

4. *Morphophonemic stage:* The term *morphophonetic* implies that morphology, in addition to phonology, plays a role in the spelling of words. Examples of words with morphophonemic spelling are *rehearsal* and *wisdom,* the pronunciation of which differs from that of their root words, *hear* and *wise.* Apparently, the spelling of words such as *rehearsal* and *wisdom* cannot be derived phonetically. Some individuals fail to master morphophonetic spellings in spite of average intelligence and many years of experience with printed language. However, a majority of children in grades 4 and 5 learn to spell many common words that have been encountered in the classroom, including those with morphophonemic spelling.

---

as metacognition. As a result, wide variation can be seen in children's writing, even in the elementary grades. Understandably, many children experience difficulty in acquiring writing skills.

Writing skill can be classified into literal and stylistic genres. Literal genre encompasses the mechanical aspects of writing, such as correct spelling, appropriate use of punctuation, and legible handwriting. Stylistic genre includes generating suitable ideas, organizing those ideas in a logical and coherent manner, using quality vocabulary, embellishing writings with metaphors and similes, and employing metacognitive skills in carrying out reviewing and editing. Generally speaking, evidence of higher order skills, such as paragraph and text organization, use of figures of speech, such as metaphors and similes, and the development of proper story structure can be expected in the writing of students in the higher grades. In the first two or three elementary grades, children are expected to have learned only the elements of literal writing.

In the higher grades, children's awareness of the qualities of good writing will enhance the quality of their own writing. Such qualities include 1) planning before starting to write, 2) being aware of the purpose of writing, 3) keeping in mind the audience for whom the message is intended, 4) anticipating the clarifications readers might seek, 5) leaving out irrelevant information, and 6) avoiding redundancies.

The complex nature of writing and the wide variability seen in students' writing skills make gathering normative data on the development of writing skills difficult. In addition, some children who are poor spellers appear to use limited vocabulary, which results in simplistic writing, but actually they are avoiding the use of big words for fear of misspelling them. It is, known, however, that direct instruction and extended practice in reading and writing improve students' writing skills. Table 5.6 shows the expected literacy skills at different grade levels.

Table 5.6. Expected literacy skills at different grade levels

By the time children leave *kindergarten*, they will be able to do the following:[a]

Phonological skills
Identify and produce rhyming words in response to an oral prompt
Identify the beginning sound in monosyllabic words
Blend vowel-consonant sounds orally to make syllables
Produce fricative and stop sounds when asked
Imitate bilabial and dental phonemes in spoken words
Count the number of syllables in words (by tapping on the desk)

Word recognition skills
Match consonant and vowel sounds to appropriate letters
Write own first name
Read a few monosyllabic words that were taught in the classroom

Comprehension skills
Be aware that a book can contain stories, poetry, or information
Indicate through action that one reads from left to right
Tell the difference between letters, words, and sentences
Relate pictures in the book to the story
Retell stories in their own words
Ask and answer simple questions
Follow one- and two-step oral directions

Vocabulary
Name color, shape, and food items when these objects are shown
Describe common objects, such as a book and an umbrella

Writing
Write their first name
Write upper- and lowercase letters independently
Show a tendency to write from left to right

By the time children leave *first grade*, they will be able to do the following:[a]

Phonological skills
Blend sounds to make words (e.g., /m/ /a/ /t/ = *mat*)
Produce more rhyming words than kindergarten children
Generate word families with similar rimes
Delete or add initial phonemes to change a word (e.g., *cat* → *at*, *rat*)
Segment common words into phonemes (e.g., *cat* = /c/ /a/ /t/)

Word recognition skills
Sound out and write all letters of the alphabet
Read monosyllabic words taught in the class
Read simple words with suffixes (e.g., *looked, played, plays*)

Comprehension skills
After listening to a story, respond correctly to *who, what* and *how* questions
Follow one-step written directions
Summarize in one or two sentences short stories they have read
After reading, tell the beginning and end of a story

Vocabulary
Demonstrate knowledge of more than 2,500 words
Name objects in the classroom
Produce words that mean the opposite of a few given words

Writing
Write from left to right
Leave space between words
Capitalize the initial letter of the first word in a sentence
Correctly spell three- and four-letter words taught in the class

By the time children leave *second grade*, they will be able to do the following:[a]

Phonological skills
Show that they know the phonemes in the English language
Articulate most of the phonemes
Delete and substitute phonemes in spoken words (e.g., *cat → at, bat, can*)

Word recognition skills
Read and sound out multisyllabic words correctly
Correctly read words with regular plurals (e.g., *run, runs; fly, flies; knife, knives*)
Read simple stories with proper intonation
Self-correct oral reading errors
Know when they encounter difficulty in word recognition and seek help
Seek help when they encounter difficulty in comprehension
Restate facts read in the passage
Associate pictures and maps in text with the reading material
Follow two-step written instructions

Comprehension skills
Use a table of contents to locate information
Verbalize their purpose for reading

Vocabulary
Understand and explain common antonyms and synonyms
Know the meaning of simple prefixes and suffixes and how they change the meaning of words
Know the meaning of abstract words such as *honesty* and *liberty*

Writing
Write in complete sentences
Write brief narratives based on their experiences
Write a narrative in a logical sequence
Write a letter to a friend with proper form for greeting and closing
Use correct word order in forming sentences
Use capitalization correctly
Spell correctly common irregular words, such as *were, said, come,* and *which*

(continued)

Table 5.6. *(continued)*

By the time children leave *third grade,* they will be able to do the following:[a]

Phonological skills

Show evidence of mastery of phonemic awareness

Word recognition skills

Decode regular multisyllabic words

Read aloud expository text fluently and with proper intonation

Decode unfamiliar words

Read simple tables

Comprehension skills

Distinguish between poetry, fiction, and nonfiction

Use higher order concepts (e.g., refer to *animals* collectively rather than *dog, cat,* and *horse* separately)

A knowledge of the difference between the main idea and supporting details

Follow multiple steps of written instruction, such as for assembling a game board

Summarize the main point of a text

Vocabulary

Understand what antonyms and synonyms mean and use them appropriately in speech and writing

Show how to use the dictionary

Demonstrate familiarity with many prefixes and suffixes and know how these change word meaning

Know about 5,000 words

Writing

Write in cursive

Adhere to margins and correct spacing between words in sentences

Produce declarative and interrogative sentences in writing

Use past, present, and future verb tenses properly

Use punctuation marks correctly

Spell irregular words encountered in the classroom

Write narratives in a chronologically coherent fashion

Sources: California State Board of Education (2006) and Indiana Phonics Taskforce (n.d.).

[a]For the 100 words children should be able to read at different grade levels, consult the Dolch Basic Word List and Fry Instant Word List. These word lists can be downloaded by using a search engine such as Google. In addition, graded lists of sight words, homophones, homographs, and other content area vocabulary words are presented in Fry, Fountoukidis, and Polk (1985).

Assignments for the Student Teacher

1. Select two kindergarten and two first-grade children. Ask them the following questions about print awareness, then write a short paragraph about their answers:
   "Do you have books at home? Can you tell me the name of the books?"
   "Do you like books? Which one do you like the most? Why do you like them?"
     (e.g., "Because they have stories")
   "Does your daddy or mommy read to you from the books?"

2. Administer the following tasks to three or four kindergarten or prekindergarten children:
   "I am going to say a word. You take away the first sound and say the word. For example, if I say *Dad,* you will say *ad.* OK? If I say *book,* what will you say? *(Ook.)* That is fine. Now, let's try these words: *ball, sit, fat, take, rat.*"
   For the preceding task, see if some phonemes are more difficult for the children to manipulate than others. If so, which ones are difficult?

   "Now I am going to say a word. You take away the last sound in the word and say the word. Are you ready? If I say *ball,* you will say *ba.* If I say *school,* what will you say? *(Schoo)* That is right. Now, let's try these words: *and, big, hand, car, calf.*
   For the preceding task, is final phoneme deletion more difficult for the children than initial phoneme deletion? Is there a relationship between these children's phoneme deletion skills and their letter knowledge?

3. Interview one or two kindergarten or first-grade teachers and ask the following questions:
   "What are the most frequently asked *wh-* questions (*what, where, when, why, which, who*) by the children in the class?"
   "Do you see any relationship between the children's cognitive maturity and the type of questions they ask?"

4. Show a picture to a few children in grades 1, 2, and 3 and ask them to describe it. Estimate their MLU. Is one child linguistically more advanced than the others? Do you see a relationship between the children's MLU and the cognitive level of their conversation?

5. With reference to the conversation in Assignment 4, how far have these children progressed in the development of grammatical morphemes (see Table 5.3)?

6. The following are 10 first-level words from the Dolch list: *his, they, you, said, was, that, the, and, she,* and *but.* Print these words in large font size (14 or 16). Ask a few children in first or second grade to read these words. Mark the words they read correctly. After a short interval, administer these words as a written spelling test. What is the ratio between the words read correctly and the words spelled correctly? What is the ratio between the words read incorrectly and spelled incorrectly? Make a qualitative analysis of the spelling errors and write a short descriptive note outlining how you would try to improve these children's spelling skills.

Reading Assignment

Read one of the following articles, discuss it, and write a one-page summary. These articles can be obtained from your college's library or downloaded by accessing the library's electronic holdings.

Boulware-Gooden, R., Carreker, S., Thornhill, A., & Joshi, R.M. (2007). Instruction of metacognitive strategies enhances reading comprehension and vocabulary achievement of third-grade students. *The Reading Teacher, 61*(1), 70–77.

Villaume, S.K., & Brabham, E.G. (2003). Phonics instruction: Beyond the debate. *The Reading Teacher, 56*(5), 478–482.

Literacy Instruction and Teaching Strategies

CHAPTER 6

Developing Basic Literacy Skills

Summary

This chapter describes specific methods and strategies for developing children's phonological awareness, phonemic awareness, and knowledge of the alphabetic principle. Basic principles and strategies for creating print awareness and fostering emergent literacy are also presented. Teachers are provided with guidelines for developing their own instructional programs. A commercially available structured program for developing phonemic awareness and decoding skills is also described.

Main ideas presented in this chapter

1. There are two major approaches to the teaching of beginning literacy: a skills approach and a meaning approach.

2. Developing listening comprehension skills in preschool children teaches them to pay attention.

3. Preschoolers' curiosity about literacy-related activities is considered a sign of emergent literacy. This inquisitiveness provides an opportunity to create print awareness in very young children.

4. Specific methods (e.g., language experience approach [LEA], finger pointing) can be used to promote print awareness.

5. The manipulation of syllables, onsets and rimes, and phonemes promotes phonological awareness.

6. The teacher can develop his or her own program for developing phonemic awareness in children. If the teacher chooses to do so, certain principles should be observed in developing such informal programs.

7. Structured programs for developing phonemic awareness and decoding skills are also commercially available.

1. What are the major approaches to beginning literacy instruction?
2. What is print awareness? How can it be developed in young children?
3. What is the significance behind the phenomenon of emergent literacy?
4. What is the language experience approach (LEA) to instruction?
5. What is phonological awareness?
6. What is phonemic awareness?
7. What basic principles should be observed in developing phonemic awareness in children?
8. What sequence should be followed in developing decoding skills in children?
9. What is a syllable? How many syllable types are there?
10. What is the alphabetic principle?

Major Approaches to Beginning Literacy Instruction

A survey of the history of reading instruction in the United States makes it clear that the teaching of beginning reading was influenced by two major philosophies, one emphasizing the acquisition of word recognition skills and the other emphasizing literacy appreciation and text comprehension. Educational practices that emerged from these two orientations are broadly described as the code approach and the meaning approach, respectively. Methods used in the code approach focus on decoding and word recognition skills and, therefore, utilize some form of a phonics approach. Approaches that emphasize meaning are less structured than the phonics approach and may use words, sentences, or whole texts as the starting point for instruction in reading. The different contemporary approaches that emphasize code and meaning are shown in Table 6.1.

Phrases such as *emergent literacy* and *print awareness* represent important concepts associated with preschoolers' reading experiences. Since most young children have not yet acquired reading skills, the preschool period can be used to develop print awareness and prepare children for later literacy skill acquisition. This period can also be used to develop good habits of listening, which can lay a foundation for comprehension skills.

Table 6.1.   Major approaches to beginning literacy instruction

Approaches with a code emphasis	Approaches with a meaning emphasis
Phonological awareness, use of syllables, onsets, and rimes	Reading to preschoolers
Print awareness	Print awareness
Phoneme awareness training	
Phonics: Alphabetic principle, decoding through synthetic phonics, decoding through analytic phonics	Whole word method
	Whole sentence method
	Whole language approach

Promoting Listening Comprehension Skills in Preschoolers

Numerous studies show that reading to very young children has many benefits, including a favorable impact on their later reading achievement. The positive effects of reading to preschoolers have been confirmed by a number of studies. One of the earliest was conducted by Durkin (1966), who found that children whose parents had read to them were already readers by the time they entered first grade. Reading to young children teaches them the wonders of written language, creates in them a desire to read themselves, and prepares them to become good readers when formal instruction begins in elementary school.

Reading to children is also an important part of the preschool curriculum. The major goal of reading to young children is to help them discover that an exciting world is hidden between the covers of a book, in the form of print, and that this world can be entered by reading the book. In addition, classroom reading can help boost children's comprehension. While reading, the teacher can help children pay attention by telling them that after hearing the story, they should be able to retell what they have heard in their own words. After the story is finished, the teacher may randomly ask one child to retell the story. The following day, after another story is read, another child can be asked to retell the story. Thus, reading aloud can be used as an opportunity to increase attentiveness. Reading to children, of course, is not limited to the preschool years but should continue to be a regular feature of reading instruction in the early elementary grades, and even beyond.

Following are some guidelines that will help make reading to children pleasurable and beneficial.

1. Teachers should read to children as often as possible, at a particular time every day.

2. The duration can range from 15 to 30 minutes or more, depending on how long children sustain interest.

3. Reading can be done with the entire class or in small groups of four or five children, depending on the class size and number of other adults available to assist.

4. Reading material should be comprehensible and interesting to children. Children love to pay attention to stories and facts that relate to their personal experiences.

5. Teachers can model the reading process by using proper intonation and emotion. Enthusiasm during reading can have an infectious effect on children.

6. Reutzel and Cooter (2003) pointed out that to be effective, reading aloud to children should be interactive. That is, teachers should pause frequently during reading, ask the children questions (particularly *who*, *what*, and *why* questions), point to pictures, encourage the children to participate, and involve them in the act of reading.

7. Teachers may explain words they think some children may not understand. This is also an opportunity to introduce new words.

8. At the end of the story, one child can be randomly selected to retell the story. If there is an opportunity, a group discussion can follow.

9. At the end, teachers can retell the story and summarize it.

Strategies for Fostering Print Awareness

Around the age of 2 or so, children begin to use spoken language to communicate with the people around them, although it is unlikely that they think consciously about spoken language as a means of communicating their needs, wishes, pleasures, and displeasures. At this age, children are less aware that written language is also a communicative tool.

What Is Print Awareness?

Understanding that the strange-looking scribbles adults call *writing* are also a means of communication is referred to as print awareness or print concepts. Print awareness also includes the knowledge that written language consists of letters, words, and sentences; books contain stories; books have a beginning and an end; and books are written by people called authors.

Although some kindergarten children know a great deal about books and stories, others do not possess such knowledge even when they enter first grade. Reading achievement at the end of first grade is related to children's awareness about print (Johns, 1980). Morrow (1993) also found that knowledge of certain aspects of printed language is necessary for successful literacy development. Taking these observations into account, Hiebert, Pearson, Taylor, Richardson, and Paris (1998) strongly advocated that teachers explicitly promote knowledge about print among preschoolers. (See Box 6.1.)

Clay (2000a) considered that print awareness consists of three different types of knowledge: that written language is informative, that written language relates to spoken language, and that written language has some unique features. The informational function of print refers to an understanding that written language is used for communicating information, that it contains stories, and that these stories were written by someone. This information can be in the form of directions, stories, or messages. One of the earliest experiences children have with the informational function of written language is seeing simple directions or warnings on signs, such as *exit, stop,* and *no smoking.* This type of written language is called **environmental print.** Young children encounter this form of written language in an informal way every day.

Box 6.1.   Print awareness

Promoting print awareness does not mean that preschool children should be taught to memorize letters of the alphabet or to read words. Rather, it means that children should be exposed to literacy materials so that they can discover that writing, like speaking and listening, is a form of communication.

The second aspect of print awareness does not come easily or automatically to children. This includes the understanding that there is a relationship between written and spoken language, that speech can be written down, that written language can be transformed into spoken language, and that written language tells us something. Such understanding is acquired from children's encounters with books, magazines, and newspapers and from seeing adults interact with these materials. A child who grows up in an environment devoid of such material will have more difficulty developing print awareness. As this aspect of print awareness develops, children will acquire more specific knowledge about print, such as understanding that peoples' names can be written down and that a written word stands for a spoken word.

The third aspect of print awareness—that written language has unique features—includes the understanding that words make up sentences; sentences start at one end of the page and move toward the other end, and they are stacked from top to bottom; punctuation marks are part of written language; books have pages, which are numbered; every story has a title; every story was written by someone referred to as the author; and every story has a beginning and an end. Some of this knowledge is not acquired naturally by many children and needs to be taught. Phrases such as *print-rich environment* and *immersion in a literacy environment* capture the essence of the instructional philosophy behind creating awareness about written language in children. This means that the classroom environment should be enriched with books, posters, pictures, and other print-related materials; there should be opportunities for children to look at books and handle them; and there should be materials for children to use for drawing and writing. Children should be able to observe the teacher and other children using books for the purpose of getting information and for enjoyment. Teachers can informally draw children's attention to book titles, author names, and poster labels. Reading the printed message on greeting cards or the labels on cereal boxes and soup cans to children are also informal means of drawing children's attention to printed language.

The Language Experience Approach

Reutzel and Cooter (2003) described several formal procedures for promoting print awareness among young children, including the LEA. The LEA can be carried out as a group experience or with one child at a time. In implementing the LEA, the teacher asks children to tell a story or to talk about a particular experience, such as a trip a child's family took or a group project such as a classroom birthday party, or a visit to the grocery store. The teacher writes any one child's story on a large sheet of paper or on the chalkboard and displays it in front of the children. The teacher may use markers of different colors to identify individual words so that children come to realize that words are independent units. After the story is completed, the teacher reads the story aloud, pointing to each word as she reads. The teacher can ask the children to read along with her as she reads it a second time. The story is stored for the day and can be read again the next day. LEA-generated stories can be rewritten on a smaller sheet of paper, copied, and sent home with the children. Or, they can be stored to be put into an album that will make them realize that spoken language can be transformed into written language and, eventually, into "books."

Strategies for Developing Phonological Awareness

Being sensitive to the phonological aspects of spoken language, particularly the internal phonological structure of words (e.g., syllables, onsets and rimes), is referred to as phonological awareness (Scarborough & Brady, 2002). There is a distinction between the two frequently encountered expressions *phonological awareness* and *phonemic awareness*. Phonological awareness includes the ability to segment words into syllables, the ability to produce rhyming words, and phonemic awareness. Phonemic awareness is the knowledge, usually implicit, that speech is made up of discrete sounds called phonemes; it also includes the ability to identify these sounds. Thus, *phonological awareness* is a comprehensive term that includes phonemic awareness.

The phonological structure of words can be analyzed at different levels, such as whole words, syllables, onsets and rimes, and phonemes. Children seem to acquire an awareness of these levels progressively. Arranged from simple to complex, the components of phonological awareness would be in the following order: rhyming, identifying words in sentences, segmenting syllables, segmenting onsets and rimes, manipulating phonemes, and blending phonemes. These components are most effectively taught in a similar order. Examples of the different components of phonological awareness are shown in Table 6.2.

Rhyming

An awareness of syllables, onset-rime, and phonemes as well as an appreciation of rhymes can be seen even in preschool children. Traditionally, young children are introduced to nursery rhyme songs that have many rhyming words. An example is the common song "Twinkle, Twinkle, Little Star." Rhyming skill appears to develop quite early in preschool children, and there appears to be a significant relationship between rhyming ability and later reading skill (Stanovich, Cunningham, & Cramer, 1984). Children can generally identify rhyming words, such as *star/are* and *high/sky* in "Twinkle, Twinkle, Little Star." They also enjoy producing a word that rhymes with a word the teacher has said.

Table 6.2. Levels of phonological awareness

Skill	Example
Rhyming	cat, rat, mat, bat
Segmenting syllables	/pen/ + /cil/
	/tea/ + /cher/
	/Christ/ + /mas/
Segmenting onsets and rimes	/d/+ /in/, + /n/ + /er/ = dinner
	/z/ + /ig/, + /z/ + /ag/ = zigzag
	/c/ + /up/, + /c/ + /ake/ = cupcake
Manipulating phonemes	/d/ + /i/ + /n/ + /n/ + /e/ + /r/
	/z/ + /i/ + /g/ + /z/ + /a/ + /g/
	/c/ + /u/ + /p/ + /c/ + /a/ + /k/

From Goswami, U. (1993). Toward an interactive analogy model of reading development: Decoding vowel graphemes in beginning. *Journal of Experimental Child Psychology, 56*(3), 460.

A similar task can also be used as the first step in creating an awareness of words by drawing children's attention to the fact that sentences are made up of words. They can clap their hands or knock on the desk for each word they hear as the teacher speaks a sentence. This activity also provides an opportunity for vocabulary development. A game that can promote rhyme awareness and vocabulary knowledge in children in first grade and older is Hink Pinks (cited by Fry, Kress, & Fountoukidis, 2000). In this game, the teacher reads a riddle question, the answer to which is a pair of words that rhyme. After demonstrating the first few examples by reading both the question and the answer, the teacher reads another question and asks the children to come up with the answer rhymes. If they cannot come up with the answer, the teacher can supply the first word in the pair and encourage children to guess the rhyming word. If the game is played again and again using the same questions, children will memorize the rhyming words. (See Table 6.3.)

For another rhyming activity, the teacher collects pairs of pictures representing the objects listed in Table 6.4. These pictures can be pasted on index cards. The teacher names one picture from the pair and asks the children to name the other. For example, the teacher shows a picture of a cat, names it, and asks the children to name the other picture (hat). Although this activity takes a little practice for children, they come to enjoy it. Later, the pictures can be replaced by written words.

The teacher can create a number of similar rhyming activities and use them year after year. For instance, the teacher can say a number from 1 to 10 and ask the children to supply a word that rhymes with that number. If the teacher says "one," the children might say "bun"; if the teacher says "two," the children might say "zoo" or "blue." Similarly, the teacher can elicit rhyming words for color words: for "red" the children might say "bed"; for "blue" they might say "true" or "flu."

Identifying Words in Spoken Sentences

Segmenting sentences into words is a skill that can be learned relatively easily by most 4- and 5-year-old children. In conversation, words in sentences do not stand out distinctly because many words run into each other. For this reason, young children may not be aware of the fact that sentences are made up of words. Activ-

Table 6.3. The Hinks Pinks game

Question	Rhyming two-word answer
Who is an unhappy father?	sad dad
What is an empty seat?	bare chair
Who is a library thief?	book crook
What is an entrance to a shop?	store door
What do you call a boring tune?	long song
What is a skyway to heaven?	air stair
Where do ducks stack their books?	quack rack
What is a chicken enclosure?	hen pen
What is a hip place for learning?	cool school
What do you call a journey by boat?	ship trip
What is a closed-up shack?	shut hut
What is a skinny hotel?	thin inn

Table 6.4. Pairs of rhyming words for use in rhyming game

rat	cat
mail	pail
bell	well
eye	pie
cake	lake
road	toad
wing	ring
hair	pair
rain	grain
nose	rose
gun	sun
boat	goat
pie	tie
pen	hen

ities designed to help children become aware that the word is a linguistic unit that can stand by itself can be helpful. The following example of such an activity requires word identification, word manipulation, and word counting.

- Is there a word *brother* in what I am going to say? "My brother and I had ice cream today."

  Can you say what I said without the word *today*?

  Can you put the word *sister* in place of *brother* and say the sentence?

- "Once upon a time a giant lived in the woods."

  Can you tell me how many words are in that sentence by knocking on your desk?

Segmenting and Blending Syllables

Words can be classified as monosyllabic, disyllabic, or multisyllabic according to the number of syllables they have. The teacher can start with monosyllabic words, such as *dog, cat, dad,* and *mom,* and children can be told that these words have only one chunk of sound and therefore cannot be broken apart. The teacher can follow this up with a demonstration by clapping his or her hand once. Following this, the teacher can demonstrate mono- and multisyllabic words by knocking on the desk or clapping his or her hands for each syllable as he or she says the disyllabic word. He or she can then say some additional words and ask the children to indicate the number of syllables in each word by clapping their hands. After the children have demonstrated their understanding of segmenting words into syllables, the teacher can ask the children to give some examples of monosyllabic and disyllabic words. Examples of disyllabic words in preschool children's vocabulary are *father, mother, table, upset, doctor, window,* and *Christmas.* Examples of multisyllabic words are *America, alligator,* and *caterpillar.* Children can repeat these words and segment the syllables by knocking on their desks or clapping their hands. Children can then be introduced to blending syllables; the teacher says the syllables in words distinctly (e.g., *win-ter*) and asks children to put the two syllables together to make the word.

As noted in Chapter 3, linguists have classified syllables into six categories (see Table 3.1). These may not be of great use in early childhood, but beyond this stage, they can increase the sensitivity of children's knowledge about words and spelling. Of the six categories, the closed and open syllables are the most frequently encountered in the primary grades. Beginning or struggling readers may have trouble reading multisyllabic words. Teachers can help children become aware of the idea of syllable by using monosyllabic words and then slowly introducing multisyllabic words.

Segmenting and Blending Onsets and Rimes

The next level of phonological awareness is the segmentation and blending of onsets and rimes. As noted in Chapter 3, onset refers to the initial consonant(s) in a monosyllabic word, and rime refers to the vowel and the consonants following it. For instance, in the words *strong, stripe,* and *straw,* /str/ is the onset and /ong/, /ipe/, and /aw/ are the rimes, respectively. In the words *would, could,* and *should,* /w/, /c/, and /sh/ are the onsets and /ould/ is the rime.

Several studies indicate that sensitivity to onsets and rimes is present in preschool children and develops before an awareness for phonemes. Analysis of English spelling by Treiman and her associates (1995) showed that more than 70% of the consistency in spelling is seen in rimes in which a vowel is followed by consonants in a digraph unit (e.g., /ack/ as in *back, hack, jack, lack, pack, rack,* and *sack*). On the basis of their analysis of books used in primary grades, Wylie and Durrell (1970) reported that nearly 500 primary grade words were derived from a set of only 32 rimes (see Table 6.5). It follows that rhymes can be used to draw children's attention first to the nature of the sounds of words and later to how they can use rhyming features to help them read and spell these words.

The teacher can use the vowel–consonant combinations shown in Table 6.5 to generate her own list of rhyming words. Once children learn how to rhyme, the teacher can say a word and ask children, one at a time, to repeat the word and produce rhyming words for it. After the children have mastered this, the teacher can merely supply a vowel–consonant unit (such as those shown in Table 6.5) and ask children to generate their own rhyming words for it.

Another useful word unit is the onset-rime combination. The teacher can introduce children to onsets and illustrate how similar onsets can have different rimes (see Table 6.6). A simple teaching aid to enhance awareness of onsets and rimes is a

Table 6.5. Wylie and Durrell's (1970) 32 rimes from analysis of words in primary grade texts

ack	ank	eat	ight	ore
ail	ap	ell	ill	or
ain	ash	est	in	uck
ake	at	ice	ine	ug
ale	ate	ick	ing	ump
ame	aw	ide	op	unk
an	ay			

From Wylie, R.E., & Durrell, D.D. (1970). Teaching vowels through phonograms. *Elementary English, 47,* 790; originally published by the National Council of Teachers of English; reprinted by permission.

Table 6.6.   Onsets that can be used for generating rimes

Onset	Word examples
/br/	br/ave, br/ew, br/ine, br/other, br/own, br/oad
/cr/	cr/ate, cr/awl, cr/ew, cr/inge, cr/ow, cr/uel
/gl/	gl/ad, gl/ee, gl/ide, gl/obe, gl/ue
/str/	str/ange, str/eet, str/ict, str/oll, str/udel

list of onsets on separate index cards and rimes written down the length of a strip of paper. An onset card can be placed in front of the strip of rimes, and children can read each onset-rime combination as the teacher slides the onset card downward.

Several years ago, the onset-rime and rhyming principles were incorporated into a method of reading instruction called a linguistic approach (Bloomfield & Barnhart, 1961). The authors did not use the terms *rime, onset,* or *rhyming* to describe their way of grouping words; instead, they called sets of rhyming words *word families.* Making children aware of the idea of word families can facilitate the acquisition of reading skills.

In addition to increasing phonological sensitivity, rhyming activities can provide an opportunity for vocabulary development. Dr. Seuss's books are also a rich source of rhymes, although many of these books contain imaginary words.

Strategies for Developing Phonemic Awareness

Chapter 1 noted that the phoneme is the basic unit of speech sound that can be manipulated to change a word. In speech, phonemes are not readily recognizable because they overlap one another. Nevertheless, because word recognition depends on the ability to relate units of spoken language to units of written language, an awareness of phonemes is of great help in learning to read. (See Box 6.2.)

A simple but interesting task for creating an awareness of sounds in language is picture sorting (Bear et al., 1996). In this task, children are asked to group pictures according to the initial or final sounds in their names. For instance, the teacher prepares a set of cards with several pictures whose names start with the

---

Box 6.2.   *Phonemic Awareness in Young Children*

In their book *Phonemic Awareness in Young Children* (1998) Adams, Foorman, Lundberg, and Beeler provided step-by-step instructions for developing children's phonological awareness, beginning with rhyming activities and culminating in word identification. Their instructional program covers awareness of words in spoken sentences, awareness of syllables, identification of phonemes in words, analysis and manipulation of phonemes, synthesis of phonemes in words, and sounding out of written words. The book also includes methods for assessing phonological awareness. Written in simple language, the book describes specific activities that can be readily implemented in kindergarten and at the beginning of first grade.

same phoneme and a few cards with different initial phonemes. The cards might show a rat, a ring, rain, and a roof as well as a ball, a box, a bat, and a goat. Children are asked to name each picture and then sort the cards into groups based on the first sound. The teacher first models the activity and guides the children as they perform the task. As children progress in this sorting task, they can sort the cards according to the final sounds in the words, and then on the basis of the rimes in the words. Children can work as individuals or in a group to do the sorting. Eventually the pictures can be replaced with words, and children can sort the cards on the basis of the letters that make up the words.

There are two ways to go about developing phonemic awareness that eventually leads to word recognition skills. One procedure is for teachers to develop their own materials and proceed in an informal fashion; the other is to follow any of the structured programs that are available commercially.

Informal Phonemic Awareness Programs

The following is a description of phonemic skills in the order in which they should be introduced to children. Teacher-developed programs for phonemic awareness should follow the order outlined here.

1. Rhyming is the first and easiest activity with which to start the program. This is followed by extensive practice in segmenting syllables in speech.

2. Sentence segmentation follows rhyming and syllable segmentation. This involves identifying words in sentences, deleting words, adding words, and counting words.

3. Activities involving rimes and onsets are introduced next. This is accomplished by introducing words that have the same onset but different rimes.

4. After students have mastered the preceding skills, phonemic awareness instruction can begin. The use of letters of the alphabet in such training is recommended, as research shows that the use of letters can add to children's success in understanding and manipulating phonemes. Furthermore, many children come to kindergarten already equipped with at least a rudimentary knowledge of the letters of the alphabet. Phonemic awareness instruction follows these steps:
    Creation of an awareness of the sounds (phonemes) in the spoken language
    Creation of an awareness that there are two kinds of sounds, consonants and vowels
    Manipulation of phonemes in spoken words by deleting and adding them; observational studies have shown that deleting initial phonemes is easier than deleting final phonemes, which in turn is easier than deleting phonemes in the middle of a word
    Synthesis of phonemes (blending of sounds in words)

5. The following steps should be observed in moving from phonemic awareness to word recognition:
    Associating sounds in the spoken word with colored blocks or tiles (for more on using colored blocks or tiles for phonemic awareness, please see the following section on the Lindamood program)
    Replacing colored blocks or tiles with letters of the alphabet
    Sounding out phonemes in written words

Blending constitutional sounds in written words and pronouncing the words
Copying words onto paper and pronouncing the words
Spelling the words from memory

A Commercial Program for Phonemic Awareness

Many commercial programs are available for phonemic awareness and word recognition instruction. One is the Lindamood Phoneme Sequencing Program for Reading, Spelling, and Speech (1998) by Patricia and Phyllis Lindamood. This program, also referred to as the LiPS, offers a multisensory approach to developing phonemic awareness and word recognition skills.

After sensitizing children to sounds in the environment, the program introduces them to 24 consonant sounds and 15 vowel sounds. Children are encouraged to feel and describe their own articulatory actions and those of their peers as they say the sounds aloud and notice how they are produced. Children notice how the mouth moves when saying sounds, by looking either in the mirror or at their peers. They also hold their hands in front of their mouth and feel the air movement as they produce individual consonant sounds and place their hands on their vocal chords to feel the vibrations as they produce the sounds. Children practice these exercises until they have learned the critical features of the sounds of the language.

Descriptive name labels are attached to consonant sounds to enable students to remember them. Examples of these labels are "Lip Poppers" (/p/, /b/), "Lip Coolers" (/f/, /v/), and "Tip Tappers" (/t/, /d/). Some consonants are introduced as "brothers": /b/, /z/, and /v/ are the "noisy brothers," and /p/, /s/, and /f/ are the "quiet brothers." Consonants such as /s/ and /z/ are "skinny," whereas digraphs such as /sh/ and /zh/ are "fat." Other consonant groups are introduced as "cousins" because they sound similar to each other, such as /m/, /n/, and /ng/; /w/, /h/, and /wh/; and /l/ and /r/. Consonants such as /c/, /x/, /qu/, and /y/ are known as "borrowers" because they can sound like other letters.

Pictures of the mouth in action are included in the manual and add a visual dimension to the sounds children are learning. For vowels, the distinguishing feature is whether the tongue placement is toward the front, the bottom, or the back of the mouth. Like consonants, vowels are given labels, such as "Smiles," "Opens," "Rounds," and "Slides." Learning of the 15 vowel sounds is aided by the use of a "vowel circle," a labeled, pictorial representation of the tongue position and mouth shape of the vowels.

Once the sounds and labels of the consonants and vowels are learned, children are given a number of exercises. For example, the teacher says a sound and the children label it (e.g., as a Lip Popper); conversely, the teacher names a label and the children supply a sound that fits that label. At this stage, phoneme manipulation activities can be introduced. This would include phoneme deletion (e.g., taking away the first sound in the word *cat* and sounding out the word that is left); phoneme addition (e.g., adding the sound /b/ to the beginning of the word *at* and sounding out the resulting word); and phoneme substitution (e.g., replacing the first sound in the word *cat* with the sound /h/).

After this level of awareness is reached, the teacher presents the names of the letters, associating each letter with its sound, label, mouth picture, and letter symbol. Introduction of the letters, however, could be delayed until a later time.

Simple syllables and words are introduced by representing the speech sounds in them visually with the help of mouth pictures, colored tiles, or blocks. This transition from **auditory processing** to a combination of auditory and visual association is called tracking and enables students to compare and contrast sequences of phonemes in syllables and monosyllabic words. No specific color is associated with any particular sound, but within a word, the same color is used to represent the same phoneme. For example, *mop* might be represented by a blue, a red, and a green tile; *mom* might be represented by a blue, a yellow, and a blue tile. These tracking exercises follow a fixed format provided in the manual.

After this stage is mastered, letters replace the colored tiles. Subsequently, pencil and paper are introduced and children are encouraged to reproduce the word they hear by writing it.

Pronunciation rules are called expectancies and are introduced by tracking with letter tiles and labeling the sounds. Three such expectancies are introduced and practiced. They are 1) the silent *e*; 2) rules such as "when two vowels go walking, the first one does the talking"; and 3) letters with multiple sounds, such as *c* and *g*. Lists of words are provided in the manual to practice four expectancies.

Once children master the basic decoding skills, they are introduced to sight word reading. The authors provide selections of words from the Dolch list (1948) and Fry list (1994). These words are arranged according to the frequency of occurrence in children's texts and complexity. The teacher selects 5 to 30 words that are appropriate for each child, writes each word on a card, and asks the child to read the words as fast as possible. The cards are then placed in three piles—slow, medium, and fast—based on how fast and how accurately the child can read the words. The slow and medium words are practiced over and over again until the child can read them instantly and without error. The child is also asked to spell these words.

The final section of the LiPS manual contains some useful tips for teaching contextual reading and writing. Throughout the program, there are opportunities for games that allow students to practice what they have learned. Teachers are provided with audio- and videotapes that assist in implementing the program.

As can be seen, the LiPS program is structured and very detailed. Teachers are required to receive training and attend workshops to use the program in their classrooms. Other phonemic awareness and reading instruction programs follow a similar overall format. Regardless of the program used, phoneme instruction should be based on a generally accepted scope and sequence, such as the one shown in Table 6.7.

Table 6.7. Scope and sequence for introduction of phonemes

1. Phonemes should be introduced in the following order: Stops (/p/, /k/, /t/, /b/, /d/, /g/) can be taught earlier than fricatives (/f/, /v/, /s/, /z/). Liquids (/l/, /r/), nasals (/m/, /n/), and glides (/w/, /j/) are introduced later.

2. Voiced consonants (e.g., /b/, /d/, /g/) are introduced before voiceless consonants (e.g., /p/, /t/, /k/).

3. Phonemes in the initial position are introduced before those in the final or medial position.

4. Because phonemes in the final position are not enunciated clearly, they are not as easily perceived as the phonemes in the initial position. Teachers should provide extended instruction for phonemes that occur in the final position.

Strategies for Introducing the Alphabetic Principle

Knowledge of the alphabetic principle exists at two levels. First, the learner becomes aware that spoken language can be represented in written form and that written language represents spoken language (known as print awareness, discussed previously). Second, the learner comes to understand that specific sounds can be represented by letters or a combination of letters of the alphabet and that particular letters represent particular sounds.

Some children learn about letters and letter names informally even before they enter kindergarten, through songs and television programs such as *Sesame Street* or through reading activities at home. Many children, however, may need specific instruction to help them match the letters with their sounds and write the letters of the alphabet when they are named (these activities can be introduced as part of Step 6 in the previously mentioned sequence as an integrated component of phoneme awareness instruction). Formal instruction in alphabet letters involves recitation of the alphabet sequence, manipulating plastic letters, and writing the letters. Materials for such instruction include an alphabet strip that can be displayed where all students can see it, an individual alphabet strip for each student, three-dimensional letters for students to handle, alphabet cards with one letter printed on each card (in both upper- and lowercase), and word cards with individual words printed on them.

Daily activities would include letter recognition, letter naming, and matching of individual three-dimensional letters with those on the alphabet strip. The teacher models these skills by picking up a three-dimensional letter, saying its sound, and placing it on the alphabet strip. The teacher might also pick up a letter and ask students to identify its sound, or he could identify the sound of a letter and have the children pick up the letter from their collection of three-dimensional letters. In addition to using three-dimensional letters, children could finger-write the letters in a tray of sand.

It is important to note that letter–sound relationships (e.g., the initial sound in the word *cat* is /k/) are introduced first. After these associations are mastered, letter–name associations are taught, using the same steps as for letter–sound associations. Letter–sound, not letter–name, association is introduced because beginning readers will acquire a tendency to pronounce words by naming the letters in words. The inconsistent relationship between spelling and the names of the letters can impede the reading process.

Games for Learning Letters and Sounds

Games can also help children learn letters and sounds. Allen and Beckwith (1999) described in detail many such activities, some of which are presented next. Allen and Beckwith recommended that these activities and games be carried out for 5–7 minutes daily until children can recite, name, and identify the letters quickly and automatically.

Name Game

The teacher writes each child's name on a sticky label and places the label on the child's shirt. The teacher says the name of a letter, and the children have to identify the child (or children) whose name starts with the letter indicated. For example, if the teacher says "Letter A," the children would point to Allison or Andrew.

Alphabet Bingo

Each student has a box in which plastic letters of the alphabet are kept. Each child selects, without looking, seven letters from the box and places them in front of him or her. The teacher says the sound of a letter, and if it is the sound of one of the child's seven letters, the child puts that letter in a separate "Bingo" pile. The child who is the first to place all seven letters in his or her Bingo pile wins. This game can also be used for teaching letter–name associations.

Guess What?

A child draws one plastic letter from his or her box of letters without looking at it. The student tries to identify the letter by feeling its shape. Every child in the classroom gets a chance. After this, a second letter is named, and so on. The student who guesses most of the letters correctly wins.

Alphabet Charade

The teacher displays the alphabet strip in front of the class, says that she has selected one letter from the strip, and asks the students to guess which letter it is. The children can ask questions to help them guess, but the questions can only be answered with a yes or no. For example, they might ask the teacher, "Is it the first letter of the alphabet?" or "Does it have only straight lines?" Through the questioning process, students eliminate the letters one by one until they guess the correct answer.

The Word Card Game

Each child takes out his or her deck of word cards, on which are printed words starting with each letter of the alphabet. The teacher asks the children to arrange the cards in alphabetical order based on the first letter in the words; for example, *ant*, *ball*, *cat*, *dog*. The student who finishes the game in the shortest amount of time wins.

The Missing Letter

The teacher writes a common word on the chalkboard but leaves one letter out. For example, the teacher may write *b_by*. The students guess which letter is missing. Next, the teacher may write *bo_k*, leaving out the second letter of the alphabet. In the next word, the teacher leaves out the letter *c* (e.g., *s_hool*). All the letters of the alphabet could thus be presented sequentially.

What Does the Research Say?

There is an impressive array of studies showing that a measure of phonological awareness in preschool children is a good predictor of their reading achievement in the early elementary grades. For instance, a study by Scarborough (1998) obtained a correlation of .46 between a phonological awareness measure at kindergarten and later reading performance. These studies include instruction conducted in English (e.g., Ball & Blachman, 1991; Bradley & Bryant, 1985) as well as in European languages (e.g., Lie, 1991; Lundberg et al., 1988).

More direct evidence of the benefits of phonological awareness instruction comes from experimental studies that assessed the impact of such training on word reading. Some of the earliest studies come from Europe. Three research reports (Bradley & Bryant, 1985; Elkonin, 1973; Lundberg et al., 1988) indicated that developing children's phonological awareness by using different techniques has a positive impact on word recognition skills. Bradley and Bryant provided phonological awareness instruction to British 4- and 5-year-olds through word sorting, rhyming, and alliteration activities. Children with the greatest gains in word recognition had been given opportunities to manipulate plastic letters of the alphabet along with the phonemic awareness instruction. The gains in reading-related skills lasted long after the training was over. Lundberg and his associates provided phonological awareness instruction to 235 Danish preschoolers through the use of games and songs. They also found that the training had a positive impact on children's word recognition skills.

Elkonin (1973), a Russian educator, likely was the first to describe a simple procedure for relating phonemes to graphemes. In this procedure, children are presented with the picture of an object and asked to say its name aloud. They then arrange colored tiles under the picture to match the phonemes in the name. For instance, children would place three tiles of different colors under the picture of a cat; for the word *mom,* children would place three tiles of only two different colors (the two *m*s would have the same color tile). Eventually, pictures are replaced by words and children would represent the phonemes in the word with colored tiles. Children would thus form an association between the letters in a word and the phonemes they represent. In the final step, when a word is uttered, children would form the word by arranging the letters in the word in the correct order. Elkonin's method has been successfully implemented in some remedial programs developed in the United States.

Several studies conducted in the United States have reported positive effects of phonemic awareness instruction on word recognition skills (e.g., Ball & Blachman, 1991; Blachman, Ball, Black, & Tangel, 2000). Torgesen, Wagner, and Rashotte (1997) provided phonemic awareness instruction to three groups of kindergarten children for 80 minutes per week. One group received multisensory phonemic awareness training in the form of synthetic phonics, the second group was taught through an embedded phonics approach, and the third group received regular classroom instruction, with no specialized program. (For an explanation of synthetic and embedded phonics, see Box 6.3.)

In the multisensory phonemic awareness training program (Torgesen, Wagner, & Rashotte, 1997), children tracked speech sounds by seeing, feeling, and touching their mouths and throats as they produced phonemes. Phonemes in a word were associated with the constituent letters of the word and were then blended to pronounce the word. In the embedded phonics program, children were taught to read real words without any sound analysis. When tested in the middle of second grade, all three groups receiving instructional support could read words at a level close to that of typical readers; however, the first group was more advanced in nonword reading than the other two groups. Ball and Blachman (1991) and Blachman et al. (2000) also reported that phonemic awareness instruction for kindergarten children

Box 6.3. Synthetic and embedded phonics

Synthetic phonics is a method of reading instruction in which beginning readers first learn the letter–sound correspondences and then how to blend these combinations. Most of the basic blending skill is expected to be mastered within a few months of the first year of school. Knowing the letter–sound correspondences and having the ability to blend letters and pronounce them enables children to read unfamiliar words.

In the embedded phonics method, letter–sound correspondence is not explicitly taught in isolation but is taught in the context of reading text. Thus, embedded phonics teaches phonics skills incidentally. The instructional approach described as whole language advocates this method.

Source: Torgesen, Wagner, Rashotte, Alexander, & Conway (1997).

from families of low income increased their letter–sound knowledge, their ability to read simple words, and their production of invented spelling.

Although phonological awareness instruction improves word recognition skills, it does not, by itself, improve reading fluency. Phonemic awareness provides a foundation on which word recognition skills can be built, but it should be followed up with reading experience. A related issue is whether phonological awareness instruction should be limited to the introduction of speech sounds or should be combined with letter knowledge. Although a few studies, such as the one by Lundberg et al. (1988), have noted positive results from sound training alone, many other studies have shown that the benefits of phonemic awareness instruction are increased when such instruction is combined with alphabet knowledge. For instance, Hammill's review of studies (2004) reached the conclusion that the greatest impact on children's reading achievement is seen when phonemic awareness training is combined with letter–sound knowledge. As noted previously, Bradley and Bryant (1985) found that the greatest gain in reading skill is seen in children who have opportunities to manipulate the letters of the alphabet along with receiving phonemic awareness instruction. Other researchers have also noted that children develop an awareness of phonemes only when they have a knowledge of letter identity. In a recent study, Foorman and her associates (2003) conducted a study of more than 4,000 kindergarten children and concluded that children who receive instruction in blending and segmenting phonemes and then explicit instruction in systematically connecting phonemes to graphemes through phonics instruction show the best reading and spelling outcomes in first grade. This is not an unreasonable conclusion, because adding written letters to phonological awareness instruction makes the instruction multisensory in nature and the task more concrete than limiting such training to learning speech sounds. Furthermore, many children come to kindergarten with some knowledge of the alphabet, and such background knowledge can be profitably utilized in phonological awareness instruction.

It must be noted, however, that a cause–effect relationship between increased phonological awareness and improved reading performance has not yet been established. It is fair to say that the relationship between phonemic awareness and letter knowledge is reciprocal. This means that exposure to written language can enhance sensitivity to phonemes; at the same time, increasing an awareness of phonemes can increase children's knowledge about written language. Many studies report that phonemic awareness instruction with young children increases their reading skills when they enter the early elementary grades. But critics have argued that many preschool children come to school with a knowledge of written letters and that no study has provided unequivocal evidence of a causal link between phonological awareness and success in reading and spelling (Castles & Coltheart, 2004). On the basis of his meta-analysis studies, Hammill (2004) concluded that the best predictors of reading are skills involving print, such as print awareness, alphabet knowledge, and knowledge of phoneme–letter correspondences. Hammill also noted that the current attention to nonprint abilities, such as phonological awareness, rapid naming, and memory, might be overemphasized. It has also been reported that some children who demonstrate good phonemic awareness skills in grades 1 and 2 have difficulty with comprehension when they reach grades 3 and 4 (Scarborough, 2005).

Assignments for the Student Teacher

1. Describe an example of emergent literacy you have personally observed.
2. Based on your observation of children, what is your estimate (in seconds and minutes) of the attention span of children in kindergarten and first grade?
3. How would you support the development of print awareness in preschool children?
4. What is the difference between phonological awareness and phonemic awareness?
5. Describe the sequence of phonological awareness development.
6. Define *onset* and *rime*. Describe, with examples, how you would use onsets and rimes to develop children's phonological awareness.
7. Imagine that you are developing a phonemic awareness program for your students. How would you structure such a program?

Reading Assignment

Read one of the following articles, discuss it, and write a one-page summary. These articles can be obtained at your college library or downloaded by accessing the library's electronic holdings.

Dykstra, R. (1968). The effectiveness of code and meaning emphasis in beginning reading programs. *The Reading Teacher, 22*(1), 17–23.

Stahl, S.A. (1992). Saying the "P" word: Nine guidelines for exemplary phonics instruction. *The Reading Teacher, 45*(8), 618–625.

CHAPTER 7

Strategies for Developing Decoding, Instant Word Reading, and Spelling Skills

Summary

This chapter addresses the transition from spoken to written language—that is, from being aware of the phonological aspects of language to relating them to written language. Strategies that facilitate children's progression from developing phonemic awareness to decoding skills are described, along with principles for teaching beginning decoding skills. This chapter also includes brief descriptions of **analytic phonics, synthetic phonics,** and linguistic phonics instructional approaches. Instructional methods for developing morphological awareness and **instant word reading** skills are presented. Several methods for teaching beginning readers or children at risk are described, along with an instructional model that integrates skills and meaning approaches. The second part of the chapter is devoted to spelling and spelling instruction; both formal and informal spelling instruction are covered. The chapter ends with a discussion of principles for teaching spelling.

Main ideas presented in this chapter

1. Many of the methods described in this chapter can be used for teaching beginning readers or children who are not making progress in the acquisition of literacy skills.

2. A mastery of phonics skills is required for acquiring coding skills. There are various ways to help children acquire phonics skills. Instant word reading and fluency in reading are built on the foundations of grapheme-phoneme conversion (decoding) skill.

3. Context plays an important role in the comprehension of sentences, but its role in word recognition is not as strong.

4. The **Reading Recovery (RR)** program may be used to teach children who show signs of reading problems in the first grade. Structured instructional programs such as Orton-Gillingham and Spalding's Writing Road to Reading can be used with beginning readers as well as children at risk.

5. The **Four Blocks Model,** a framework for instruction rather than a teaching method, allows the integration of meaning and skills approaches into the teaching of literacy skills.

6. Like phonological awareness, morphological awareness contributes to word recognition skills.

7. English spelling is not as chaotic as sometimes thought and is influenced by several factors. Children's attention should be drawn to the fact that phonology, morphology, etymology, and dialect have shaped today's English spelling.

8. Spelling instruction can follow informal as well as formal procedures. The discovery method of teaching spelling is one way to teach children how to spell.

9. **Qualitative assessment of spelling** provides practical hints for helping children to become better spellers.

**After reading this chapter,
you will be able to answer the following questions:**

1.   What is the difference between synthetic phonics and analytic phonics?

2.   What are the important features of the RR program?

3.   How does the Orton-Gillingham method of instruction differ from Spalding's Writing Road to Reading?

4.   What are the Four Blocks in Cunningham's Four Blocks Model?

5.   What factors have helped shape English spelling?

6.   What are spelling rules? Does a knowledge of these rules contribute to spelling performance?

7.   What are the differences between informal spelling instruction and formal spelling instruction?

8.   When would you use quantitative assessment of spelling, and when would you use qualitative assessment? What are the advantages of these two approaches?

9.   What is the discovery method of teaching spelling?

10. What are some of the basic principles to be followed in teaching spelling?

Strategies for Developing Decoding and Word Recognition Skills

Instructional strategies designed to promote word recognition skills can be broadly classified into two categories: phonics-based strategies and morepheme-based strategies.

Phonics-Based Strategies

Children who have been exposed to reading by being read to, by handling books, and by observing older siblings and parents read can more easily relate phonics instruction to the reading process than children who have little conception of what reading is all about. According to Stahl (1992), letter–sound instruction will make no sense to these children. Therefore, teachers should help children see that phonics instruction and mastery of phonics skills will lead to the ability to read—for meaning, for information, and for enjoyment.

There are several phonics approaches to teaching reading. Three are widely recognized and used to varying degrees: synthetic phonics, analytic phonics, and linguistic phonics.

Synthetic Phonics

Synthetic (*syn* means "together") phonics introduces letter sounds first and then teaches putting these sounds together by blending them into syllables and words. Thus, synthetic phonics teaches grapheme–phoneme relationships as the first step.

The LiPS, the Orton-Gillingham method, and Spalding's Writing Road to Reading all use the synthetic phonics approach. The LiPS was described in the previous chapter; the other two methods are described later in this chapter.

The use of syllables, rather than letters, as the basic unit in word recognition training has been advocated by some educators, although it has not gained much support as the main means of developing word recognition skills. However, syllabication training (i.e., breaking multisyllabic words into syllables) is used in developing word recognition skills at a later stage. According to Tierney, Readence, and Dishner (1995), using syllable knowledge for word recognition involves three steps:

1. The teacher provides training in syllable knowledge and syllabication.

2. The children practice with teacher-provided exercises.

3. The children apply what they have learned to actual reading of text.

Gleitman and Rozin (1973) reported that some children who were instructed in the use of the syllable as the basic unit of word identification achieved word recognition skills that they were not able to achieve through the phonics approach, which focused on individual phonemes. Apparently, these children found the syllable to be a better cue for word identification than the letters of the alphabet and their phonemes. Indeed, some written languages, such as Japanese, use the syllables as part of their orthography. However, Tierney et al. (1995) cautioned that readers cannot depend solely on syllables for word identification because the vast number of syllables can strain memory capacity. English is an alphabetic system, and using syllables as the basic unit of reading instruction will introduce additional difficulties.

Analytic Phonics

Analytic phonics (*ana* comes from the word *analysis* and means "taking apart"), in contrast to synthetic phonics, introduces a few words first, and students are then taught to take the constituent sounds apart. Instruction usually begins with teaching children to read a set of preselected words by sight. Although this method seems similar to the whole word method of teaching reading, there is an important difference between the two. Analytic phonics uses whole words only as a means to an end, the end being knowledge of grapheme–phoneme associations. In contrast, the whole word method does not involve further word analysis. According to Aukerman (1984), many, though not all, basal readers (see Appendix B) of the 1980s introduced phonics as an addition after teaching children to recognize a list of selected words by sight.

After learning a few words by sight, children are taught to identify letters and letter patterns in these words. This can be carried out at the consonant level, at the syllable level, or in terms of rimes and onsets. Thus, children who know the words *car* and *ball* should be able to pronounce the word *call*.

In "pure" analytic phonics (although such a form may not actually be practiced), the teacher would proceed along the following lines. First, the teacher would select a number of sound patterns to teach. Then she would select words in the children's vocabulary that contain these patterns. She would present these words to students several times and encourage them to read the words by sight as whole words. For example, the teacher would write the words *can, cat,* and *cap* on the chalkboard and teach them as sight words. The teacher would then ask the children how these words are alike. She would stress the fact that they all start with the /k/ sound. After this, she would introduce another set of words, such as *ball, bat,* and *bed,* and teach these as sight words. Next the teacher would write a new word, such as *cab,* on the board and ask the students to pronounce it. As students learn more and more words this way, the analysis could be moved up to the onset and rime level. For example, after learning the words *lamp, camp,* and *ramp* in addition to the words *bad, mad,* and *dad,* children should be able to read words such as *damp* and *map.*

Unlike synthetic phonics, very few patented methods based on analytic phonics have been developed. However, some schools in Scotland use analytic phonics. Methods using onset–rime analysis and word families fall into the broad category of analytic phonics. One such procedure is the Glass Analysis for Decoding Only, developed by Glass and Glass in 1976. In one study, Foorman, Francis, Shaywitz, Shaywitz, and Fletcher (1997) found that children taught through a synthetic phonics program attained greater skill in phonological analysis and synthesis than did their peers in a combined synthetic/analytic phonics program or a sight word program. However, the sight word group did attain greater skill in spelling and word reading and also demonstrated higher spelling achievement than the synthetic/analytic phonics group. It appears that sight word instruction helps children learn certain orthographic or spelling patterns more readily than synthetic/analytic phonics.

Analytic phonics may be quite helpful under special circumstances. Some children, such as those with severe autism or with **Down syndrome,** may find it difficult to identify phonemes and manipulate them, rendering efforts at developing phonemic awareness unsuccessful. These children can be first taught to name familiar objects and pictures. Subsequently, these objects and pictures can be associated with the corresponding written words. Once the children are taught to sound out a small number of written words, they can be taught to sound out constituent letters of the words, and then, if possible, letter sounds.

Any instructional activity that starts at word-level analysis and moves to phoneme-level analysis can be broadly described as following the analytic phonics strategy. Accordingly, word-sorting exercises can be viewed as part of analytic phonics instruction. Word sorting is similar to picture sorting, described in Chapter 6. The teacher selects words that are within the vocabulary level of the students, writes each word on an index card, and makes several sets of the cards for the classroom. (Alternatively, the teacher can write the words on the chalkboard and ask students to copy them onto individual cards.) Students sort the cards according to the criterion established by the teacher, such as initial phonemes, final phonemes, long and short vowels, vowel and consonant digraphs, prefixes and suffixes, and so on. The teacher models the procedure first and provides guided practice sessions. Once students understand the idea of word sorting, they can work individually or in groups.

Linguistic Phonics

A variation of analytic phonics is the linguistic phonics method. The linguistic method, in a strict sense, does not have much to do with classic linguistics but introduces words with similar pronunciation and orthographic patterns as a family.

Box 7.1. **Phonograms**

A *phonogram* consists of a vowel sound plus a consonant sound, but it is often less than a syllable. Examples are *ab* as in *cab*, *gab*, and *crab* and *ack* as in *back*, *rack*, and *snack*. In their book *The New Reading Teacher's Book of Lists*, Fry, Fountoukidis, and Polk (1985) presented a list of 28 phonograms along with words that contain these phonograms.

For example, words such as *can, man, ban,* and *van,* which have a short vowel sound, are taught before words with a long vowel sound, such as *cake, make,* and *bake.* Nonwords that conform to this sound pattern may also be introduced. An underlying premise of the linguistic phonics system is that language is systematic, and drawing children's attention to the features shared by words facilitates word recognition because children are pattern learners. Some of these shared features are rhyming syllables, onsets and rimes, and affixes. Some authors recommend the use of phonograms to develop word recognition skills (see Box 7.1).

Books such as *Let's Read: A Linguistic Approach* (Bloomfield & Barnhart, 1961) and *Linguistics and Reading* (Fries, 1963) were the major publications that introduced word recognition instruction along the lines of a linguistic phonics approach. Even though these strategies did not become major instructional methodologies, teachers can use them as part of their instructional program. In fact, the *Merrill Linguistic Readers* (Wilson & Rudolph, 1986) were based on the belief that recurrent writing patterns in English can be exploited as strategies for teaching children to read.

Regardless of the strategies used, good results can be expected if the following recommendations made by researchers are implemented. After describing word sorting and similar exercises designed to promote word recognition skills, Bear et al. (1996) presented guiding principles for implementing such word recognition exercises.

- Children learn consonant sounds more readily than vowels because consonants, in general, have more consistent grapheme–phoneme correspondence. In addition, a majority of words encountered by children start with consonants. Vowels, therefore, require additional instructional attention, and teachers should not be surprised if children find it more difficult to master vowel usage than consonant usage.

- During literacy instruction, stop consonants (e.g., /p/ in *pen*), and fricatives (e.g., /f/ in *father*) can be introduced before liquids, (e.g., /r/ in *hard*) nasals (e.g., /ng/ in *king*), and glides (e.g., /tu/ in *tune*). Stop consonants can be introduced at the kindergarten level.

- Although short vowel sounds do not "say the name" of their associated letter, as long vowel sounds do (e.g., *mat, cut,* and *hostel* versus *mate, cute,* and *hotel*), observation shows that children master words with short vowels before those with long vowels. Short vowels also can be introduced at the kindergarten level.

- Blends and digraphs can be introduced sometimes in the middle of first grade, although it is more difficult to learn reading of digraphs than reading of blends. This is understandable because blends are letter groups in which the constituent letter sounds can be identified (e.g., /bl/ as in *blue,* /fl/ as in *flat,* /br/ as in *brother,* and /tr/ as in *tree),* whereas digraphs are letter groups in which the constituent letter sounds are not distinct (e.g., /ch/ as in *chair,* /th/ as in *that,* and /ng/ as in *going*). Diphthongs (e.g., /oi/ in *oil)* and schwas (e.g., /a/ in *about* and /i/ in *pencil),* which are barely perceptible in speech, are mastered even later than blends.

- Words whose spelling is consistent with their pronunciation are learned earlier than words whose spelling is not consistent with their pronunciation. Inconsistent words are usually short, but they occur frequently in written language and can be learned as whole words. Frequently occurring phonograms, such as *ght, ing,* and *tion,* can be introduced as units after consonants and vowels are learned.

Several strategies for teaching phonics are introduced in this chapter. Teachers should flexibly use any of these methods and strategies, alone or in combination, as the situation demands.

Morpheme-Based Strategies

The morpheme is the basic linguistic unit of meaning. Morphemes are similar to words, but these are not synonyms. Morpheme-based instruction can focus on words (rather than phonemes) in the text but also can make use of a knowledge of word structure. As noted in Chapter 3, a knowledge of the structure of words and how they are formed is referred to as morphological awareness. Similar to phonological awareness, morphological awareness is also helpful in acquiring word recognition skills and vocabulary knowledge.

In recent years, the role of morphological awareness in reading has received much attention (e.g., Carlisle & Nomanbhoy, 1993) because it plays an important role in the acquisition of reading skills (Snow, 1990). According to Carreker (2005a), morphological awareness not only facilitates decoding but also provides a springboard for vocabulary development.

Language Experience Approach

The language experience approach (LEA), described in Chapter 6 as a way to encourage print awareness in preschool children, can also be used to teach word recognition skills to beginning readers. When using the LEA for this purpose, teachers should observe the principles shown in Box 7.2.

Fingerpointing

LEA-generated stories provide an opportunity to implement fingerpointing, which creates an awareness of words as literary units. According to Uhry (2002), who found that fingerpointing enhances letter and word recognition, this is a kindergarten and early first-grade activity in which the teacher shares an LEA story or a storybook with children by reading it aloud. As she reads, the teacher demonstrates the fingerpointing procedure by moving her finger along the sentence, briefly stopping at each word in the sentence as she reads it. The teacher may also stress the initial phonemes in the words as she reads or emphasize the

Box 7.2. Principles for using the Language Experience Approach (LEA) for developing word recognition skills

1. Establish a good relationship with the learners.

2. As you proceed, ask questions as needed to help enrich the story.

3. Make the written material easy to see and read.

4. Use color to highlight important words.

5. Write or print slowly so that the children can follow the process.

6. Write the children's words just as they say them, but use standard spelling.

7. After the story is written, read each sentence aloud, pointing to each word as you read (fingerpointing).

8. Have each child read the story aloud, pointing to each word.

9. Repeat the process until the children attain fluency in reading the story.

10. Ask the children to copy the story and keep it in their own files, and ask each child to read his or her story periodically.

From Newman, A.P. (1980). *Adult basic education* (p. 63). Boston: Allyn & Bacon.

stressed vowels in syllables, as children frequently do not notice stress patterns in speech and miss vowels when they write words. After participating in repeated shared reading, many children memorize the material and are able to carry on fingerpoint reading by themselves. A child may be chosen to use fingerpointing with an LEA story, pointing her finger at each word as the teacher reads the story aloud.

Children can also use fingerpointing to read their own stories they have written. Although for very young children these "stories" may be merely scribbles or simple drawings, nevertheless the stories can be put together into a book, of which the child is the author. Another way for children to create stories is using the computer. Children can also dictate stories to the teacher, teacher's assistant, or a parent volunteer, who can either write or type and print out the stories on the computer, bind them into books, and give them to children to take home and share with their parents.

Read-Aloud Exercises: Echoic Choral Reading and Shared Reading

Once children have been introduced to the basics of reading in first grade, teachers can use such techniques as echoic choral reading and shared reading. According to Reutzel and Cooter (2003), in echoic choral reading the teacher reads aloud a line or a few sentences and the children repeat them, like an echo. Children should have their own copies of the material the teacher is reading. Thus, echoic choral reading involves teachers and students reading together orally but not at the same time. The reading should end with summarization either by the teacher or the students and, when possible, a discussion of what has been read.

In shared reading, the teacher and students read from a book simultaneously. According to Reutzel and Cooter, the best books for shared reading contain repetition, rhymes, and rhythm sequences, as these attract children's attention. The teacher models oral reading and encourages children to imitate his intonation, pauses, and stress patterns. As with echoic choral reading, the passage or story can be discussed and summarized at the end of the reading. Eldredge, Reutzel, and Hollingsworth (1996) found that shared reading experiences resulted in substantial progress for second-grade children in word recognition, vocabulary, comprehension, and fluency when compared with other forms of oral reading practice. Reading aloud, regardless of the format used, should start with a brief introduction of the material by the teacher. This will not only motivate children to listen and read but also activate their schema, or background knowledge, and thus render what they read or hear meaningful. The reading should end with a summary (either by the teacher or the children) and, when possible, a discussion of what has been read.

Word Structure and Word Recognition

Morphology refers to the structure of words, which includes root words, prefixes, and suffixes. When children write and read aloud, they have a tendency to omit affixes in words, possibly because in word recognition, the word is divided into its root morpheme and the affix, and these two units are processed separately. Since affixes have no meaning, they are usually discounted. For this reason, drawing children's attention to root morphemes and their affixes can increase the probability of success in reading and writing these words.

Etymology of Root Words

Because knowing the meaning of words facilitates word recognition and retention of words in memory, drawing students' attention to the origins of root morphemes (etymology) and their meaning will help improve word recognition. As noted in Chapter 3, the origin of many English words can be traced to Latin and Greek. The list in Box 7.3 contains examples of words derived from Latin and

---

Box 7.3.   **Latin and Greek roots of English words**

Common Latin Roots

audi (to hear)—*auditory, audience, audit, auditorium, audible, audition*
vis (to see)—*vision, visual, visit, vista, visualize, visionary, supervisor, invisible*
spect (to watch)—*spectator, inspect, respect, spectacle, spectacular*
tract (to pull)—*tractor, traction, attraction, subtraction, extract, retract*

Common Greek Roots

auto (self)—*automobile, automatic, autograph, autobiography, autocracy*
graph (write)—*graphic, graphite, geography, photograph, phonograph*
ology (study of)—*geology, biology, psychology, zoology, meteorology, technology*
photo (light)—*photography, photosynthesis, phototropism, photogenic*

From Carreker, S. (2005a). Teaching reading: Accurate decoding and fluency. In J.R. Birsh (Ed.), *Multisensory teaching of basic language skills* (2nd ed., pp. 243–244). Baltimore: Paul H. Brookes Publishing Co.; adapted by permission.

Greek and can be helpful in promoting children's morphological awareness (for a more detailed list of common root words, see Henry, 2003).

Instant Word Reading and Fluency

According to Ehri (1992, 1998), sight words are words that the reader has encountered before, perhaps several times, and has read accurately. This means that the reader has in her memory information about the word, such as its spelling and pronunciation, that enables her to recognize the word instantly without investing much attention. This memory helps the reader avoid confusing the word with many other words of similar spelling and even pronunciation (e.g., *fourth* versus *forth*). Discriminating the target word from other words that resemble it requires remembering the letters in the word, because it is the arrangement of the constituent letters that makes a word unique. Ehri (1992) proposed that sight word reading (or instant word reading) is accomplished through the connections formed between a word's specific features and its pronunciation and meaning. Foremost among such word-specific features is the word's spelling. It was noted in Chapter 2 that when a word is read, the reader samples all the letters in it. It is reasonable, therefore, to conclude that memory of letter–sound relationships functions as a cuing system that bonds the written form of a word to its pronunciation in memory. Once such a grapho–phonic association is built, children can build a lexicon of sight words quickly.

Several studies support the theory that understanding letter–sound relationships is very important for building sight word vocabulary and thereby developing fluency. In their study of kindergarten children, Share, Jorm, Maclean, and Matthews (1984) compared 39 measures for their ability to predict word-reading skills after 1 and 2 years. They found that phoneme segmentation and letter-name knowledge were the best predictors of word-reading ability. In Chapter 6, several studies were discussed that reported that training in phonological awareness combined with letter identification training has a positive impact on word reading. Also, Aaron et al. (1999) found that children in the first five elementary grades who had difficulty decoding words also had poor sight word reading skills, and those who had poor sight word skills also had difficulty decoding words. It appears, therefore, that efforts to build sight vocabulary by circumventing grapheme–phoneme associations are not likely to be successful. That is, exposing children who do not have sufficient decoding skills to words written on cards (the flashcard method) repeatedly may not be nearly as productive as first building the children's decoding skills.

Phonological Conversion of Written Words

A related issue regarding sight word reading and fluency is whether phonological conversion of written words is necessary for recognizing words by sight. In other words, can words be recognized instantly by circumventing the phonological process? This question dominated reading research during the 1970s and 1980s. Most of this research was influenced by the "dual route theory" of word recognition (Coltheart, 1978). The dual route theory proposes two strategies, or pathways, for recognizing a written word: the sequential, phonological processing of the letters in a word and the simultaneous visual processing of all letters in the word. Sequential processing of letters in a word results in constructing the pronunciation of the word, whereas processing the word as a single unit by processing all of the letters in the word simultaneously results in accessing the meaning and pronunciation of the word without resorting to a letter-by-letter decoding strategy. In the former case, word pronunciation is *assembled;* in the latter case, word meaning is *addressed.* These two strategies are analogous to decoding and sight word reading, respectively. Many researchers propose that both of these routes are essential for word recognition. Phonological processing is necessary for decoding unfamiliar words. The simultaneous visual processing is necessary to identify irregular words that cannot be pronounced accurately by applying phonology. For instance, words such as *rave, cave,* and *pave,* which have a similar spelling pattern, can be sounded out phonologically, but the word *have* cannot be correctly pronounced by using the same letter–sound relationship. It is thought, therefore, that pronunciation of such words must be accessed as a whole.

Nevertheless, phonological conversion (decoding) of written words is necessary for reading. One reason for this is that beginning readers, having had limited exposure to written words, must rely on decoding skills for recognizing unfamiliar words. Another important reason phonological conversion is necessary is that during reading, the reader starts at one end of the sentence, which often contains the subject, and processes several words until reaching the final word in the sentence. To comprehend the sentence, the reader must remember the subject near the beginning of the sentence. Numerous studies in cognitive psychology show that auditory memory is better suited for retaining words in short-term memory (STM) than visual memory is. Thus, although a word could be identified as a sight word without being decoded, subsequent to its identification it must be converted into its phonological form for the reader to retain it in STM and comprehend the sentence. The question, therefore, is not whether phonological conversion is necessary but at what stage it takes place: before or after the word is recognized. For a beginning reader, phonological conversion of the written word takes place *before* the apprehension of its meaning. A skilled reader must convert many of the words processed as sight words into their phonological form *after* comprehending their meaning.

In addition, the number of words humans can remember by sight is limited, perhaps not exceeding 3,000 to 6,000 items. Readers overcome this cognitive limitation by using phonology-based strategies rather than memorizing entire words as visual patterns. (See Box 7.4.)

One of the strategies often recommended for increasing reading fluency is rereading. Children who have difficulty decoding words the first time they encounter the words have noticeably less difficulty the next time they come across

---

Box 7.4. **Building sight vocabulary**

There are two requirements for the development of sight vocabulary. First, children should have a good foundation of decoding skills. Second, they should be provided with plenty of reading experiences. The benefits of reading practice cannot be overstated.

those words. Reading the same text or story again and again improves word recognition skills considerably and increases fluency. However, a question that remains unanswered is whether fluency gains that accrue as a result of rereading will transfer to new passages.

Using Context to Determine Meaning and for Word Recognition

In addition to morphological knowledge, the context in which a word appears in a sentence is helpful for word recognition. Context effect is useful in two ways: to understand the meaning of sentences and to recognize written words (however, context-based recognition of words is less reliable than decoding).

The role of context in understanding sentences is obvious. For example, the word *eat* has different meanings depending on the context in which it is used. Consider the following sentences:

- I eat only when I feel hungry.
- A combination of acid and air eats metals.
- Inflation will eat our savings.

In each of these sentences, the word *eat* is used in a different context and thus carries a different meaning. Context, therefore, is an important factor for the correct comprehension of words in sentences, and children should be instructed in using context to determine meaning.

The evidence for the role of context in word decoding, however, is much less robust. Studies by Juel (1991) and Share and Stanovich (1995) indicate that good readers do not use context as a primary strategy to recognize words. Good readers in primary grades rely on decoding for recognizing words. In fact, only individuals with impaired decoding skills rely on context for identifying words. Observation of the reading behavior of poor readers shows that they rely on minimal cues, such as one or two letters at the beginning of a word, and then guess the word. This often leads to errors such as reading *basketball* as "baseball" and *house* as "horse" (Aaron & Joshi, 1992). Gough (1983) reported that only about 10% of content words, and only one out of four words of all types, can be accurately predicted by using contextual cues. The use of context to decode the written word is an unreliable strategy (Share & Stanovich, 1995); therefore, teaching children to use context is unlikely to improve their word recognition skills. Yet the use of context is essential for comprehending the meaning of the sentences in which the words appear. Teachers should therefore instruct children about utilizing context for comprehending text.

Instructional Programs for Teaching Children at Risk

Approximately 10%–20% of children experience difficulty in learning to read (Ysseldyke & Algozzine, 1995), mainly because they have trouble decoding printed words. This condition is described by various labels, including *learning disability (LD)*, *specific reading disability*, and *dyslexia*. Since it was first recognized that some children with typical mental ability experience great difficulty in learning to read, specialized methods for teaching these children have been developed and promoted. Fernald and Keller (1921), Monroe (1932), and Orton (1937) were pioneers of these instructional methods, which focused primarily on developing word recognition skills through systematic phonics instruction. This section presents a variety of programs developed for children at risk for reading problems.

The Reading Recovery Program

Reading Recovery (RR) was developed by Marie Clay (1985, 1993) in New Zealand and became a nationwide program there in 1979. It was introduced in the United States and Australia in 1984. Designed to be preventive in nature, the program is actually implemented soon after reading problems are recognized during the first year of school. Unlike many other programs for at-risk readers, RR emphasizes meaning rather than a rigid sequential phonological format. According to Clay (1993), salient features of the RR program include the following:

- It is designed for at-risk readers in the first grade, especially those scoring in the lowest 20% for reading.

- The program is individually designed for each child, and there is no standardized or scripted program of instruction. RR teachers spend a considerable amount of time identifying each child's weaknesses and strengths.

- The program is based on the belief that children learn to read best by reading meaningful materials, such as stories and messages. Therefore, RR uses storybooks rather than highly structured books or worksheets.

- Children are tutored individually. However, in some school systems, children are tutored in groups of two or three. In some school systems, RR is for children who are not very weak in reading (Briggs & Duncan, 2006).

- The instructional program lasts about 30 minutes a day and is supplementary to the general classroom instruction, with classroom teachers and RR teachers working as a team.

- RR is temporary and lasts until the child reaches a level of reading skill expected for her grade level. Typically, this period is about 12 weeks.

- RR teachers are required to undergo special in-service training, which may be of a year's duration. They also continue to participate in in-service programs.

- RR instruction may also help children use letters and phonological code for word recognition in 10 to 20 weeks (Briggs & Duncan, 2006). Initially, however, many children are encouraged to use their oral language strengths to read simple books by looking at language patterns and text illustrations. Building on students' strengths is a basic principle of RR instruction.

According to Manzo and Manzo (1995), RR "is not a step-by-step plan, but one that unfolds more like an extended conversation between teacher and child" (p. 433). The initial screening of a child for the RR program is based on information provided by the classroom teacher, the opinion of the kindergarten teacher, and the child's performance on tasks such as letter identification, word reading, concepts about print, written vocabulary, and phonemic knowledge. A running record of text reading, in which the nature of the child's reading errors is documented as well as the words he can read with 90% accuracy, is used for diagnostic purposes. This information, along with teacher observation, is used to tailor the instructional strategy for the child. Diagnostic procedures are ongoing and do not cease when the child is discontinued from the program. Ongoing diagnosis helps teachers note the progress the child makes, both in the program and after leaving the program.

Every RR lesson has the following seven components:

1. *Familiar rereading of books:* The teacher keeps a running record of the child's reading errors and may draw the child's attention to these errors at a later time.

2. *Keeping a running record:* Using the running record of the previous day's reading, the teacher may ask the child to again read the previous day's assignment and encourage the child to think aloud as she reads. The teacher asks questions, such as "Does it make sense?" "Why do you think so?" "Is that what that word says?" "How would you say that?" and so on. The goal is to help the child develop self-correcting strategies that will help her become an independent reader.

3. *Letter identification; word making and breaking:* Children who need to learn letter names are taught with the aid of magnetic letters. When letters are mastered, simple words are introduced.

4. *Story writing and segmentation of sounds in words:* A child-generated written story is used to help the child think about the order of sounds in spoken words. Sometimes phoneme segmentation is used, and letters corresponding to phonemes are placed in separate boxes. Initially, tokens may be used instead of letters for this purpose so that the child is prevented from associating a single sound with a single letter. That is, as many tokens as there are phonemes in a word are placed in the box. Thus, there will be three tokens for the word *cat* and two tokens for the word *though.*

5. *Segmentation of words in sentences:* Great emphasis is placed on segmentation in the RR program. The cutup story exercise provides practice in segmenting words in sentences. In this exercise, the teacher selects a few sentences from a story and makes two copies of these sentences. The child reads one sentence at a time, and the teacher cuts up one copy of the sentence into words. The child puts the words together to reassemble the sentence, initially by looking at the second copy of the sentence as a guide; later, the child does this without looking at the completed sentence.

6. *New book reading:* The teacher first provides background (schema) for a new story and introduces new words and their meanings. The child then reads the story. The teacher keeps a running record of the child's errors while reading and may draw the child's attention to them at a later time.

7. *New book reading attempted:* Books that cannot be read independently by the child but could be read with help from the teacher are used in this component of the RR program. To become an independent reader, the child should read as many books as possible.

Detailed descriptions of these strategies can be found in Clay (1993).

The Orton-Gillingham Approach

This approach was first presented in 1936 by Anna Gillingham, a close associate of Samuel Orton, and by Bessie Stillman. In the 1920s and 1930s, Orton practiced medicine as a neuropsychiatrist in Iowa and gained extensive experience in dealing with children who had educational problems. Orton hypothesized that reading disability was caused by an uneven development of cerebral hemispheric dominance, with sequential processing losing ground to simultaneous processing strategies of the brain. This, Orton believed, led to the bad habit of processing written words as "ideograms," or wholes, to the neglect of sequential, phoneme-by-phoneme processing. He felt that remedial methods should therefore focus on helping children develop sequential processing skills (i.e., phonics) and wean them from the bad habit of processing words as wholes. Gillingham, an educator and associate of Orton, helped develop the phonics-based method while they were operating a clinic in New York.

The original publication by Gillingham and Stillman was revised several times, until the seventh edition appeared in 1979 under the title *Remedial Training for Children with Specific Disability in Reading, Spelling, and Penmanship* (Gillingham & Stillman, 1979). Several versions of the Orton-Gillingham approach have been developed in recent years. One of these, Spalding's Writing Road to Reading, is described later in this section. Another version that follows a phonics approach was developed by Henry and Redding (2005). Although the Orton-Gillingham method is intended for children in grade 3 and above, it is also used for younger children as well as adolescents. Professionals working in the area may associate this method with remedial instruction; however, the Orton-Gillingham approach is equally relevant for all beginning readers.

The three important features of the Orton-Gillingham approach are that 1) it teaches phonics directly by introducing letter names and their sounds first, and blending skills soon after; 2) it uses a multisensory approach by teaching letter–sound associations through auditory, visual, and kinesthetic modalities; and 3) it follows a systematic, step-by-step approach that proceeds from simple to complex tasks.

Instruction is usually conducted on a one-to-one basis but occasionally occurs in groups of two or three children. To teach letter–sound associations, individual letters printed on cards are exposed to the child one at a time, and the *name* of the letter is spoken by the teacher and repeated by the student. After this, the *sound* of the letter is produced by the teacher, and the student repeats it. Then the teacher produces the sound represented by a letter, and the child is encouraged to tell the name of the letter. Following this, the pupil traces the letter with her finger and copies it onto a sheet of paper. Thus, the child learns letter sounds through three kinds of associations: visual–auditory, visual–kinesthetic, and auditory–kinesthetic.

Initially, two vowels and eight consonants are introduced with the aid of key words (e.g., *a* as in *apple*). Once these associations are well formed, three-letter words are introduced, and the same three kinds of associations are practiced. These words are preselected and stored on printed cards in a file box referred to as the Jewel Case. Each set of words in the Jewel Case is intended to teach one letter–one sound association. For example, the Jewel Case might contain the words *don, dad, dug, dam, dim, dash, bid, hid,* and *kid* to teach the letter–sound association of *d* and /d/.

Each lesson lasts 40 to 60 minutes a day, and usually no more than two new letters are introduced in a day. Only one sound of a letter is introduced at a time because it is believed that introducing more than one sound (e.g., /k/ in *cat* and /s/ in *city*) will confuse children. Some digraphs, such as /th/ and /br/, are introduced before some of the single letters because, having a fixed sound, these digraphs are easier to learn than letters with multiple sounds. Once a certain number of words in the Jewel Case are learned, the child learns to spell the words. Simple sentences in the form of stories are then formed from the words in the Jewel Case, words that are regular in the sense that they have consistent pronunciations. The stories come from the teacher's manual and, as the authors admit, may sound infantile. Once the child learns to read these stories, the stories are used for dictation. Gradually, the teacher introduces phonetically irregular words and multisyllabic words, following the same procedures used for introducing single-syllable regular words.

The Slingerland Method

A closely related method for teaching children with specific reading disability through a multisensory approach was developed by Slingerland (1977), who also developed a screening test for the early diagnosis of potential reading problems (1974). The Slingerland reading method, according to its author, is most effective when used as a preventive measure. It starts with the introduction of single letters of the alphabet. During the initial stages, a special time block is arranged for learning the names of the letters. The teacher shows the children specially prepared cards that display a letter, a word that starts with that letter, and a picture of the object the word represents. Each child in the group is called on to pronounce the letter. This is the auditory method.

This is followed by a kinesthetic exercise in which the teacher writes the letter on the chalkboard and asks the children to copy the letter on a sheet of paper and trace the letter with their finger as they pronounce it. After the children have mastered several letters, they are asked to reproduce them from memory by writing the letters on paper. The teacher then draws children's attention to the sound the letters make.

Following this, children are asked to pronounce letters written on the chalkboard. After the children have learned several consonants and vowels, the teacher writes three-letter words on the board. The teacher pronounces each word, and the children repeat it. The teacher introduces the concept of blending, and tracing and spelling exercises are carried out simultaneously. Eventually, simple sentences are introduced.

Spalding's Writing Road to Reading

The Writing Road to Reading program was developed by Romalda Spalding and first published in 1957. It has been widely tested, with positive results. A fifth revised edition of the program has been recently published (Spalding, 2003). The program is a structured method of teaching phonics and is presented in a single book, which makes implementation of the procedures relatively easy. Although this method is intended for use in the general education classroom, it is equally valuable for students needing remedial assistance. The Spalding program is also called the Unified Phonics Method because it incorporates hearing, speaking, and writing as well as reading comprehension.

Although much of the material in Writing Road to Reading is borrowed from the Orton-Gillingham approach, it differs in two important respects: emphasis on letter sounds rather than letter names, and emphasis on spelling through writing. According to Spalding and Spalding (1986), the core of the method is a technique in which children are taught how to write the sounds of the spoken language in isolation and then in combination. Once this skill is mastered, children can pronounce any printed word. In implementing the Spalding method, children are taught the sounds of graphemes, or, to use the author's terminology, phonograms. According to Spalding and Spalding (1986), a phonogram is a single letter or a combination of letters that represents a single sound, such as /b/, /p/, /qu/, /th/, and /ough/ as in the words *rough* and *though*. According to the authors, the English language contains 70 phonograms representing 45 basic sounds.

Each phonogram is printed on a card, and the teacher shows one phonogram at a time to the children and pronounces it. Children repeat the sound in unison. The children then write the phonogram on paper. The correct pronunciation of the phonogram and a word that represents it are printed on the back of the card for the teacher's use. Children are not shown the words until they have mastered the phonograms. The method prohibits using letter names because in many English words, letter names and the sounds do not correspond with each other. Children's mastery of the phonograms is frequently tested by having children write the correct phonogram when the teacher says its sound.

As soon as children have learned the phonograms fairly well, the teacher dictates words from a prescribed list and asks children to write the words and say them at the same time. After writing the word, they pronounce the word again. Writing and pronunciation of the written word are stressed because the authors recognize, quite correctly, that accurate spelling is more dependent on the ability to pronounce a word than to visualize it. After a word has been learned, the teacher discusses its meaning with the help of pictures. A system of spelling rules and notations is also introduced to help children read and spell more difficult words.

After children have mastered the 70 phonograms and have learned to write and read a few hundred words, they are encouraged to read and write sentences. Book reading does not begin until children have learned enough common words to comprehend the meaning of simple sentences. At this point, children may be introduced to textbooks or storybooks.

The Slingerland manual provides a helpful list of phonograms arranged by grade level, along with suggestions for teaching the spelling of these words in which the phonograms appear. The manual also contains lists of decodable books and children's literature titles.

Wilson Reading System

Introduced in 1988, the Wilson Reading System (WRS; Wilson, 1994) is a structured reading and writing program intended as an intervention approach for children from grades 2 through 12 who are struggling with reading. There is also a level for ESL students. The WRS is based on the Orton-Gillingham multisensory approach and provides a well-organized, incremental, and cumulative 12-step instructional structure. Steps 1 through 6 provide students with the basics of decoding and encoding and create a solid foundation; Steps 7 through 12 focus more on word analysis, vocabulary development, comprehension, and metacognition. The system provides extensive instruction in phonemic awareness, phonics, fluency, vocabulary, and comprehension, and students are directly and explicitly taught to decode and encode. Comprehension is taught from the beginning through visualization techniques that are used during reading from controlled text. The instructional design and content of the program are aligned with current reading research, although empirical support for the WRS is limited.

Direct Instructional System for Teaching Arithmetic and Reading

Direct Instructional System for Teaching Arithmetic and Reading (DISTAR) was developed by Siegfried Engelmann and Wesley Becker in 1964 and was intended primarily for children who were socioeconomically disadvantaged. However, it has also been used with children who have reading disability. DISTAR can be implemented as a stand-alone program or as part of a schoolwide reform effort. The initial implementation of the program was carried out by Bereiter and Engelmann (1964). Currently, it is published as *Reading Mastery* (SRA/McGraw-Hill, 2008). DISTAR received much attention during Project Follow Through (1967–1995), a large, federally funded experiment in public education, which ranked the model high in achievement for students from disadvantaged backgrounds and also for students who were not from disadvantaged backgrounds.

The features of DISTAR include the following:

- Explicit, systematic instruction based on scripted lesson plans
- Ability grouping, in which students are grouped and regrouped based on their ability and rate of progress
- Emphasis on the pace and efficiency of instruction; lessons are designed to bring students to mastery level as quickly as possible
- Frequent assessment using curriculum-based tools
- Professional development and coaching for instructors

The use of DISTAR has been debated since its inception. Empirical support is generally in favor of the program; however, some teachers are not comfortable with the highly scripted, high-pressure nature of the program and its inflexibility.

The Four Blocks Model

One of the biggest challenges classroom teachers face is the disparity in children's reading skills. Some children may be good decoders but comprehend poorly; others may be able to comprehend spoken language well but have difficulty decoding written language. Under these circumstances, should teachers focus on skills instruction or comprehension? The pressures of the classroom leave little time to individualize instruction (Meek, 2003). Educators have started to recommend a balanced approach to teaching reading to children in early elementary grades. One strategy for achieving this balance is to spend part of each reading lesson on standard phonics, then move to literacy appreciation (Calfee, 1998). Another strategy is to gradually shift from a phonics emphasis in first grade to a focus on comprehension skills by about the third grade. However, these approaches have been tried for many years and do not work well for students with reading disabilities.

Another solution to this dilemma is the Four Blocks Model developed by Patricia Cunningham (1999a), an instructional model that integrates the skills and meaning approaches. This model, according to the author, avoids the pendulum swing between skills and meaning orientations and at the same time meets the needs of children with a wide range of literacy skills without placing them in ability groups. With the Four Blocks Model, instructional time is divided fairly evenly among the following four major instructional strategies (called Blocks):

- Guided Reading
- Self-Selected Reading
- Writing
- Working with Words

Each block is allotted 30 to 40 minutes each day. Instruction within each block is made as multilevel as possible to meet the needs of children who are at different reading skill levels.

The Guided Reading Block

The purpose of this block is to expose children to a wide range of literature, teach comprehension, and teach children how to read materials that become increasingly harder. A variety of literacy materials, including basal readers, magazines, and trade books, is used. Each session usually begins with a teacher-led discussion to build background knowledge for the materials children will be reading. The reading is done individually, in small groups, or with partners. Children are not placed in fixed ability groups, although a child who is weak in reading may be paired with a better reader. Each week, the teacher selects and assigns one grade-level text and one text that is easier to read. Rereading is practiced to enable children who could not read the text fluently the first time to achieve fluency after reading the same material several times. The teacher meets with small groups of children to practice rereading; these teacher-supported small groups change on a daily basis and include children at a variety of reading levels. In addition to these activities, the teacher can schedule a 10-minute session with children who are lagging behind and use easy reading materials with them. Thus, every child, regardless of reading level, receives some guided reading instruction every day in material at his instructional level or an easier level. Comprehension strategies are also taught and practiced during this block.

The Self-Selected Reading Block

During this block, children choose what they want to read and participate in reading activities. This block includes a read-aloud period by the teacher, following which the children read material at their own level from a variety of books. While the children read, the teacher has conferences with several children. The block usually ends with a few children sharing their book in a reader's circle format. The teacher encourages children to choose materials at their reading level and on a subject they are interested in.

The Writing Block

This block of activity begins with a mini-lesson, during which the teacher writes and models writing. Before and during writing, the teacher thinks aloud. For instance, she might sound out a word aloud as she writes and frequently look at the **word wall** (see "The Working with Words Block") for spelling assistance. After this demonstration, children carry out their own writing. Like reading, writing is also carried out at multilevels because children choose their own topic and work on their topic for as many days as needed. While the children write, the teacher holds conferences with individual children. When they are finished with their writing, the teacher helps children polish up their stories by making suggestions and correcting mistakes. Children can then "publish" their stories by making the stories available to their classmates. The block ends with an author's chair time, in which some students share their completed work or work in progress. An additional opportunity for meeting children's individual needs is during publishing conferences, when both advanced and struggling writers are nudged forward. According to Cunningham (1999b), the best avenue for some children to become readers is for them to write their own experiences and read back what they have written. Often, children who struggle with even the simplest reading material can read everything they themselves have written because they are writing about their own experiences.

The Working with Words Block

During the daily implementation of the words block, children learn to read and spell high-frequency words and practice strategies for decoding and spelling. The word wall is part of the instructional procedure of this block. Wagstaff (2005) described the word wall as "an interactive, ongoing display (on a chart, bulletin board, or other exhibition medium) of words and/or parts of words, used to teach spelling, reading and writing strategies, letter–sound correspondence, and more. Word Walls . . . are useful work in progress, built over time as words are harvested from meaningful contexts."

Cunningham (1999a) made several recommendations for developing and using a word wall: 1) Words selected for the word wall are common words that children use often in writing and reading; 2) words are added gradually, about five a week; 3) words are written in big letters, with commonly confused words written in different colors; 4) words are displayed so children can easily see them; 5) words are reviewed and practiced frequently; and 6) students are encouraged to use words from the wall in their writing and to do so correctly by sounding them out and copying them.

Word walls should be used for daily wordplay activities, such as word sorts, word hunts, and spelling exercises or games. There are many ways to build a word wall. What key words to add and when to add them depends on what the students need. The words may come from the textbook used in the classroom, or the teacher may select words that are related to a current classroom theme. A classroom can have more than one word wall. For instance, one word wall could be constructed for language arts, one for social studies, and one for science. Of course, space may be a limiting factor. One of the advantages of a word wall is that it is in full view of children all day and can be utilized again and again.

To make the words on the wall meaningful and familiar to children, the teacher selects about five words daily and puts each word in a sentence, then reads them to the children. The teacher might call out a word from the wall and ask a child to locate and point out that word. All the children chant the spelling of this word and write it on their own sheet of paper. The teacher usually calls out several words in one session. Generally, the first 10 minutes of the Working with Words block are spent in word wall activities. (For more information on word walls, see Chapter 8 and the resources listed in Box 7.5.)

In the remaining 20–30 minutes of the block, students participate in decoding and spelling activities, such as "making words," "using words you know," "guess

Box 7.5.   Resources on word walls

More information about word walls can be obtained from the following sources:

Cunningham, P.M. (2004). *Phonics they use: Words for reading and writing* (4th ed.). Boston: Allyn & Bacon.

Green, J. (2003). *The word wall: Teaching vocabulary through immersion* (2nd ed.). Don Mills, ON, Canada: Pippin Publishing.

Spann, M.B. (1999). *Portable file-folder word walls: 20 Reproducible patterns for thematic word walls to help kids become better readers, writers and spellers.* New York: Scholastic.

Wagstaff, J.M. (1999). *Teaching reading and writing with word walls.* New York: Scholastic.

Additional information can be accessed on the Internet by using a search engine.

the word," or other game-like activities. In "making words," a hands-on activity, children learn how changing and adding letters to a word changes the word. Children are also asked to sort rhyming words from the word wall into rhyming word groups or to sort the words on the basis of their orthographic patterns. Children are also provided with a few letters of the alphabet and asked to make as many words as they can. More details about these activities are described by Cunningham (1999b).

Although phonemic awareness and direct phonics instruction are not specifically mentioned as instructional tools in the Four Blocks Model, the model is flexible enough for teachers to implement skills-related instruction during the Working with Words Block.

What Does the Research Say About These Reading Methods?

Scholars of literacy have come to give credence mainly to studies that can be backed by scientific evidence. Phrases such as *evidence based, scientifically proven,* and *empirically established* reflect this tendency. Opinions of practitioners that are based on classroom experience, however, cannot be dismissed as irrelevant. It should also be noted that science is in a constant state of flux and what appears to be irrefutable truth today can be overturned tomorrow by new findings. In addition, data collected through well-controlled studies can be subject to more than one interpretation. Cattell's (1886) study of the unit of word recognition, discussed in Chapter 2, is a case in point. It is important to keep these caveats in mind while examining studies that tested the validity of methods of teaching reading.

Reading Recovery

According to Tierney et al. (1995), RR has been acclaimed as one of the most successful early intervention programs for students at risk. The Ohio Reading Recovery sites reported an average of 82% success rate in 1986–1987 and a success rate of 86% for the 1987–1988 period. At the end of first grade, more than two thirds of the children who had completed the program were reading at or above first-grade level. Tierney and colleagues, however, noted that these data are based on children who had successfully completed the RR program, not on the total population of students who had received RR instruction. In addition, progress in RR is measured by informal rather than standardized tests. There is the additional possibility that the effects may diminish after students exit the program. Another concern with RR is the extensive training teachers have to undergo and the one-to-one format of the program, both of which may not be cost-effective for schools.

Review studies that have been published more recently have reiterated these concerns. For example, Farrall (2002) noted that RR lacks independent research that validates the program's success; RR does not measure progress objectively using standardized measures; students in RR programs do not perform better than students in Title I programs; RR is selective in admitting students into the program; and RR is not cost-effective. Other researchers note that RR does not raise overall reading performance of the school (Hiebert, 1994) and that only about 6.5% of the students in the program reach national norms in reading (Pollock, 1996). In another review study, Grossen, Coulter, and Ruggles (1996) expressed the same concerns about the RR program. They also noted that fewer students benefit from RR than actually claimed and that children who are initially successful in RR often are not successful later. Furthermore, they added that some compensatory reading programs are more effective than RR. Hiebert (1994) pointed out that about 30% of the students who begin the RR program do not complete it and their performance is disregarded in the final evaluation of the program, which introduces bias. According to Center, Wheldall, and Freeman (1992), the evaluation procedures used in RR are subjective because predictable texts are used for both teaching and assessment and the strategies taught and tested are closely aligned.

It should also be noted that there cannot be a single archetypical RR program because teachers, depending on the circumstances and their own experience, may depart from a strict adherence to the RR program. For instance, some teachers may stress phonics instruction if they find that the students they teach are weak in word recognition skills, whereas other teachers may emphasize book reading. This makes an objective evaluation of the RR program difficult.

The Orton-Gillingham Method

According to Clark (1988), although the Orton-Gillingham method has been practiced extensively with children and adolescents with dyslexia, very few research studies have been conducted to validate its effectiveness. The primary reason for the paucity of research is that this method is used primarily in clinical settings on a one-to-one basis, which does not generate extensive data that can be statistically analyzed (Clark, 1988). However, two studies, one by Kline and Kline (1978) and another by Joshi, Dahlgren, and Boulware-Gooden (2002), reported successful outcomes. Of the 92 children with dyslexia taught through the Orton-Gillingham approach in the Kline and Kline study, only 4.4% failed to show improvement; older children gained in reading as much as younger children did. This study also noted that at least 2 years of remedial instruction was necessary to produce substantial gains. In their 2002 study, Joshi et al. compared the performance of 24 first graders from an inner-city school who were taught through an Orton-Gillingham-based multisensory alphabetic phonics approach with the performance of another group of first graders who used a basal reader program. At the end of the academic year, children in the treatment group showed significantly greater gains on standardized reading tests in phonemic awareness and decoding skills than the comparison group. Children in the treatment group also showed improvement on tests of comprehension, though not more than the children in the comparison group.

The Slingerland Method

The effectiveness of the Slingerland approach has been more thoroughly studied than the Orton-Gillingham method. Clark (1988) described three studies that found the Slingerland method to be more effective for young children with and without reading disability than conventional teaching.

Spalding's Writing Road to Reading

As noted previously, the Writing Road to Reading has been shown to be effective. According to Aukerman (1984), it had been tried and used in a number of schools across the United States. Aukerman further stated that "a significant and up-to-date body of data has been assembled showing the indisputable success that many schools are enjoying with the Spalding method" (p. 541). In support of this conclusion, Aukerman provided statistics collected in grades 1 through 6 from 20 different schools widely separated geographically from Hawaii to Illinois. Two further editions of the Writing Road to Reading have been published since Aukerman's writing; however, research data are sparse on these editions.

The Wilson Reading System

Two studies (Banks, Guyer, & Banks, 1993; O'Connor & Wilson, 1995) have shown that students using the WRS performed better on comprehension and spelling measures than a control group using other methods.

The Direct Instructional System for Teaching Arithmetic and Reading System

In general, empirical support favors DISTAR as a remedial instructional method. A meta-analysis by Adams and Engelmann (1996) found a mean effect size of .75, which indicates that the overall effect is substantial. A follow-up study of preschool students who were socioeconomically disadvantaged, each of whom had participated in one of three different preschool programs, found that through age 15, students using DISTAR tested superior in IQ scores and academic abilities to students in the other programs, although the margin of difference was not significant (Schweinhart, Weikart, & Larner, 1986). This study, however, was based on only 54 students.

The Four Blocks Model

As previously noted, the Four Blocks Model provides instruction through a variety of methods, such as literature use, experience in writing, and exposure to written words. As a result, its merits cannot be evaluated as a method. Studies do show that instruction carried out under the Four Blocks Model resulted in superior reading achievement for a wide range of children (Cunningham & Allington, 1999; Cunningham, Hall, & Defee, 1998). It should be noted, however, that these studies were conducted by the author of the Four Blocks approach.

Strategies for Promoting Spelling Skills

During its early history, American education did not distinguish between reading instruction and spelling instruction. In fact, some schoolbooks used during the 17th and 18th centuries were called spellers, and an inability to spell well was considered a sign of poor education. Schools were urged, therefore, to pay special attention to spelling. For instance, in 1897, a physician named Rice developed his own spelling tests and administered them to hundreds of children in schools in the Midwest. He was appalled by children's spelling performance and urged schools to take special steps to improve spelling instruction. Despite such reports, the importance given to spelling as a cohort of reading skills, however, diminished over the years, and until recently, spelling was taught as an independent skill.

Improving spelling skills results in a corresponding improvement in reading skills. This was recognized by Romalda Spalding, who assigned spelling instruction a central role in the reading instruction program Writing Road to Reading. The correlation between spelling and word reading skills is quite high, ranging from .84 to .86 (Greenberg, Ehri, & Perin, 1997; Guthrie, 1973). In a longitudinal study, Mann, Tobin, and Wilson (1987) administered an invented spelling task to groups of children at the end of kindergarten. A year later, the children were tested on word identification and word attack skills. Kindergarten spellings predicted between 37% and 47% of the variance in first-grade reading performance. This suggests that an invented spelling task could be used at the end of kindergarten as a rough predictor of reading performance in first grade.

Sometimes it is claimed that an individual can be a bad speller but a good reader. It is possible for some adults who have had a great deal of reading experience to develop a substantial sight vocabulary. This would make them appear to be good readers, but upon close examination it would be found that they do have some difficulty with reading. Joshi and Aaron (1991) assessed the reading skills of college students who claimed to be good readers but poor spellers. They found that these students performed below average on a nonword reading test; the students also read slowly. The quality of spelling performance is more readily noticeable than that of reading performance because spelling is public, and errors are therefore more readily noticeable than in reading, which is private. Furthermore, spelling, a recall task, results in more errors than reading, which is a recognition task.

Because children's spelling provides a window into their phonological and word recognition potential, spelling performance can be used as a diagnostic tool for designing instruction (Treiman, 1998). When analyzing children's spelling errors, it is helpful to remember that incorrect spelling is not the product of visual processing difficulties, such as confusion between *v* and *w* or between *b* and *d*; rather, it reflects children's efforts to represent words on the basis of their phonological and orthographic knowledge. If students' knowledge in these areas is weak, spelling errors will result. On the basis of her study of two groups of 43 beginning readers from an Indianapolis school, Treiman (1993) concluded that learning to spell is not, as often thought, memorization of the visual sequence of letters in a word but an attempt to represent a word's sound in written form. Spelling errors are, therefore, logical reflections of the speller's linguistic ability and are informative to teachers.

Spelling instruction uses a variety of strategies and can be classified as informal or formal. The following sections describe each type.

Informal Spelling Instruction

Neither mere exposure to print nor reading experience alone is likely to make poor spellers become better spellers. Spelling must be explicitly taught (Treiman, 1998). In the preschool years, children show a tendency to "write" on their own. The product of these spontaneous efforts is described as invented spelling. Treiman (1993) suggested that teachers, while encouraging children in this endeavor, should nevertheless downplay the correctness of spelling in these early years. Children at this age are not going to be perfect spellers; however, eventually most of them will master the elements of good spelling. Focusing on the accuracy of spelling at this stage would thwart children's creativity or cause them to use only words that they know how to spell. However, teachers should help even young children understand that there is an agreed-upon spelling system, that spelling patterns can be seen in most words, and that these patterns follow certain conventions.

Children progress through several levels in their development of spelling. Initially, letters of the alphabet are produced in a random fashion. Drawings of objects and animals often accompany such writings. Next, spelling reflects children's efforts to represent phonemes through letters, albeit imperfectly. Some letters are incorrectly represented, and others are left out. This leads to a level of mastery of phoneme–grapheme relationships in which incorrect spellings, as well as phonetic misspellings, are seen, such as "sed (*said*)," "bal (*ball*)," and "rum" (*room*). The result is that most regular words are spelled correctly, and the misspelled regular words can be guessed by the reader. However, at this level of mastery many irregular words are misspelled. The ability to correctly spell even irregular words in their vocabulary is ultimately reached by most, if not all, children.

An understanding of the development of spelling skills can help teachers determine a child's level of phonological skills and why the child misspells words in a particular way. For instance, a child might have misspelled a word because he or she was not able to relate phonemes to their corresponding graphemes or because the student had difficulty in perceiving the phonemes themselves. A child's age must be considered when evaluating his or her strength or weakness in spelling, because not all phoneme–grapheme connections are learned at the same time. Spellings involving glides and liquids, for instance, are learned much later than those involving stops and fricatives. Spellings with digraphs are also mastered much later. In addition to chronological age, vocabulary knowledge plays a role in spelling skill. Children as well as adults are more likely to misspell a word they have never encountered.

A correct interpretation of spelling errors can not only indicate the source of the errors but also provide guidance for remedial instruction in both spelling and reading. For example, the word *got* may be spelled as "cot" because the speller is not sensitive to the differences between voiced and unvoiced phonemes. However, the reason for some spelling errors is not so obvious. For example, Treiman (1993) found that some children spell *truck* as "chruck" and *train* as "chrain" because the /t/ /r/ combination sounds like /ch/ due to the position of articulation of these phonemes (as in the word *fortune*).

Children more often misspell vowels than consonants ("thay" or "thy" for *they*; "fod" for *food*; "hape" for *happy*). The errors in these examples represent vowel omission and substitution. Vowel digraphs, such as *ai* in *said*, and semivowels, such as *y* in *you* and *w* in *now*, are often misspelled. Consonant clusters may be misspelled ("helpt" for *helped*) more often than individual consonants. Children who speak dialects other than Standard English are likely to commit spelling errors that reflect dialectal influence. As Shefter (1976) noted, accurate spelling and proper pronunciation go hand in hand.

With a knowledge of English phonology, teachers can draw children's attention to the types of errors seen in their spelling and encourage them to spell correctly the words they misspelled when they use those words in their future writings. This should be done informally, in a way that will not dampen children's enthusiasm for writing. If a child uses strictly nonphonetic spellings, phonemic awareness instruction should be the first step to take with that child.

Teachers can follow these key steps to help children improve their spelling (Treiman, 1993):

1. Determine what the student meant to write by immediately asking him what he wrote.

2. Analyze the misspelling and make a reasonable guess about why the child spelled the word the way he did.

3. Decide what help the child needs in order to spell the word, and similar words, correctly.

Formal Spelling Instruction

As noted in the previous section, spelling instruction enhances reading proficiency, and learning to spell requires explicit instruction (Carreker, 2005b). Spelling requires a good grasp of the phoneme–grapheme correspondence, a knowledge of morphology, and visual memory for words such as homophones (e.g., *beat/beet, rain/reign*) and irregular words.

When a teacher asks a student, "Does the way you wrote that word look right to you?" the teacher is asking whether the spelling the child has produced matches the one the child has in her memory. Although it is known that visual memory for words does play a role in spelling some aspects of words, the exact nature of this visual memory is unknown. This memory may be limited to orthographic patterns of two or three letters in a word and not extend to an entire word of five or seven letters. Support for this statement comes from a study of deaf children and adolescents whose spelling errors were primarily limited to omission or displacement of two or three clusters of letters (Aaron, Keetay, Boyd, Palmatier, & Wacks, 1998). The relatively minor role played by visual memory is also supported by the observation that good and poor spellers do not differ greatly in visual memory ability. In fact, some great artists, such as Auguste Rodin and Charles Russell, were not good spellers (Aaron, Phillips, & Larsen, 1988). Nor is spelling ability related to IQ score. Some of the great authors, such as Hans Christian Andersen and Agatha Christie, were also poor spellers (Aaron, Joshi, & Ocker, 2004).

In contrast, the connection of phonology to spelling is stronger and more obvious. Even skilled readers misspell words with unstressed syllables (e.g., *nega-*

tive), double letters (e.g., *necessity*), and morphemic junctions (e.g., *misspelling, nineteenth*)—instances where phonetic cues become unreliable.

Teachers often come across students who can remember and spell all 20 words in a homework list given the previous day but promptly forget the spellings the next day. Empirical studies show that simply looking again and again at words does not make one a good speller. Although flashcards can help, they too cannot be relied on as the sole means of spelling instruction. However, attention to the phonological, semantic, and morphological features of words *is* helpful in building spelling skills because these linguistic cues are useful in generating spellings when rote memory fails, which it almost always does. Formal instruction in spelling should, therefore, include methods that develop or increase phonological awareness, morphological awareness, and a knowledge of orthographic patterns (traditionally referred to as the rules of spelling). In addition, children's attention should be drawn to the meaning of words as well as to their history. Teaching of these linguistic features can be augmented by personal writing, dictation, and word sort games.

Carreker (2005b) noted that there are many words with more than one spelling pattern (e.g., *forth/fourth, brake/break*). The spelling pattern may be based on the position of the sound in a word, the length of the word, the influence of surrounding sounds, or a combination of these factors. Knowing the conditions under which a spelling pattern occurs can be of help in spelling. See Table 7.1.

When spelling is taught through orthographic patterns, letter sounds that occur frequently in written language are introduced first; less frequent sounds are introduced later. Teachers can follow the order presented in Table 7.2.

The Discovery Method of Teaching Spelling

Spelling patterns can be introduced through the discovery method, in which the teacher asks questions that lead students to discover the spelling patterns (Carreker, 2005b). The teacher reads five to seven words, some of which contain the same sound and spelling pattern. After listening, students should discover the sound that is the same in most of the words. When they have identified this sound, the teacher asks the students how the sound might be spelled. The teacher then writes the words that contain this spelling pattern on the chalkboard, and students compare their spelling prediction to the actual spelling. The students then copy the words in their notebook. For example, the teacher may say the following words: *book, cook, took,* and *look*. The spelling pattern to be discovered is *ook*. After the students have mastered the *ook* spelling pattern, the teacher may use another list of words: *back, clock, pick, peck,* and *truck*. The spelling pattern to be discovered here is *ck*.

The discovery method can also be used to teach the spelling of irregular words. The teacher would include words such as *echo* and *bike* with the previous list of *ck* words; these two words also have the /k/ sound, but it is spelled in a different way. During discovery teaching of unusual patterns, the teacher asks the children to copy these words, draws children's attention to the unusual spelling pattern, and then asks them to circle the unusual pattern. A scope and sequence chart for teaching spelling on the basis of letters and letter blends is suggested by Moats (1995); see Table 7.3 for an example.

Table 7.1. Some selected spelling rules[a]

Rule	Examples
k and *c* rules	
• Place *k* before *e, i,* or *y.*	• *keg, kid, milky*
• Place *c* before *a, o, u,* and any consonant.	• *cat, cop, cup, clip, crop*
Final /k/ rule	
• Place *ck* after a short vowel.	• *black, neck, duck*
• Place *ke* after a long vowel.	• *make, broke, like*
• Place *k* after a consonant or a vowel digraph.	• *milk, bank, week, book*
• Place *c* at the end of a word with two or more syllables.	• *garlic, picnic, magic*
er and *or* rules	
• Use *er* at the end of words that refer to basic necessities.	• *baker, brewer, barber, sharecropper*
• Use *or* at the end of words that refer to higher level professions.	• *doctor, professor, actor*
Silent /e/ rule	
• *e* at the end of a word makes the preceding vowel long (makes the vowel "say its name").	• *make, more, gate*
e rule	
• When a root word ends with *e*, drop the *e* before adding a suffix that starts with a vowel.	• *take → taking, give → giving*
ll, ff, ss, and *z* rule	
• Double final *l, f,* and *s* immediately following a vowel in a monosyllabic word.	• *tell, staff,* and *grass* but not *sail* and *pail*
/j/ rule	
• /j/ is spelled with a *g* before *y.*	• *gym, gypsy, apology*
• In other instances, /j/ is spelled with a *j.*	• *jalopy, jog, jungle*
/ch/ rule	
• Use *tch* after a short vowel in monosyllabic words.	• *batch, match*
• Use *ch* after a consonant or vowel digraph.	• *bench, beach*
Final /j/ rule	
• After a short vowel in monosyllabic words, use *dge.*	• *budge, grudge*
oi/oy rule	
• *oi* is generally used at or near the beginning or middle of a syllable.	• *oil, boil*
• *oy* is generally used at the end of a syllable.	• *boy, toy*
ou/ow rule	
• *ou* is generally used at the beginning or the middle of a syllable.	• *out, our*
• *ow* is generally used at the end of a syllable.	• *cow, bow*
Double letter rule	
• In a one-syllable word with a short vowel, double the final consonant before adding a suffix that starts with a vowel.	• *fit → fitted*
Prefix rules	
• When a prefix ends in a consonant and the root word also begins with a consonant, retain both consonants.	• *misspell, unnecessary*
• When the prefix ends in a consonant and the root word starts with a vowel, the consonant is not doubled.	• *disappoint*
• When the prefix ends in a vowel and the root word begins with a consonant, the consonant is not doubled.	• *prefer, repeal*

(continued)

Table 7.1. *(continued)*

Rule	Examples
Suffix rules	
• When a suffix that starts with a vowel is added to a word ending in a silent *e*, the *e* is usually dropped.	• *coming*
• When a suffix is added to a word ending in consonant *-y*, the *y* is usually changed to *i*.	• *heartily, tardiness*
• When a suffix is added to a word ending in vowel *-y*, the *y* is usually retained.	• *swayed, player*
• Words ending with a double consonant usually retain both consonants when a suffix is added.	• *enrolled, added*

ªChildren are not expected to memorize these rules. However, an understanding of the rules can create an awareness that there is some logic behind English spelling.

Role of Morphology and Etymology

Knowing the structure and etymology of words can also be helpful in spelling some words. This knowledge can help students understand why some words, such as *debt* and *receipt,* are spelled in what appears to be an illogical way. Examples of such words are shown in Table 7.4. Teachers have reported that an active study of spelling words, involving writing, analyzing, and categorizing the words, helps students achieve better spelling than merely looking at the words (Moats, 1995).

Principles for Teaching Spelling

Spelling instruction will be most optimal if teachers follow these principles (adapted from Moats, 1995):

1. Provide spelling exercises and tasks according to children's vocabulary level rather than their chronological age.
2. Provide phonemic awareness instruction if necessary.
3. Use as many modalities as possible for spelling instruction.
4. Embed spelling words in a sentence to make them more meaningful and to build vocabulary knowledge.
5. Focus on letter patterns, such as word families.

Table 7.2. Order of teaching spelling sounds

1. /o/ as in *hot*	11. /u/ as in *cube*	21. /oi/ as in *oil*
2. /u/ as in *up*	12. /e/ as in *athlete*	22. /oi/ as in *boy*
3. /k/ as in *kitten*	13. /i/ as in *fly*	23. /ch/ as in *chip*
4. /k/ as in *cup*	14. /e/ as in *penny*	24. /ch/ as in *witch*
5. /k/ as in *truck*	15. /ay/ as in *tray*	25. /ou/ as in *out*
6. /j/ as in *Jim*	16. /e/ as in *even*	26. /ou/ as in *cow*
7. /ee/ as in *feet*	17. /i/ as in *iris*	27. /ow/ as in *snow*
8. /a/ as in *cake*	18. /o/ as in *open*	28. /j/ as in *giant*
9. /i/ as in *five*	19. /u/ as in *unit*	29. /j/ as in *judge*
10. /o/ as in *rope*	20. /k/ as in *music*	30. /ue/ as in *statue*

From Cox, A.R. (1992). *Foundations for literacy: Structures and techniques for multisensory teaching of basic written English language skills* (p. 23). Cambridge, MA: Educators Publishing Service; Copyright © 1992 Educators Publishing Service. Used by permission of Educators Publishing Service, 800-225-5750.

Table 7.3. A spelling scope and sequence chart

Grade level	1	2	3
Beginning consonants	b, c, d, f, h, j, k, l, m n, p, r, s, t v, w, y, z g (girl)	y, z, s	g (gem)
Consonant digraphs	wh, kn, wr, ck	ph, tch, ch, gn, mb	(d)ge
Consonant blends	br, cr, dr, fr, gr, cl, fl, sl, tw, ld, nd	gl, pr, qu, kw sk, sm, sn, sp sw, sch, nk	shr, ss, ng, str, thr
Short vowels	a, e,i, o, u	w,y	
Long vowels	a, e, i, o, u		
r-controlled vowel	ar, er, ir	or, ur, oor (door) our (four)	
Vowel digraphs	ay, ea, ee, oa, ow	aw, oo (boot)	oo (foot), ie
Vowel diphthongs	oi	ou, au, ow	
Letter clusters	alk, eigh, ind ook	old, ough, ful ness	tion, sion, able ment
Schwa	ago	every	about, commerce
Ending suffixes	s, ed, ing	ly, ful, ness	tion, sion

6. When preparing lists of words for spelling tests, keep in mind each student's spelling skill level. Tests may have to be individualized in terms of number and complexity of words.

7. Introduce four or five spelling words per day to students in the lower grades and to those in higher grades who experience difficulty in spelling.

8. Test students on these words the day after introducing them. Include missed words on the following day's spelling list.

9. Analyze spelling errors and direct students to compare the misspelled word with the correct spelling. Explain to students why they might have misspelled the word. It is desirable to give immediate feedback.

In spite of teachers' best efforts, some children continue to have difficulty with spelling. It is important to remember that spelling does not reflect general intelligence. Furthermore, at a different time in history, or in a different geographical

Table 7.4. The origin of the irregular nature of selected English words

Word	Origin
Debt	debit (Latin)
receipt	receptacle (Latin)
calendar	calendara (Latin)
definite	fin (Latin)
negative	negation (Greek)
cousin	cosin (French)
guard	garde (French)

> **Box 7.6. Spelling changes with time and distance**
>
> Johnny's teacher gave him a spelling test, which consisted of the words *blessed, kingdom, earth, will, bread, trespass, mercy, lead,* and *become.* Johnny spelled these words "blessid," "kyngdom," "erthe," "wile," "bred," "trespas," "merci," "lede," and "becume." Johnny got all of them correct, and his teacher gave him an "A." Johnny lived a thousand years ago, and this is how these words were spelled in medieval England.
>
> Which word within each of the following pairs is spelled correctly?
>
> *caligraphy, calligraphy*
>
> *ecstacy, ecstasy*
>
> *supercede, supersede*
>
> *surprize, surprise*
>
> All these words are spelled correctly, depending on whether you live in England or the United States.

location, students who chronically misspell words might have been considered typical spellers. For the reason why, see Box 7.6.

What Does the Research Say About Spelling?

Research indicates that training in spelling is one of the most effective ways to improve children's decoding skills. In a study by Ehri and Wilce (1987), preschool children in one group were taught to spell words phonetically; students in a control group practiced isolated phoneme–grapheme associations. When children were later tested on words with similar spelling, investigators found that the spelling-trained children were able to read significantly more words than children in the control group. A review of Dutch research (Bosman & Van Orden, 1997) showed that direct spelling instruction, including such activities as copying words, spelling them out, or forming words by using letter tiles, were superior approaches to learning spelling than mere reading experience. Commenting on this and related studies, Treiman (1998) arrived at a similar conclusion.

Conversely, letter–sound instruction also improves spelling performance (Arra & Aaron, 2001; Foorman, Francis, Novy, & Liberman, 1991). In the Arra and Aaron study, 46 children from grade 2 were instructed in spelling by drawing their attention to the phonological basis of their spelling errors (psycholinguistic group). A comparison group of 47 children were shown the correct spelling of their misspelled words without any accompanying instruction (visual group). Posttests showed that children taught through a psycholinguistic and phonemic awareness approach outperformed the visual feedback group in spelling.

Assignments for the Student Teacher

1. Observe a second- or third-grade classroom. How does the teacher help the students develop morphological awareness?

2. Interview two teachers who have been trained in RR and have used it to teach children. Based on this interview, prepare answers to the following questions:
   In their opinion, how effective is RR?
   What is the most attractive feature of RR?
   What problems have they encountered with RR?

3. Collect spelling samples from children in the second and third grades. Analyze them and answer the following questions:

   What changes do you see in children's spelling from one grade to the next?

   What percentage of children in these grades are good spellers? What percentage are very poor spellers?

   How do the reading skills of good spellers compare with those of poor spellers?

   Perform a qualitative analysis of these children's spelling errors to identify the phonemes that led to the errors. What do you think are the underlying reasons for these errors?

   How would you design spelling instruction to make use of the findings from your analysis of spelling errors?

Reading Assignment

Read one of the following articles, discuss it, and write a one-page summary. These articles can be obtained at your college library or downloaded by accessing the library's electronic holdings.

Hudson, R.F., Lane, H.B., & Pullen, P.C. (2005). Reading fluency assessment and instruction: What, why, and how. *The Reading Teacher, 58*(8), 702–715.

Pikulski, J., & Chard, D.J. (2005). Fluency: Bridge between decoding and reading comprehension. *The Reading Teacher, 58*(6), 510–519.

CHAPTER 8

Strategies for Developing Vocabulary Knowledge, Comprehension Skills, and Writing Skills

Summary

This chapter deals with three topics: vocabulary instruction, comprehension instruction, and guidelines for writing exercises. It describes several programs and activities to help students encounter new words as well as aids for retaining these words in memory. The second part of the chapter lists obstacles to optimal reading comprehension and highlights strategies for overcoming these barriers. Methods for teaching students how to use comprehension strategies are presented. The last part of the chapter discusses the relationship between reading and writing and offers suggestions for improving students' writing skills.

Main ideas presented in this chapter

1. For vocabulary growth to occur, learners need to encounter new words and retain them in memory. Most vocabulary comes from incidental learning, but some students require direct instruction in the classroom.

2. Memorizing lists of words and definitions is an ineffective way to acquire new vocabulary; classroom games and word walls are effective tools for encountering and understanding words.

3. Students should be taught how to identify both root words and affixes.

4. There is a difference between knowing words and knowing about words.

5. To comprehend a passage, the reader needs background knowledge about the material presented.

6. Readers must be able to use appropriate comprehension strategies. Instruction in this area can be structured and teacher driven, or teachers can serve as guides while students select strategies. Teacher use of modeling and think-alouds is an effective way to teach comprehension strategies.

7. Awareness about **story grammar** can improve children's reading comprehension, as can writing exercises.

8. Planning the final product should be a main component of the writing process so that only one aspect of writing is the focus at any given time.

1. What are the two major requirements for acquiring vocabulary knowledge?

2. How might a third-grade teacher select which vocabulary words to teach?

3. What are **connotative meaning** of words and **denotative meaning** of words?

4. How can word walls be used in vocabulary instruction? What other activities can be used in vocabulary instruction?

5. What are some of the characteristics of a good vocabulary program?

6. What is orthographic awareness? What are the four requirements for reading comprehension to proceed smoothly? What is the role of metacognition in this process?

7. How do prereading activities facilitate reading comprehension?

8. What are some principles of comprehension strategy instruction?

9. How can story grammar be used for improving reading comprehension?

10. Is it necessary to teach comprehension strategies in the same sequence they are presented in the chapter?

To comprehend a passage of text, readers must know the meaning of the words that make up the passage. Many research studies show that reading achievement and vocabulary size are highly correlated (e.g., Anderson & Freebody, 1979; Stanovich, Cunningham, & Feeman, 1984). In a study of reading comprehension in 15 countries, the correlation between vocabulary and reading comprehension ranged from .66 to .75 (Thorndike, 1973). Biemiller (2005) reported a correlation of .81 between vocabulary size and reading comprehension across grades 1 through 5. Furthermore, oral vocabulary size in grade 1 is a good predictor of reading comprehension in grade 11 (Cunningham & Stanovich, 1997). Considering the crucial role vocabulary plays in reading, it is only logical that vocabulary instruction has received considerable attention in recent years.

Chapter 4 described the Matthew effect, or the concept that intensive reading practice leads to enriched vocabulary knowledge. The importance in vocabulary knowledge in reading comprehension can similarly be described as the **John effect,** after this verse: "In the beginning was the Word" (John 1:1, New King James Version).

To develop vocabulary, students must encounter new words and remember what they mean. Vocabulary instruction, therefore, should be designed to help students accomplish these two goals by creating opportunities for students to encounter words and creating conditions for them to remember the words they have come across. Knowing a word is not an all-or-none phenomenon but comes by degrees: Children move from not knowing a word, to being somewhat acquainted with it, to attaining a deeper and richer knowledge of the word (Blachowicz & Fisher, 2006).

Encountering Words

Instructional strategies that enable children to encounter written words can be classified as direct and indirect. Direct instruction is teacher guided and takes place in the classroom. Indirect instruction does not target vocabulary learning as the primary goal of instruction but occurs when students read stories and expository materials and also when they listen to such material read by the teacher or by other adults.

Direct Vocabulary Instruction

Vocabulary instruction is not merely teaching a list of words and their meanings. As part of such instruction, students should use the vocabulary they are learning for text comprehension and in their written work. Vocabulary words, therefore, have to be learned in depth. This means that students should learn multiple meanings of words as they occur in different contexts, along with their derived and inflected forms. Vocabulary instruction, therefore, should not be limited to knowing the words but should also create conditions for knowing *about* the words.

Because most children in the early grades do not read extensively on their own yet, in these grades direct instruction becomes the primary means of achieving vocabulary growth. Furthermore, environmental factors play an important role in vocabulary development, and children from low-income homes, compared with children from affluent homes, have a more limited oral and written vocabulary. For these students, direct teaching of vocabulary becomes essential.

Direct vocabulary instruction can be made effective by the following:

- Providing repeated exposure of words

- Engaging children in a discussion of words

- Embedding newly introduced words in sentences and using the words in several sentences in a variety of contexts to make the words meaningful

- Encouraging students to create their own sentences using newly learned words

- Engaging students in activities such as word games and dictionary games

- Having each child bring one word from home every day to share with the class; displaying these words in the classroom along with students' names

Indirect Vocabulary Instruction

Estimates of children's vocabulary knowledge vary, but according to one study, by the end of second grade children know about 6,000 root words. By the time they reach the end of grade 6, the word count increases to 10,000 (Biemiller, 2005). No classroom instructional program can be expected to teach such a vast number of words through direct instruction, and textbooks—the primary source of direct vocabulary instruction—may limit the range of vocabulary acquired in the primary grades. This leaves indirect instruction, also known as extensive reading (in content areas and through students' own reading initiatives), and reading aloud by the teacher as the two major sources of enriching vocabulary (Johnson, 2001). This is particularly true for children in the higher grades, because spoken language is not as rich in vocabulary as written language and the development of vocabulary knowledge beyond the seventh-grade level depends on reading (Cunningham, 2005).

The benefits of reading aloud to children are well documented. In a study by Elley (1989), children were read a text containing target words and were given pre- and posttests of vocabulary knowledge. The 7- and 8-year-olds showed vocabulary gains of 15% after hearing a story on three different occasions with no student participation or teacher explanation. However, when teacher explanation accompanied the story, 8-year-olds demonstrated vocabulary gains of 40%. This study illustrates that shared reading can be used to introduce new words incidentally but in a meaningful way. Shared reading is also reported to be beneficial to children with limited vocabularies, those with language delays, and children from economically disadvantaged backgrounds (Hiebert & Kamil, 2005). Reading aloud to children in the first two grades is an important source of vocabulary development because these children are still learning to decode written words, and their oral vocabulary far exceeds their reading vocabulary. Listening to teacher-read material, however, should not be a passive affair; as the Elley study illustrated, accompanying teacher explanation greatly enhances the chances that children will learn and remember new vocabulary words. Children should be taught how to listen with a purpose, how to discuss what they heard, and how to ask questions about what they heard (Hiebert & Kamil). Before beginning the story, the teacher can prepare the students to listen by telling them that after hearing the story they will be expected to answer some questions and carry on a discussion.

Indirect learning of vocabulary also occurs when students complete assignments given by the teacher or read outside the classroom on their own. Content-area reading, such as social studies, science, and history texts, provides additional opportunities for vocabulary development, particularly for students in the higher grades.

Vocabulary instruction is not merely teaching a list of words and their meanings but helping students use vocabulary knowledge for text comprehension and writing. Vocabulary words, therefore, have to be learned in depth. This means knowing multiple meanings of words, as they occur in different contexts, along with their derived and inflected forms. Thus, vocabulary instruction should not be limited to knowing the words; it also should create conditions for knowing about the words.

Principles for Delivering Vocabulary Instruction

Some basic principles need to be observed when delivering vocabulary instruction, regardless of whether it is direct or indirect. These are summarized in the following section.

Direct Instruction of Vocabulary

Direct instruction can be made effective by following these guidelines:

- Providing repeated exposure to words
- Engaging children in discussion of words
- Embedding the newly introduced words in sentences and using the words in different sentences in different contexts to make the words meaningful
- Encouraging students to create sentences that include the newly learned words

- Engaging students in activities such as word and dictionary games
- Asking each child to bring one word from home every day and explain it to the class
- Displaying the words from home, along with the names of the students who contributed them, in the classroom

Indirect Instruction of Vocabulary

Indirect instruction, also known as wide reading, can be accomplished by the following means:

- The teacher's initiation of shared reading in the classroom
- The reading that the student chooses to do independently
- The student's reading as part of classroom assignments
- The student's parents reading to and with him or her
- The student's reading in science, social studies, and history classes

Despite the instructional appeal of the acquisition of vocabulary through reading outside the classroom, children in the early primary grades cannot be expected to indulge in wide reading on their own. Therefore, in these grades direct instruction becomes the primary means of achieving vocabulary growth. Furthermore, environmental factors play an important role in vocabulary development and children from low-income homes, who, when compared with children from affluent homes, have a much more limited vocabulary, both oral and written (Nelson-Herber, 1986). Thus, leaving vocabulary development to self-initiated wide reading and chance encounters may not have a substantial effect on children from low-income homes. Under these circumstances, direct teaching of vocabulary becomes essential to build an optimal level of the children's vocabulary.

Choosing Which Words to Teach

Teachers generally select vocabulary words from books used in the classroom. However, the words in textbooks are selected with the "typical" child in mind, and in any classroom there is wide variation in children's vocabulary knowledge.

Beck, McKeown, and Kucan (2002, 2005) provided guidelines for selecting words for vocabulary instruction by classifying words into three tiers. This classification is based on two criteria: the frequency with which words occur in books and the usefulness of the words. Words in Tier 1 are those in the spoken vocabulary of most children and that occur frequently in children's storybooks. Examples of Tier 1 words are *play, school,* and *come.* Words in Tier 2 are less common than Tier 1 words and are often found in children's textbooks. Tier 2 words for the fourth or fifth grade include *tended, mention, emerging, haunting,* and *sinister.* Tier 3 words occur with low frequency in children's textbooks and are not usually encountered in informal conversation. Examples of fourth- or fifth-grade Tier 3 words are *entomologist, metamorphosis,* and *phobia.* Children might encounter many of the words in Tier 3 for the first time in a written passage or in upper-grade content textbooks.

Naturally, classification of words into these three tiers depends on grade level, children's maturity, and their reading skills. An unfamiliar Tier 2 word to a first grader is likely to be a Tier 1 word to a second grader. There are no rules for classifying words into these three categories, and teachers should use the categorization flexibly as a guide to selecting words for vocabulary instruction.

Another way to select words for instruction is described by Blachowicz and Fisher (2006). These authors classified words into the following four categories: comprehension words, useful words, generative words, and academic words. Comprehension words are essential for understanding the selection to be read. Examples include *consequently, in spite of,* and *contrary to.* Useful words may not be crucial for understanding the text but have high utility for general use. Generative words have root words and word parts that lead to further word learning, wherein other words with the same root are encountered. Academic words, generally not encountered in expository text, direct students to take actions such as thinking critically, making judgments, and evaluating what has been read. Examples of academic words are *analyze, consider,* and *contrast.*

The selection of words for vocabulary instruction should not be a random process but should take into account the grade level and the level of vocabulary knowledge of the students.

Examining What Is in a Word

In addition to the selection of words, other factors enter into vocabulary instruction. For example, presenting words in different contexts, using words in sentences, and discussing the meaning of words will enhance children's vocabulary learning. A majority of English words have more than one meaning. To understand which meaning is being conveyed in a text, the words have to be considered in context. For instance, the meaning of the common word *run* changes according to the context in which it occurs, as the following sentences illustrate:

- If Mr. Wilson decides to *run* for the election, he is not likely to win.
- Babe Ruth accumulated the most *runs* as a baseball player.
- I have to fix the *run* in my hose.
- Cheetahs can reach a speed of 40 miles per hour when they *run*.

Consider also the word *base.* It can refer to a base in baseball, base for makeup application, the base on which a statue is placed, or an air force base. Words also acquire different meanings over time. With the advent of the computer, the following words have acquired different meanings from the original: *bug, web, chip, crash, dish, net,* and *mouse* (Diamond & Gutlohn, 2007). To understand different shades of meaning, then, readers have to encounter words in different contexts. Known as connotative meaning, these context-dependent meanings differ from denotative meaning, which is simple, direct meaning without associated subtleties. Denotative meaning conveys the literal meaning of a word.

Because connotative meaning indicates different shades of meaning as desired by the writer, connotative words are said to be loaded. Consider the following two sentences:

- John is a *young* boy, and therefore his behavior is understandable.
- John is an *immature* boy, and therefore his behavior is understandable.

Notice the words in italics. Which of these two words is denotative and which is connotative? Do they create different impression of John in your mind? Again, consider these two sentences:

- Upon her husband's death, Hatshepsut *seized* the throne and became the pharaoh.

- Upon her husband's death, Hatshepsut *succeeded* to the throne.

Although students in the early elementary grades will not grasp the connotative meanings of many such words, teachers in the upper grades can draw students' attention to both the denotative and connotative meanings of words.

Another aspect of vocabulary instruction concerns affixes. Many root words take on prefixes and suffixes, which alter the meaning of the words. Some changes in meaning are slight, as in the words *play* and *replay*, but other changes are more drastic, as in *happy* and *unhappy*. Teachers can explain that affixes can be grouped together into "families" because suffixes and prefixes belonging to the same family "look like each other," just as people from the same family often resemble each other (Baumann, Font, Edwards, & Boland, 2005). One example of this family resemblance is the family of negations. Members of this family are *dis, un, in, im, ir,* and *non,* forming such words as *dislike, undo, inability, impolite, irresponsible,* and *nonliving.* An interesting list of number prefixes of Latin and Greek origin is provided by Diamond and Gutlohn (2007) and is shown in Table 8.1.

Some common suffixes are *ed* as in *walked*, *ing* as in *running*, and *er* as in *taller*. Whereas prefixes generally do not change the grammatical status of a root word, suffixes sometimes do. For example, *divide* is generally used as a verb, whereas *division* is a noun; *educate* is a verb, whereas *education* is a noun; and *imagine* is a verb, whereas *imaginary* is an adjective. Of course, students must be alerted to the fact that the beginning and ending of some words may look like prefixes and suffixes but are not. For example, *dis* in *dismal*, *un* in *under*, and *in* in *interest* and *industry* are not prefixes; *ed* in *bleed*, *er* in *hammer*, and *able* in *table* are not suffixes. A general rule for distinguishing words with and without affixes is to strip the prefix or suffix and see if the remainder of the word is a root word. If it is not, then the word is not a derived word. Teachers can also introduce root words and ask students to generate new words by adding prefixes and suffixes to the root words. Some common affixes that occur in children's textbooks are shown in Table 8.2.

Prefixes and suffixes can be portrayed visually, as shown in Figure 8.1. The root word is placed in the center of the chart, and derived words with one suffix or prefix are placed in the first box. Words derived with more than one affix are placed in the second box. For example, in Figure 8.1, *form* is the target root word. The word *informs* is placed in the first box; the word *informed* is placed in the sec-

Table 8.1. Number prefixes of Latin and Greek origin

Numeral	Greek	Latin	Related words
1	uni-	mono-	unicycle, monotone
2	bi-	di-	bilingual, dichotomy
3	tri-	tri-	triangle, triple
4	quad-	tetra-	quadrangle, tetrahedron
5	quint-	penta-	quintuplet, pentagon
6	sex-	hex-	sextuplet, hexagon
7	sept-	hept-	September, heptagon
8	octa-	octo-	octagonal, octopus
9	non-, nove-	ennea-	November, Ennead
10	deci-	dec-	decimal, decathlon

Diamond, L., & Gutlohn, L. (2007). *Vocabulary handbook* (p. 173). Baltimore: Paul H. Brookes Publishing Co.; adapted by permission.

Table 8.2.   Common prefixes and suffixes

Prefix	Example	Suffix	Example
ab-	abnormal	-ible	edible
anti-	antibiotic	-ment	government
bi-	bicentennial	-ous	studious
mis-	misspell	-ed	walked
pre-	pretest	-ing	running
un-	unhappy	-er	taller
im-	impossible	-tion	education
il-	illegal	-sion	division
in-	inhuman	-ness	happiness
dis-	disagree	-al	accidental
mis-	misread	-ary	imaginary
re-	replay	-able	readable
trans-	transport	-ly	lovely
non-	nonfiction	-est	biggest
de-	deface	-ful	helpful

ond box. A comprehensive list of prefixes and suffixes is provided in *Unlocking Literacy: Effective Decoding and Spelling Instruction* (Henry, 2003) and in *Vocabulary Handbook* (Diamond & Gutlohn, 2007).

Creating Opportunities for Encountering Words

A simple though possibly not very effective means of providing direct vocabulary instruction is to construct a list of words, particularly from a textbook used in the classroom, and include the dictionary meaning for these words. Students are asked to learn the words and the meanings. Research by Stahl and Vancil (1986) and several others, however, shows that such instruction fails to significantly improve vocabulary growth. Dictionary instruction is a form of associative learning and is not very useful in helping students remember vocabulary words because it does not

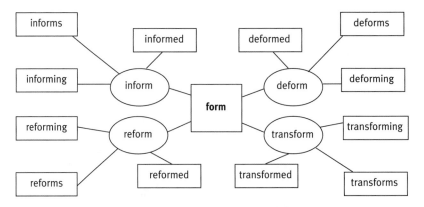

Figure 8.1.   Root web 2. This intermediate web adds words with inflected endings for verbs, *-ed, -s,* and *-ing*. (From Lubliner, S. [2005]. *Getting into words: Vocabulary instruction that strengthens comprehension* [p. 25]. Baltimore: Paul H. Brookes Publishing Co.; reprinted by permission.)

allow students to process the words in depth. Words can be processed in depth by associating them with several meanings and by encountering them in different contexts.

If the dictionary approach *is* used as one means of developing vocabulary, it is important to remember that children require repeated exposure to words before the words become part of their vocabulary. An early study by Gates (1930) indicated that a typical first grader needs 35 repetitions of a word to learn it. This figure appears to be somewhat high, and others have come up with more modest estimates. When "learning a word" is defined in terms of how much it helps in reading comprehension, McKeown, Beck, Omanson, and Pople (1985) found that the number of repetitions required for a word to become part of a child's vocabulary is about 12. Regardless of the variation in these estimates, repetition is necessary before a word becomes part of students' vocabulary knowledge. Teachers can provide repetition by discussing the word several times, embedding the word in different sentences, and using synonyms and antonyms to illustrate the meaning of the word.

Presenting such lessons in a game-like format can make the material more interesting for children. Following are several vocabulary development activities that can be used either on an individual basis or in small groups. Group competition can be incorporated into many of the activities. Although some educators may express concern about using competition in the classroom, it can be an effective motivating force when it is rewarded by a feeling of achievement. Children enjoy competition, especially in a group format, and even reluctant readers become motivated to participate when there is an element of competition.

Find the Word Game

The teacher gives a selected list of words to students and asks them to locate the words and their meaning in the dictionary. The first team to locate the words wins. In first and second grades, the teacher may have to provide guidance during the activity. In addition to teaching the meaning of words, this game reinforces spelling as students must use the correct spelling of a word to locate it quickly in the dictionary. The teacher may also use this opportunity to teach children that many words have more than one meaning. After the children have learned several words, they can construct their own glossary, grouping words into categories along with their meaning.

Vocabulary Bingo Game

For Vocabulary Bingo (Reutzel & Cooter, 2003), the teacher prepares bingo cards made up of words already introduced in the class. Students may play the game as individuals or in teams of three or four. The teacher calls out the definition of a word and the students cross out the word on their bingo card that matches that definition. The first student or team to cross out all the words is the winner.

My Personal Dictionary and Word Bank

Children write the words introduced during a lesson, along with their meaning and a sentence for each, on a single sheet of paper with the first letter of the word written in the left corner. Over a period of time, these sheets can be bound or stapled together to make a personal dictionary. Words can also be written on index cards and stored in shoeboxes with students' names written on them. Alphabet dividers can be used to separate the words. Reutzel and Cooter (2003) called these word banks.

The Cloze Game

This procedure is based on the Cloze form of tests of reading comprehension. The teacher selects sentences from a class textbook and deletes some of the words in the sentences. The teacher writes these sentences on transparent film and projects them by using an overhead projector. The students fill in the missing words. Students can be divided into small groups for this activity, and the groups can compete with one another.

Word Wall Activities

One of the most effective means of repeatedly presenting vocabulary words in the classroom is a word wall (see Chapter 7). Since the reference to the word wall by Patricia Cunningham (1999a), its importance to vocabulary development came to be appreciated quickly, and it has become an ubiquitous feature in American classrooms. A word wall provides an opportunity for teachers to expand on words selected systematically, on the basis of a topic or a theme, and to make frequent use of them. Wagstaff's (2005) description appears in Chapter 7 (see p. 175).

As each word is added to the wall, the teacher may give the meaning of the word, present its relatives (words derived from the root word), and use the word in two or three sentences. In first and second grades, pictures that relate to the word can be cut out from magazines and pasted next to the words. In the upper grades, the teacher can encourage students to create their own sentences using the words on the wall.

Some fourth- and fifth-grade teachers prefer not to use a word wall because they believe that students encounter a sufficient number of words in their textbooks. However, students will not become saturated with vocabulary by relying on textbooks alone. Furthermore, in any classroom there are students whose vocabulary knowledge is more limited than that of their peers, and these children can benefit much from word walls. The remaining vocabulary activities in this section involve words from the word wall.

Mind Reader

The teacher tells the students that she has selected a word from the word wall and will give them five clues about the word. After each clue, students try to guess the word and write it down in their notebook. The first student or team to correctly guess the word is the winner. The following is an example of a series of word clues:

1. It is one of the words on the word wall.
2. It has six letters.
3. It begins with the letter *s*.
4. It has two vowels.
5. It appears in the sentence "I go to _____ five days a week."

Word Wall Bingo

Each child is given a bingo card with six blank spaces. The teacher gives clues about the type of words students should write in the spaces. For instance, the teacher may say, "The words we are going to use in today's bingo game have to do with traveling to other countries, so select words that describe travel or words that tell about other countries," or "Today's words will all be animal [or plant] names." Children copy one word from the word wall into each blank space, based on the clues given by the teacher. Then the teacher calls out six words, one at a time. Children cross out the words that appear on their card, and the first child to cross out all six words wins.

Who Am I?

The teacher gives a definition or description of a word from the word wall and asks children to guess the word and write it down in their notebook. For instance, the teacher may say, "I am a color," "I have five letters," "My name starts with the second letter of the alphabet," "I have the vowel *o* in me." "Who am I?"

Simple Dictation Game

The teacher calls out a number of words, one at a time, and the students write each word down on index cards. If they do not know the correct spelling, they can look it up on the word wall. The teacher collects the children's written spellings.

Word Wall Baseball

The class is divided into two teams. Seats in the room are arranged roughly like a baseball diamond, with a chair to represent each base. The teacher writes words from the word wall on index cards, shuffles them, and asks a child from one of the teams to pull one card. If the child can read the card correctly (or define the word, depending on the rules of the game), she moves to the first base. If she fails to read it, she is out. Words other than those used on the word wall can also be used.

Story Writing

Students are asked to make up a story using a certain number of words from the word wall and a certain number of sentences. Children can save the sheets of paper they write their sentences on and make a book out of their stories over time.

Donate a Word

Children are asked to bring a word from home to the classroom, perhaps relating to a topic being discussed in class. Children write the word they bring and paste it on the word wall. They may also make up a sentence using their word and read it to the class.

Word Gathering

The teacher chooses a topic, such as Thanksgiving, and asks students to select as many words from the word wall as they can that are related to the topic. They then write a meaningful sentence for each word, either on their own or as a group. This activity, of course, requires that a substantial number of words related to the topic be posted on the word wall.

Word Election

The teacher tells the students that they are going to play a voting game and that the word that is liked by a majority of the students will be the winner. Each student in the class then chooses one word from the word wall and speaks on behalf of the word, explaining its characteristics and why the student likes it. For instance, the student may give the meaning of the word, report how often it occurs in texts, and provide any other reason why he likes the word. After the election propaganda, each student votes for one word. The student who has lobbied for the word that receives the largest number of votes is also a winner.

Remembering Words

Meaningful words are remembered much more easily than meaningless (nonsense) words. The first set of psychological studies to establish the validity of this fact was conducted in the late 19th century by Herman Ebbinghaus (1885/1913), a German psychologist. He also noted that repeated study of word lists improved memory of the words.

As noted previously, repetition and meaning promote the retention of vocabulary words. Students' active involvement with words when they create word webs, play word games, select synonyms, and construct sentences gives them repeated exposure to vocabulary words and makes the words more meaningful. These strategies are likely to be more effective than mere associative learning. Good vocabulary instruction should focus not only on the breadth of students' knowledge (i.e., how many words students know) but also on the depth of their knowledge (i.e., how much students know about these words).

Words become meaningful when they are associated with several aspects of the concept the word represents. A basic principle in making words meaningful is to relate new words to the ones children already know. For example, the word *legend* can be introduced by relating it to common words such as *story* and *tale*. Thus, words can become more meaningful to students by relating them to their dictionary meaning, relating them to words with similar meaning, relating them to words with the opposite meaning, and more importantly, embedding them in sentences so that their meaning in context becomes explicit. In addition, knowing about words, word parts, and word history makes words meaningful. When word associations are made in these ways, words are processed in depth and are anchored in memory. This can be illustrated with a tent analogy. To secure a tent on a camping site against gusty winds, the tent needs to be anchored with several pegs. Similarly, the more "pegs" a word is anchored to, the more secure it becomes in the learner's memory. The following "pegs" are useful in vocabulary instruction and are discussed in detail in this section:

• Knowledge of the denotative meaning of words

• Knowledge of the synonyms and antonyms of words

• Knowledge of word parts, word origins, and morphological status

• Knowledge of the connotative meaning of words

- Knowledge of the relationships among words through graphic representation such as semantic and cluster maps

Knowledge of the Denotative Meaning of Words

A prereading vocabulary exercise can help children become familiar with words they are about to encounter. Before reading a text, children scan it and highlight or call out the words they are not familiar with. If students are reluctant to do this initial assignment, the class can be divided into small groups and each group can come up with a list of unfamiliar words. This will produce a sizeable body of words, which the teacher writes on the chalkboard. Students copy the target words in their notebook along with the sentences in which they appear. The teacher gives a simplified version of the dictionary definition of the words, explains the meaning of these words in her own words, and demonstrates them in sentences. If the words have multiple meanings, the teacher explores these meanings with students by using the words in a variety of sentences. In addition, the teacher can use the target words to build schema by asking students questions and by drawing their attention to the context of the words. The teacher can write the words and sentences on individual cards and use them as flashcards to periodically test students' understanding of them. These words can also become part of the word wall.

Knowledge of Synonyms and Antonyms of Words

Although difficult for young children, producing synonyms and antonyms can help children better understand word meanings. In general, students find it easier to generate antonyms than synonyms. Examples provided by the teacher can be helpful. For instance, the teacher might say, "The opposite of *day* is *night,* and the opposite of *good* is *bad.* Can you give me a word that is the opposite of *tall* and the opposite of *big?*" Some children in grade 2 and above can successfully produce a few antonyms. Students in grades 4 and above can understand and produce many synonyms. Students can also be taught to use the thesaurus to generate synonyms and antonyms. If there is a computer in the classroom, an electronic thesaurus can be accessed readily.

Knowledge of Word Parts, Word Origin, and Morphological Status

Nagy, Anderson, Schommer, Scott, and Stallman (1989) noted that more than 60% of new words encountered by readers have a relatively transparent morphological structure. That is, if a student can identify the root of a word by analyzing its root and its affixes, she can gain a broad understanding of the word's meaning. Blanchfield (2004) described a simple model for introducing word parts in the upper elementary grades. First, the concept of a root word and affixes is introduced. Then students are asked to select a root word, take a sheet of paper, and draw a picture of a tree with its root and branches. Next they are asked to mark its root with the root word given. The students can use a dictionary and find as many words as they can by adding prefixes and suffixes to the root word. The students can then write the new words on the branches of the tree. The resulting pictures are shared and put on display in the classroom.

The tree model can also be used to group words according to their etymological origin, such as Greek, Latin, or French. A list of root words of Latin and Greek origin is shown in Table 8.3. More root words and affixes can be obtained by accessing the Internet through a search engine. A comprehensive list of root words of Greek, Latin, and French origin is provided in *Unlocking Literacy: Effective Decoding and Spelling Instruction* (Henry, 2003).

The morphological status of many English words changes according to context. More specifically, some words can function as nouns as well as verbs. The morphological status of words can change the meaning of the sentences in which they appear. Examples of words that can function as nouns as well as verbs are seen in the following sentences:

- Farmers *produce* the *produce*.
- The bandage should be *wound* around the *wound*.
- The *present* is the best time to *present* the *present*.
- The *wind* was so strong we could not *wind* the sails.
- We will *ship* the cargo by *ship*.
- The witch cast a *spell* after which he could not *spell* any word.

In fact, a large number of English words can function as both nouns and verbs. Students can play a game in which they come up with words that function as nouns and verbs.

Knowledge of the Connotative Meanings of Words

Embedding vocabulary words in a variety of sentences is one of the most effective ways to make words meaningful for students. This activity also provides an opportunity for students to use context to understand the meaning of unfamiliar words. It may take several different sentences for students to grasp the meanings. An example is the word *page*. The teacher might say, "The word *page* has more than one meaning. It can refer to the page on which a story appears in your book. Or, it can refer to a young person undergoing training under an official. It can also mean to call a person over the intercom. For example, I can say, 'Turn to *page* 25 for the lesson we are going to read today.' Or, I can say, 'My brother is serving as a congressional *page* in Washington, D.C.' Or, I can say, 'When I visit the hospital,

Table 8.3. A selected list of Greek and Latin roots and their English derivatives

Latin roots and derivatives	Greek roots and derivatives
aqua: *aquarium*	anti: *antidote*
aud: *audible, laudable*	astro: *astronomy, astrology*
cent: *centennial* (but not *decent*)	bio: *microbiology, bionics*
liber: *liberty, liberation*	geo: *geology, geometry*
pedis: *pedestrian, bipedal*	graph: *biography, photography*
port: *portable, deport* (but not *portion*)	hydro: *hydroplane*
trans: *transfer, transport* (but not *transparent*)	mono: *monotone, monopoly*
uni: *uniform*	octo: *October, octopus*
vis: *visual, vision*	phon: *telephone, phonics*
voca: *vocal, vocalic*	tele: *telegraph, telepathy*

I hear doctors being *paged* on the intercom.'" In the higher grades, students can also learn the idiomatic meaning for *page,* as in "He turned a new *page* in his life."

Children with limited reading skills have limited vocabulary knowledge, and their knowledge of words is limited compared with that of skilled readers. That is, although poor readers may be aware of the literal meaning of words, they may not be aware of the connotative meaning. The following activities can help students with this.

The Embedding Game

The teacher says a word and asks students to construct as many sentences as they can with the word in them. Each sentence should reflect a different meaning of the word. The teacher may need to give numerous examples before students grasp the concept of multiple meanings of words. The teacher should keep in mind that, at best, most children will produce one or two sentences, and children in grades 1 and 2 may have great difficulty doing even this. This activity may be most successful when used as a group game.

Word Sort Game

Knowing that more than one word can have the same meaning can also enhance an awareness of the connotative meaning of words. The teacher writes words and their synonyms that have been introduced in the class on index cards. There should be a set of cards for each group of students. For a *closed sort*, the groups sort the word cards into piles according to the criteria set up by the teacher, such as words with similar meanings, words with similar affixes, science words, and so on. For an *open sort*, the students sort the word cards according to categories they themselves choose.

Knowledge of the Relationship Among Words Through Visual Representation

When a word and its relatives are presented to students in some form of visual representation, students remember the words better than when they merely hear them or are told their meaning. There are several ways in which the relationships among words can be visually represented.

Pictures

The teacher or students select a picture from a magazine, and students select words from the word wall that go with the picture. An alternative is to have students select their own words and illustrate them by drawing pictures.

Semantic Map

The teacher selects a word from the word wall and writes it on the chalkboard. Then he writes *Synonyms* on one side of the target word and *Antonyms* on the other side. Students call out words that have the same meaning (synonyms) or the opposite meaning (antonyms), and the teacher writes the words in the appropriate column. For example, if the target word is *morning,* words such as *early* and *sunrise* would go under *Synonyms,* and words such as *evening, late,* and *sunset* would go under *Antonyms.* These words are then connected to the target word by drawing lines.

Cluster Map

A slightly modified version of the semantic map is the cluster map. To produce a cluster map, the teacher asks students to suggest words that are somehow related to the target word but not necessarily synonyms or antonyms. In the case of the word *morning,* words such as *getting up, breakfast,* and *alarm clock* might be included on the cluster map. Depending on the degree of relationship to the target word, these words are written either very close to the target word or farther away. As with the semantic map, lines can be drawn between the target word and the newly generated words (e.g., see Figure 8.1).

Word Web

The word web is also a modified version of the semantic and cluster maps. Drew (2005) gave an example of using a word web. After selecting a target word, *went,* children are told that the word is a verb and that they should come up with verbs or adverbs, but not nouns, that are related to this word. The words that children might generate for *went* include *ran, hurried, quickly, skipped,* and *walked.*

The target word can be written on the chalkboard and the generated words connected to the target word by drawing lines. Once the children seem to have exhausted their word knowledge, they can look in the dictionary to see if they can find additional words. The word web also provides an opportunity to introduce the basic elements of grammar and, therefore, is suitable for grades 3 and up.

Vocabulary Matrix

On the chalkboard or overhead projector, the teacher constructs a matrix of rows and columns. The teacher selects four or five related target words and writes them in the left-hand column, one below the other. On the top row, the teacher writes certain descriptors or properties that would fit some but not all of the words in the column. For example, as shown in Figure 8.2, the target words are *oars, motor,* and

BOATS	oars	motor	sails	anchor	mast	crew
ferry	–	+	–	+	–	+
sailboat	–	+	+	+	+	+
kayak	+	–	–	–	–	–
rowboat	+	–	–	+	–	–
cruise ship	–	+	–	+	–	+
schooner	–	+	+	+	+	+
tugboat	–	+	–	+	–	+
canoe	+	–	–	–	–	–

Figure 8.2. Vocabulary matrix. (From Diamond, L., & Gutlohn, L. [2007]. *Vocabulary handbook* [p. 62]. Baltimore: Paul H. Brookes Publishing Co.; reprinted by permission.)

so forth. The words in the column are *ferry*, *sailboat*, and so forth. Students read the words in the column and check each word against the properties in the top row. In the intersecting box of a word and property, students mark a + sign if the property is true of that word, a − sign if the property is not true of that word, or a question mark if the students are not sure. For instance, a rowboat has oars, so a + mark is given under *oars*; it has no motor and therefore gets a − mark in the *motor* column. A detailed description of the vocabulary matrix is presented by Nagy (1988).

The Alphabet Book

Each student is given a sheet of paper. The teacher announces a letter of the alphabet and the students write down words that begin with that letter. They can illustrate the words or cut pictures from a magazine and paste them next to the words. These worksheets are saved and later stapled to make a picture dictionary for each student.

Characteristics of a Good Vocabulary Instruction Program

What does a good vocabulary program look like? Blachowicz and Fisher (2006) listed a number of characteristics of a strong vocabulary program. An adapted version of their list is presented below.

- The teacher engages in daily read-aloud activities.
- The classroom has a "word of the day" or "word activity of the day."
- The teacher shows enthusiasm for words and learning about words.
- The classroom has word walls and word charts.
- The classroom has books on words and dictionaries.
- Word games, puzzle books, and student-made word books are present.
- Students show enthusiasm for word learning.
- Students can name a favorite book and a word game.
- Students can use the dictionary at the appropriate level.
- Students have strategies for dealing with unknown words.
- Students have an adequate knowledge of word parts.
- Visual graphics are used for instruction.
- Students are provided opportunities for multiple exposure to words.
- Students engage in word play and participate in vocabulary-building activities.
- Teachers periodically assess the breadth and depth of students' vocabulary knowledge.

For information on using computer programs for vocabulary instruction, see Box 8.1. See Appendix C for more information on using computers in instruction.

Promoting Reading Comprehension

Comprehension is the ultimate goal of reading. The National Reading Panel appropriately concluded that reading comprehension is the essence of reading because it is important not only to academic learning but also to lifelong learning

---

Box 8.1. **The computer and vocabulary instruction**

There are several software programs designed to promote children's vocabulary knowledge. Many are in game format to hold children's interest. Computer programs for literacy instruction are more fully described in Appendix C; the following is a list of selected commercially available software.

- Merit Software: http://www.meritsoftware.com/software/index.php
- Laureate Learning Systems: http://www.laureatelearning.net/professionals602/products/prodsby/category.html#vocabcon%20Anchor
- Inspiration Software: http://www.inspiration.com

(National Reading Panel, 2000). Reading comprehension has not received much research attention and, consequently, much less is known about it than about word recognition processes. This is partly due to a belief that comprehension is an aspect of intelligence and cannot be taught. This view has changed dramatically in recent years, and reading comprehension, as a research topic, has received a good deal of attention. As a result, more has been learned about teaching comprehension since 1990 than at any point in history (Block, Gambrell, & Pressley, 2002).

According to Carlisle and Rice (2002), about one fifth of the students in most elementary classrooms in which students are not grouped by achievement show moderate to severe difficulty with reading comprehension. Students can experience difficulty in comprehending written text for four reasons: 1) They do not have adequate word recognition skills, 2) they do not have the vocabulary knowledge needed for comprehending the text, 3) they do not have the required schema or background knowledge to understand the text, and 4) they do not use strategies for optimal comprehension. Improving students' reading comprehension requires attention to these four factors.

In addition to these factors, limited awareness of morphological patterns and poor metalinguistic abilities can hinder comprehension (Carlisle & Rice, 2002). Morphological awareness refers to sensitivity to prefixes and suffixes in written words, not memory for an entire sequence of letters in a word. An example of such a morphemic suffix is *tion*. Once the reader possesses a knowledge of this unit, he can more easily identify and comprehend words such as *prevention, attention,* and *occupation*. Words that have similar onsets represent orthographic patterns. Examples of words with the onset *str* are *strike, strong,* and *strange*. Processing these morphological and orthographic units without having to invest much attention frees up the reader's attention to focus on the meaning of words and sentences.

Metalinguistic abilities refer to reflecting on one's own language and monitoring comprehension and other language-related activities. An integral component of metalinguistic ability is sensing when comprehension is being hindered and taking corrective action. For instance, as a student reads, she may encounter an unfamiliar word. She should be able to say to herself, "Oh, I don't know this word; I wonder what it means." This awareness must be followed up by efforts to determine the meaning of the word. These efforts may include trying to guess the word from context, asking the teacher, or referring to a dictionary. Absence of meta-linguistic awareness precludes further efforts by the student to comprehend text.

As mentioned previously, reading comprehension depends on four factors: word recognition skill, vocabulary knowledge, background knowledge, and the use of comprehension strategies. Word recognition was discussed in Chapter 7. The following section describes very briefly an aspect of the role of vocabulary in reading not described in the previous section on vocabulary development; it also expands on the remaining two essential factors in comprehension, namely, the role of schema and the deployment of reading comprehension strategies.

The Role of Vocabulary Knowledge in Reading Comprehension

Vocabulary and reading comprehension have a reciprocal relationship: Vocabulary knowledge affects reading comprehension, and reading experience promotes vocabulary development. Studies show that the more children read, the greater their vocabulary knowledge; the larger their vocabulary knowledge, the greater their interest in reading. On the other hand, the less they read, the more limited their vocabulary knowledge, which leads to diminished interest in reading. In one study, Anderson, Wilson, and Fielding (1988) found that a typical child with a reading score at the 50th percentile read only 4.6 minutes per day, and a child at the 20th percentile read less than 1 minute a day. In contrast, a child at the 80th percentile read 14.2 minutes daily, more than 20 times as much as the child at the 20th percentile. Thus, good readers read more and develop larger vocabularies, which in turn enhances their comprehension skills. Poor readers read less, stunting their vocabulary growth and causing them to fall further and further behind in their ability to understand what they read.

Knowing the words in a text does not guarantee comprehension. Readers are also expected to infer meaning from what they read and to use their background knowledge in making such inferences. In addition, they must use context to interpret the meaning of a word correctly. Gray (2003) noted that "according to the Oxford English Dictionary, the 500 words used most in the English language each have an average of 23 different meanings."

Furthermore, words may be figuratively used in idioms, and a literal interpretation can lead to a misunderstanding of the text. Examples of idioms are *strike a bargain, break a date, throw a party, jump the gun, hit the road, robbed blind,* and *cold hearted.* The relationship between vocabulary and comprehension can be summed up in this way: Vocabulary knowledge is a necessary but not sufficient condition for comprehension.

The Role of Schema in Reading Comprehension

In Chapter 2, schema was described as the reader's background knowledge. The reader interprets what she reads in light of the information she already has about the topic. Because individuals develop various schema as a result of their daily experiences, the reader's age is closely associated with the quantity and quality of schema. Culture and environment also shape the reader's schema. Reading comprehension can be adversely affected by a lack of relevant schema or by a failure to activate the appropriate schema and use it for comprehension. The effect on comprehension of not having the appropriate schema was illustrated in Chapter 2.

Furthermore, the type of schema activated during reading can have a profound influence on comprehension. Pichert and Anderson (1977) asked three groups of college students to read about what two boys did at one of the boys' homes while skipping school. The reading material contained a description of the boy's home. Although all three groups of readers were given the same reading material, their schema were manipulated by assigning the groups different perspectives: One group of students was instructed to read the story from the viewpoint of a potential home buyer; another group from that of a burglar. The third group was given no special instructions. When the participants had finished reading, the reading material was withdrawn and the participants were asked to recall the story. Not surprisingly, the assigned frame of reference had a powerful influence on memory and recall. The "home buyer" group recalled many items about the quality of the home, such as the kitchen gadgets, the bathroom layout, the size of the master bedroom, and so on, whereas the "burglar" group recalled many details relevant to entry into the house and escape from it, such as the number of windows and doors, the kind of locks used to secure the windows and doors, and the alarm system. The descriptions given by the control group did not show any such biases.

Reading comprehension instruction should first focus on activating the appropriate schema; if the teacher believes that students may not have the appropriate schema, or that it may be lacking in some way, he should try to develop it. Of course, in any classroom there will be wide variation in children's background knowledge on a particular subject.

There are several strategies for activating and developing the appropriate schema. One is to draw students' attention to the topic to be read and discuss it. For instance, say the students in grade 5 are to read a passage about kangaroos. The teacher can tell the students that they are going to read about kangaroos and ask them what they know about kangaroos. There will be an assortment of responses from the students, and the teacher can elaborate on these answers and fill in any missing information.

Having thus developed background knowledge for the subject of kangaroos, the teacher can further help students understand the text by presenting the text. An important variable in doing so is taking into account students' maturity level. In the first two or three grades, the teacher may simply discuss basic facts about kangaroos, such as where kangaroos are found, the way they move, their feeding habits, and the unique way they raise their young. In the higher grades, the teacher might develop the main idea that animals have adopted different strategies to take care of their newborns. The kangaroo, for instance, accomplishes this by rearing the immature young in a pouch in the mother's body for several weeks. The birth of the young one at an immature stage avoids prolonged pregnancy and the associated risk factors. Animals that raise young ones in a body pouch are called marsupials.

The teacher might elicit statements from the children about marsupial pregnancy, safety of the young kangaroos, and so on by asking the children questions. After the activation of the marsupial schema, the children can read the assigned passage. Students usually seek and find the main idea primed by the teacher during prereading schema-activating exercises. This facilitates text comprehension.

Appropriate schema can also be developed and activated by showing relevant pictures or a film or, in the case of the kangaroo lesson, even visiting a zoo to see the kangaroos. Because the level of reading comprehension varies, the teacher can adjust the level of schema development to students' understanding.

Comprehension Strategy Instruction

One of the earliest publications to focus on comprehension strategy instruction was by Palincsar and Brown (1984). These investigators selected a set of strategies and taught students in small groups to use them. The instructional procedure included the teacher's explanation of the nature of the strategies and demonstration of their use as the text was read. The strategies taught were predicting, questioning, clarifying, and summarizing. That is, as students read, they anticipated what was coming next, asked themselves if they understood what they had read so far, cleared up ambiguities by asking the teacher or checking with the dictionary, and eventually summarized in one or two sentences the main idea contained in the passage. After several sessions of practicing these strategies one by one, the students assumed a leading role and functioned as role models to other students in the group. Palincsar and Brown called this **reciprocal teaching** because the teacher and the student exchange roles as model and learner.

Variations of this method have been reported. Carlisle and Rice (2002) gave brief descriptions of four models that differ from reciprocal teaching in the degree to which the teacher's role varies. One such variation is called transactional strategies instruction, developed by Pressley and his colleagues (1992). Many other studies on the effects of strategy instruction on comprehension have been conducted since Palincsar and Brown's (1984) study, and most have reported positive effects on students' comprehension and reading habits. Examples of such studies are those conducted by Aaron, Joshi, Gooden, and Bentum (in press); Baumann and Ivey (1997); Block (1993); and Dole, Brown, and Trathen (1996).

Questions About Comprehension Strategy Instruction

Three questions are often raised in connection with strategy instruction: 1) Is strategy instruction meant only for struggling readers, or is it effective with all readers? 2) At what grade level can these strategies be successfully implemented? 3) Which strategies make reciprocal teaching effective, and under which conditions?

It is reasonable to conclude that strategy instruction conforms to sound principles of teaching and learning. After examining several meta-analysis studies, Vaughn, Gersten, and Chard (2000) concluded that "in all cases where interventions have demonstrated significant positive effects for students with LD, they have resulted in at least as high (and often higher) effect sizes for all other students, including average and high achieving students" (p. 108). It would, therefore, be safe to conclude that strategy instruction is effective regardless of students' ability level.

Strategies such as activating schema, visualizing (discussed later in this chapter), and seeking help can be successfully taught to children in grades 1 and 2. Brown and Palincsar (1987) were able to use the reciprocal teaching procedure with children whose word recognition skills were not fully developed by reading the text aloud to them. According to Carlisle and Rice (2002), explicit strategy instruction with teacher assistance may be the best general model for teaching comprehension to very young children and children with learning disabilities. Strategy instruction, therefore, can be used at every level, with adaptations as necessary.

Numerous studies have investigated the strategies most effective in improving reading comprehension. In a major review of research between 1963 and 1997, Swanson (1999b) identified the following strategies as having a significant impact on reading comprehension:

- Directed questioning/response: The teacher directs students to generate questions about the topic at hand. After discussion of these questions, the teacher in turn asks questions. This activity results in greater comprehension of the text subsequently read.

- Control of task difficulty: The level of difficulty of the reading task is controlled either through the degree of assistance provided by the teacher or by adjusting the difficulty of the text.

- Elaboration: The teacher provides additional information or explanation of the topic studied.

- Teacher modeling: The teacher demonstrates the comprehension studies that the students are to follow.

- Small-group instruction: Students work in small groups with other students or with the teacher.

- Strategy cues: The teacher reminds students to use strategies and encourages them to think aloud when doing so.

In the Reading Comprehension Improvement Project, Aaron et al. (in press) provided remedial reading instruction for students in grades 2 through 5. Pretesting revealed that some students had low scores in decoding and others had better word recognition scores but below-average reading comprehension scores. The students with comprehension difficulties received comprehension strategy instruction 1 hour per day, 4 days a week for one semester; the students with word recognition difficulties received instruction designed to improve decoding skills. The strategies used are shown in Table 8.4.

The data reported in the study came from seven groups of children taught over a period of 7 years. Posttreatment testing showed that students who received comprehension strategy instruction scored significantly higher in reading comprehension than a comparison group of children in learning disability resource rooms who did not receive differentiated instruction.

Format of Comprehension Strategy Instruction

The Aaron et al. study (in press) suggests the following steps for teaching all students, regardless of ability level. Comprehension strategy instruction is designed for groups of three to five students.

Table 8.4. Strategies taught in the Reading Comprehension Improvement Project

Strategy	Reader asks self this question
1. Being aware of the purpose of reading	Why am I reading this?
2. Schema activation	What do I already know about this?
3. Visualization	Are there pictures and maps that I should look at?
4. Seeking help	Do I know the word? If not, I should raise my hand.
5. Comprehension monitoring	Stop and think: What have I learned so far?
6. Summarizing	Will I be able to tell what I have read in one or two sentences without looking in the book?
7. Critical thinking	Do I have a question for the author or my teacher?

From Aaron, P.G., Joshi, R.M., Gooden, R.B., & Bentum, K. (in press). The outcome of the Component Model-based reading remedial instruction: An alternative to the discrepancy model-based treatment of learning disabilities. *Journal of Learning Disabilities*; adapted by permission.

1. Prereading activities: Each student in the group should be on the same page from the same book. The teacher selects a passage and asks the students to look at the lesson and, using a felt pen, highlight the words they do not know. This requires some practice because children often think that admitting they do not know the meaning of a word is a revelation of their ignorance. With some practice, they open up and are able to generate a list of words they do not know. In the face of persistent reluctance, the teacher can ask the entire group to identify difficult words. This way, unknown words are not associated with any particular student. The teacher then selects each word, reads it aloud, explains the meaning of the word, and uses it in a sentence. This prereading exercise serves three purposes: It provides an opportunity for vocabulary development, it provides an opportunity for discussion, and it is helpful for building schema.

2. The teacher draws students' attention to the seven strategies that will help them with comprehension (Table 8.4). These strategies can be written on the chalkboard, shown on the overhead projector, or printed on sheets of paper the students can use again and again. These strategies should be on display every time comprehension instruction is conducted. The teacher explains what each strategy means and asks the students to memorize the strategies. Memorizing the strategies is relatively easy, but actually applying them to reading is much more difficult. The most effective way for the teacher to help students use the strategies is to model them while thinking aloud. Modeling has to be done again and again, each time a new lesson (or passage) is introduced.

3. The teacher reads a passage that is different from the one assigned to the students but similar in vocabulary, content, and level of difficulty. The teacher models reading while thinking aloud, revealing what is going through her mind as she reads. A student in the group (the reader model) then reads the assigned passage aloud and models his thinking while the other students in the group follow along by reading the passage silently. If the reader model skips any of the strategies, the teacher as well as the other students remind him to use the skipped strategy. Every student in the group is given an opportunity to model the strategies.

4. Students ask themselves the purpose for reading the passage. This is the first comprehension strategy, as shown in Table 8.4. As Sweet and Snow (2002) pointed out, every reader should have a purpose, one that is either externally imposed by the teacher or internally generated by the student. The purpose for reading may be to enjoy a story, learn about a particular topic, or prepare for a test. But many children are not aware of these different purposes; many think that the sole purpose of reading is to get through the text as fast as they can without making any errors. Students need to be made aware of the reason they are reading. Consequently, this is the first strategy children have to master in reading for comprehension.

5. Students activate schema by asking themselves the question "What do I already know about this?" Since the appropriate schema was built during Step 1, students should be able to activate the schema quite readily.

6., 7., and 8. The next three strategies—visualization, seeking help, and comprehension monitoring—need not follow each other in a fixed sequence but should be used flexibly depending on the situation. Students should also be ready to use these strategies during the entire reading process when they are needed.

Visual imagery helps students retain information in memory. Studies show that memory is enhanced by constructing visual imagery (e.g., Sadoski, Goetz, & Fritz, 1993). This strategy is not limited to activating a visual image pertaining to the reading material; it also includes the ability to use information from maps and pictures present in the text.

Students seek help when they do not know the meaning of a word or if they have any questions by raising their hand to ask the teacher, consulting with their peers in the group, or referring to a dictionary or a thesaurus.

Comprehension monitoring involves the use of metacognitive skills. Students are taught to self-question by asking "Do I understand what I have read so far?" Students should be able to recognize when what they have read so far does not make sense and then take the necessary corrective actions, such as rereading or seeking help from the teacher or their peers. Without such metacognitive realization, self-correction cannot take place.

9. Students express in one or two sentences the central message in the lesson. Summarizing is one of the most difficult strategies for students to successfully master. It is important to impress on students from the beginning that after reading, they will have to tell from memory what they have read in one or two sentences. Students have a tendency to look in the book or the passage they have just read and read one or two sentences from it. Often, this will be a sentence that does not reflect the main idea. For this reason, students are asked to close the book and, without looking at the passage, come up with one or two key sentences of their own. This instruction is given at the beginning of every lesson and must be repeated several times. Students require repeated practice with summarizing and need many sessions of modeling by the teacher. If students fail to summarize successfully, they can be asked to recall the most important word or words they remember from reading the text. The teacher can then use these key words to develop the main idea in the story. When students realize that they will have to summarize what they are going to read, it keeps their attention focused on the reading task.

10. Students apply critical thinking to the text they have read, separating facts from opinions and opinions from author bias. This strategy can be taught to students in grades 4 and above. The text selected for reading may be narrative, descriptive, expository, or persuasive. Persuasive text will be particularly useful for implementing the critical thinking strategy. Students who have difficulty in using this strategy can be encouraged to ask the teacher a few questions about the passage or story they have read.

Story Grammar and Reading Comprehension

Another model recommended as a tool in comprehension instruction is story grammar, which can be used along with reciprocal teaching. Story grammar refers to story structure or the skeletal elements of a text. Stories, in general, share some common features. These include a setting, heroes, villains, a plot, conflict, and a resolution. Students' attention can be drawn to the fact that stories have a structure by pointing out these basic elements of stories. Knowledge of story grammar is claimed to improve students' reading comprehension (Beck, Omanson, & McKeown, 1982). The teacher can create an awareness of story grammar by asking students to remember to look for the answers to a number of *wh-* questions as they read: *who, what,*

Box 8.2. The use of *wh-* questions in comprehension instruction

Story	Story elements (on sticky note)
Once upon a time, in Rome, a slave named Androcles escaped from his master and fled to the forest. As he was wandering about, he came upon a lion lying down moaning and groaning. At first Androcles turned to run, but finding that the lion did not pursue him, he turned back and went up to him. As he came near, the lion put out his paw. Androcles found that a huge thorn had gotten into it and was causing all the pain. He pulled out the thorn, and the lion was able to rise and walk. Shortly afterwards, both Androcles and the lion were captured by the Roman soldiers. Androcles was sentenced to be thrown to the lion as punishment. The Roman emperor and his court came to see how Androcles would be killed by the lion. Soon, the lion was let loose from his cage, and he rushed towards Androcles. But as soon as he came near to Androcles he recognized his friend and licked his hands. The emperor, who was surprised at this, summoned Androcles to him. Androcles told him the whole story, whereupon Androcles was freed and the lion let loose to go to his native forest.	Where? Who? What did he do? Who else? What happened? What happened? What happened? Where? Who? Why? What was the end?

---

where, when, how, why, and *what happened.* Basing their instruction on the concept of story elements, Short and Ryan (1984) taught fourth-grade students to ask themselves questions such as "Who was the main character?" "Where and when did the story take place?" "What did the main characters do?" and "How did the story end?" In another study, Beck et al. found that students who were trained to ask themselves these questions recalled more information than students who did not receive such training. Several other investigators have reported similar positive results.

Story grammar can supplement reciprocal teaching and serve as a scaffolding device for comprehension. The *wh-* questions can be written on sticky notes and pasted next to the story so that as students read, they will be reminded to find answers to the *wh-* questions. The *wh-* questions also can be printed on a sheet of paper and used again and again. Answers to the questions will result in the gist of the story, reflecting the reader's comprehension of the essence of the story. An example of the use of story elements for developing comprehension is shown in Box 8.2.

Principles for Comprehension Strategy Instruction

Regardless of the method or methods used, comprehension instruction should follow some general principles of reading instruction:

- Students are taught to take charge of the comprehension process gradually.
- The text should be challenging for students but not overwhelming.

- Preferably, the text or story should be of such length that it can be completed in one session. Children lose interest when they have to read long stories that cannot be completed in one instructional session.

- The strategy training should be part of everyday instruction.

- When the teacher feels that the students have grasped the basic notion of using comprehension strategies, the responsibility for using all seven strategies can be gradually shifted to students. Comprehension instruction must be neither too prescriptive nor too free flowing (Block & Johnson, 2002). When the teacher is too dominant, students may not learn how to apply strategies without being prompted. Alternatively, when instruction is sparse or unmonitored, pupils do not develop the tools to think strategically as they read.

- Within any classroom there will be wide variation in skill level among students. Students can therefore be grouped according to ability. Some teachers, however, may prefer to form groups composed of students with varying levels of reading ability.

- Repeated modeling by the teacher is a vital element in strategy instruction. Several practice sessions will be required before students feel comfortable using the comprehension strategies.

Teachers should adjust their assistance and guidance according to students' needs. More assistance can be provided to students who are struggling by scaffolding their comprehension skills to a higher level. This practice is broadly described as guided reading. Under such circumstances, the teacher may place students with similar ability in small groups and select a text at their reading level. In guided reading, the teacher plays a more supportive role (scaffolding) than what is used during the reciprocal teaching procedure. When introducing the lesson, the teacher may select words the students may not know and explain the words with a number of illustrations. The students then read the text, with the teacher asking individual students to read aloud so that he can informally assess their level of comprehension as well as their level of fluency. After oral reading, the teacher engages students in a discussion of the text. The teacher may weave in the seven comprehension strategies, starting with the purpose for reading. The teacher may draw students' attention to the main and subordinate ideas in the text. Each student makes a summary statement of the text, with the teacher guiding the students to the most suitable summary. Guided reading, when combined with explicit instruction and group discussion, is considered to be a good model for teaching comprehension strategies to students with learning disabilities (Swanson, 1999a).

If the children are at the beginning of the first grade or are very limited in their ability to decode written words, preliminary training in comprehension can be given orally by modeling the strategies shown in Table 8.4. Use of these strategies can improve listening comprehension and, ultimately, reading comprehension.

Promoting Writing Skills

Considerably more research exists on reading than on writing. This may be due to the thought that once reading is mastered, writing will automatically follow. Writing is an important life skill, but it is also linked to academic success, as the recent introduction of a writing component to the SAT shows. The National Assessment of Educational Progress (1995) rated only 28% of fourth-grade and 31% of eighth-grade students as being proficient in writing.

Foundation for Good Writing Skills

Writing skills can be classified as basic level and higher level skills. Basic level skills include spelling, punctuation, capitalization, and grammar; higher level skills include planning, organization, following the structure of story grammar, and the ability to review the written product and revise it if necessary. Good writing depends on the quality of the theme and the ideas contained, not just an understanding of the basic mechanical aspects.

One reason for the poor writing ability seen in many students may be due to their being so concerned with the mechanics of writing that they define good writing as the absence of spelling and grammar errors. However, good writing encompasses much more. It requires content knowledge, knowledge of the forms of writing, an awareness of the purpose of writing, sensitivity to the audience for whom the writing is intended, and the ability to evaluate one's own writing (MacArthur, 2006). Other requirements for good writing are described next (MacArthur, 2006):

1. Good oral language skills: This includes a wide range of vocabulary, good syntactical skills, and extensive reading experience. Reading exposes students to different styles and formats of writing, and this reading experience has a direct impact on students' own writing. The benefits of extensive reading should not be underestimated.

2. Transcription skills: These include spelling, handwriting, and punctuation. Spelling can be a problem for many students. Uncertainty about the spelling of some words may limit some students to using only words that are easy to spell. As a result, students' written products tend to be simplistic.

3. Knowledge about writing itself: This includes knowledge about the topic the students are writing about, because unlike reading—in which knowledge is gained—the goal of writing is to communicate information. The writer must therefore have something to write about. Proficient writers also know the features of good writing. Good writers always have their readers in mind, anticipate questions from the reader, and avoid ambiguities in their statements.

4. Organization skills: Good writers think and plan what they are going to write about. They are also keenly aware of the concept of story grammar and organize their product to conform to good story structure. When writing essays, students clearly present the main idea, use a good beginning, and offer a clear-cut ending with a well-defined summary. A well-organized product is the result of detailed planning.

5. Evaluation throughout the writing process: Good writers keep their audience in mind at all times. To some extent while writing, authors detach themselves from being writers and examine their writing from the reader's point of view. Whenever necessary, the written material is revised and ambiguities clarified.

Writing to Improve Reading

Good writing is strongly associated with good reading comprehension. Just as reading improves writing skills, extended practice in writing will improve reading comprehension. Although the close relationship between reading and writing is well recognized (Tierney & Shanahan, 1991), most of the studies that have explored this relationship have investigated the effect of reading experience on writing. Studies of the influence of writing on reading are relatively rare. One of the few was by Molner (cited in Hefflin & Hartman, 2002), who found that writing activities that preceded reading had positive effects on later recall of text.

Most of the studies reviewed by Hefflin and Hartman (2002) started the prereading writing exercise with an introduction of the topic by the teacher, followed by student contributions that the teacher wrote on the chalkboard or an overhead projector. This procedure was based on such methods as the language experience approach (LEA), dialogue journals, and author circles. These activities can be used to improve comprehension through students' writing, as discussed below.

The LEA, which was described in Chapter 6, is a generic approach with many variations. But the essence of the approach is as follows. The teacher selects a topic, the students orally discuss it and report their experiences, and the teacher writes these experiences on the chalkboard or the overhead projector, or uses the computer. The students read this written material and copy it in their notebook. The written material is saved and becomes part of the students' portfolio. (See Chapter 10 for information on **portfolio assessment.**)

Dialogue journals provide an opportunity to communicate informally with the teacher or other students in the class through writing. E-mail can be used profitably for this purpose. The teacher can select a topic that is related to a lesson students are going to study, or the students can write to one another on a topic of their own choice. Teachers should be aware that strict evaluation of the products of this type of communication through the assigning of grades or correcting of grammar and spelling may discourage students from further communication efforts.

Author circle is part of a larger approach called the authoring cycle (Short, Harste, & Burke, 1996). In author circle, students express themselves through various sign systems, such as writing, drawing, or painting (Hefflin & Hartman, 2002). In small groups, students explore and reflect on their products by making self- and peer-directed revisions to better articulate the substance and form of the product they are authoring. Finally, they share and present their product to the entire class. The teacher can relate the author circle to reading comprehension by selecting a topic that is related to a lesson students will be studying.

Guidelines for Promoting Writing Skills

When writing is chosen either as a prereading exercise or as part of literacy learning, adhering to the following principles will be helpful.

- Writing should have a purpose that makes it meaningful. Using writing primarily as an exercise to promote literacy skills can be uninteresting and make writing seem a chore to students. Writing becomes meaningful when the writer has an audience and a story to tell or a message to convey. The teacher can implement this principle more readily in the upper elementary grades than in the first two grades, as young children may not have a clear understanding of the message and its meaning. Examples of meaningful writing are writing a letter or sending a greeting to a friend, to parents, or to classmates. The computer provides a good opportunity for such writing; it also makes revision easy.

- After deciding on the audience and the topic, students should spend a considerable amount of time planning what they are going to write about. The importance of planning before writing cannot be overemphasized. Planning would include answers to self-generated questions, such as "What am I going to write about?" "What is interesting about the topic I have chosen?" "What is my introduction going to be?" "What is the body of the story going to be?" "Is there a hero in the story?" "Is there a villain in the story?" "What action took place; who did what to whom?" "Is there a conflict in the story?" "Is there a resolution to the conflict?" and "What is the end going to be?" This prewriting activity enables students to form a mental representation of the story they are going to write.

  Once the students have spent time on planning, they can develop an outline showing the details of their plan for writing. The outline can be interspersed with as many *wh-* and other self-generated questions as possible. When students begin writing, they should be guided by the outline as they fill in the answers to their questions. In the early elementary grades, students can start with writing down the most important question. After thinking about answering this question, they can add other questions to the main question and think about answering them.

- Students focus only on the theme of the story and follow the plan already laid out. At this stage, they do not focus on grammar or spelling.

- Next, students go through their writing and fix grammatical errors; they may even recast the sentences to reflect better syntactical structures. At this phase of writing, students can use grammar templates, which show the elements of syntactically acceptable sentences. At the basic level, a syntactically acceptable simple sentence has a subject, a verb, and an object (SVO), in that order. In the early elementary grades, students can examine each of their sentences to see if they conform to this template. The teacher can create a template with subject, verb, and object, display it to the class, and ask the students to check each of their sentences for the presence of a subject, verb, and object. Students can also be taught to ensure that the suffixes of the nouns and verbs agree with each other. Students in the higher grades can be expected to use more complex templates, which have, in addition to SVO, adjectives, prepositions, conjunctions, and pronouns. Table 8.5 shows an example of such a template.

Table 8.5. Model of a basic syntax template

Part of speech	Definition and examples
Noun	Names a person, place, or thing *(John, New York, car)*
Pronoun	Replaces a noun *(he, we, it, which, none, you)*
Adjective	Describes a noun *(red, big, many)*
Article	Points to a noun *(a, an, the)*
Preposition	Links nouns, pronouns, and phrases; usually indicates temporal, spatial, and other relationships *(on, of, for, beside, during, without, along, where, when)*
Adverb	Modifies a verb and tells how, when, and where *(quickly, boldly, slowly)*
Conjunction	Joins words, phrases, or clauses *(and, but, if, since, not only, but, also, neither, nor)*

From Carreker, S. (2006). The parts of speech: Foundation of writing. *Perspectives, 32*(2), 8–12; adapted by permission.

Table 8.6. Selected items from the Writing Process Checklist

I identified who would read my paper.
I started planning my paper before I started writing it.
I tried to remember everything I already knew about the topic before I started to write.
I thought about the reader as I wrote.
I continued to plan as I wrote.
I revised my paper as I wrote.
I revised the first draft of my paper.
I checked to make sure that the reader would understand everything I had to say.
I made my paper better by adding, dropping, changing, and rearranging parts of my paper.
I corrected spelling, capitalization, and punctuation errors.

From Graham, S., & Harris, K.R. (2005). *Writing better: Effective strategies for teaching students with learning difficulties* (p. 143). Baltimore: Paul H. Brookes Publishing Co.; adapted by permission.

- As a final step, students go over their work to see if it conforms to the generally accepted story grammar format. At this stage, they may replace words, clauses, and phrases, and they may even add or delete sentences. Revision, which puts the writer in the place the reader, is an important aspect of good writing.

Graham and Harris (2005) have provided a checklist for writers to use as guidance for writing. Selected checklist items are shown in Table 8.6.

Assignments for the Student Teacher

1. Interview teachers of third and fifth grades (or second and fourth grades). Find out the information below and write out your answers.
   —What techniques do the teachers use to teach vocabulary to students? Does the vocabulary instruction vary according to the grade level?
   —Do the teachers follow, formally or informally, the methods of vocabulary instruction described in this chapter?
   —What kind of games and activities do these teachers use to teach vocabulary?
   —What instructional procedures do the teachers use for improving students' comprehension skills? Does their instruction vary according to grade level?
   —Do the teachers follow, formally or informally, the comprehension strategy instruction described in this chapter?
   —What do these teachers think are the biggest impediments to children's reading comprehension?
   —Do the second- and third-grade teachers have word walls in their classroom? If so, what criteria do they use for adding words to the wall?
   —Do the fourth- and fifth-grade teachers have word walls in their classroom? If they do, is the word wall used differently in grades 2 and 3 than in grades 4 and 5? If the teachers in the upper grades do not have word walls in their classrooms, what explanation do they have for this?
   —How do the teachers make use of the word wall to improve children's vocabulary knowledge?
2. Interview a few children from various grades. Select about 10 grade-level words from any word list. Ask the children what the words mean.

Reading Assignment

Read one of the following articles, discuss it, and write a one-page summary. These articles can be obtained at your college library or downloaded by accessing the library's electronic holdings.

Duke, N.K., Purcell-Gates, V., Hall, L.A., & Tower, C. (2006). Authentic literacy activities for developing comprehension and writing. *The Reading Teacher, 60*(4), 344–355.

Richek, M. (2005). Words are wonderful: Interactive, time-efficient strategies to teaching meaning vocabulary. *The Reading Teacher, 58*(5), 414–423.

CHAPTER 9

Reading Disability and Attention-Deficit/ Hyperactivity Disorder

Summary

Nearly 80% of the children in general education classrooms learn to read without much difficulty. The remaining 20% encounter difficulties in learning to read and spell. It is not readily apparent why some children have difficulty learning to read; therefore, this is sometimes described as unexpected reading failure. Other terms used include *learning disability (LD), reading disability, specific reading disability,* and *dyslexia.* (This chapter uses *reading disability* and *LD* interchangeably to refer to the condition.) Survey studies of reading performance report that 5%–10% of U.S. school-age children have such difficulties.

This chapter starts with a brief historical account of the study of reading disability and explains why, in the early years of its discovery, physicians were interested in studying this condition. Definitions, the diagnostic process, and both traditional and alternative models of reading disability are discussed.

A second major disability that can affect reading is **attention-deficit/hyperactivity disorder (ADHD).** Reading disability and ADHD are hard to define and diagnose with precision and therefore difficult to distinguish. Yet because the two call for different treatment approaches, this chapter deals with differential diagnosis and how best to teach reading to these children.

Main ideas presented in this chapter

1. Historically, physicians explained reading disability in neurological terms and educators explained reading disability in educational and psychological terms.

2. Reading disability has been called *unexpected reading failure, learning disability (LD), specific reading disability,* and *dyslexia.* The terms often are used interchangeably and have no firm definitions yet can be explained by considering decoding as the problem.

3. Decoding difficulties reflect an inability to effortlessly associate sounds (phonemes) with symbols (graphemes). Decoding is a skill that is distinct from general intelligence.

4. Training in phonemic awareness and in the use of comprehension strategies can improve the word recognition skills of beginning readers. Identifying and focusing instruction on the weak component in reading, as done in the Component Model of Reading, is a promising way to teach struggling readers.

5. The **discrepancy model** for diagnosing LD has many drawbacks. This led to the development of alternatives such as **response to intervention (RTI)** and the Component Model.

6. Inconsistent attention can negatively affect reading performance. Attention problems can be a sign of ADHD. When impulsive behavior accompanies attention problems a diagnosis of ADHD, predominantly inattentive type (ADHD-I) may be made. It is difficult to identify when problems are caused by reading disability and when they are caused by ADHD-I.

Reading Disability: Medical Focus

A survey of educational journals published between 1890 and 1895 reveals that the reading difficulties experienced by some children were not perceived as a major problem by educators of that time. The few reading-related articles found in educational journals such as *Journal of Education* (New England), *Ohio Educational Monthly*, and *Indiana School Journal* were concerned primarily with issues such as whether it was more effective to use whole sentences or single words as the basic unit of reading instruction. The handful of research articles that appeared about this time were concerned primarily with topics such as eye movements and the rate of reading. Even when it was recognized that some children were slow in learning to read, this was attributed to extrinsic factors, such as inadequate teaching, inadequate teaching materials, and the limited amount of time devoted to reading in the classroom. The only reference to any form of reading disability appeared as a small newsbrief in the 1887 issue of *American Journal of Psychology* concerning Berlin's description of the loss of reading ability in an adult neurological patient. This lack of pedagogical interest in reading disability is understandable. At the time, reading instruction was aimed at helping children learn to read the Bible and the history of the United States; it was not considered essential for one's livelihood.

The Rise of Interest in Reading Disability

A quarter of a century later, however, the situation slowly began to change. According to Harris and Sipay (1985), the first report in the United States of an attempt to diagnose and treat individual reading problems was published in 1916 by Uhl. This was followed by a number of articles and books published by educators and psychologists about reading-related difficulties experienced by children. In 1917, Bronner described several cases of reading disabilities that, interestingly, resembled the two kinds of struggling readers described in the Component Model of Reading in Chapter 1: those with word recognition difficulties and those with comprehension difficulties. In 1922, three monographs addressing the issue of reading difficulties from an educational perspective were published (Gates, 1922; C.T. Gray, 1922; W.S. Gray, 1922).

Interestingly, Gates used the term *disability* in his monograph titled "The Psychology of Reading and Spelling with Special Reference to Disability." Before this period, several reports of reading failure caused by neurological impairment in literate adults had been published in medical journals; some educators, undoubtedly influenced by such publications, tended to describe developmental reading difficulties along those lines by using such terms as *congenital word blindness* and *developmental alexia* (e.g., Dearborn, 1925; Fernald & Keller, 1921; Schmitt, 1918).

Although it might be too simplistic to consider a single event as providing the impetus for this emergence of interest in reading disability, the use of such terms by some educators suggests that articles written earlier by British physicians, such as Morgan (1896) and Hinshelwood (1895, 1917), might have influenced the thinking of educators. It has been suggested by Pelosi (1977) that the conceptualization of reading disability as a condition worthy of educational investigation could be traced to the publication of reading disability in a young boy under the title *A Case of Congenital Word-Blindness* (Morgan, 1896). At this point, it is worthwhile to explore the origin of the phrase *word blindness* and the connection between reading failure in literate adults and the failure to learn to read in children.

During the latter part of the 19th century, reports of isolated instances of sudden but limited loss of reading ability as a result of neurological impairment in literate adults began to appear in medical journals. The most complete account of such loss, along with postmortem findings, was provided in 1891 and 1892 by M. Dejerine, a French neurologist (as cited in Geschwind, 1974). These reports aroused a great deal of interest because the issue of localization of functions in the brain was a much debated issue at that time, and Dejerine's findings appeared to indicate that the ability to read was localized to a particular region of the brain. Dejerine's reports reveal that the two patients he studied were good readers before they had had a stroke; afterward, they were unable to read even single words. The patients had no difficulty in understanding spoken language, and their cognitive ability remained unaffected; their difficulty was limited solely to reading. From these cases, Dejerine concluded that both the visual cortex and the angular cortex of the brain played an important role in the act of reading.

In 1895, Hinshelwood, an ophthalmologist from Glasgow, reported the case of a 58-year-old teacher who suddenly lost his ability to read written material. Hinshelwood called this condition "word blindness." According to Shaywitz (2003), the term *Wortblindheit* was first introduced in 1877 by Adolf Kussmaul, a German physician; the term *dyslexia* was used by Rudolf Berlin in 1887 to describe partial reading failure in adults. Hinshelwood noted that the clinical picture presented by his patient was very similar to the one described by Dejerine. Even though Hinshelwood did not provide an anatomical explanation for the reading failure, he made a very important observation regarding the effect of training on the patient's reading skill. Nearly 7 months after the initial diagnosis, Hinshelwood advised the patient to relearn to read using a child's primer and to practice reading daily. After 6 months of such training, the patient regained some of his reading skill, although his reading was slow and laborious. His spelling skill, however, did not show a corresponding improvement.

As noted in Chapter 1, during the following year (1896), Pringle Morgan, another English physician, published a report of a healthy 14-year-old boy in whom he observed a set of symptoms similar to the ones described by Dejerine and Hinshelwood in adults. Morgan called the boy's condition *congenital word blindness*, meaning that a weakness was present at the time of birth, to contrast it from *word blindness*, which was used to describe the loss of reading ability in adults. Morgan, who was familiar with Hinshelwood's paper, was quick to observe the similarities between the traumatic and congenital forms of reading failure. According to Morgan, the boy was bright and intelligent; he could read and write all the letters of the alphabet although he had great difficulty in reading even common monosyllabic words. His spelling was very poor; he substituted word suffixes ("winder" for *winding*) and transposed letters within words ("Precy" for *Percy*). The boy experienced no difficulty in reading multidigit numbers, such as 785852017, and correctly solved problems such as $(a + x) (a - x) = (a^2 - x^2)$. Because the boy's health history revealed no illness or injury, Morgan considered the etiology of the reading disability to be congenital and attributed it to defective development of the left angular gyrus of the brain.

By 1905, a sufficient number of cases of individuals with word blindness had accumulated to enable Thomas, another British physician, to provide a summary of the condition. His summary was based on nearly 100 cases of congenital word blindness that were recorded in case books at special schools in England. The publication foreshadowed many of the current descriptions of reading disability. Thomas noted that congenital word blindness was more frequent than had been suspected. In many instances, more than one member of a family was affected; it occurred three times more frequently in boys than in girls; and the condition was frequently associated with good visual memory, intelligence, and a typical ability for arithmetic calculations. Thomas's suggestions for treatment are similarly illuminating. He recommended that the child with disability be taught on a one-to-one basis and that initial teaching of the alphabet be accomplished through touch by encouraging the child to handle large letters carved in wood. Following this, the visual–sound association of letters could be developed. Thomas was optimistic about prognosis, citing the case of an excellent surgeon who "practically did no reading, but acquired all his knowledge by the ear at grinds and lectures" (p. 384). A few years later, Hinshelwood (1917) himself published a monograph in which he described several cases of congenital word blindness, thus making reading disability a medical syndrome.

In the United States, two reports of developmental reading disability were published in 1906, one by Clairborne in the *Journal of the American Medical Association* and another in the *American Journal of Medical Science* by Jackson. During the following decades, several more reports of reading disability were published by physicians. Following the lead provided by the British physicians, physicians in the United States explained children's reading difficulties in terms of a failure of certain parts of the brain, which mediated word recognition, to develop optimally.

Orton, Brain Dominance, and Specific Reading Disability

In 1930 Samuel Orton, a neuropsychiatrist from Iowa, offered a radically different neurological explanation of reading disability. Orton felt that the term *word blindness* was a poor choice of wording, as many children who experienced reading difficulties had excellent vision. In its place, Orton used terms such as *strephosymbolia* ("twisted symbols") and *specific reading disability.* Ironically, Orton's term strephosymbolia was later criticized by others because mirror writing and reversals in reading are not the salient symptoms of specific reading disability. (See Box 9.1.) Orton himself took pains to point out that "reversals are not an outstanding feature" of specific reading disability (1937, p. 93) and used the term *specific reading disability* more often than strephosymbolia.

Orton proposed his own hypothesis to replace that of the congenital defect of the angular gyrus. In his clinical experience, Orton had observed a high incidence of left-handedness among children who experienced reading difficulties and among members of their families. This observation, in combination with the many published clinical reports that the left hemisphere of the human cortex is responsible for many aspects of language processing, led Orton to propose that the functions of speech, reading, and writing are concentrated in the left hemisphere of the brain. Thus, reading is carried out by the left hemisphere, and failure to establish language dominance in the left hemisphere could result in word images being present in both hemispheres, one being the mirror image of the other. The presence of two images in the two hemispheres could lead to confusion in reading words and writing letters. Furthermore, a lack of dominance could also result in left-handedness or mixed-handedness. Today, many researchers do not hold to a literal version of Orton's hypothesis because there is no reason to believe that images of words and letters are present in the two hemispheres of the brain as mirror images. Studies have also failed to establish a clear relationship between reading disability and handedness. However, the explanation of using a right hemisphere strategy for processing written words as gestalts and not as a string of letters is still viable.

Many of Orton's insightful observations in connection with specific reading disability are worth mentioning. Orton (1937) emphasized the purity of the symptoms of the reading deficit. He noted that many children show no deficit other than reading, spelling, and written language and that the most searching examinations revealed no deviations in brain functions. In this connection, he also pointed out that the auditory development of these children was usually quite typical, as was their ability to understand spoken words and to acquire speech. Furthermore, he

---

Box 9.1.   Letter reversals: Cause for concern?

Many parents, and some teachers, believe that a child who reverses letters in writing has specific reading disability, or dyslexia. Clinical observations such as the one by Orton, as well as those from recent research, show that letter reversal in writing is not a reliable symptom of reading disability. Letter reversal is seen in many children of kindergarten age. Some children in the first and second grades also reverse letters even though they are good readers. Conversely, some children who are poor readers do not reverse or transpose letters in their writing. Letter reversals can be explained as a tendency to view words as pictures, not as a string of letters; pictures and photographs can be recognized regardless of their left–right orientation. Letter reversal is best viewed as a developmental phenomenon rather than as a sign of disability.

observed that the spoken language could be typical or even superior to other children's. These children were no less bright than typical readers, and in fact some ranked high in intelligence. Orton emphasized the distinction between children with specific reading disability and children with an overall intellectual impairment, limiting the term specific reading disability to the former. He also noted that there are degrees of severity of the impairment. Children with milder cases gradually learn to read, but as they progress in school, both the volume and the demands of reading surpass their ability, and their slow rate of reading impedes academic progress. Orton also believed that a hereditary factor was involved in specific reading disability and noted that boys were affected 3.5 times more often than girls.

A considerable portion of Orton's 1937 book was devoted to the treatment of specific reading disability. He did not offer a blanket prescription but recommended capitalizing on readers' auditory competence by teaching them the phonetic equivalents of printed letters and combining this with the kinesthetic approach. In general, he favored a phonetic approach and stressed training in word attack, blending, and written spelling skills. He noted that "because the great majority of the children whom we studied had already been unsuccessfully exposed to the sight or flash-card method of teaching reading, . . . we came to feel not only that repeated flash exposure of the whole word was not effective, but that it might in certain children even increase the tendency to confusion and failures of recognition" (p. 158).

The history of reading disability prior to the 1920s is notable for two features. First, the pioneers who studied reading disability, being physicians, tended to explain it in neurological and biological terms. Second, many of these physicians were also interested in developing and trying out remedial methods. During these early years, some educators also used the terms used by physicians, such as special disability and word blindness (e.g., Dearborn, 1925; Lord, 1925). Eventually these terms fell into disuse, and educators preferred to explain reading disability in terms of educational, psychological, sociological, and linguistic concepts. Often, they used descriptive language rather than labels. For instance, Fernald and Keller (1921) reported four cases of students of "normal mentality who have failed to learn to read after three or more years in the public schools" (p. 357). Gates (1929), after studying more than 400 children who were poor readers, concluded that he had "not yet encountered a case of disability which seemed to be best described as word-blindness" (p. 272). Instead, he used terms such as *deficiency in word analysis* and *deficiency in phonetic analysis* to describe this condition. A closer look at the children Gates described, however, indicates that many could be described as having congenital word blindness or specific reading disability.

Eventually, reading difficulties came to be called *dyslexia*. However, attempts to define dyslexia have not resulted in a single definition that is acceptable to all. Orton's influence on the study of specific reading disability is exemplified by the establishment of the Orton Dyslexia Society (now known as the International Dyslexia Association), which holds international and regional meetings and provides a forum for physicians, psychologists, and educators to meet and share their knowledge in the field of reading research and practice.

Learning Disability: Educational Focus

Following the publications by educators such as Dearborn (1925), Fernald and Keller (1921), Gates (1922), and Monroe (1932) and physicians such as Morgan

(1896) and Orton (1937), the fact that some children with average or above-average IQ scores found learning to read extremely difficult came to be nationally recognized. In April 1963, at the conference Explorations into the Problems of the Perceptually Handicapped Child, Samuel Kirk from the University of Illinois introduced the term *learning disabilities (LD)* to collectively refer to reading disability and related difficulties. During the following year (1964), the Association for Children with Learning Disabilities, now known as the Learning Disability Association of America, was founded. Learning disabilities as an impairment gained official status with the passing of the Education for All Handicapped Children Act of 1975 (PL 94-142), which defined learning disability as a "disorder in one or more of the basic psychological processes involved in understanding or in using spoken or written language, which may manifest itself in an imperfect ability to listen, think, speak, write, spell or to do mathematical calculations." The federal definition further stated that learning disabilities included "such conditions as perceptual disabilities, brain injury, minimal brain dysfunction, dyslexia, and developmental aphasia" (p. 1).

According to this definition, learning disabilities do not include learning problems that are primarily the result of visual, hearing, or motor disabilities; intellectual disability (mental retardation); or environmental, cultural, or economic disadvantages. As can be seen, the definition is inclusive (perceptual disabilities, brain injury, and developmental aphasia) but also exclusionary in the sense that the definition hinges on what learning disabilities are not. The term *dyslexia* is also included in this definition. Furthermore, the term *learning disability* fits what had been historically described as specific reading disability.

Learning Disability and Dyslexia

Although the legal definition of LD includes impairment in a variety of areas, when children are referred for assessment and evaluation, invariably the diagnostic conclusion is based on their reading performance. As a result, nearly 80% of children identified as having LD have reading disability. Some children are said to have mathematical disability; however, this condition has not been fully researched. Furthermore, when children in the upper grades demonstrate difficulty with math story problems, the level of reading involved makes it difficult to distinguish whether children have trouble solving the problems because of math LD or because of reading disability. For instructional purposes, LD, specific reading disability, and dyslexia can be viewed as practically the same educational problem. In reading research literature, the terms *specific reading disability* and *dyslexia* are often used interchangeably. It is, therefore, worthwhile to examine whether dyslexia can be defined in more precise terms than LD. As you read the definitions of dyslexia, see if you can differentiate dyslexia from LD.

The following definition of dyslexia has been adopted by the International Dyslexia Association in 2002 and used by the National Institute of Child Health and Human Development:

> Dyslexia is a specific learning disability that is neurological in origin. It is characterized by difficulties with accurate and/or fluent word recognition and by poor spelling and decoding abilities. These difficulties typically result from a deficit in the phonological component of language that is often unexpected in relation to other cognitive abilities and the provision of effective classroom instruction. Secondary

consequences may include problems in reading comprehension and reduced reading experience that can impede growth of vocabulary and background knowledge.

Studies show that individuals with dyslexia process information in a different area of the brain than do non-dyslexics.

Many people who are dyslexic are of average to above average intelligence.

The British Dyslexia Association defines dyslexia in the following way:

> The word 'dyslexia' comes from the Greek and means 'difficulty with words.'
>
> Definition: Dyslexia is a specific learning difficulty which mainly affects the development of literacy and language related skills.
>
> It is likely to be present at birth and to be lifelong in its effects.
>
> It is characterized by difficulties with phonological processing, rapid naming, working memory, processing speed, and the automatic development of skills that may not match up to an individual's other cognitive abilities.
>
> It tends to be resistant to conventional teaching methods, but its effects can be mitigated by appropriately specific intervention, including the application of information technology and supportive counselling.

The following definition of dyslexia is among those collected by the Singapore Dyslexia Association:

> Dyslexia is a specific difficultly in reading, writing, and spelling, it is not caused by a lack of intelligence or a lack of opportunity to learn. It has been estimated that 3% to 5% of Singaporeans may be dyslexic. The difficulties caused by dyslexia can be overcome with specialist teaching and the use of compensatory strategies.

These definitions lead to two conclusions. One is that dyslexia (or reading disability) exists worldwide. Second, dyslexia, specific reading disability, and LD are not different from one another and cannot be defined or even described with any degree of precision. The vagueness of definitions makes it difficult to diagnose dyslexia (or LD) with any precision. Parents generally come to the conclusion that their child has dyslexia or LD when the child is not progressing well in the classroom. The possibility that the child's lack of progress in reading could be due to other reasons, such as poor motivation, overall low cognitive ability, or limited reading practice, is often overlooked by parents. As a result, terms such as LD and dyslexia are used as a pretext and have lost much of their usefulness. This vagueness in the use of reading disability-related terms can be traced back to 1921, when Fildes conducted a "psychological inquiry into the nature of the condition known as congenital word-blindness." He studied 26 children, 25 of whom had IQ scores that ranged from 55 to 88. From this sample, only one child with an IQ score of 111 could be considered a typical case of congenital word blindness by the Morgan-Hinshelwood standards. Fildes, nevertheless, concluded that "word blind individuals reveal special difficulties in dealing with material other than words" (p. 304). In addition to being fuzzy, the terms used to describe reading difficulties do not tell the classroom teacher what, exactly, is causing the student's difficulty, nor do they give the teacher any guidance for remedial instruction. The definitions and descriptions of learning disability, specific reading disability, and dyslexia include a variety of developmental deficiencies. As a result, they have come to be used casually by both laypersons and professionals.

Occasionally, the term *unexpected reading difficulty* is used for describing dyslexia. It is unexpected in the sense that children with dyslexia have average or above-average IQ scores and their spoken language is good to excellent, yet they

If dyslexia is caused by a deficiency in decoding skill, why spend time and energy in formulating a definition of dyslexia? Why not describe this condition as poor reading performance due to weak decoding skill and provide word recognition instruction? This will avoid controversies surrounding the definition of LD and dyslexia.

have difficulty learning to read. Although this term appears to be more operationally fitting than the other terms discussed so far, it also is not satisfactory, for the following reason. Decoding and spelling are dissociable from general intelligence. According to Spearman (1904), intelligence is made up of one general factor (the "g" factor) and many specific factors ("s" factors). When a person is described as being bright or smart, this description refers to the "g" factor. Decoding and spelling can best be understood as one of Spearman's "s" factors and comprehension as Spearman's "g" factor. Of course, poor decoding interferes with reading comprehension but not listening comprehension. When this explanation is taken into account, reading disability seen in bright children is *not* unexpected because they possess average or above-average levels of "g" factor of intelligence and are deficient only in some "s" factor(s).

This does not mean that reading disability is not a genuine academic problem. There is ample evidence showing that reading disability is distinct from reading difficulties caused by low cognitive ability and limited reading experience. This evidence comes not only from behavioral studies but also from neuroimaging studies. For instance, Shaywitz, Mody, and Shaywitz (2006), using fMRI procedures, found that the parieto-temporal region of the brain in children who could not integrate strings of letters and perceive them as words was not activated well by printed words. Fortunately, these brain imaging studies also show that the neural systems for reading are malleable and respond to effective reading instruction. In contrast, neuroimaging shows a poorly activated left frontal gyrus in Broca's area of the brain in poor readers with lower cognitive ability and a disadvantaged background. Now there is overall consensus that LD or dyslexia is caused by deficiencies in the phonological component of language, which leads to weak decoding skills (Adams, 1990; Ball & Blachman, 1988; Ehri, 1998).

Diagnosis of Learning Disability and Dyslexia

The official recognition that LD is a form of disability made the privileges and accommodations to which individuals with disabilities are entitled accessible to individuals with reading problems. It became necessary, therefore, to develop an objective means of identifying and diagnosing LD, particularly in children in the school system.

The Discrepancy Model

Because LD was defined as having average or above-average intelligence but lower reading performance, it appeared that a logical means of diagnosing it would be to assess the IQ of children thought to have LD and compare their reading achievement scores with their IQ scores. If an individual's IQ score was in the average or above-average range but reading achievement was noticeably lower, the individual was diagnosed as having LD. The diagnostic criterion is the discrepancy between the IQ score and the reading score. This way of identifying LD has therefore come to be referred to as the discrepancy model-based diagnosis. In many schools, children identified as having LD on the basis of the discrepancy formula are placed in resource rooms to receive special instruction, although there is a trend toward teaching children with LD in the general education classroom. But to what extent has this diagnostic procedure been helpful?

The absence of clear descriptions of reading-related developmental disorders can, perhaps, be overlooked if somehow these descriptions have produced positive educational outcomes. Unfortunately, they have not (Aaron, 1997). The disappointing outcome of the discrepancy model-based educational policy naturally impelled researchers to examine the potential reasons for its failure (e.g., Lyon et al., 2001). Two major classes of reasons have been identified. One includes the validity of certain assumptions on which the discrepancy model is based, and the other involves the nature and quality of resource room instruction.

One of the assumptions underlying the foundation of the discrepancy formula is that IQ scores and reading achievement scores are intimately related to each other; IQ scores can therefore be used for predicting the reading achievement score. For this expectation to be valid, the correlation between IQ scores and reading scores would need to be high. However, the correlation coefficient between IQ scores and reading achievement scores is about 0.5, indicating that IQ scores can explain only about 25% of the variance seen in the reading scores of all students (Stanovich, Cunningham, & Feeman, 1984). It can be concluded, therefore, that IQ score is not a reliable predictor of reading achievement score. A measure of listening comprehension, for instance, is a much better predictor; the correlation between these two variables ranges from 0.65 to 0.8.

Another assumption is that there is a cause-and-effect relationship between IQ score and reading achievement. In other words, the relationship is unidirectional and IQ score is causally related to reading achievement. However, it is known that the relationship between these two variables is reciprocal rather than unidirectional. That is, reading experience can also affect IQ score, because many IQ tests use language-related measures such as vocabulary and general information. Children who are avid readers are likely to obtain higher scores on these subtests (Bishop & Butterworth, 1980).

An additional assumption is that there are qualitative differences between children with LD and poor readers whose scores do not evidence the discrepancy stipulated by the school system. Studies investigating this problem have failed to substantiate this assumption, noting that all poor readers, regardless of the labels attached to them, have deficits in the phonological area and do not differ from each other in cognitive profile (Algozzine, 1985; Kavale & Forness, 1994; Ysseldyke, Algozzine, Shinn, & McGue, 1982). Yet another problem with the discrepancy model is the lack of agreement about the extent of the discrepancy between IQ scores and reading achievement scores that marks LD. States and school districts differ on the degree of discrepancy that is indicative of LD.

As noted earlier, the most formidable problem with the discrepancy formula and the concept of LD is that children who are identified as having LD and receive instruction in resource rooms fail to show improvement in reading skills (Bentum & Aaron, 2003; Carlson, 1997; Fuchs & Fuchs, 1995; Haynes & Jenkins, 1986; Moody, Vaughn, Hughes, & Fischer, 1998; Wleklinski, 1993). In fact, some of these studies showed that children who received instruction in resource rooms tended to decline in their word attack and spelling scores over a long period of time.

There could be several reasons for the lack of success of resource room instruction. Among these are the high pupil–teacher ratio in resource rooms and the mixing of children with reading difficulties with children who have behavioral and emotional problems. One other reason for the ineffectiveness of instruction in resource rooms may be that remedial instruction is not initiated until the child fails, which may be too late for instruction to be effective. The research reports mentioned earlier, however, indicated that a major reason for the poor outcome of LD instruction is the unsystematic way children are taught in many resource rooms. More specifically, there is a lack of uniformity of instructional methods for teaching children with LD, because the discrepancy model does not provide LD teachers with guidelines for instruction. In a review study, Vaughn, Levy, Coleman, and Bos (2002) synthesized studies on students with LD and reported that the quality of reading instruction was poor, with excessive time allocated to seatwork and worksheets but limited time given to reading itself. After observing instruction in resource rooms, Haynes and Jenkins (1986) and Moody et al. (1998) noted that it was not based on a skills approach but was driven by the whole language philosophy and relied mainly on group work, disregarding individual needs.

Reading Research Beyond the Framework of the Discrepancy Model

In light of the shortcomings of the discrepancy model of LD, researchers have attempted to study instructional methods that are not dependent on LD diagnostic procedures and are outside the parameters of the discrepancy model. These studies fall into two broad categories: those focused on phonemic awareness and those targeting comprehension skills.

Attempts to Improve Reading Skills Through Phonemic Awareness Training

A large body of research findings has documented the effectiveness of phonological awareness training in promoting reading skills in beginning readers (e.g., Ball & Blachman, 1988, 1991; Bradley & Bryant, 1985; Byrne & Barnsley, 1995; Lovett, Ransby, & Barron, 1988; Olson, Wise, Ring, & Johnson, 1997; Torgesen, Wagner, & Rashotte, 1997). In one of the earlier studies, Bradley and Bryant (1985) examined the effectiveness of phonemic awareness instruction with 65 British 6-year-olds. The children were divided into two experimental and two control groups. Children in one of the experimental groups received training in sound categorization, which was carried out by teaching alliteration and rhyming skills first and then creating an awareness of phonemes with the help of pictures (e.g., Question: In what way do the names of these pictures sound alike: *cat, car, cup?* Answer: The beginning sounds of these words are the same). Children in the second experimental group received this training plus practice in constructing words with plastic letters. Children in the two control groups received either concept categorization training or no training. The concept categorization training involved teaching concepts such as words like *bat, cat* and *rat* all refer to animals. The training was provided one session per week for a period of 2 years. At the end of the training period, children who received phonological training obtained higher scores on standardized tests of reading and spelling than children in the control groups. Children in the second experimental group, who received letter–sound training, did better than those in the first experimental group, who received only sound categorization training. These children were tested again, and the advantages persisted over a period of 5 years.

In a study of the effectiveness of phonemic awareness, Ball and Blachman (1991) randomly assigned 90 kindergarten children at risk for reading failure to one of three conditions: 1) phonemic awareness training in segmenting words into phonemes, along with training in sound–letter association, 2) training in sound–letter association only, or 3) no special instruction. After 7 weeks of training, the phonemic awareness group performed significantly better on measures of reading and spelling than either of the other groups.

Phonemic awareness training studies reporting a positive impact on children's reading achievement are too numerous to describe here. Some of the studies conducted prior to 1996 were summarized by Aaron (1997). A review of studies conducted since then has reached the conclusion that the greatest impact on children's reading achievement is seen when phonemic awareness training is combined with letter–sound knowledge (Hammill, 2004). It may be impossible to study the effect of phonemic awareness training on reading in isolation because almost all children are exposed to printed language during their preschool years.

Attempts to Improve Reading Skills Through Comprehension Training

A number of studies of students with adequate decoding skills but poor comprehension have demonstrated that these students' reading comprehension skills can be improved. Methods used explicitly to teach comprehension skills are known by labels such as transactional strategy instruction (Pressley et al., 1992), self-regulated strategy development (Graham & Harris, 1993), reciprocal teaching (Palincsar & Brown, 1984), and Component Model–based reading instruction (Aaron et al., in press). All of these approaches attempt to improve comprehension by teaching readers to use selected strategies, to monitor their use of these strategies, and to take corrective action when comprehension fails. Many of these strategies were described in Chapter 8.

Some of these studies provided training in one or two comprehension strategies, such as activating schema, developing story maps, predicting upcoming events in the text, visualizing, or summarizing, and reported positive outcomes. Other studies, which used a combination of these strategies, also found improvement in reading comprehension. For instance, Dermody and Speaker (1995) investigated the effects of metacognitive strategy instruction and reciprocal teaching on 41 fourth graders with and without reading problems. On the basis of their performance on the Stanford Diagnostic Reading Test (Karlsen & Gardner, 1995), the students were classified into the following three categories: those with average decoding and comprehension skills, those with above-average decoding but below-average comprehension, and those who were below average in both decoding and comprehension. The students were then trained in comprehension strategies for 9 weeks. The results of the training procedure indicated that the group with above-average decoding but below-average comprehension scores had the highest gain on the reading comprehension subtest of the Stanford Diagnostic Reading Test.

Rosenshine, Meister, and Chapman (1996) performed a meta-analysis of studies that used reciprocal teaching and found effect sizes of .30 when standardized comprehension tests were used and .86 when experimenter-developed tests were used. Swanson, Carson, and Saches-Lee (1996) reviewed 78 intervention studies that met stringent selection criteria. Of these 78 studies, 30 focused on reading comprehension. Children involved in these studies were all poor readers. After reviewing these studies, the authors concluded that cognitive instructional procedures that focused on comprehension strategies produced the highest effect size (1.07), followed by direct instruction (0.91). The review also found that word recognition and spelling skills did not improve when instruction focused on cognitive instruction. (See Aaron, 1997, for a summary version of several other cognitive strategy instruction studies.)

Instructional Methods for Learning Disability

The previously mentioned limitations of LD instruction have led researchers and educators to look for better methods of teaching students who experience difficulty in learning to read and write. RTI is one such approach (Bradley, Danielson, & Doolittle, 2005; Fuchs, Fuchs, & Speece, 2002; Fuchs, Mock, Morgan, & Young, 2003; Haager, Klingner, & Vaughn, 2007). Another is the Component Model of Reading (Aaron et al., in press).

Response to Intervention Approach: The New Kid on the Block

RTI is embedded in a multitiered model, with assessment, intervention, and progress monitoring implemented at these levels (Kovaleski, 2004). These tiers are also referred to as phases. During the initial phase, a determination is made of whether effective instruction is in place in the classroom. If a large number of students fail to perform well on reading tasks, the classroom reading instruction receives a thorough examination, and if necessary, instructional changes are implemented. If only a handful of students in the class experience reading difficulties, these children become the object of further attention and instruction. During the next phase, intense instruction is provided to students at risk who have not made progress, and its effect is measured. Individualized instruction is then provided for those students whose progress is still below average. During the final phase, the students who continue to make no progress are further tested or their previous history reviewed. Based on the outcome of this evaluation, students may be referred for special education services.

Compared with existing LD services, RTI has some beneficial features. One is the early identification of literacy problems; children need not wait until they fall behind to receive services. Early identification can occur in kindergarten or first grade, perhaps by evaluating children's letter knowledge and level of phonemic awareness. Another attractive feature is the use of short reading probes and monitoring of students' progress on a continual basis. Assessment modeled after curriculum-based measures can be used for this purpose. Yet another feature built into RTI is frequent informal evaluation of the effectiveness of classroom instruction. If, during the first phase, many children in the classroom demonstrate typical progress in reading and only a few lag behind, ineffective instruction can be ruled out as a possible source of poor reading performance of some children. However, if there are many children in the classroom who do not make progress in reading, the quality of instruction may be scrutinized. It should be noted, however, that many variables, such as family background and family income, also contribute to reading achievement and that ineffective teaching may not be the only source of children's reading difficulties.

As an alternative to the discrepancy model, RTI looks promising and is being tried out in many school systems. Some unanswered questions, however, remain. In its present form, RTI appears to be primarily an alternate process for the identification of learning disabilities. An examination of several published reports indicates that the focus of RTI is still identification of LD and not the method of instruction designed for children on a case-by-case basis. According to Fletcher, Coulter, Reschly, and Vaughn (2004),

> Recent consensus reports concur in suggesting major changes in the federal regulatory approach to the *identification of learning disabilities* (LD). These reports recommend abandoning the IQ-discrepancy model and the use of IQ tests for identification, and also recommend incorporation of response to instruction (RTI) as one of the *identification* criteria. (p. 305)

Although providing effective instruction is often mentioned in the context of RTI, such instructional procedures are seldom specified. Another question that may defy a satisfactory answer is how RTI differs from what teachers typically do with struggling readers in the general education classroom. Again, is it not, in the first place, because the child was not responding to instruction that the classroom teacher referred the student for evaluation by the school psychologist? According to Gerber (2005), the RTI policy is simply urging the educational system to try harder and to invest more effort in students who are difficult to teach and manage. According to Kavale (2005), RTI simply reoperationalizes LD instead of redefining it. Furthermore, there are several variants or models of RTI (Fuchs & Fuchs, 2006), which indicates that a consensus about the method of implementation of RTI has not yet emerged. Several other issues remain unresolved. For example, what constitutes response and no response to intervention; is it the same for a poor reader who starts at a higher level of reading and a poor reader who starts at a lower level of reading? Should a child who has improved by only 0.25 standard score in one semester be considered a responder or a nonresponder? Should children at risk be taught in a one-to-one setting, in groups of three to five, or in larger groups of 10 or more? How much time should be spent every day on instruction?

In the RTI model, children who fail to respond even to the most intensive instruction will be moved into special education classes. In this respect, RTI is similar to the Reading Recovery Program (RR; see Chapter 7), which is criticized for relegating children who do not make sufficient progress to special education (Grossen, Coulter, & Ruggles, 1996). This policy of dropping nonresponders, proposed by RTI and practiced by RR, may not fulfill the intent of the No Child Left Behind Act of 2001.

The Component Model of Reading

Several studies show that all poor readers are *not* alike and that reading difficulties have different causes and vary in nature (Catts, Hogan, & Fey, 2003; Swanson, Howard, & Saez, 2006). From a cognitive perspective, this means that the cause of reading difficulty may be poor decoding skill, poor comprehension skill, or limited vocabulary knowledge. Thus, a single instructional strategy cannot be used successfully with all poor readers. Instructional methods must be tailored to deal with the source of the reading difficulty.

As discussed in Chapter 1, the assessment procedures and instructional methods based on the Component Model of Reading fulfill the two requirements that the process to be assessed is elementary in nature and independent of other processes. Component Model–based remedial instruction applies to all children, regardless of their ability and achievement. It does not categorize weak readers into LD and non-LD categories. The model identifies the source of a student's reading problem and designs instructional methods that address the cause of the reading difficulty without regard to the child's IQ. It encompasses the idea that all poor readers can become better readers regardless of the degree of progress they make. The Component Model–based instruction was described in Chapter 1, and the successful outcome of one study is described by Aaron et al. (in press). The Component Model–based instruction is founded on three philosophies. First, poor readers are not classified into categories such as LD and non-LD, nor are labels attached to children. Second, the weak component that leads to reading difficulties is identified (whether decoding, word recognition, comprehension, or vocabulary) and targeted by instruction. Third, it is assumed that all children can make progress in reading, albeit to varying degrees. All poor readers may not become accomplished readers, but all poor readers can become better readers.

The Component Model–based study by Aaron et al. (in press) described in Chapter 8 provided remedial reading instruction for students in grades 2 through 5 who experienced difficulty in learning to read. Students were tested to find the source of their reading difficulties, whether it was in word recognition or comprehension. The students who had comprehension difficulties received comprehension strategy instruction; students who had word recognition difficulties received instruction in phonemic awareness and letter–sound association designed to improve decoding skills. Posttests showed that students who received comprehension strategy instruction scored significantly higher on tests of reading comprehension than a comparison group of children from LD resource rooms where such differentiated instruction was not provided. Similarly, children who received instruction in word recognition had significantly higher word-attack scores than a comparison group of children identified as having LD (see Figure 9.1).

Students in the study who showed improvement in word recognition skills also showed improvement in reading comprehension. This is logical, because word recognition functions as a factor that enhances or limits comprehension, and improvement in word recognition skill naturally results in improvement in reading comprehension. However, improvement in comprehension did not result in an increase in word recognition skills. Similar to the conclusion drawn in the previous section on the outcome of phonemic awareness training, studies of comprehension strategy instruction show that children's reading comprehension can be improved through comprehension strategy training without resorting to labeling students.

When parents ask their child's teacher, "Does my child have LD?" or "Is my child dyslexic?" the teacher can respond, "Your child experiences difficulty in decoding and recognizing words" or "Your child has difficulty in comprehending written language" and "I will be working with your child to improve this particu-

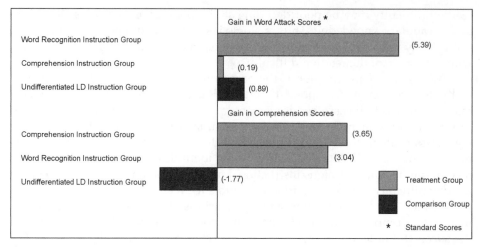

Figure 9.1. Gains in word attack and comprehension scores by treatment and comparison groups. (From Aaron, P.G., Joshi, R.M., Gooden, R.B., & Bentum, K. [in press]. The outcome of the Component Model-based reading remedial instruction: An alternative to the discrepancy model-based treatment of learning disabilities. *Journal of Learning Disabilities*; reprinted by permission.)

lar skill." The teacher should then design instruction that addresses the child's weakness. This is what makes the teacher a professional reading teacher. The Component Model of Reading empowers the teacher to accomplish these goals.

Inconsistent Attention as a Source of Reading Difficulties

At the beginning of this chapter, it was noted that the two major developmental disabilities experienced by school-age children are reading disabilities and ADHD. The prevalence rate of reading disability reportedly varies from 5% to 17.5% (Shaywitz, Fletcher, & Shaywitz, 1994), making it a high-incidence disorder. Investigations of ADHD report that nearly 3% to 5% of school-age children experience difficulty in maintaining sustained attention (American Psychiatric Association, 1994). Furthermore, ADHD can coexist as a comorbid condition with reading disability (Pisecco, Baker, Silva, & Brooke, 2001); estimates of comorbidity range from 10% to 45%. This means that 10%–45% of poor readers have a deficit in both areas. It is generally agreed that reading disability is a language-based disorder, whereas ADHD is not. More specifically, these two disorders are associated with different cognitive processes: Reading disability is caused by weakness in phonological processing and comprehension strategy use, and ADHD is associated with deficits in executive functioning and impulse control (Hall, Halpern, Schwartz, & Newcorn, 1997; Pennington, Groisser, & Welsh, 1993). There is good reason to believe that these two impairments are distinct from each other because they respond to different forms of treatment—reading disability to phonemic awareness and comprehension strategy instruction, and ADHD to drug therapy or a combination of drug therapy and **cognitive behavior therapy.**

When a reader does not pay attention to what he reads, his comprehension will be compromised. Thus, in addition to poor word recognition and comprehension skills, inconsistent attention can also lead to poor performance in reading tasks and on reading tests. It was noted previously that an "imperfect ability to listen" was included as a symptom of reading disability in one of the definitions of

LD. Although it is true that lack of attention can result in poor reading performance, the converse situation—difficulty in recognizing words and comprehending text—could also make the reader's attention wander. This makes it difficult to pinpoint whether the source of poor reading performance is a deficiency in a reading component or inconsistent attention.

ADHD is thought to comprise two interrelated behavioral conditions, hyperactivity/impulsivity and inattention. Both conditions are present in a large number of children with ADHD, although some children manifest only the inattentive form of ADHD. Because it was not clear whether the inattentive group represented a subtype of ADHD or an entirely different disorder, the *Diagnostic and Statistical Manual of Mental Disorders, Fourth Edition* (*DSM-IV*; American Psychiatric Association, 1994) labeled this ADHD, predominantly inattentive type (ADHD-I). After reviewing the limited research relevant to this issue, Barkley (1997) noted that children with ADHD-I experience difficulty in selectively attending to relevant features of information, have difficulty in maintaining focused attention, are often inaccurate in information processing, and may also have memory retrieval problems.

Attention deficit, which dominates ADHD-I, does not mean there is a total absence of attention (Breggin, 1998). This is indicated by the fact that *DSM-IV* prefaced all nine symptoms of ADHD with the qualifier *often* or *frequently*. Furthermore, individuals with ADHD do attend to external and internal stimuli, although often in an inconsistent manner and not to what the teacher wants them to attend. Thus, the nature of the task is one of the variables that causes fluctuations in attention (Reason, 1999). Because of the difficulty in clearly defining ADHD and diagnosing it objectively, some researchers have questioned the validity of calling inconsistent attention a disorder (e.g., Breggin, 1998; Diller, 1998). It is true that even adults' attention wanders during reading a passage or listening to a lecture, depending on factors such as the nature of the material, the purpose of reading, and how tired they are. Even as you read this chapter, it is doubtful if you were able to attend to every sentence in a consistent manner. It is best to view lapses in attention in the classroom as inconsistent attention and to remove the impediments that make attention wander.

Distinguishing Learning Disability from Attention-Deficit/Hyperactivity Disorder

Both reading disability and ADHD-I manifest themselves in poor reading performance, albeit for entirely different reasons, which often leads to one being mistaken for the other. This is because children with reading disability have weak word recognition skills and, therefore, devote an excessive amount of attention to decoding the print. When they are required to read lengthy passages, they often lose their focus, become frustrated, and indulge in off-task behaviors. As a result, their behavior appears similar to children who have ADHD-I. For instance, research by Pennington et al. (1993) showed that reading disability can interfere with the reading process and cause inattention in some children. Children with ADHD-I, unable to maintain sustained attention, also indulge in off-task behavior. As a result, they process information in an inconsistent manner and thus perform poorly on reading tasks and tests, making it appear that they have reading disability. A study of a large sample of children from New Zealand by Fergusson and Horwood (1992) and DuPaul and Stoner (1994) provided additional support for the existence of a reciprocal relationship between attention and reading performance. It appears, therefore, that regardless of which disorder a student may have—ADHD-I or reading disability—the outcome is the same, namely, impaired reading performance.

Distinguishing reading disability from ADHD-I is not a useless undertaking, however, because as previously noted, the two conditions require different treatments. Yet, efforts to distinguish the two have not been greatly successful. In an effort to establish differential diagnostic procedures, researchers have relied on a variety of procedures and tests. Reading performance, of course, can be assessed by a variety of standardized tests of phonemic awareness and comprehension. However, optimal performance in these tests also requires attention. For instance, tests of phonemic awareness require students to listen and delete a phoneme in a series of words or manipulate phonemes in word lists. Many children find it difficult to keep test instructions in memory and maintain attention during this test. Similarly, tests of reading comprehension, particularly those in paragraph format, are attention demanding. Consequently, it is difficult to tell with certainty whether poor performance on tests is due to poor reading skill or inconsistent attention. Studies that have attempted to separate reading disability from ADHD by using tests of phonemic awareness are subject to this criticism (e.g., Felton & Wood, 1989; Pennington et al., 1993).

Diagnosing Deficits in Attention

Attention is usually evaluated by using three types of tools: **rating scales** and questionnaires, tests of fluctuation of attention, and tests of executive function.

Rating Scales

Rating scales, in general, use the nine criteria set up by *DSM-IV* and are used by psychologists, parents, and teachers to rate a student on these criteria. Examples of these criteria are behaviors such as *often fidgets with hands or feet or squirms in seat; is often on the go or often acts as if driven by a motor; often has trouble waiting one's turn;* and *often blurts out answers before the question has been finished.* If six or more of the nine symptoms have been present for at least 6 months, it leads to a diagnosis of ADHD-I.

The *DSM-IV*–based rating scale has many criticisms, one being that the process of establishing objective diagnostic standards for ADHD has itself been quite subjective (Diller, 1998). According to DuPaul and Stoner (1994), a limitation of the *DSM-IV* is that the reliability and validity of the various diagnostic criteria are not well established. For instance, Reid and Maag (1994), in a critique of behavior rating scales for identifying students with ADHD, asked "How many fidgets is pretty much?" Furthermore, rating is a subjective process.

Questionnaires

Questionnaires are usually completed by the teacher and parents of the child believed to have ADHD-I. Like rating scales, questionnaires carry an element of subjectivity (Reid & Maag, 1994). A study by Wolraich and Hannah (1996) found only a 52% agreement among teachers about which children had ADHD. In addition, there is also the possibility that the off-task behavior exhibited by children with reading disability can be mistaken for ADHD-I by teachers as well as parents. In spite of these limitations, questionnaires are consistently used by psychologists to evaluate children for ADHD-I. Some of the commonly used questionnaires are the Conners' Parent Rating Scale and Child Behavior Checklist, Third Edition (2004); the Attention Deficit Disorder Evaluation Scale by McCarney (2004); and the ADHD Rating Scale–IV (DuPaul, Power, Anastopoulos, & Reid, 1998).

Tests of Fluctuation of Attention

ADHD is also assessed by using continuous performance tests (CPT), which measure fluctuation of attention. One of the most frequently used CPT is the Conners' Continuous Performance Test II (Conners, 2000). In this test, letters of the alphabet are presented on a laptop computer one at a time for 250 milliseconds, and the student is asked to press the space bar for the letter X and no other letter. When the student fails to hit the bar when X appears on the screen, it is an error of omission; when the student hits the bar when a letter other than X appears, it is an error of commission. The speed with which the student responds is yet another measure used in this task. In one study, indices of variance (standard deviation) of both accuracy scores and reaction time were found to be a better measure of consistency of attention than errors of omission and commission (Aaron et al., 2002).

Test of Executive Function

The Stroop Color Word Test (Stroop, 1935), which assesses the reader's ability to direct attention, has also been used as a measure of attention. The Stroop test is, therefore, considered to be a measure of executive function of memory. A list of words is presented, printed in colors that do not match the names of the colors. For example, the word *red* is printed in green, and the word *green* is printed in blue. The student is first asked to read the words as quickly as he can, and the time is recorded. Following this, the student is asked to name the color in which the words are printed rather than the words themselves. This part of the test requires the student to suppress the tendency to read the words and instead to name the colors. The difference in the time it takes to name the words and to name the colors is taken as an index of the student's ability to control his impulse to read the word instead of the color. Studies show that in typical readers, reading has become automatized and overlearned to the point that they find it difficult to suppress the tendency to read words and to name the color in which the words are printed. Consequently, they take more time to name the colors than to name the words. In individuals with reading disability, word reading has not become automatized to the same extent; therefore, the difference between the time they take to name the colors and name the words is less than that seen in typical readers. Some studies have shown that individuals with ADHD-I have a tendency to perform more poorly on the Stroop test than individuals without ADHD-I (Bush et al., 1999; Willcut et al., 2001). Thus, students with a reading impairment show less color interference only when compared with students who have ADHD.

Additional Diagnostic Considerations

A logical way to distinguish reading disabilities from ADHD-I is to administer reading-related tasks that vary in the degree of attention they demand while holding the decoding level of the reading task constant. It is expected that individuals with ADHD-I will perform more poorly on reading-related tasks that place heavy demands on attention than on tasks that demand less attention. Such a difference may not be seen in the performance of children with a reading disability only. Listening is more attention demanding than reading; if a word is missed in a test of listening comprehension, the missed word cannot be retrieved. In contrast, if a student misses a word while she is reading because of a lapse in attention, she can go back and check the word. This suggests that on standardized tests, individuals with ADHD-I will perform more poorly on tests of listening comprehension than on tests of reading comprehension. Conversely, individuals with weak word-recognition skills will perform better on tests of listening comprehension than on reading comprehension. Scores obtained by students on standardized tests of reading and listening comprehension can, therefore, provide clues for distinguishing reading disability from ADHD-I. It is important to use the reading and listening comprehension tests from the same battery because the tests are standardized on the same population.

Standardized tests of reading that use paragraph-length material to assess comprehension are more attention demanding than tests that employ the cloze procedure, which generally use single sentences. (In the cloze procedure, the reader is required to furnish words that have been systematically deleted from sentences. The assumption is that the reader cannot supply the correct word unless she has grasped the meaning of the sentence.) For this reason, individuals with ADHD-I are expected to perform more poorly on tests of paragraph length, such as the Stanford Diagnostic Reading Test and the Gates-MacGintie Reading Tests, Fourth Edition (MacGinitie, MacGinitie, Maria, Dreyer, & Hughes, 2000), than on tests in a cloze format, such as the Woodcock Language Proficiency Battery–Revised (Woodcock, 1991/1994). These expectations were confirmed in two studies by Aaron et al. (2002) and Aaron, Joshi, and Phipps (2004). Scores obtained by students on paragraph-based tests of reading comprehension and on cloze procedure-based reading comprehension tests can, therefore, be used as one source of information to distinguish reading disability from ADHD-I. Table 9.1 provides a list of informal cues for differentiating between reading disability and ADHD-I.

Table 9.1. Informal cues for distinguishing reading disability from attention-deficit/hyperactivity disorder, predominantly inattentive type (ADHD-I)

Reading disability	ADHD-I
Results of parent–teacher rating scales	Results of parent–teacher rating scales
Listening comprehension score is higher than reading comprehension score	Reading comprehension score is higher than listening comprehension score
No noticeable difference between reading comprehension scores on cloze test and paragraph-length test	Reading comprehension score on cloze test is higher than score on paragraph-length test
No noticeable difference between word-naming time and color-naming time on the Stroop test	Color-naming time is noticeably slower than word-naming time on the Stroop test

Assignments for the Student Teacher

1. Interview two or three teachers from the first three grades. Ask them what percentage of children reverse letters when they write. Does the tendency to reverse letters when they write decrease with age?

2. Interview two or three fourth- and fifth-grade teachers.
   Find out how many children in their classes are taking medication to treat ADHD.
   Has ADHD diminished in these children since they began treatment?
   Has their academic performance improved because of the treatment?

3. How are learning disabilities diagnosed in the school you have access to?

4. How are children with LD taught in the school in which you do your practice teaching?
   If the children are taught in a resource room, visit the resource room and note how many children are taught at any one time.
   Do all children in the resource room have LD, or are there students with different disabilities?
   If the children are included in general education, describe how they are taught in the general education classroom.

5. Interview the general education classroom teachers and find out what difficulties they encounter in including children with LD.

6. How do teachers define or describe dyslexia? Do they think letter reversal is indicative of dyslexia?

7. How does the school psychologist collaborate with the classroom teacher in assessing reading difficulties and in designing remedial instruction?

Reading Assignment

Read one of the following articles, discuss it, and write a one-page summary. These articles can be obtained at your college library or downloaded by accessing the library's electronic holdings.

Hudson, R.F., High, L., & Al Otaiba, S. (2007). Dyslexia and the brain: What does current research tell us? *The Reading Teacher, 60*(6), 506–515.

Valencia, S.W., & Buly, M.R. (2004). Behind the test scores: What struggling readers really need. *The Reading Teacher, 57*(6), 520–531.

Assessment in Literacy Instruction

CHAPTER 10

Testing
and Assessment
of Literacy Skills

Summary

There is a distinction between testing and assessment. Testing involves standardized tests administered for comparison of performance with students in other schools. Assessment provides comparison with students in the same classroom and guidance on teaching individuals who have specific difficulties. This chapter discusses the controversy surrounding testing and assessment and the advantages and disadvantages of both. It outlines basic concepts of testing procedures and the types of standardized tests used for measuring reading, listening, writing, and spelling skills. Procedures that the teacher can use to test individual children's progress are also described. The chapter concludes by discussing the strengths and weaknesses of some frequently used standardized tests.

Main ideas presented in this chapter

1. There is a difference between testing and assessment.

2. Tests can be classified as formal or informal. Formal tests are standardized on a nationwide basis; **informal tests** are quasi-standardized. Tests can also be classified as achievement tests and diagnostic tests.

3. Assessment tools are criterion-referenced rather than norm-referenced.

4. The criteria used for evaluating standardized tests are validity, reliability, and norms.

5. Test performance is expressed as standard scores, percentile scores, and scaled scores.

6. Methods exist for testing phonological and phonemic awareness, levels of morphological and syntactic development, word recognition skills, reading and listening comprehension, vocabulary, spelling, and fluency.

7. Assessment procedures can yield qualitative and quantitative information.

Testing and Assessment: What Is the Difference?

Although the terms *testing* and *assessment* are generally used interchangeably, they
are not synonyms. Testing is usually accomplished by administering one or more
written or oral tests, the results of which are expressed in quantitative terms. These
quantitative measures are usually statistical in nature, the most frequently used statistics being averages (mean), **standard deviations (SDs),** standard scores, and percentiles. These units allow comparison of the performance of different groups of
children, different school systems, different states, and even different countries.

Tests of reading and related tasks that generate quantitative data can be
placed under two broad categories: standardized tests and informal tests. Standardized tests are standardized on a nationwide sample, allowing comparisons of
performance among students of the same age from across the nation. Informal
tests are often developed by the teacher using the classroom curriculum. Although
there may be some exceptions, both standardized tests and informal tests rely on
quantitative measures to determine students' performance. Because informal tests
rely on materials and information taught in the classroom, they are also called curriculum-based tests; the testing procedure is **curriculum-based measurement
(CBM).** The results of standardized tests as well as curriculum-based tests are expressed in numbers; however, standardized tests use statistical measures such as
standard scores and percentiles, whereas curriculum-based tests may use descriptors such as averages and above and below averages. Generally, informal tests do
not use elaborate statistical descriptors.

As noted, the scores obtained from nationally standardized tests provide an
opportunity to compare performance of students or even entire schools with the
performance of similar populations across the nation. In contrast, the purpose of
informal curriculum-based tests is to measure the progress made by individual
children. Standardized tests, then, are designed for comparisons to be made
among individual students and schools, whereas curriculum-based tests enable
teachers to make judgments about an individual student's level of performance
and rate of progress.

In contrast to standardized and informal tests, outcomes of assessment procedures are expressed in qualitative terms. Assessment procedures are relatively informal and include observation, interviews, informal inventories, and students' collected works (portfolios). Generally speaking, assessment leads to educational decisions regarding classification, instructional planning, and evaluation of students' progress. Assessment, therefore, is the process of collecting comprehensive information about the strengths and weaknesses of individual students (Salvia & Ysseldyke, 2004).

A common way of assessing children's performance in the classroom is by using **informal inventories.** This procedure is mainly based on teacher observation and recording of children's performance as they read and spell. This performance is often expressed in descriptive terms, such as *slow reader, struggling reader,* or *skilled reader.* This method of assessment provides information about the nature of students' reading or writing errors. Informal inventories are also described by terms such as *miscue analysis* and *running records.* Thus, teachers have access to three types of evaluation tools: standardized tests, informal (or curriculum-based) tests, and assessment procedures that use informal inventories and portfolios (see Table 10.1).

Controversy Over Testing

In recent years, the view that schools should be held accountable for children's academic performance and that such accountability should be determined by administering standardized tests has gained momentum. Although this might appear to be valid, it has led to a great deal of controversy in educational circles. Criticisms some educators have leveled against establishing accountability through standardized tests include the following:

* The testing enterprise has led teachers and parents to distrust their own ability to see, observe, and evaluate children (Meier, 2002).

* Academic achievement is the product of several factors, such as children's home background, socioeconomic status, and culture. This creates an uneven playing field in the testing arena and sets up unfair comparisons of children and schools through standardized tests (Crain, 2004).

Table 10.1. Different forms of tests and assessment tools

Type	Features	Outcome measures
Standardized tests	Standardized on national level	Mean, percentiles, standard scores
Informal tests (curriculum based)	Standardized on local level	Number of words read correctly in one minute
		Number of words misread
		Number of words recalled from the text read
Assessment	Informal inventories	Verbal descriptions of performance, such as *reads fluently, comprehends well, reads at frustration level,* and *guesses words*
	Not standardized	

- The use of standardized tests causes teachers to teach to the test, often using scripted texts, and miss the lofty goals of education.

- Standards are politically determined, often by the state, which is far removed from the schools (Meier, 2002).

- Imposition of standardized tests leads to a large number of students failing to obtain a high school diploma because graduation requirements may be linked to attaining a certain level of test scores. This prevents students from entering college.

- Many parents do not know how to interpret standardized test scores.

- The standardization procedure is designed to fulfill an accountability function rather than an instructional function. (Behuniak, 2002).

- Standardized testing does not promote a child-centered atmosphere, and education should be child centered to create a desire in children to learn.

Reasonable as they seem to be, these concerns should be viewed from the perspective of a growing fear that today's students are not performing at the level expected of them and that some students who graduate from high school appear to be functionally illiterate (Anderson, Hiebert, Scott, & Wilkinson, 1985). A precipitating event for the testing controversy was the publication of *A Nation at Risk* in 1983 (National Commission on Excellence in Education), which noted that the schools represent a "rising tide of mediocrity that threatens our very future as a nation and a people" (p. 5). Even though this report drew its conclusions from secondary education, there is an awareness that academic decline starts early in the elementary grades. Standardization and accountability, therefore, seem to be the only means of stemming this decline in academic competence. An awareness of this state of affairs resulted in programs such as Early Reading First (2001) and legislation such as the No Child Left Behind (NCLB) Act of 2001 (PL 107-110), which mandates yearly standardized testing of children in reading and math in grades 3 though 8. Advocates of accountability also point out that no business or agency can be run successfully without knowing whether it is making a profit or sustaining a loss, although thus far educational institutions have been not operated like this. As will be noted later, standardized tests are value neutral; their value depends on the purpose for which they are used, whether to help children become better learners or to penalize institutions for lagging behind national norms.

Both standardized testing and informal assessment procedures are valuable, depending on how the results are used. Informal assessment gives teachers immediate feedback and helps them design appropriate instruction tailored to the needs of their classroom or an individual child. If teachers want to compare a child's ability to that of the child's peers outside the classroom, standardized tests can be administered. In this chapter, these two forms of tests are treated as complementary.

Tests

In this section, basic concepts about standardized tests are provided so that preservice and in-service teachers can understand why these tests are used to assess the literacy skills of students.

Standardized Tests: Statistical Concepts

Validity, Reliability, and Norms

To qualify as a standardized test, the test should, at minimum, satisfy the following three criteria: have good validity, reliability, and well-established norms. Validity is determined by confirming that the test measures what it claims to measure. For instance, a standardized test of reading vocabulary should measure word knowledge but not decoding skills. This form of validity, also known as content validity, is the one presented most often by test manuals. There are also other forms of validity, such as concurrent validity and predictive validity. Concurrent validity indicates how well a test correlates with another well-established test that measures the same skill. Predictive validity refers to the extent to which a test can predict future performance. For instance, the Graduate Record Examination (GRE) is expected to predict how well a student will perform in graduate school; it therefore shows predictive validity.

Test validity is generally expressed as a coefficient of correlation which can range from –1.00 to +1.00. A correlation of +1.00 indicates a perfect positive relationship between two variables. For instance, the correlation between height and weight is about +0.7. A correlation coefficient of –1.0 indicates a perfect negative relationship between two variables. That is, as one variable increases, the other decreases. An instance of negative correlation would be the relationship between the time a child spends on video games and the grades he gets in the classroom. Most published tests have a validity coefficient around +0.70. Tests with lower validity may be contaminated by factors other than the one the test is intended to measure. For example, a test of decoding with a validity of about +0.4 might not be very valid and may contain too many familiar words that can be read without decoding the words. Under such conditions, the test may be confounded by word familiarity. If a test does not provide information about its validity, it is best to treat the test as an informal tool of assessment.

Reliability refers to whether a test gives the same results time after time. In other words, it indicates to what extent the results of the test are stable over time. Thus, a test administered in California in January should provide similar results if it is administered in North Carolina in April, so that the results are generalizable. Reliability is also expressed as a coefficient, which can theoretically range from –1.0 to +1.0. It is desirable to select a test that has a reliability coefficient of +0.80 or higher.

The **reliability of a test** can be established in more than one way. One way is to administer the test on two different occasions, separated by a month or two. This is referred to as test-retest reliability. Another form of reliability is called alternate form reliability, which is determined by administering a second test of items similar to the ones in the target test and then computing the correlation between the scores obtained on these two tests. Yet another way of calculating the reliability of a test is to divide the test into two shorter forms by selecting alternate items in the test and then computing the correlation coefficient between the scores obtained on the two short forms of the test. The outcome of this form of computation is referred to as split half reliability. In order to obtain satisfactory levels of split half reliability, the level of difficulty should be uniform from beginning to end.

Norms are usually established by administering a test to a large number of individuals, usually a few hundred, from various parts of the country who are of different ethnic, cultural, and socioeconomic background. This ensures that the test is suitable for individuals of all backgrounds, the results are generalizable, and the test is not biased. Norms are average scores, but norms tables also contain statistics such as *SD* and **standard error of measurement (SEM)**. *SD* is a measure of variability, and *SEM* is an index that indicates to what extent the score is free of errors of measurement and to what extent the score is a measure of the skill tested. For example, the *SD* of a spelling test will be quite high if the scores of the 20 children in Classroom A range from a low of 2 to a high of 20. On the other hand, if all scores of the 20 children in Classroom B tend to aggregate toward the mean and range only from 15 to 18, the *SD* will be low. This means that the children in Classroom B are more homogeneous than the children in Classroom A as far as their spelling performance is concerned. Standard error is an expression of the consistency of the *SD*. If, upon repeated administration of the spelling test, the *SD*s obtained vary widely from one occasion to another, the standard error will be high. If this is the case, it is assumed that the spelling test is influenced by some variable other than spelling skill.

Most standardized tests present norms, or averages, on a grade-by-grade and age-by-age basis. An age-based mean score gives a more accurate picture of a child's skill level than a grade-based mean score. To illustrate, take the vocabulary scores of two children, Jack and Ben, from grade 1. Both have obtained a standard score of 80 out of a possible 100. Does it mean both children have developed vocabulary skills at the same rate? The answer depends on the chronological age of the two children. For instance, if Jack is 9 years old and Ben is 7 years old, the answer is no; Jack is lagging behind his age mates.

Norm-Referenced and Criterion-Referenced Tests

Tests are classified as norm referenced or criterion referenced. Standardized tests are usually referred to as norm-referenced tests and compare the score of an individual with the scores of similar individuals who took the same test. By using a norm-referenced test score, teachers can tell where their students stand compared with other children in the country. To give an extreme illustration, a child might have obtained a score of 70 points out of 100 and still be considered a skilled reader because 95% of the normal population scored less than 70 on that particular test. Without this reference point, the teacher may think that this child is a poor reader, which is not true. In contrast, a teacher may think that her students are very proficient in reading, only to find from a comparison to national norms that the class is well below average. A norm-referenced test generally does not convey how much students know; it simply provides a comparative measure.

In contrast to the norm-referenced test, a criterion-referenced test measures the content mastered by an individual student. For example, a third-grade teacher may set a standard of reading 60 common words per minute for his students. When the teacher administers this test, he can easily identify the children who fail to meet this criterion. If a majority of children fail to read at the stipulated rate, the teacher can lower his expectation to 50 words per minute. Criterion-referenced tests are, therefore, more flexible than standardized tests, but their results are not generalizable beyond a particular classroom.

In selecting tests for classroom use, the teacher should first decide what results are expected from testing: norms for comparison or criteria to evaluate individual students' skills. In addition, the teacher should look at the validity, reliability, and *SEM* of a standardized test. Ease of administration, duration of the test, and ease of scoring are other factors to consider when selecting tests.

Standard Scores, Percentile Scores, and Scaled Scores

One of the problems some parents encounter when viewing the results of standardized tests is that the numbers on the report are confusing. There are raw scores, **standard scores,** percentiles, stanines, and scaled scores. Teachers should not only understand these various results themselves but also be able to explain them to parents in simple, understandable language. This is particularly true during case conferences, when decisions are made regarding students' individualized educational programs and possible placement of these students in special instructional settings.

A standard score is obtained by converting the raw score on a test into a commonly accepted format that has the same mean and *SD* as most other key tests. The standard score puts scores from different tests on the same footing so that they can be compared. For example, suppose a teacher administers a test of word reading and a test of comprehension to students. The word reading test has 40 items and the comprehension test has 20 items. Is a score of 15 on the first test comparable to a score of 5 on the second test? With these scores, does the student have equal skills in both functions, or is she better in one or the other? This question cannot be answered by looking at the raw scores because the number of questions on the two tests varies. To make the two test scores comparable, the test scores have to be put on a common plane. This can be accomplished by converting the word reading score of 15 out of 40 to a base of 100 and the comprehension score of 5 out of 20 also to a base of 100. The corresponding standard scores are 37.5 and 25.0, respectively. Now these two scores can be compared directly with each other; the student's word reading score is higher than her comprehension score.

Most standardized tests are designed in such a way that the mean score of the population on which the test is normed is 100, with a *SD* of 15. As previously noted, *SD* is a number that expresses the variability of scores. An *SD* of 15 obtained for the scores in a classroom indicates that the children in that classroom are no more heterogeneous or varied than what is seen in the general population. If, however, the *SD* for a particular class is 30, the reading skills of children in that classroom are more varied than would be expected. There may be several good readers and several poor readers but very few average readers in that class. In other words, the scores of the children are scattered widely. Standardized tests are constructed in such a way that approximately 34% of the individuals obtain scores within 1 *SD* of the mean; approximately 14% score between 1 and 2 *SD*s; and about 2% score between 2 and 3 *SD*s from the mean. Thus, approximately 68% of the individuals score between ±1 *SD* above and below the mean and approximately 96% score between ±2 *SD*. In turn, on a test with a mean of 100 and *SD* of 15, 68% of the students score between 85 to 115, and 96% score between 70 and 130. This example also shows that standard scores can be converted into percentile scores and vice versa (see Figure 10.1).

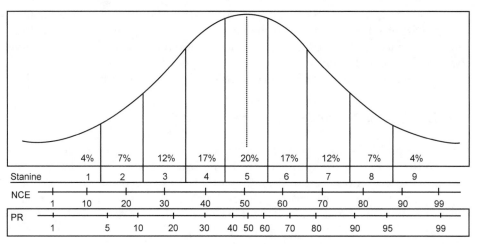

Figure 10.1. The normal distribution curve. (*Key:* NCE = normal curve equivalent; PR = percentile.)

SEM, as noted, is an estimate of possible measurement error involved in the scoring and interpretation of a test. Tests in general are not perfect, psychological tests particularly so. If a student is administered the same test twice, say a week apart, he is not likely to obtain identical scores on those two occasions. He may get a score of 102 the first time and 105 the second time. The question then is this: Is the 3-point difference a true difference in the child's performance, or is it due to chance? Such fluctuation in test scores is referred to as error of measurement. This question can be answered only by knowing the *SEM* of the test. For instance, if the *SEM* of this particular test, as reported by the test makers, is 10, the 3-point difference, being lower than 10, is due to chance and therefore cannot be interpreted to indicate a true difference in skill level. Scores obtained by an individual on psychological and educational tests, at a particular time, should be seen as an estimate of the individual's true score. Thus, *SEM* makes interpretation of scores relatively more objective. If one has to choose between tests with differing *SEM*s, it is advisable to select the test with the smaller *SEM*.

Usually, scores obtained on tests are viewed to fall within a range. For example, the Woodcock Reading Mastery Test–Revised (WRMT–R; Woodcock, 1987) has a mean standard score of 100 and a *SD* of 15; any score between 85 and 115 is considered within the normal range. The same is true of IQ tests, such as the Wechsler Intelligence Scale for Children (Wechsler, 1991). This means that an IQ score between 85 and 115 is considered within the average range.

Standardized tests also often express scores as percentile scores. A percentile score indicates how many students with a similar background fall above and below the given score. Percentile scores can be age based or grade based. For instance, an age-based percentile score of 90 indicates that out of 100 children of comparable age, 10 have scores above the child who has the score of 90. A grade-based percentile score of 90 indicates that 10 children from the same grade have scores above the child who has the score of 90.

Test scores are sometimes expressed as scaled scores. This is true of some subtests in test batteries, such as the Wechsler Intelligence Scale for Children. Scaled scores have a mean of 10 and a *SD* of 3. A child whose scaled score is 7 on an intelligence battery subtest such as digit span is considered to have a score within the average range.

Standardized Tests: Achievement Tests and Diagnostic Tests

Depending on the goals of assessment, standardized tests of literacy skills can be classified as achievement tests or diagnostic tests. Achievement tests attempt to measure the amount of information or knowledge a student has gained over a period of years; diagnostic tests evaluate a student's strengths and weaknesses. The origins of contemporary achievement tests can be traced to Horace Mann, secretary of Education for the Commonwealth of Massachusetts, who in 1845 recommended the use of written examination in place of oral examination. Mann argued that written examinations establish a uniform condition of testing and, at the same time, eliminate examiner bias. Beginning around 1910 under the leadership of Edward Thorndike, standardized achievement tests designed to measure reading comprehension, spelling, and other related skills were developed at Columbia University.

The speed with which reading achievement tests were produced and utilized in the United States during the early years of the 20th century can be appreciated by noting the different tests used by Arthur Gates in his 1922 study of the relationship between intelligence and literacy. The list of tests used by Gates includes Holley's Sentence Vocabulary Test, Burgess Reading Test, Brown's Reading Test, Curtis Silent Reading Test, Monroe's Silent Reading Test, Thorndike-McGall Reading Test, Gray's Reading Test, and Stanford-Binet Intelligence Test. Since then, hundreds of literacy achievement tests have been developed and marketed; test construction procedures have also undergone many technical refinements.

Diagnostic tests attempt to identify the source of the weaknesses of students whose performance is below average. Consequently, diagnostic tests focus on skills such as word recognition, reading comprehension, vocabulary, and math operations.

By about 1920, educators realized that some children experienced a great deal of difficulty in learning to read. Instead of describing a child as a poor reader in global terms, it became necessary to describe her performance more precisely in terms of subskill areas, such as word recognition, vocabulary, spelling, and comprehension. However, in the area of reading, a rigid distinction cannot be drawn between achievement tests and diagnostic tests because the scores obtained on many achievement batteries can also be used for diagnostic purposes. For instance, the Stanford Diagnostic Reading Test (Karlsen & Gardner, 1995), described by its developers as a diagnostic test, contains subtests of phonetics and comprehension skills that inform the teacher about the strengths and weaknesses of students in these subskill areas. In contrast, scores obtained on the word attack, reading vocabulary, listening vocabulary, reading comprehension, and listening comprehension subtests of the Woodcock Language Proficiency Battery (WLPB-R; Woodcock, 1991/1994), which is an achievement test, also tell the teacher the strengths and weaknesses of the students.

Areas Covered by Achievement Tests

This section presents some of the subtests included in achievement tests. One of the fundamental skills that should be mastered to later become a fluent reader is phonological awareness, including phonemic awareness.

Phonological Awareness and Phonemic Awareness   Studies that have probed word recognition skills suggest that phonological and phonemic awareness contribute to word recognition skills. Because phonemic awareness is a strong correlate of reading skill (Ball & Blachman, 1991; Bradley & Bryant, 1985; Muter, 1998; Stahl & Murray, 1993) and a good predictor of the later reading skills of kindergarten children, it is often assessed. Among the standardized tests for phonemic awareness are the Test of Phonological Awareness (Torgesen & Bryant, 1995), and the Comprehensive Test of Phonological Processing (CTOPP; Wagner, Torgesen, & Rashotte, 1999). Tests of phonemic awareness include tasks of phoneme identification and phoneme manipulation. Phoneme identification tasks require the child to indicate the number of phonemes in a spoken word by knocking that many times on the desk. Phoneme manipulation is the ability to identify and deal with individual phonemes in a word. Phoneme manipulation can be tested in more than one way. The child might be asked to delete the initial phoneme in a word and sound out the rest of the word (e.g., take away the first sound from the word *cat* and sound it out; the answer is /a/ /t/), or the child may be asked to take out the final sound in a word and sound the rest of the word. In testing phoneme substitution skill, the child is asked to remove a sound from a word and substitute another sound (e.g., take away the first sound in the word *bat* and put /k/ in its place; the answer is *cat*). Phoneme substitution is more difficult for children than phoneme deletion. All these tasks test children's ability to deal with individual phonemes.

When preschool children are administered a test of phoneme awareness, it is important to make sure that they understand the nature of the task. Tasks such as phoneme substitution and manipulation can be difficult for some children to understand, which could lead to incorrect responses. Low scores obtained on these tests may, therefore, be due to a lack of phonemic skills or to misunderstanding the task. Providing children with several practice trials can help them understand what they are being asked to do.

Letter knowledge is another good predictor of kindergartners' reading skill when they reach first grade. There is evidence to show that children who do not have alphabetic knowledge by the middle of first grade are likely to experience problems in reading as they progress through the grades (Adams, 1990; Juel, 1994).

Word Recognition   The first component of the cognitive domain of the Component Model of Reading, word recognition, is also referred to by several related terms, such as decoding, lexical processing, and grapheme–phoneme conversion. Decoding skill can be assessed with a test of nonword reading and a spelling test. Nonwords are also referred to as pseudowords; *daik* and *brane* are examples of nonwords. Nonword reading (or pseudoword reading) is a recognition task, whereas spelling is a recall task. Spelling requires that all the letters corresponding to the phonemes in a word be recalled in the correct sequence. This makes spelling a more sensitive test of decoding skill than nonword reading.

There is a misconception that all pseudowords are alike. Some, however, can be read not by decoding them but by using words that rhyme. For example, the nonword *dake* can be read more easily if the child is familiar with rhyming words with the *ake* ending, such as *cake, bake,* and *take*. Thus, *dake* has many "neighbors," which makes it a "friendly" nonword. In contrast, a nonword such as *daik* has few neighbors and is therefore unfriendly. Unfriendly nonwords cannot be decoded by using the analogy strategy. For this reason, it is essential that nonword lists designed to test decoding skill use as many unfriendly nonwords as possible. Many word attack subtests used in standardized tests of reading do not take this precaution. Word attack subtests can be found in many standardized tests, such as The Woodcock–Johnson–Revised Tests of Achievement (Woodcock & Johnson, 1989) and the WLPB-R (Woodcock, 1991).

A spelling test can also be used as a rigorous test of decoding skill. Very poor spelling performance is the first indication that a child has word recognition difficulty. When using spelling performance as a measure of decoding skill, teachers should be careful to use only words children have encountered in the classroom. When children misspell unfamiliar words, it will be hard to determine if it indicates poor spelling skill or lack of familiarity with the spelled word.

Sight word reading is a familiar term to many. *Instant word recognition* is another term that refers to the same process, namely, quick and accurate recognition of the written word. The latter is preferred, because the term *sight word reading* gives the impression that quick and accurate recognition of written words is primarily a visual task, with phonology being relegated to a subordinate position. However, this is not entirely true. As previously noted, instant word recognition skill is built on the foundation of phonological and alphabetic knowledge. A fluent reader must possess good decoding skills, adequate comprehension skills, and the ability to process information at an optimal rate. In a review of 17 studies, Compton and Carlisle (1994) found that students with weak word recognition skills were slower in naming words and nonwords. This led them to conclude that word reading speed, or fluency, is an important factor in differentiating individuals with reading disability from readers with typical reading ability.

Until the third grade, many children rely on decoding letters or syllables to recognize words. Beyond third grade, many children become exposed to many words that they can recognize instantly, quickly, and automatically. In other words, they have become instant word readers. When words are recognized instantly and automatically, it frees up the reader's attention to be invested in comprehension. For this reason, fluency is an important requirement for reading. Some children who are given ample training in decoding and phonics may be able to pronounce pseudowords accurately but do so slowly and laboriously. Under such circumstances, unless the time it takes to finish the task is taken into account, test scores alone will give an incorrect impression that the child has adequate decoding skills. In one study (Joshi & Aaron, 2002), 37 fifth graders were administered the word attack subtest from the WLPB-R (Woodcock, 1991/1994). This is not a timed test. When word recognition skill was evaluated by using a composite index of accuracy and time, it was found that many children who had average decoding scores in fact had composite scores in the lowest quartile. These children, who were slow but accurate decoders, could escape diagnosis as poor decoders and, therefore, represented instances of false negatives. For this reason, when measuring decoding through the use of nonwords, both speed and accuracy must be taken into consideration.

A simple way to come up with a composite index that combines both decoding skill and speed of processing is to administer a timed, standardized word-naming test. The Test of Word Reading Efficiency (TOWRE; Torgesen, Wagner, & Rashotte, 1999) is a good example of such a test. The TOWRE has two subtests. One subtest is for sight word efficiency, which assesses the number of printed words that can be accurately identified within 45 seconds; the second subtest measures the number of nonwords that can be decoded within 45 seconds.

Aaron et al. (1999) demonstrated that children in grade 2 took longer to name a common word than to name a letter of the alphabet, the difference being statistically significant. However, students in grade 3 and up, including college students, named both letters and words at about the same rate. This indicates that by about the third grade most children have mastered decoding skills and have become instant word readers. The time it takes to name a letter of the alphabet and a common content word, therefore, could be used to assess instant word reading skill. When a list of 20 common monosyllabic content words (nouns, verbs, and adjectives) is named as rapidly as a list of 20 letters, it can be concluded that these words are read as sight words. Classroom teachers can prepare a list of words that students have encountered many times in the classroom and use it to assess instant word reading skill. Of course, the word list would vary from grade to grade. It must be noted that in the early elementary grades children encounter more difficulty with grammar words, such as prepositions and conjunctions, than with content words, such as nouns, verbs, and adjectives. Although grammar words are high-frequency morphemes, children take longer to name them and commit more errors when attempting to do so. This is so because grammar words, unlike content words, are abstractions. It is, therefore, preferable not to include grammar words in teacher-made lists of words.

Spelling   Why is spelling considered to be so important by researchers? With the availability of computer spell checks, are not good spelling skills superfluous? As early as 1940, Spache noted that children who are poor spellers also are deficient in decoding skills. In a study that specifically examined the question of whether children use similar processes to read and spell words, Waters, Bruck, and Seidenberg (1985) found that third-grade children, regardless of ability level, used spelling–sound correspondences for both reading and spelling. Excessive spelling errors, therefore, often indicate a weakness in phonological skill and should not be interpreted as an indication of poor visual memory without strong evidence (Joshi & Aaron, 1991). In spite of its usefulness as a diagnostic tool, spelling is seldom utilized as a test of decoding skill.

Traditionally, spelling ability is assessed by dictating a list of words to children and then scoring their output as right or wrong. This kind of quantitative assessment has two drawbacks. First, it is quite possible that children tend to spell unfamiliar words phonetically, which often leads to spelling errors. These spelling errors do not reflect an impairment in spelling skill per se but rather limited vocabulary knowledge. Dialect also has an effect on spelling. Studies show that some of the spelling errors committed by children who use African American English dialect can be traced to their dialect.

The effect of familiarity with words on spelling tests was studied by comparing the scores obtained by using the traditional procedure (number of words from a list that were spelled correctly) and the alternate form of scoring (number of words spelled correctly that were also read correctly; Joshi, 1999; Joshi & Aaron, 2002). It was found that 5 out of 39 children from third grade scored higher when the alternate scoring method was used. This represented approximately 13% of the children who might have been misclassified as poor spellers. Thus, familiarity with words, as indicated by the ability to pronounce them, has to be taken into account when spelling lists are constructed. Spelling scores derived from standardized spelling tests are particularly susceptible to this type of misinterpretation. A mistake of this nature can be avoided if teachers use as spelling tests only those words already introduced in the classroom (Joshi & Aaron, 2003).

The ability to spell words falls on a continuum; therefore, spelling errors cannot be dichotomized as right or wrong. Such a quantitative assessment of spelling can yield an incomplete and distorted picture of a child's spelling skill. For instance, a child who spells "kat" for *cat* has better knowledge of letter–sound correspondence than a child who spells *cat* as "tca," even though both are incorrect when scored right or wrong. Further, dichotomizing spelling performance as right or wrong may not give a comprehensive picture of the source of children's spelling difficulty. Quantitative assessment also does not inform the teacher of the specific problem a student may have in spelling.

A quasi-qualitative assessment procedure was provided by Tangel and Blachman (1995). Under this procedure, a score of 0 is assigned to a spelling that is an array of random symbols with little or no alphabetic representation; a score of 6 is given to correct spelling. Scores 1 through 5 are assigned depending upon the degree of proximity to the correct spelling of the word (see Table 10.2). While administering a qualitative analysis of spelling, teachers should keep in mind that correctly spelling the word *cat* will earn the same 6 points as spelling *dinosaur*. This inequality factor can be controlled in two ways. Children can be tested on words that have been introduced in the classroom, or the teacher can select words that occur with the same frequency in textbooks.

Several studies indicate that the acquisition of grapheme–phoneme conversion (GPC) skill follows a developmental trend in moving from a mastery of simple to complex spelling–sound relationships (Calfee, Venezky, & Chapman, 1969; Ehri, 1992, 1998; Moats, 1995; Treiman,1993, 1998; Venezky, 1976). For instance, hard *c* (as in *cat*) is mastered earlier than soft *c* (as in *city*), and hard *g* (as in *girl*) is learned before soft *g* (as in *gem*). A list of words designed to test decoding skill should, therefore, contain words that assess a wide range of GPC rules, utilized by children as they grow older. Based on this observation, Shearer and Homan (1994) suggested that spelling development could be gauged by examining children's spelling errors. A child could be in the phonemic, letter-name spelling, early phonetic, phonetic, or correct spelling stage. Of course, children's misspellings usually occur in more than one stage.

Table 10.2. A model for qualitative assessment of spelling

Score criteria	Example	Target word
0. No alphabetic representation; random	trpqr	book
1. A letter representing a phoneme in the word present	kllmo	book
2. Initial phoneme correct	blnk	book
3. More than one phoneme present, but not all	sowe	snow
4. Many phonemes or phoneme-related letters	chran	train
5. All phonemes with one or two missing	snoing	snowing
6. Correct spelling		

From Tangel, D.M., & Blachman, B.A. (1995). Effect of phoneme awareness instruction on kindergarten children's invented spelling. *Journal of Reading Behavior, 24,* 233–261; adapted with permission of the National Reading Conference and Darlene M. Tangel.

Furthermore, qualitative analyses of spelling errors can be helpful in designing corrective instruction. A detailed phonological analysis of spelling errors, such as substitution of consonant phonemes, omission of consonants in blends, omission of unaccented vowels (schwa), or syllable omission, can be useful in identifying the source of children's spelling (and decoding) errors, and their attention can be drawn to those errors (Joshi & Aaron, 2003). In sum, spelling, being a recall task, is a more rigorous test of decoding skill than nonword reading. The validity of spelling tests can be improved by administering only those words children can read aloud correctly and by using qualitative or quasi-qualitative analyses of spelling errors.

Vocabulary   Although vocabulary is not a separate component in the Component Model of Reading, vocabulary knowledge is a prerequisite for comprehension. As previously noted, the coefficients of correlation between vocabulary and reading comprehension range from 0.66 to 0.75 (Just & Carpenter, 1987). A meta-analysis of vocabulary studies by Stahl and Fairbanks (1986) suggested that vocabulary knowledge very likely plays a causal role in comprehension. Not surprisingly, the reading vocabulary of children with specific reading disability tends to be lower than that of their typically achieving peers. This is not surprising, as reading experience is an important source of vocabulary development, particularly in the upper grades, and poor readers tend to avoid reading. However, the poor reading vocabulary score of a child with reading disability could be the result of decoding problems rather than the consequence of impoverished vocabulary. In order to obtain a true estimate of students' vocabulary knowledge, it is desirable to administer tests of both reading and listening vocabulary. The WLPB-R (Woodcock, 1991/1994) has subtests of both listening and reading vocabularies.

Listening Comprehension   *Comprehension* is a generic term used to refer to both reading and listening comprehension. Although reading comprehension is the ultimate goal of reading, listening comprehension is given much importance in this textbook. One reason is that listening comprehension and reading comprehension are closely related. A number of studies have shown that except for modality differences, reading comprehension and listening comprehension are mediated by the same cognitive processes. As previously noted, the correlation between reading and listening comprehension is impressively high. Savage (2001) found that the correlation coefficient between listening and reading comprehension is about 0.74. Listening comprehension, therefore, can be used to assess comprehension without being confounded by decoding skill. The discrepancy between reading comprehension and listening comprehension can indicate whether poor decoding is the source of a reading problem or if the comprehension component itself is impaired.

Listening comprehension can be assessed by more than one test; consequently, results can vary somewhat depending on the test used (Joshi, Williams, & Wood, 1998). As previously noted, the WLPB-R has listening and reading comprehension subtests; both were normed on the same population and use the same cloze format. This makes the reading and listening comprehension comparable. The Diagnostic Achievement Battery–Third Edition (Newcomer, 2001) and the Wechsler Individual Achievement Test–Second Edition (WIAT-II; Wechsler, 2001) also have subtests of listening comprehension.

Reading Comprehension Many tests of reading comprehension are available. Are they all the same? What difference does it make if the teacher uses one test rather than another test? All standardized tests of reading comprehension are *not* alike; they differ in the strategy they use for assessing comprehension. For example, the Stanford Diagnostic Reading Test–Fourth Edition (Karlsen & Gardner, 1995) and Gates-MacGintie Reading Tests (MacGintie et al., 2000) ask students to read passages and answer questions in multiple-choice format. In such a format, the ability not only to comprehend but also to remember the passage read plays a role in performance. Memory ability, therefore, can become a confounding factor.

Another strategy used for assessing reading comprehension is the cloze procedure. Tests that follow this format usually do not impose a time restriction. A weakness of this form of assessment is that tests in a cloze format are somewhat removed from the reading of a paragraph or story and comprehending text. Thus, scores obtained using sentences in a cloze format may not yield an ecologically valid comprehension measure. The WRMT-R (Woodcock, 1981), the WLPB-R (Woodcock, 1991/1994), and the Woodcock Diagnostic Battery–Revised (Woodcock, 1997) have subtests that assess reading comprehension using the cloze format.

The Peabody Individual Achievement Test–Revised (PIAT-R; Markwardt, 1998) follows a different technique to assess reading comprehension. The student reads a sentence and chooses one picture from among the four that fits the sentence. Although this form of testing reduces the memory load, correct understanding of the pictures requires a good deal of reasoning ability. This is particularly true in the test for the higher grades, which appear to be tests of intelligence.

Many of the tests described here take 45 minutes or more to complete and are meant to be administered in a single session. Blanchard, Di Cerbo, Oliver, and Albers (2001) found that when a test was split into two parts and administered in two separate sessions, reading comprehension scores improved. This was particularly true for students with reading disabilities.

Selected Standardized Tests

The following sections describe some of the commonly used standardized tests for assessing the different components of reading.

Group-Administered Reading Tests As the name implies, achievement tests, assess how much children have mastered the area in which they are being tested. Thus, there are achievement tests in reading, math, science, and social studies. Almost all standardized achievement tests have a reading subtest. A few are described in this section.

1. California Achievement Tests, Fifth Edition

The California Achievement Tests, Fifth Edition (CAT/5; CTB/McGraw-Hill, 2007) are suitable for kindergarten through grade 12 and are both norm-referenced and criterion-referenced. Decoding is measured by testing students' ability to identify unfamiliar words. Vocabulary is measured by asking students to select synonyms and antonyms presented in a multiple-choice format. Three types of comprehension—literal, inferential, and evaluative—are assessed by requiring students to find the meaning of sentences and passages. Spelling is measured by students' ability to identify incorrectly spelled words embedded in sentences.

2. Stanford Achievement Test–Tenth Edition

The Stanford Achievement Test–Tenth Edition (SAT 10, Harcourt Assessment, 2003) is intended for grades 1 through 9. Decoding, vocabulary, and literal and inferential comprehension are measured by multiple-choice test items. Spelling is measured by having students identify, from a choice of words, the correctly spelled word. See Case (2003) for information regarding test accommodations for students with disabilities.

3. Metropolitan Achievement Test–Eighth Edition

The Metropolitan Achievement Test–Eighth Edition (MAT-8, Harcourt Assessment) is both a norm-referenced and criterion-referenced test suitable for kindergarten through grade 12. Decoding skill is measured by having students identify consonant sounds, vowel sounds, and word parts. Vocabulary is measured by having students select the correct meaning of words shown in a sentence context. Several aspects of comprehension, such as literal comprehension, knowledge of cause-and-effect relationships, and the ability to identify the main idea, are measured by multiple-choice test items.

4. Iowa Test of Basic Skills

The Iowa Test of Basic Skills (ITBS; Hoover, Dunbar, & Frisbie, 2001) is both a norm-referenced and criterion-referenced test that can be used in kindergarten through grade 8. Decoding tasks require students to identify initial, medial, and final sounds in words. Vocabulary is measured by determining how well students know the meaning of words in context. Literal and inferential comprehension are assessed by requiring students to read passages and answer multiple-choice questions.

All of these tests have acceptable levels of validity and reliability and are fairly widely used in schools. Because these tests are both norm referenced and criterion referenced, they can be used as group tests for a wide range of age groups, from kindergarten through high school.

Individually Administered Reading Tests   Achievement tests described in this section are administered to one student at a time.

1. Kaufman Test of Educational Achievement–Second Edition

The Kaufman Test of Educational Achievement–Second Edition (KTEA-II; Kaufman & Kaufman, 2003) is a norm-referenced test suitable for students in grades 1 to 12. It has extended norms for individuals through age 22. Decoding is measured by letter identification, word identification, and pronunciation tasks. Spelling is measured by asking the student to spell 50 words of increasing difficulty, dictated by the examiner. Reading comprehension is measured by asking the student to read a passage and respond orally to the teacher's questions.

2. Peabody Individual Achievement Test–Revised

The Peabody Individual Achievement Test–Revised (PIAT-R; Markwardt, 1998) is a norm-referenced test suitable for students in grades 1 to 12. It has extended norms for individuals through age 22. Decoding measures include matching letters and pronouncing words of increasing difficulty. Reading comprehension, which consists of 82 items, requires the student to silently read a sentence on one page and then select from among four pictures on another page the picture that best represents the meaning of the sentence. Spelling is measured by asking the student to select the correctly spelled word from among four choices.

3. Wechsler Individual Achievement Test–Second Edition

The Wechsler Individual Achievement Test–Second Edition (WIAT-II; Wechsler, 2001) is suitable for ages 5 through 19 and measures basic reading, decoding, spelling, reading comprehension, and listening comprehension skills. Basic reading is measured through sight word recognition, and decoding is measured through pseudoword naming. Vocabulary knowledge is included in the comprehension assessment, which also includes measures of word, sentence, and passage comprehension. Spelling is measured by asking the student to write the words dictated by the examiner.

4. Wide Range Achievement Test–Third Edition

The Wide Range Achievement Test–Third Edition (WRAT-3; Wilkinson, 1993) is meant for individuals from 5 to 74 years of age and measures word recognition, spelling, and arithmetic. Word recognition is assessed by asking the individual to read a list of words, and spelling is measured by asking the student to write the word dictated by the examiner. There are no other reading subtests.

5. The Gates-MacGintie Reading Tests, Fourth Edition

The Gates-MacGintie Reading Tests, Fourth Edition (MacGinitie et al., 2000), are widely used tests of silent reading. Developed for use from kindergarten through grade 12, the Gates-MacGintie Reading Tests, Fourth Edition, measure vocabulary and comprehension. There are approximately 45 questions on each of the vocabulary and comprehension portions, which are presented in a multiple-choice format. This is a fairly well-standardized test and easy to use.

Oral Reading Tests   Oral reading tests assess reading accuracy, speed, and comprehension.

1. Gray Oral Reading Tests, Fourth Edition, and Gilmore Oral Reading Tests

Two widely used oral reading achievement tests are the Gray Oral Reading Tests, Fourth Edition (GORT-4; Wiederholt & Bryant, 2001) and the Gilmore Oral Reading Test (Gilmore & Gilmore, 1968). The GORT-4 is suitable for children ages 6 through 18 years; it measures rate and accuracy of passage reading. The Gilmore measures accuracy, comprehension, and reading rate. When the student orally reads passages, errors (also called miscues or deviations from print), such as mispronunciations, substitutions, additions, reversals, and omissions, are noted. Thus, these tests provide an opportunity for qualitative assessment.

2. Slossan Oral Reading Test–Revised

The Slossan Oral Reading Test–Revised (SORT-R; Slossan & Nicholson, 1990) is a test of somewhat limited use. It provides a quick survey of oral reading (i.e., pronunciation) skill only. It has 10 lists ranging from primer to high school level, and each list has 20 words. This is a survey test that estimates grade level and should be used and interpreted accordingly.

Diagnostic Reading Tests   As previously stated, diagnostic tests can be used for making recommendations about remedial teaching by assessing students' strengths and weaknesses. Because they measure a variety of reading skills, they generally take longer than achievement tests to administer and score.

1. Durrell Analysis of Reading Difficulty, Third Edition

The Durrell Analysis of Reading Difficulty, Third Edition (DARD; Durrell & Catterson, 1980) is an individually administered test suitable for kindergarten through grade 6. Decoding is measured by a student's ability to pronounce sounds in letters, blends, phonograms, and affixes when presented in isolation. Decoding is measured by asking the child to read a list of words under both timed and untimed conditions. An additional feature of this test is the listening comprehension subtest. Spelling is measured by the number of words correctly written to dictation. Caution is advised in interpreting the results from this test as the information on the standardization procedures, as well as on the validity, reliability, and the population used for developing norms, is at best average.

2. Diagnostic Reading Scales

Diagnostic Reading Scales (Spache, 1981) is an individually administered diagnostic reading test for children in grades 1 through 8. Decoding skill is measured by testing the child's knowledge of initial consonants, blends, and vowel sounds. Word recognition skill is measured by asking the child to read lists of words in isolation. Literal and inferential comprehension are measured by asking questions from passages read orally or silently. Similar to the DARD, the standardization information of this test is inadequate.

3. Diagnostic Achievement Battery–Third Edition

The Diagnostic Achievement Battery–Third Edition (DAB-3, Newcomer, 2001) is an individually administered test for 6- to 14- year-old children and measures listening comprehension, vocabulary, alphabet and word knowledge, spelling, and reading comprehension. This is a fairly well-standardized test, but it can be time consuming to administer and score.

4. Woodcock Reading Mastery Test–Revised

The Woodcock Reading Mastery Test–Revised (WRMT-R; Woodcock, 1987) is probably one of the most widely used tests and consists of six subtests, including word identification, word attack, and word and reading comprehension for ages 5 to 75 and older. It is a well-standardized test, but scoring can be tedious because several tables have to be used. However, computer scoring is available, which makes scoring easy. This test also does not include a test of listening comprehension, which is a better measure than IQ scores for identifying children with reading disability.

5. Woodcock Diagnostic Reading Battery–Revised

The Woodcock Diagnostic Reading Battery–Revised (WDRB-R; Woodcock,1997) is an individually administered diagnostic reading test that consists of 10 subtests taken from other Woodcock tests. The subtests include letter recognition, word attack, reading vocabulary, passage (reading) comprehension, phonological awareness, oral vocabulary, listening comprehension, and reading aptitude. Simon (1998–1999), in a review of the WDRB-R, mentioned that it was more comprehensive than the WRMT-R and easier to use than the Woodcock–Johnson–Revised Tests of Achievement (Woodcock & Johnson, 1989).

6. Woodcock Language Proficiency Battery–Revised

The WLPB-R (Woodcock, 1991) is a battery of tests, many of which can be found in other Woodcock tests. In addition to oral and reading vocabulary, it also has a test of listening comprehension. The fact that the tests of reading comprehension and listening comprehension were normed on the same population and use the same format (cloze) means that the scores obtained from the two tests are readily comparable. This test can be computer scored.

7. Woodcock-Johnson III Tests of Achievement

The Woodcock-Johnson III Tests of Achievement (WJ-III; Woodcock, McGrew, & Mather, 2001) is a widely used, individually administered norm-referenced test for ages 6 to adult. It measures general intellectual ability, specific cognitive abilities, oral language, and reading achievement. There are separate cognitive and achievement batteries, each of which has a standard and an extended battery. The standard battery includes letter word identification, reading fluency, passage comprehension, and spelling; the extended battery includes word attack and reading vocabulary. WJ-III has been well standardized and is similar to the WIAT-II. The different subtests have been standardized on the same population, which makes the scores on the achievement and cognitive tests comparable.

8. Stanford Diagnostic Reading Test–Fourth Edition

The Stanford Diagnostic Reading Test–Fourth Edition (SDRT-4; Karlsen & Gardner, 1995) is a group administered diagnostic test that is both norm referenced and criterion referenced. The SDRT-4 has six levels, each designed for different grade levels up to college-entry level. Decoding is measured primarily through the ability to analyze words on the basis of phonetic identification and segmentation. Vocabulary knowledge is measured by having students select the correct word from a list of words. Reading comprehension is measured through the students' understanding of the meaning of sentences and passages by answering questions in a multiple-choice format. In addition to decoding, vocabulary, and comprehension, the SDRT-4 measures the rate of reading, which can be of diagnostic value. This test is often preferred by schools because it is a group-administered test and can be given to an entire classroom.

Strengths and Weaknesses of Frequently Used Tests It was noted previously that tests of listening comprehension and reading comprehension play a key role in the identification of the weak component of reading. For this reason, standardized batteries that have a test of reading comprehension and listening comprehension have an advantage. Two examples of such tests are the WLPB-R (Woodcock, 1991/1994) and the WIAT-II. In addition, the WIAT-II is linked to the Wechsler Intelligence Scale for Children–Third Edition (WISC-III; Wechsler, 1991), which makes a comparison of achievement and IQ scores possible.

Precautions to be taken when evaluating tests of decoding and spelling were noted previously. That is, tests of word reading should take into consideration the length of time it takes for a student to read the nonwords. In addition, nonwords used as test items of decoding skill should not have many similar sounding or rhyming cohorts.

Tests of reading comprehension use different strategies to assess comprehension. Each strategy has its advantages and disadvantages. Tests that use the cloze strategy reduce the reader's memory load, but tests in cloze format are somewhat removed from the real reading process. Being limited to one or two sentences, cloze tests are also not suitable for assessing inferential comprehension and, therefore, provide information about literal comprehension. Some tests are not timed and may make some slow readers appear more like typical readers. Tests such as the Stanford Diagnostic Reading Test–Fourth Edition (Karlsen & Gardner, 1995) and the Gates-MacGintie Reading Tests, Fourth Edition (MacGintie et al., 2000) use paragraphs of varying lengths followed by multiple-choice test questions. Performance on these types of tests depends not only on the reader's comprehension ability but also on the reader's memory capacity. A major weakness of tests in multiple-choice format is that they allow for guessing, which can misrepresent the reader's true ability. For instance, under ordinary circumstances, if there are four choices for every question, the chances of guessing the correct answer is 25%. The chances of successfully guessing increase when the questions are independent of the passage to be read and answered (passage independent). These questions are those that can be answered correctly from past experience and prior knowledge, without reading the passage. The level of passage independence of tests of reading comprehension is a factor that test users should take into consideration when selecting tests. This can be accomplished by inspecting the questions in the test. For instance, questions such as "What do we do in a restaurant?" and "What did John wear during the snowstorm?" can be answered without reading the passage, which was about a visit to the restaurant or a day in winter. The problem of passage independent comprehension was studied as early as 1964 (Preston), but the topic has not been investigated on a consistent basis (Hanna & Oaster, 1978; Katz, Lautenschlager, Blackburn, & Harris, 1990). Nevertheless, it has been recognized as a confounding factor that test users should take into consideration when selecting tests.

Another strategy for testing reading comprehension has been adopted by the PIAT-R (Markwardt, 1998). Although selecting one item out of four in a multiple-choice format may benefit individuals who may not be able to respond orally but who can point to pictures that correspond to sentences, the reading comprehension subtest involves a great deal of reasoning. At higher levels, some of the test items are very similar to items seen on tests of intelligence. Moreover, the picture format cannot be used to assess comprehension of central ideas and themes contained in connected prose.

Informal Tests that Measure Student Progress

Tests described under this heading can be administered quickly, with some taking only about 10 minutes per child. For this reason, these tests can be administered as often as once a week. When administered so frequently, the test informs the teacher about student progress.

Curriculum-Based Measurement

CBM involves tests that are based on the curriculum taught in the classroom and act as quasi-standardized criterion-referenced measurement tools. They are standardized in the sense that they give information about children's average reading speed. CBM is based on the premise that assessment and decision making are valid because they are based on the standard curriculum. That is, students' performance on these tests indicates their level of competence with the local school curriculum. In addition, CBM also provides a measure of students' rate of progress. In CBM, reading and spelling (as well as math) tests are developed using classroom textbooks.

Assessment of literacy skills that are based on the CBM model involves administering a series of short passages as a test of oral reading. These passages can be selected from the textbook used in the classroom. Information collected includes oral reading rate per minute, errors in reading, and comprehension scores. The teacher and the student each have a sheet of paper with the passage to be read; the teacher's copy contains numbered lines, comprehension questions, and answers. Each student is required to read three such passages, selected according to his grade level. The student is told that he will be asked to orally read the passage for 1 minute and will then be asked to answer a few questions at the end. The teacher marks the spot in the passage at the end of 1 minute, but the student continues to read until he finishes the passage. Then the comprehension questions are asked and the score is entered as percent correct. The teacher also scores the number of words read correctly during the one minute reading time and the number of words misread. The **median** score from the three passages is the score for word recognition, reading errors, and comprehension.

Detailed procedures about the CBM can be downloaded by accessing http://www.interventioncentral.org. Additional web sites describing CBM can be accessed by typing "curriculum-based measurement" in an Internet search engine.

Dynamic Indicators of Basic Early Literacy Skills

The Dynamic Indicators of Basic Early Literacy Skills (DIBELS; Good & Kaminski, 2002) is also a quasi-standardized test that yields quantitative measurements. The DIBELS includes two types of assessments: 1) benchmark assessments, designed to be administered to all students three times a year; and 2) progress monitoring measures, designed to be administered often to students receiving intervention. The progress monitoring tests are administered more frequently, at least once in 2 weeks.

The DIBELS measures three areas relevant to early literacy acquisition: phonological awareness, knowledge of alphabetic principle, and fluency and comprehension in reading connected text. The tests are meant for children from kindergarten through grade 3. The teacher assesses children's performance in these areas once a week or once in 2 weeks and records the progress made by the children. The advantages of DIBELS are that the test does not take much time to give and is simple enough to be administered by a paraprofessional or a trained volunteer. The DIBELS test informs the teacher of the level of students' performance in the stated areas of beginning reading; it does not tell the teacher what to teach or how to teach reading. Specific areas assessed by the DIBELS are discussed next.

Letter Naming Fluency   The child is presented with a page of upper- and lowercase letters arranged in a random order and asked to name as many letters as she can. The child is allowed 1 minute to produce the letter names. Children are considered at risk if they perform in the lowest 20% of children in their district. In general, a child who had been introduced to the letters of the alphabet but can name no more than four letters during the early months of kindergarten is thought to be at risk for reading difficulties.

Initial Sound Fluency   This is a standardized, individually administered measure of phonological awareness that assesses a child's ability to recognize and produce the initial sound in orally presented words. The examiner shows four pictures (e.g., sink, cat, gloves, and hat) to the child, sounds out the name of each picture, and then asks the child to point to the picture that begins with the sound produced orally by the examiner. The administration time is 3 minutes. There are a total of 20 alternate forms. Students who do not score above 10 by the middle of the kindergarten year may need intensive training in phonemic awareness and phonological skills.

Phoneme Segmentation Fluency   This is a standardized, individually administered test of phonemic awareness. It assesses a child's ability to fluently segment three- and four-letter spoken words into individual phonemes. For example, the examiner says "sat," and the student says "/s/ /a/ /t/" to receive three possible points. This test takes about 2 minutes to administer. Students who score below 10 in the spring of kindergarten and fall of first grade may need additional instructional support.

Nonsense Word Fluency   This is a standardized, individually administered test of knowledge of letter–sound correspondence and the ability to blend letters into words. This test can be administered from mid-kindergarten through the beginning of second grade. It can also be used for monitoring the progress of older children who have poor decoding skills. A written nonword (e.g., "dat") is presented, and the student is required to pronounce the word or to name each letter in the word. The duration of the test is 2 minutes. Since it takes more time to name the letters in the word than to pronounce the nonword itself, those who follow a letter-by-letter strategy receive a lower score.

Oral Reading Fluency   This is also a standardized, individually administered test with two parts. Part I is designed to measure accuracy and fluency of reading connected text; Part II is meant for assessing the ability to retell what has been read (comprehension). This subtest contains standardized sets of passages that are calibrated for each grade level. The student is told that he will read the passage aloud and after a minute will have to retell what he read. The number of correct words read per minute from the passage is the oral reading fluency rate (Part I). When the student has read the passage, he is asked to tell about what he read (Part II). The number of words the student can produce within 1 minute is a measure of comprehension. Test scores from both Part I and Part II are used for assessing reading proficiency. Although the number of words read per minute gives an indication of reading fluency, in order to consider that figure as a true index of reading proficiency, the student should be able to recall at least 50% of the words he has read. For example, a student in first grade who reads 60 words per minute and recalls 30 words he has read is typically achieving. If he can recall only 20 words out of the 60 he read, he is not proficient in reading comprehension.

Other assessment options similar to CBM and DIBELS are also available. Some of these are described next.

Once children have mastered decoding skills, they should be able to recognize words quickly and effortlessly. That is, they should become fluent readers. Both curriculum-based measurement (CBM) and Dynamic Indicators of Basic Early Literacy Skills (DIBELS; Good & Kaminski, 2002) can be used by the teacher to monitor students' fluency development.

Fox in a Box: An Adventure in Literacy

Fox in a Box: An Adventure in Literacy (Adams & Treadway, 2002) is a criterion-referenced early literacy assessment system designed to measure children's reading development in kindergarten through second grade. Based on the recommendations outlined by the National Research Council's *Preventing Reading Difficulties in Young Children* (Snow, Burns, & Griffin, 1998), Fox in a Box assesses four sets of literacy skills: 1) phonemic awareness, 2) phonics, 3) reading and oral expression, and 4) listening and writing. The package is attractive, examiner friendly, classroom oriented, and based on current scientifically based research findings.

Texas Primary Reading Inventory

The Texas Primary Reading Inventory (TPRI; Foorman et al., 2002) is an early reading instrument designed for children in kindergarten through grade 3. The TPRI consists of measures that assess five reading components: 1) phonemic awareness, 2) graphophonemic knowledge, 3) reading accuracy, 4) listening/reading comprehension, and 5) reading fluency. At each grade level, it has two parts: a screener part and an inventory part. According to Rathvon (2004),

> Developed by a leading team of researchers and based on state-of-the art test construction practices, TPRI combines high predictive accuracy with outstanding usability. The TPRI is a cost-effective choice for out of state users and earns high marks in terms of ease of administration, scoring, and interpretation, examiner supports, and links to interventions. (p. 294)

Assessment

It appears that standardized tests can provide all the information teachers may need to identify students' level of functioning and measure their progress. What, then, are the advantages of informal, or qualitative, assessment? One advantage is the informal nature of the assessment procedure. Another is that children's performance during assessment resembles the natural reading process. The assessment procedures are relatively easy to use and less time consuming than standardized tests. Assessment procedures yield information and data that are essentially qualitative in nature, but quantitative data can also be derived.

Computers can play an important role in assessment, record keeping, and literacy instruction. Computer-assisted instruction is described in Appendix C at the end of the book.

Informal Reading Inventories

Qualitative information about the student is obtained primarily through interviews and observations, whereas quantitative data are obtained by administering informal tests based on the curriculum material taught in the classroom. Qualitative information about reading performance is often collected through informal reading inventories (IRIs), which usually require children to read passages aloud, pronounce words, and answer comprehension questions.

As noted earlier, procedures such as miscue analysis and running records can also be used as part of informal assessment. Oral reading provides information to the teacher about a child's word recognition skills and fluency. The child's answers to questions after the reading provide a measure of reading comprehension skill. IRIs are easy to administer, take a few minutes, and do not require extended training to administer. In general, IRIs use graded word lists and graded passages to measure word recognition and comprehension skills. Since IRIs require oral reading, they must be administered individually. The IRIs are meant to be used for screening purposes, and a child's performance on these tasks is used for making informed judgments such as whether the child can read and comprehend text independently without assistance (independent level), can perform with some instructional help from the teacher (instructional level), or has great difficulty in reading (frustration level). Because IRIs provide measures of these three levels of reading, they can be of great help to the teacher in selecting appropriate instructional methods and materials.

Although school psychologists, reading specialists, and educational diagnosticians prefer to use standardized tests, information obtained from informal tests can often provide additional help in instruction decision making, particularly for the classroom teacher. Informal inventories are generally constructed without following the rigorous standardization procedures of establishing validity, reliability, and norms. The face validity of the inventories is estimated by eye-balling the test. That is, the validity of the test is taken at face value and not determined through statistical analysis. The IRIs are used for screening purposes only, not for making decisions regarding instructional placement.

The following IRIs have been recently published and are commonly used by teachers and clinicians:

- Analytical Reading Inventory–Seventh Edition (Woods & Moe, 2003)
- Qualitative Reading Inventory–Fourth Edition (Leslie & Caldwell, 2006)
- Basic Reading Inventory–Ninth Edition (Johns, 2005)
- Ekwall/Shanker Reading Inventory–Fourth Edition (Shanker & Ekwall, 2002)
- Classroom Reading Inventory–Tenth Edition (Silvaroli & Wheelock, 2001)
- Reading Inventory for the Classroom–Fifth Edition (Flynt & Cooter, 2004)

Another assessment technique in the informal reading inventory category is the running record. Running records are a record of a student's reading behaviors, jotted down by the teacher as the student reads. Developed by Marie Clay (2000b), this form of evaluation is an organized way for teachers to quickly and easily assess a student's reading performance. Recording forms can be downloaded by accessing a search engine and typing "running records."

Reading miscue analysis, a term proposed by Goodman (1973), is useful in examining the errors made by children as they read and for making inferences about the strengths and weaknesses of the students' reading skill. The procedure is to ask a student to read a passage from a book; as he reads, the teacher records the errors committed during reading. Error categories include misreading a word, skipping a word, and not being able to read a word. Important cues to observe are whether the student experiences difficulty in decoding written words, relies on context for decoding words, and self-corrects the misread words. Excessive dependence on context indicates a decoding weakness. Self-correcting an oral error indicates that the student is monitoring her own comprehension, a good sign. When a word is substituted for a target word and the student leaves it uncorrected, it shows that the student is not monitoring her own comprehension. For example, the student may read the sentence "The house that Jack built is on the seashore" as "The horse that Jack built is on the seashell." If the student does not go back and correct the misread words, she is not paying attention to her own comprehension. When a student substitutes one word for another and the substitution does not alter the general meaning of the sentence, it can be concluded that her decoding skill is weak but her comprehension is not impaired. An example is when a student reads the sentence "I like to play basketball" as "I like to play baseball." Keeping a record of these errors, along with an interpretation of the errors, provides insight into students' weaknesses and helps teachers keep track of students' progress in literacy skills, as running records can be obtained every week or every month. A quantitative record of children's performance can be obtained by using a passage of 100 words and noting the percent of words students were not able to read correctly. In addition, the teacher may ask children questions about the passage read, and the percent of correct responses can be used as a measure of reading comprehension.

Portfolio Assessment

Literacy portfolios document students' performance over time, allowing teachers to monitor literacy skills development. Literacy portfolios contain a record of activities that are in some form associated with the development of literacy skills. For example, a student may write an essay in November about Thanksgiving dinner at home, another essay in December about how he celebrated Christmas, and another essay in March about his plans for the summer. These products are kept in a file, which becomes part of the portfolio. The teacher can assess the growth of the student's writing skills by looking through the portfolio. Portfolios focus on student accomplishments rather than on students' weaknesses. Excessive attention to mistakes in writing and spelling can discourage students from further activities. Portfolios need not contain only written materials; students can tape-record their experiences in conducting a project and include the tapes in the portfolio. Portfolios may also contain other artifacts, such as maps and photographs of a project. The project may be a collaborative effort between the student and his parents, a desirable feature of portfolios because they can provide opportunities for parental involvement. Portfolios need not be limited to long-term projects only; students can include in their portfolio a description of a brief experience, such as a visit to the zoo. There are no rigid rules about the degree of guidance the teacher provides in the development of students' portfolios. Of course, teachers in the lower grades may provide more guidance than those in the higher grades. For instance, a third-grade teacher may ask the students to write summaries of stories they have read during school time and keep them in student portfolios. On the other hand, a fifth-grade teacher may ask the students to write summaries of stories they have read on their own, after school hours.

Students have some freedom in choosing the contents of their portfolios. Because of this, evaluation of literacy achievement is more subjective than objective. Educators suggest that teachers develop a checklist or a rubric about what is expected from students, communicate it to the students, and use it for evaluation. However, evaluation is not the main goal of portfolios; the major objective is to stimulate students' interest in literacy-related activities and to nurture growth in literacy skills.

Assignments for the Student Teacher

1. Administer the DIBELS or a similar informal test and monitor the progress made by a child in the second or third grade over a period of 4 weeks. Interpret the results of your assessment procedures. Recommend some instructional strategies if the child is found to have difficulties in some area of reading.

2. Construct a 12-word spelling test. Adjust the spelling list according to the reading level of the children you plan to test. Make sure the list contains monosyllabic and bisyllabic words as well as regular and irregular words.

   Administer the spelling test to the children. First read a word, then embed it in a sentence, and then read the word again.

   Score the spelling responses both quantitatively and qualitatively. Compare the outcome of both forms of scoring. How can you use the results of qualitative scoring to improve the children's spelling skills?

3. Administer an oral reading test to a child and keep a running record. Calculate the percentage of words read accurately and determine the type(s) of strategy (decoding or reliance on context) the child is using to sound out unfamiliar words. Also note whether the child is able to monitor her own comprehension.

4. Administer an informal reading inventory to one child in the primary grades and one child in the intermediate grades. Determine whether each child's reading level is frustration, instructional, or independent.

5. Determine the listening comprehension level of a child. Is there a difference between his level of reading comprehension and his level of listening comprehension? Interpret the results and note how you will use this information in instruction.

6. Select 20 content words and 20 function words (grammar words) from the textbooks used in grades 2 and 3. Print these words on sheets of paper and administer them as oral reading tests to groups of children from these grades. Note the accuracy and time needed for reading these word lists. What is the average number of content words and function words the children can read per minute? Are there differences in accuracy and speed between the content word list and the function word list?

Reading Assignment

Read one of the following articles, discuss it, and write a one-page summary. These articles can be obtained at your college library or downloaded by accessing the library's electronic holdings.

Opitz, M.F., & Ford, M.P. (2006). Assessment can be friendly. *The Reading Teacher, 59*(8), 814–816.

Walpole, S., & McKenna, M.C. (2006). The role of informal reading inventories in assessing word recognition. *The Reading Teacher, 59*(6), 592–594.

References

Aaron, P.G. (1989). *Dyslexia and hyperlexia*. Boston: Kluwer Academic Publishers.

Aaron, P.G. (1995). Differential diagnosis of reading disabilities. *School Psychology Review, 24*(3), 345–360.

Aaron, P.G. (1997). The impending demise of the discrepancy formula. *Review of Educational Research, 67*(4), 461–502.

Aaron, P.G., & Joshi, R.M. (1992). *Reading problems: Consultation and remediation*. New York: Guilford Press.

Aaron, P.G., & Joshi, R.M. (2006). Written language is as natural as spoken language. *Reading Psychology, 27*, 263–311.

Aaron, P.G., Joshi, R.M., Ayotollah, M., Ellsberry, A., Henderson, J., & Lindsey, K. (1999). Decoding and sight-word naming: Are they independent components of word recognition skill? *Reading and Writing: An Interdisciplinary Journal, 11*, 89–127.

Aaron, P.G., Joshi, R.M., Boulware-Gooden, R., & Bentum, K. (in press). The outcome of the Component Model-based reading remedial instruction: An alternative to the discrepancy model-based treatment of learning disabilities. *Journal of Learning Disabilities*.

Aaron, P.G., Joshi, R.M., Hyyon, P., Smith, N., & Kirby, E. (2002). Separating genuine cases of reading disabilities from reading difficulties caused by attention deficits. *Journal of Learning Disabilities, 35*(5), 425–435.

Aaron, P.G., Joshi, R.M., & Ocker, E. (2004). Summoning up the spirits from the vast deep: LD and giftedness in historic persons. In T.A. Newman & R. Sternberg (Eds.), *Students with both gifts and learning disabilities* (pp. 199–234). Boston: Kluwer Academic Publishers.

Aaron, P.G., Joshi, R.M., Palmer, H., Smith, N., & Kirby, E. (2002). Separating genuine cases of reading disability from reading deficits caused by predominantly inattentive ADHD behavior. *Journal of Learning Disabilities, 35*(5), 425–435, 447.

Aaron, P.G., Joshi, R.M., & Phipps, J. (2004). A cognitive tool to diagnose predominantly inattentive ADHD behavior. *Journal of Attention Disorders, 7*(3), 125–135.

Aaron, P.G., Keetay, V., Boyd, M., Palmatier, S., & Wacks, J. (1998). Spelling without phonology: A study of deaf and hearing children. *Reading and Writing: An Interdisciplinary Journal, 10*, 1–22.

Aaron, P.G., & Kotva, H. (1999). Component Model-based remedial treatment of reading disabilities. In I. Lundberg, F.E. Tonnessen, & I. Austad (Eds.), *Dyslexia: Advances in theory and practice* (pp. 221–244). Boston: Kluwer Academic Publishers.

Aaron, P.G., Phillips, S., & Larsen, A. (1988). Specific reading disabilities in historically famous persons. *Journal of Learning Disabilities, 21*, 521–584.

Adams, G., & Engelmann, S. (1996). *Research on direct instruction: 25 years and beyond DISTAR*. Seattle: Educational Achievement Systems.

Adams, M.J. (1990). *Beginning to read: Thinking and learning about print*. Urbana-Champaign, IL: Center for the Study of Reading.

Adams, M.J., Foorman, B.R., Lundberg, I., & Beeler, T. (1998). *Phonemic awareness in young children: A classroom curriculum*. Baltimore: Paul H. Brookes Publishing Co.

Adams, M.J., & Treadway, J. (2002). *Fox in a box: An adventure in literacy*. Monterey, CA: CTB/McGraw Hill.

Adger, C.T., Wolfram, W., & Christian, D. (2007). *Dialects in schools and communities*. Mahwah, NJ: Lawrence Erlbaum Associates.

Adlof, S.M., Catts, H.W., Hogan, T.P., & Little, D.T. (2005). *The role of fluency in reading comprehension: Should fluency be included in the simple view of reading?* Paper presented at the annual meeting of the Society for the Scientific Study of Reading. Toronto.

Algozzine, B. (1985). Low achiever differentiation: Where is the beef? *Exceptional Children, 52,* 72–75.

Allen, K.A., & Beckwith, M.C. (1999). Alphabet knowledge. In J.R. Birsh (Ed.), *Multisensory teaching of basic language skills* (pp. 85–117). Baltimore: Paul H. Brookes Publishing Co.

Allen, K.A., Neuhaus, G.F., & Beckwith, M.C. (2005). Alphabet knowledge: Letter recognition, naming, and sequencing. In J.R. Birsh (Ed.), *Multisensory teaching of basic language skills* (2nd ed., pp. 113–150). Baltimore: Paul H. Brookes Publishing Co.

Allington, R.L. (2002). *Big brother and the national reading curriculum.* Portsmouth, NH: Heinemann.

American Federation of Teachers (1991). *Teaching reading is rocket science.* Washington, DC: Author.

American Psychiatric Association. (1994). *Diagnostic and statistical manual of mental disorders* (4th ed.) Washington, DC: Author.

Anderson, R., & Freebody, P. (1979). *Vocabulary knowledge* (Technical Report No. 136). University of Illinois at Urbana-Champaign: Center for the Study of Reading.

Anderson, R.C., & Freebody, P. (1981). Vocabulary knowledge. In J. Guthrie (Ed.), *Comprehension and teaching: Research reviews* (pp. 77–117). Newark, DE: International Reading Association.

Anderson, R.C., Hiebert, E.H., Scott, P., & Wilkinson, D. (1985). *Becoming a nation of readers: The report of the Commission on Reading.* Champaign, IL: The National Institute of Reading, The Center for the Study of Reading.

Anderson, R.C., Wilson, P., & Fielding, L.G. (1988). Growth in reading and how children spend their time outside of school. *Reading Research Quarterly, 23,* 285–303.

Anisfeld, M. (1984). *Language development from birth to three.* Hillsdale, NJ: Lawrence Erlbaum Associates.

Arra, C.T., & Aaron, P.G. (2001). Effects of psycholinguistic instruction on spelling performance. *Psychology in the Schools, 38,* 357–363.

Au, K.H. (1980). Participation structures in a reading lesson with Hawaiian children: Analysis of a culturally appropriate instructional event. *Anthropology and Education Quarterly, 11,* 91–115.

Aukerman, R.C. (1984). *Approaches to reading.* New York: John Wiley & Sons.

Baddeley, A.D. (1966). The influence of acoustic and semantic similarity on long-term memory for word sequences. *Quarterly Journal of Experimental Psychology, 18,* 302–309.

Baddeley, A.D. (1982). *Working memory.* New York: Oxford University Press.

Bailet, L.L. (1990). Spelling rule usage among students with learning disabilities and normally achieving students. *Journal of Learning Disabilities, 8,* 162–165.

Baker, L., Fernandez-Fein, S., Scher, D., & Williams, H. (1998). Home experiences related to the development of word recognition. In J.L. Metsala & L.C. Ehri (Eds.), *Word recognition in beginning literacy* (pp. 263–287). Mahwah, NJ: Lawrence Erlbaum Associates.

Ball, E.W., & Blachman, B.A. (1988). Phoneme segmentation training: Effect on reading readiness. *Annals of Dyslexia, 38,* 208–225.

Ball, E.W., & Blachman, B.A. (1991). Does phoneme segmentation training in kindergarten make a difference in early word recognition and developmental spelling? *Reading Research Quarterly, 26,* 49–66.

Banks, S.R., Guyer, B.P., & Banks, K.E. (1993). Wilson Reading System: Spelling improvement by college students who are dyslexic. *Annals of Dyslexia, 43,* 186–193.

Baratz, J. (1973). Teaching reading in an urban Negro school system. In R.H. Bentley & S.D. Crawford (Eds.), *Black language reader* (pp. 55–69). Glenview, IL: Scott Foresman & Co.

Baratz, J., & Povich, E. (1967). *Grammatical constructions in the language of the Negro preschool child.* Paper presented at the annual meeting of the American Speech and Hearing Association, Washington DC.

Barkley, R.A. (1997). *ADHD and the nature of self control.* New York: Guilford Press.

Barnhart, C.L. (Ed.). (1956). *The American college dictionary.* New York: Random House.

Barton, P. (1992). *America's smallest school: The family.* Princeton, NJ: Educational Testing Service.

Barton, P. (1994). *Becoming literate about literacy.* Princeton, NJ: Educational Testing Service.

Baumann, J.F., Font, G., Edwards, E.C., & Boland, E. (2005). Strategies for teaching middle-grade students to use word-part and context cues to expand reading vocabulary. In E.H. Hiebert & M.L. Kamil (Eds.), *Teaching and learning vocabulary: Bringing research to practice* (pp. 179–205). Mahwah, NJ: Lawrence Erlbaum Associates.

Baumann, J.F., & Ivey, G. (1997). Delicate balances: Striving for curricular and instructional equilibrium in a second-grade literature, strategy-based classroom. *Reading Research Quarterly, 32,* 244–275.

Bear, R.D., Invernizzi, M., Templeton, N., & Johnston, F. (1996). *Words their way: Word study for phonics, vocabulary, and spelling.* Columbus, OH: Merrill.

Beck, I., McKeown, M.G., & Kucan, L. (2002). *Bringing words to life: Robust vocabulary instruction.* New York: Guilford Press.

Beck, I., McKeown, M.G., & Kucan, L. (2005). Choosing words to teach. In E.H. Hiebert & M.L. Kamil (Eds.), *Teaching and learning vocabulary: Bringing research to practice* (pp. 209–222). Mahwah, NJ: Lawrence Erlbaum Associates.

Beck, I., McKeown, M.G., & Omanson, R.C. (1987). The effects and uses of diverse vocabulary instructional techniques. In M.G. McKeown & M.E. Curtis (Eds.), *The nature of vocabulary acquisition* (pp. 147–163). Mahwah, NJ: Lawrence Erlbaum Associates.

Beck, I., Omanson, R.C., & McKeown, M.G. (1982). An instructional redesign of reading lessons: Effects of comprehension. *Reading Research Quarterly, 17,* 462–481.

Beck, I., Perfetti, C., & McKeown, M. (1982). Effect of long-term vocabulary instruction on lexical access and reading comprehension. *Journal of Educational Psychology, 74,* 506–521.

Behuniak, P. (2002). Consumer-referenced testing. *Phi Delta Kappan, 84*(3), 199–207.

Benbow, C., & Stanley, J. (1983). Sex differences in mathematical reasoning ability: More facts. *Science, 222,* 1028–1031.

Bender, R.L., & Bender, W.N. (1996). *Computer-assisted instruction for students at risk.* Boston: Allyn & Bacon.

Bennett, J.A., & Berry, J.W. (1987). The future of Cree syllabic literacy in Northern Canada. In D.A. Wagner (Ed.), *The future of literacy in a changing world* (pp. 172–185). New York: Pergamon Press.

Bennett, J.A., & Berry, J.W. (1991). Cree literacy in the syllable script. In D.R. Olson & N. Torrance (Eds.), *Literacy and orality* (pp. 90–104). New York: Cambridge University Press.

Bentum, K., & Aaron, P.G. (2003). Does reading instruction in learning disability resource rooms really work? A longitudinal study. *Reading Psychology, 24,* 361–382.

Bereiter, S., & Englemann, S. (1964). *DISTAR reading.* De Soto, TX: SRA Corrective Reading.

Bergeron, B. (1990). What does the term 'whole language' mean? Constructing a definition from literature. *Journal of Reading Behavior, 22*(4), 301–329.

Berko, J. (1958). The child's learning of English morphology. *Word, 14,* 150–177.

Berlin, C.J. (1887). Alexia in an adult. *American Journal of Psychology, 1*(1), 548.

Berninger, V.W., & Swanson, H.L. (1994). Modification of the Hayes & Fowler model to explain beginning and developing writing. In E. Butterfield (Ed.), *Advances in cognition and educational practice: Children's writing: Toward a process theory of development of skilled writing* (Vol. 2, pp. 57–82). Greenwich, CT: JAI Press.

Berry, B., Hoke, M., & Hirsch, E. (2004). The search for highly qualified teachers. *Phi Delta Kappan, 85*(9), 684–689.

Berry, J.W., & Bennett, J.A. (1989). Syllabic literacy and cognitive performance among the Cree. *International Journal of Psychology, 24,* 429–450.

Bertelson, P., & de Gelder, B. (1988). Learning about reading from illiterates. In A. Galaburda (Ed.), *From neurons to reading* (pp. 240–269). Cambridge, MA: MIT Press.

Biemiller, A. (2005). Size and sequence in vocabulary development: Implications for choosing words for primary grade vocabulary instruction. In E.H. Hiebert & M.L. Kamil (Eds.), *Teaching and learning vocabulary: Bringing research to practice* (pp. 223–242). Mahwah, NJ: Lawrence Erlbaum Associates.

Birsh, J.R. (Ed.). (2005). *Multisensory teaching of basic language skills* (2nd ed.). Baltimore: Paul H. Brookes Publishing Co.

Bishop, D.V., & Butterworth, G.E. (1980). Verbal performance discrepancies: Relationship to birth risk and specific reading retardation. *Cortex, 16,* 375–389.

Blachman, B.A., Ball, E.W., Black, R., & Tangel, D.M. (2000). *Road to the code: A phonological awareness program for young children.* Baltimore: Paul H. Brookes Publishing Co.

Blachowicz, C., & Fisher, P. (2006). *Teaching vocabulary in all classrooms* (3rd ed.). Columbus, OH: Merrill.

Blanchard, J.S., Di Cerbo, K.E., Oliver, J., & Albers, C.A. (2001, July). Can divided time administration raise test scores? *The relation between attention and standardized reading comprehension tests.* Paper presented at the annual meeting of the Society for the Scientific Studies of Reading, Boulder, CO.

Blanchfield, C. (2004). Word tree posters. In G.E. Tompkins & C. Blanchfield (Eds.), *Teaching vocabulary: 50 creative strategies* (pp. 47–48). Upper Saddle River, NJ: Merrill-Prentice Hall.

Blatchford, P., Moriarty, V., Edmonds, S., & Martin, C. (2002). Relationships between class size and teaching: A multimethod analysis of English infant schools. *American Educational Research Journal, 39*(1), 101–132.

Block, C.C. (1993). Strategy instruction in a literature-based reading program. *Elementary School Journal, 94,* 139–151.

Block, C.C., Gambrell, L.B., & Pressley, M. (2002). *Improving comprehension instruction: Rethinking research, theory, and classroom practice.* San Francisco: Jossey-Bass.

Block, C.C., & Johnson, R.B. (2002). The thinking process approach to comprehension development. In C.C. Block, L.B. Gambrell, & M. Pressey (Eds.), *Improving comprehension instruction: Rethinking research, theory, and classroom practice* (pp. 54–79). San Francisco: Jossey-Bass.

Blok, H., Oostdam, R., Otter, M.E., & Overmaat, M. (2002). Computer-assisted instruction in support of beginning reading instruction: A review. *Review of Educational Research, 72,* 101–130.

Bloomfield, L. (1933). *Language.* New York: Holt, Rinehart, & Winston.

Bloomfield, L., & Barnhart, C. (1961). *Let's read: A linguistic approach.* Detroit, MI: Wayne State University Press.

Bode, B. (1989). Dialogue journal writing. *The Reading Teacher, 42*(8), 568–571.

Bohannon, J.N., & Bonvillian, J.D. (2001). Theoretical approaches to language acquisition. In J.B. Gleason (Ed.), *The development of language* (5th ed., pp. 254–314). Boston: Allyn & Bacon.

Bond, G., & Dykstra, R. (1967). The cooperative research program in first grade reading instruction. *Reading Research Quarterly, 2,* 5–42.

Bosman, A.M., & Van Orden, G.C. (1997). Why spelling is more difficult than reading. In C.A. Perfetti, L. Rieben, & M. Fayol (Eds.), *Learning to spell: Research, theory, and practice across languages* (pp. 173–194). Mahwah, NJ: Lawrence Erlbaum Associates.

Bowden, J.H. (1911). Learning to read. *The Elementary School Journal, 12*(1), 21–33.

Bowers, P.G., & Newby-Clark, E. (2002). The role of naming speed within a model of reading acquisition. *Reading and Writing: An Interdisciplinary Journal, 15,* 109–126.

Bradley, L., & Bryant, P.E. (1985). *Rhyme and reason in reading and spelling.* Ann Arbor, MI: University of Michigan Press.

Bradley, R., Danielson, L., & Doolittle, J. (2005). Response to intervention. *Journal of Learning Disabilities, 38,* 485–486.

Breggin, R.P. (1998). *Talking back to Ritalin*. Monroe, ME: Common Courage Press.

Briggs, C., & Duncan, S. (2006). Letter to the editor. *Journal of Learning Disabilities, 39*(4), 290–291.

British Dyslexia Association. (2007). *What is dyslexia?* Retrieved December 3, 2007, from http://www.bdadyslexia.org.uk/whatisdyslexia.html

Bronner, A.F. (1917). *The psychology of special abilities and disabilities*. Boston: Little Brown & Co.

Brown, A.L., & Palincsar, A.S. (1987). Reciprocal teaching of comprehension strategies: A natural history of one program for enhancing learning. In J.D. Day & J.G. Borkowski (Eds.), *Intelligence and exceptionality: New directions for theory, assessment, and instructional practice* (pp. 81–132). Norwood, NJ: Ablex.

Brown, R. (1973). *A first language*. Cambridge, MA: Harvard University Press.

Bush, G., Frazier, J.A., Rauch, S.L., Seidman, P.J., Seidman, L., Whaten, J., et al. (1999). Dysfunction in attention deficit hyperactivity disorder revealed by fMRI and the counting Stroop. *Biological Psychiatry, 45*(12), 1542–1552.

Butler, K.A. (1988). How kids learn: What theorists say. *Learning, 17*, 28–43.

Byrne, B., & Barnsley, R. (1995). Evaluation of a program to teach phonemic awareness to young children: A 2- and 3-year follow up and a new preschool trial. *Journal of Educational Psychology, 87*(3), 488–503.

Calfee, R. (1998). Phonics and phonemes: Learning to decode and spell in a literature-based program. In J.L Metsala & L.C. Ehri (Eds.), *Word recognition in beginning literacy* (pp. 315–340). Mahwah, NJ: Lawrence Erlbaum Associates.

Calfee, R., Venezky, R., & Chapman, R. (1969). *Pronunciation of synthetic words with predictable and unpredictable letter–sound correspondences* (Technical Report, No.11). Madison: University of Wisconsin, Research and Developmental Center.

California State Board of Education. (2006). *Content standards: English-language arts*. Retrieved October 2007 from http://www.sdcoe.k12.ca.us/score/stand/std.html

Cameron, J., & Pierce, D. (1994). Reinforcement, reward, and intrinsic motivation. *Review of Educational Research, 64*(3), 363–423.

Carbo, M. (1983). Research in reading and learning style: Implications for exceptional children. *Exceptional Children, 49*, 486–493.

Carle, E. (1987). *Have you seen my cat?* New York: Scholastic.

Carle, E. (1996). *Brown bear, brown bear, what do you see?* New York: Henry Holt and Company.

Carlisle, J.F. (1988). Knowledge of derivational morphology and spelling ability in fourth, sixth, and eighth graders. *Applied Psycholinguistics, 9*(3), 247–266.

Carlisle, J.F., & Nomanbhoy, D.M. (1993). Phonological and morphological awareness in first graders. *Applied Psycholinguistics, 14*, 177–190.

Carlisle, J.F., & Rice, M.S. (2002). *Improving reading comprehension: Research-based principles and practices*. Baltimore: York Press.

Carlson, E. (1997). *In school and post-school outcomes of students declassified from special education*. Unpublished doctoral dissertation, College of William and Mary, Williamsburg, VA.

Carreker, S. (2005a). Teaching reading: Accurate decoding and fluency. In J.R. Birsh (Ed.), *Multisensory teaching of basic language skills* (2nd ed., pp. 213–255). Baltimore: Paul H. Brookes Publishing Co.

Carreker, S. (2005b). Teaching spelling. In J.R. Birsh (Ed.), *Multisensory teaching of basic language skills* (2nd ed., pp. 257–295). Baltimore: Paul H. Brookes Publishing Co.

Carreker, S. (2006). The parts of speech: Foundation of writing. *Perspectives, 32*(2), 31–34.

Case, B.J. (2003). *Accomodations on Stanford 10 for students with disabilites*. San Antonio, TX: Harcourt Assessment.

Castles, A., & Coltheart, M. (2004). Is there a causal link from phonological awareness to success in learning to read? *Cognition, 91*(1), 77–111.

Cattell, J.M. (1886). The time taken up by cerebral operations. *Mind, 11*, 220–242, 377–392, 524–538.

Catts, H.W., Hogan, T.P., & Fey, M.E. (2003). Subgrouping poor readers on the basis of individual differences in reading-related abilities. *Journal of Learning Disabilities, 36*, 151–165.

Center, Y., Wheldall, K., & Freeman, L. (1992). Evaluating the Reading Recovery: A critique. *Educational Psychology, 12*, 263–273.

Chafe, W.L. (1985). Linguistic differences produced by differences between speaking and writing. In D.E. Olson, N. Torrance, & D. Hildyard (Eds.), *Literacy, language, and learning* (pp. 105–123). New York: Cambridge University Press.

Chall, J.S. (1967). *Learning to read: The great debate.* New York: McGraw Hill.

Chall, J.S. (1996). *Learning to read: The great debate* (Rev. Ed.). New York: McGraw Hill.

Chall, J.S., & Squire, J.R. (1991). The publishing industry and textbooks. In R. Barr, M. Kamil, P. Mosenthal, & D. Pearson (Eds.), *Handbook of reading research* (Vol. 2, pp. 120–146). New York: Longman.

Chaney, C. (1992). Language development, metalinguistic skills, and print awareness in 3-year-old children. *Applied Psycholinguistics, 13*(4), 485–514.

Charity, A.H., Scarborough, H.S., & Griffin, D.M. (2004). Familiarity with school English in African American children and its relation to early reading achievement. *Child Development, 75*(5), 1340–1356.

Cho, J.R., & McBride-Chang, C. (2005). Correlates of Korean Hangul acquisition among kindergartners and second graders. *Scientific Studies of Reading, 9*(1), 3–16.

Chomsky, C. (1970). Reading, writing, and phonology. *Harvard Educational Review, 40*, 287–309.

Chomsky, N. (1965). *Aspects of the theory of syntax.* Cambridge, MA: MIT Press.

Chomsky, N. (1975). *Reflections on language.* New York: Pantheon.

Chomsky, N., & Halle, M. (1968). *The sound pattern of English.* New York: Harper & Row.

Clairborne, J.H. (1906). Types of congenital amblyopia. *Journal of the American Medical Association, 47*, 1813–1816.

Clark, D. (1988). *Dyslexia: Theory and practice of remedial instruction.* Baltimore: York Press.

Clay, M. (1966). *Emergent reading behavior.* Unpublished doctoral dissertation, University of Auckland, New Zealand.

Clay, M. (1985). *The early detection of reading difficulties* (3rd ed.). Portsmouth, NH: Heinemann.

Clay, M. (1993). *Reading Recovery: A guidebook for teachers in training.* Portsmouth, NH: Heinemann.

Clay, M. (2000a). *Concepts about print: What have children learned about the way we print language.* Portsmouth, NH: Heinemann.

Clay, M. (2000b). *Running records for classroom teachers.* Portsmouth, NH: Heinemann.

Clements, A.M., Rimrodt, S.L., Abel, J.R., Blankner, J.G., Mostofsky, S.H., Pekar, J.J., et al. (2006). Sex differences in cerebral laterality of language and visuospatial processing. *Brain & Language, 98*(2), 150–158.

Coe, M.D. (1999). *Breaking the Maya code.* New York: Thames & Hudson.

Coleman, J.S., Campbell, E.Q., Hobson, C.J., McPartland, J., Mood, A.M., Weinfield, F.D., et al. (1966). *Equality of educational opportunity* (Superintendent of Documents, Catalog No. FS 5238: 38001). Washington DC: U.S. Office of Education.

Coles, G. (2000). *Misreading reading: The bad science that hurts children.* Portsmouth, NH: Heinemann.

Coltheart, M. (1978). Lexical access in simple reading tasks. In G. Underwood (Ed.), *Strategies of information processing* (pp. 228–256). New York: Academic Press.

Compton, D.L., & Carlisle, J.F. (1994). Speed of word recognition as a distinguishing characteristic of reading disabilities. *Educational Psychological Review, 6*, 115–140.

Conners, C.K. (2000). *Conners' Continuous Performance Test II.* North Tonawanda, NY: Multi-Health Systems.

Conners, C.K. (2004). *Conners' Parent Rating Scale and Child Behavior Checklist, Third Edition.* North Tonawanda, NY: Multi-Health Systems.

Cooper, D.H., Roth, F.D., Speece, D.L., & Schatschneider, C. (2002). The contribution of oral language to the development of phonological awareness. *Applied Psycholinguistics, 23*, 399–416.

Cornelius, J.D. (1991). *When I can read my title clear: Literacy, slavery, and religion in Antebellum south.* Columbia: University of South Carolina Press.

Costello, P.A. (1992). *The effectiveness of class size on reading achievement.* East Lansing, MI: National Center for Research on Teacher Learning. (ERIC document, ED 400035)

Coulmas, F. (1996). *The Blackwell encyclopedia of writing systems.* Malden, MA: Blackwell Publishing.

Coulmas, F. (Ed.). (1997). *The handbook of sociolinguistics.* Malden, MA: Blackwell Publishing.

Cox, A.R. (1992). *Foundations for literacy: Structures and techniques for multisensory teaching of basic written English language skills.* Cambridge, MA: Educators Publishing Service.

Craig, H.K., Thompson, C.A., Washington, J.A., & Potter, S.L. (2004). Performance of elementary-grade African American students on the Gray Reading Tests. *Language, Speech, & Hearing Services in Schools, 35*, 141–154.

Crain, W. (2004). *Theories of development* (5th ed.). Upper Saddle River, NJ: Prentice Hall.

Cronbach, L.J., & Snow, R.E. (1977). *Aptitudes and instructional methods.* New York: Irvington.

CTB/McGraw Hill. (2007). *California Achievement Tests, Fifth Edition (CAT/5).* Monterey, CA: Author.

Cunningham, A. (2005). Vocabulary growth through independent reading. In E.H. Hiebert & M.L. Kamil (Eds.), *Teaching and learning vocabulary: Bringing research to practice* (pp. 458–468). Mahwah, NJ: Lawrence Erlbaum Associates.

Cunningham, A.E., & Stanovich, K.E. (1997). Early reading acquisition and its relation to reading experience and ability 10 years later. *Developmental Psychology, 33*, 934–945.

Cunningham, P.M. (1999a). *The teacher's guide to the Four Blocks.* Greensboro, NC: Carson-Dellosa Press.

Cunningham, P.M. (1999b). What should we do about phonics? In L.B. Gambrell, M. Morrow, S.B. Neuman, & M. Pressley (Eds.), *Best practices in literacy education* (pp. 68–89). New York: Guilford Press.

Cunningham, P.M. (2004). *Phonics they use: Words for reading and writing* (4th ed.). Boston: Allyn & Bacon.

Cunningham, P.M., & Allington, R.L. (1999). *Classrooms that work: They can all read and write.* New York: Harper Collins.

Cunningham, P.M., Hall, D., & Defee, M. (1998). Non-ability grouped multilevel instruction: Eight years later. *The Reading Teacher, 51*, 652–664.

Dale, E., & O'Rourke, J. (1981). *The living word vocabulary.* Chicago: World Book/Children International.

Daniels, P.T. (1996). The study of writing systems. In P.T. Daniels & W. Bright (Eds.), *The world's writing systems* (pp. 1–2). New York: Oxford University Press.

Darwin, C. (1871). *The descent of man and selection in relation to sex.* London: J. Murray.

Dearborn, W.F. (1925). The etiology of word blindness. In E. Lord, L. Carmichael, & W.F. Dearborn (Eds.), Special disabilities in learning to read and write. *Harvard Monographs in Education: Vol. II* (1, Series 1).

Deci, E.L., Koestner, R., & Ryan, R. (1999). A meta-analytic review of experiments examining the effect of extrinsic motivation. *Psychological Bulletin, 125*(1), 627–668.

DeFord, D.E. (1980). Young children and their writing. *Theory into Practice, 19*, 157–162.

Dejerine, J.C. (1891). Sur un cas de cecite verbale avec agraphie, suivi d'autopsie. *Memoirs of the Society of Biology, 3*, 197–201. (Cited in N. Geschwind [Ed.], [1974]. *Selected papers in language and the brain.* Boston: Reidel.)

Dejerine, J.C. (1892). Des Differentes Varietes de Cecite berbale. *Memoirs of the Society of Biology,* 1–30. (Cited in N. Geschwind [Ed.] [1974]. *Selected papers in language and the brain.* Boston: Reidel.)

Dermody, M., & Speaker, R.B. (1995). Effects of reciprocal strategy training in prediction, clarification, question generating, and summarization on fourth graders' reading comprehension. In K.A. Hinchman, D.J. Leu, & C.K. Kinzer (Eds.), *Forty- fourth yearbook of the National Reading Conference* (pp. 190–196). Rochester, NY: National Reading Conference.

De Silva, M.S. (1982). Some consequences of diglossia. In W. Hass (Ed.), *Standard languages, spoken and written.* Manchester, United Kingdom: Manchester University Press.

Diamond, L., & Gutlohn, L. (2007). *Vocabulary handbook.* Baltimore: Paul H. Brookes Publishing Co.

Diller, L.H., (1998). *Running on Ritalin.* New York: Bantam Books.

Dodd, B., Holm, A., Hua, Z., & Crosbie, S. (2003). Phonological development: A normative study of British English-speaking children. *Clinical Linguistics & Phonetics, 17*(8), 617–643.

Dolch, E.W. (1948). *Problems in reading.* Champaign, IL: Garrard Press.

Dole, J.A., Brown, K.J., & Trathen, W. (1996). The effects of strategy instruction on the comprehension performance of at-risk students. *Reading Research Quarterly, 31,* 202–224.

Donnelly, A. (1999). *Self-questioning: A comparative analysis of what teachers and students report about the use of this reading comprehension strategy.* Unpublished doctoral dissertation. The Center for Education, Widener University, Chester, PA.

Dorr, R.E. (2006). Something old is new again: Revisiting language experience. *The Reading Teacher, 60*(2), 138–146.

Drew, S. (2005). Collecting verbs for revising writing. In G.E. Tompkins & C. Blanchfield (Eds.), *Teaching vocabulary: 50 creative strategies* (pp. 90–92). Upper Saddle River, NJ: Merrill/Prentice Hall

Dunn, R. (2000). Learning styles: Theory, research, and practice. *National Forum of Applied Educational Research Journal, 13*(1), 3–22.

DuPaul, G.T., Power, T.J., Anastopoulos, A.D., & Reid, R. (1998). *ADHD Rating scale–IV.* New York: Guilford Press.

DuPaul, G.T., & Stoner, G. (1994). *ADHD in the schools: Assessment and intervention strategies.* New York: Guilford Press.

Durkin, D. (1966). *Children who read early: Two longitudinal studies.* New York: Teachers College Press.

Durkin, D. (1993). *Teaching them to read* (6th ed.). Boston: Allyn & Bacon.

Durrell, D., & Catterson, J. (1980). *Durrell Analysis of Reading Difficulty, Third Edition (DARD).* San Antonio, TX: Harcourt Assessment.

Dykstra, R. (1974). Phonics and beginning reading instruction. In C.C. Walcutt, J. Lamport, & G. McCracken (Eds.), *Teaching reading: A phonics/linguistic approach to developmental reading* (pp. 91–110). New York: MacMillan.

Ebbinghaus, H. (1913). *Memory.* (H.A. Ruger & C.E. Bussenius, Trans.). New York: Teachers College Press. (Original work published 1885)

Education for all Handicapped Children Act of 1975, PL 94-142, 20 U.S.C. §§ 1400 *et seq.*

Ehri, L.C. (1986). Sources of difficulty in learning to spell and read. In M.L. Wolraich & D. Routh (Eds.), *Advances in developmental and behavioral pediatrics* (pp.127–158). Greenwich, CT: Jai Press.

Ehri, L.C. (1992). Reconceptualizing the development of sight word reading and its relationship to recoding. In P.B. Gough, L.C. Ehri, & R. Treiman (Eds.), *Reading acquisition* (pp. 107–143). Mahwah, NJ: Lawrence Erlbaum Associates.

Ehri, L.C. (1998). Grapheme-Phoneme knowledge is essential for learning to read words in English. In J.L. Matsala & L.C. Ehri (Eds.), *Word recognition in literacy* (pp. 3–40). Mahwah, NJ: Lawrence Erlbaum Associates.

Ehri, L.C., & Wilce, L.S. (1987). Does learning to spell help beginners learn to read words? *Reading Research Quarterly, 22,* 47–65.

Eldredge, J.L., Reutzel, D.R., & Hollingsworth, P.M. (1996). Comparing the effectiveness of two oral reading practices: Round-robin reading and the shared book experience. *Journal of Literacy Research, 28*(2), 201–225.

Elkonin, D.B. (1973). Reading in the U.S.S.R. In J. Downing (Ed.), *Comparative reading*. (pp. 68–88). New York: MacMillan.

Elley, W.B. (1989). Vocabulary acquisition from listening to stories. *Reading Research Quarterly, 24*(2), 174–187.

Falkenstein, A. (1964). Das Sumerische. Reprint from *Handbuch der Orientalistik*. Leiden, The Netherlands: Brill.

Farrall, M. (2002). Reading recovery: What do school districts get for their money, A review of the research. Retrieved August 2007 from http://www.wrightslaw.com

Feingold, A. (1993). Cognitive gender differences: A developmental perspective. *Sex Roles, 29*, 91–112.

Felton, R.H., & Wood, F.B. (1989). Cognitive deficits in reading disability and attention deficit disorder. *Journal of Learning Disabilities, 22*, 3–22.

Ferguson, C.A. (1959). Diglossia. *Word, 15*, 325–340.

Fergusson, D.M., & Horwood, L.J. (1992). Attention deficit and reading achievement. *Journal of Child Psychology and Psychiatry, 33*, 375–385.

Fernald, G., & Keller, H. (1921). The effects of kinesthetic factors in development of word recognition in the case of nonreaders. *Journal of Educational Research, 4*, 357–377.

Fildes, L.G. (1921). A psychological inquiry into the nature of the condition known as congenital word blindness. *Brain, 44*, 286–304.

Finegan, E. (1987). English. In B. Comrie (Ed.), *The world's major languages* (pp. 47–86). New York: Oxford University Press.

Fischer, S.R. (2001). *A history of writing*. London: Reaktion Books.

Fisher, D., & Frey, N. (2007). Implementing a school-wide literacy framework: Improving achievement in an urban elementary school. *The Reading Teacher, 61*(1), 32–43.

Flesch, R. (1955). *Why Johnny can't read*. New York: Harper & Row.

Fletcher, J.M., Coulter, W.A., Reschly, D.J., & Vaughn, S. (2004). Alternative approaches to the definition and identification of learning disabilities: Some questions and answers. *Annals of Dyslexia, 54*(2), 304–331.

Flynt, E.S., & Cooter, R.B. (2004). *Reading Inventory for the Classroom–Fifth Edition*. Upper Saddle River, NJ: Pearson Merrill Prentice Hall.

Foorman, B., Chen, D., Carlson, C., Moats, L., Francis, D., & Fletcher, J.M. (2003). The necessity of the alphabetic principle to phonemic awareness instruction. *Reading and Writing: An Interdisciplinary Journal, 16*, 289–324.

Foorman, B., Fletcher, J.M., Francis, D.J., Carlson, C.D., Chen, D.T., Mouzaki, A., et al. (2002). *Texas Primary Reading Inventory (TPRI)*. Houston: Center for Academic and Reading Skills, University of Texas–Houston Health Science Center & University of Houston.

Foorman, B., Francis, D.J., Fletcher, J.M., Schatschneider, C., & Mehta, P. (1998). The role of instruction in learning to read: Preventing reading failure in at-risk children. *Journal of Educational Psychology, 90*, 37–55.

Foorman, B., Francis, D., Novy, D., & Liberman, D. (1991). How letter–sound instruction mediates progress in first-grade reading and spelling. *Journal of Educational Psychology, 83*, 456–469.

Foorman, B., Francis, D.J., Shaywitz, S.E., Shaywitz, B.A., & Fletcher, J.M. (1997). The case for early reading intervention. In B. Blachman (Ed.), *Foundations of reading acquisition and dyslexia: Implications for early intervention* (pp. 243–264). Mahwah, NJ: Lawrence Erlbaum Associates.

Foss, F.D., & Hakes, D.T. (1978). *Psycholinguistics: An introduction to the psychology of language*. Englewood Cliffs, NJ: Prentice Hall.

Fountain, S.R. (2006). *Dialect and spelling in fourth grade students*. Florida State University D-Scholarship Repository. Retrieved October 2007, from http://dscholarship.lib.fus.edu/undergrad/183

Fries, C.C. (1963). *Linguistics and reading*. New York: Holt, Rinehart, & Winston.

Frith, U., & Snowling, M. (1983). Reading for meaning and reading for sound in autistic and dyslexic children. *British Journal of Developmental Psychology, 1*, 320–342.

Fry, E.B. (1994). *1000 words: The most common words for teaching reading, writing, and spelling.* Laguna Beach, CA: Laguna Beach Educational Books.

Fry, E.B., Fountoukidis, D.L., & Polk, K.J. (1985). *The new reading teacher's book of lists.* Englewood Cliffs, NJ: Prentice Hall.

Fry, E.B., Kress, J.E., & Fountoukidis, D.L. (2000). *The reading teacher's book of lists* (4th ed.). San Francisco: Jossey-Bass.

Fuchs, D., & Fuchs, L. (1995). What's so "special" about special education? *Phi Delta Kappan, 76,* 552–530.

Fuchs, D., & Fuchs, L. (2006). Introduction to response to intervention: What, why, and how valid is it. *Reading Research Quarterly, 41,* 93–99.

Fuchs, D., Mock, D., Morgan, P., & Young, C. (2003). Responsiveness-to-intervention: Definitions, evidence, and implications for learning disabilities construct. *Learning Disabilities Research & Practice 18*(3), 157–171.

Fuchs, L., Fuchs, D., & Speece, D. (2002). Treatment validity as a unifying construct for identifying learning disabilities. *Learning Disability Quarterly, 25,* 33–45.

Gates, A.I. (1922). The psychology of reading and spelling with special reference to disability. *Teachers College Contributions to Education* (No. 129). New York: Columbia University.

Gates, A.I. (1929). *The improvement of reading.* New York: MacMillan.

Gates, A.I. (1930). *Interest and ability in reading.* New York: MacMillan.

Gelb, I.J. (1974). *A study of writing.* Chicago, IL: University of Chicago Press.

Gentry, J.R. (1982). An analysis of developmental spelling in GNYS AT WRK. *The Reading Teacher, 36,* 192–200.

Gerber, M.M. (2005). Teachers are still the test: Limitations of response to instruction strategies for identifying children with learning disabilities. *Journal of Learning Disabilities, 38,* 485–486, 516–524.

Geschwind, N. (Ed.). (1974). *Selected papers in language and the brain.* Boston: Reidel.

Geva, E. (1995). Orthographic and cognitive processing in learning to read English and Hebrew. In I. Taylor & D.R. Olson (Eds.), *Scripts and literacy* (pp. 277–294). Boston: Kluwer Academic Publishers.

Geva, E., & Siegel, L. (1991). The role of orthography and cognitive factors in the concurrent development of basic reading skills in bilingual children. Paper presented at the meeting of the International Society for the Study of Behavioral Development, Minneapolis, MN.

Geva, E., & Siegel, L. (2000). Orthographic and cognitive factors in the concurrent development of basic reading skills in two languages. *Reading and Writing, 12,* 1–30.

Gillingham, A., & Stillman, B.W. (1936). *Remedial work for reading, spelling, and penmanship.* New York: Sachett Wilhelms.

Gillingham, A., & Stillman, B.W. (1979). *Remedial training for children with specific disability in reading, spelling, and penmanship.* Cambridge, MA: Educators Publishing Service, Inc.

Gilmore, J.V., & Gilmore, E.C. (1968). *Gilmore Oral Reading Test.* San Antonio, TX: Harcourt Assessment.

Gilyard, K. (1996). *Let's flip the script: An African American discourse on language, literature, and learning.* Detroit, MI: Wayne State University Press.

Glass, G.G., & Glass, E.W. (1976). *Glass Analysis for Decoding Only: A teacher's guide.* Garden City, NY: Easier to Learn.

Gleason, J.B. (2001). *The development of language* (5th ed.). Boston: Allyn & Bacon.

Gleitman, E.J., & Rozin, P. (1973). Teaching reading by use of a syllabary. *Reading Research Quarterly, 8,* 447–483.

Good, R.H., & Kaminski, R.A. (Eds.). (2002). *Dynamic Indicators of Basic Early Literacy Skills (DIBELS)* (6th ed.). Eugene, OR: Institute for Development of Educational Achievement.

Good, T.L., & Brophy, J.E. (1994). *Looking in classrooms* (6th ed.). New York: HarperCollins.

Good, T.L., & Brophy, J.E. (2008). *Looking in classrooms* (10th ed.). Boston: Allyn and Bacon.

Goodman, K. (1973). *Miscue analysis: Applications to reading instruction.* Urbana, IL: National Council of Teachers of English.

Goodman, K. (1986). *What's whole in whole language?* Portsmouth, NH: Heinemann.

Goodman, K., Shannon, P., Freeman, Y., & Murphy, S. (1988). *Report card on basal readers.* Katonah, NY: Richard C. Owen, Publishers.

Goody, J. (1968). *The logic of writing and organization of society.* New York: Cambridge University Press.

Goswami, U. (1993). Toward an interactive analogy model of reading development: Decoding vowel graphemes in beginning. *Journal of Experimental Child Psychology, 56*(3), 443–475.

Goswami, U. (1998). The role of analogies in the development of word recognition. In J.L. Metsala & L.C. Ehri (Eds.), *Word recognition in beginning literacy* (pp. 41–63). Mahwah, NJ: Lawrence Erlbaum Associates.

Gough, P.B. (1983). Context, form and interaction. In K. Rayner (Ed.), *Eye movements in reading: Conceptual and language processes* (pp. 203–211). San Diego: Academic Press.

Gough, P.B., & Tunmer, W. (1986). Decoding, reading, and reading disability. *Remedial & Special Education, 7,* 6–10.

Graddol, D. (1996). English manuscripts: The emergence of a visual identity. In D. Graddol, D. Leith, & J. Swann (Eds.), *English: History, diversity and change.* London: Routledge.

Graham, S., & Harris, K.R. (1993). Self-regulated strategy development: Helping students with learning problems develop as writers. *The Elementary School Journal, 94*(2), 169–181.

Graham, S., & Harris, K.R. (2005). *Writing better: Effective strategies for teaching students with learning difficulties.* Baltimore: Paul H. Brookes Publishing Co.

Grainger, J., & Whitney, C. (2004). Does the human mind read words as a whole? *Trends in Cognitive Science, 8,* 58–59.

Gray, C.T. (1922). *Deficiencies in reading ability: Their diagnosis and remedies.* Boston: D.C. Heath.

Gray, J. (2003). *Collection of ambiguous or incomplete/inconsistent statements.* August 27, 2007, from http://www.gray-area.org/Research/Ambig

Gray, W.S. (1922). Remedial cases in reading: Their diagnosis and treatment. *Educational Monographs Supplement* (No. 221). Chicago: University of Chicago Press.

Green, J. (2003). *The word wall: Teaching vocabulary through immersion* (2nd ed.). Don Mills, ON, Canada: Pippin Publishing.

Green, L. (2004). *African American English: A linguistic introduction.* New York: Cambridge University Press.

Greenberg, D., Ehri, L.C., & Perin, D. (1997). Are word-reading processes the same or different in adult literacy students and third–fifth graders matched for reading level? *Journal of Educational Psychology, 89,* 262–275.

Grissmer, D.W., Kirby, S.N., Berends, M., & Williamson, S. (1994). *Student achievement and the changing American family.* Santa Monica, CA: RAND Institute on Education and Training.

Grossen, B., Coulter, G., & Ruggles, B. (1996). Reading Recovery: An evaluation of benefits and costs. *Effective School Practices, 15*(3), 1–30.

Gunning, T.G. (2000). *Best books for building literacy for elementary children.* Boston: Allyn & Bacon.

Guthrie, J. (1973). Models of reading and reading disability. *Journal of Educational Psychology, 65,* 9–18.

Haager, D., Klingner, J., & Vaughn, S. (2007). *Evidence-based reading practices for response to intervention.* Baltimore: Paul H. Brookes Publishing Co.

Hall, S.J., Halpern, I.M., Schwartz, S.T., & Newcorn, J.H. (1997). Behavioral and executive functions in children with attention deficit hyperactive disorders and reading disability. *Journal of Attention Disorders, 1,* 235–247.

Halpern, D.F., Benbow, C., Geary, D.C., Gur, R.G., Hyde, J.S., & Gernsbacher, M.A. (2007).

The science of sex differences in science and mathematics. *Psychological Science in the Public Interest, 8*(1) 1–51.

Hammill, D.D. (2004). What we know about correlates of reading. *Exceptional Children, 70*(4), 453–464.

Hanna, G.S., & Oaster, T.R. (1978). How important is passage dependence in reading comprehension? *Journal of Educational Research, 71*(6), 345–348.

Harcourt Assessment. (2002). *Metropolitan Achievement Tests, Eighth Edition (MAT 8)*. San Antonio, TX: Author.

Harcourt Assessment. (2003). *Stanford Achievement Test–Tenth Edition (SAT 10)*. San Antonio: TX: Author.

Harris, A.J., & Sipay, E.R. (1985). *How to increase reading ability* (8th ed.). New York: Longman.

Harste, J., & Burke, P. (1982). Predicabilidad un universal de la lecto-escritura. In E. Ferreiro & M. Gomez (Eds.), *Nuevas perspectivas sobre los procesos de lectura y escritura* (pp. 110–118). Mexico: Siglo XXI.

Hart, B., & Risley, T. (1995). *Meaningful differences in the everyday experience of young American children*. Baltimore: Paul H. Brookes Publishing Co.

Hatta, T., & Hirose, T. (1995). Reading disabilities in Japan: Implications from the study of hemisphere functioning. In I. Taylor & D.R. Olson (Eds.), *Scripts and literacy* (pp. 231–246). Boston: Kluwer Academic Publishers.

Hawelka, S., & Wimmer, H. (2005). Impaired visual processing of multi-element arrays is associated with increased number of eye movements in dyslexic reading. *Vision Research, 45*, 855–863.

Haynes, C.W., & Jennings, T.M. (2006). Listening and speaking: Essential ingredients for teaching struggling writers. *Perspectives, 32*(2), 12–16.

Haynes, M.C., & Jenkins, J.R. (1986). Reading instruction in special education resource rooms. *American Educational Research Journal, 23*, 161–190.

Hedges, L.V., & Nowell, A. (1995). Sex differences in mental test scores, variability, and numbers of high-scoring individuals. *Science, 269*, 41–45.

Hefflin, B.R., & Hartman, D.K. (2002). Using writing to improve comprehension: A review of the writing-to-reading research. In C.C. Block, L.B. Gambrell, & M. Pressey (Eds.), *Improving comprehension instruction: Rethinking research, theory, and classroom practice* (pp. 199–228). San Francisco: Jossey-Bass.

Henderson, E. (1981). *Learning to read and spell: The child's knowledge of words*. DeKalb, IL: Northern Illinois University Press.

Henry, M.K. (1999). A short history of the English language. In J.R. Birsh (Ed.), *Multisensory teaching of basic language skills*. Baltimore: Paul H. Brookes Publishing Co.

Henry, M.K. (2003). *Unlocking literacy: Effective decoding and spelling instruction*. Baltimore: Paul H. Brookes Publishing Co.

Henry, M.K. (2005). A short history of the English language. In J.R. Birsh (Ed.), *Multisensory teaching of basic language skills* (2nd ed., pp. 151–170). Baltimore: Paul H Brookes Publishing Co.

Henry, M.K., & Redding, N. (2005). *Patterns for success in reading and spelling*. Austin, TX: PRO-ED.

Hewes, G.W. (1983). The invention of phonemically based language. In E. de Grolier (Ed.), *Glossogenetics: The origin and evolution of language* (pp. 143–162). New York: Harwood Academic Publishers.

Hiebert, E.H. (1994). Reading recovery in the United States: What difference does it make to an age cohort? *Educational Researcher, 23*(9), 15–25.

Hiebert, E.H., & Kamil, L.M. (2005). *Teaching and learning vocabulary: Bringing research to practice*. Mahwah, NJ: Lawrence Erlbaum Associates.

Hiebert, E.H., Pearson, P.D., Taylor, B., Richardson, B., & Paris, S.G. (1998). *Every child a reader*. Ann Arbor, MI: Center for the Improvement of Early Reading Achievement.

Hinshelwood, J. (1895). Word-blindness and visual memory. *The Lancet, 1*, 1506–1508.

Hinshelwood, J. (1917). *Congenital word-blindness*. London: Lewis.

Hittleman, D.R. (1988). *Developmental reading, K–8* (3rd ed.). Columbus, OH: Merrill.

Hohn, W.E., & Ehri, L.C. (1983). Do alphabet letters help pre-readers acquire phonemic segmentation skill? *Journal of Educational Psychology, 75*, 752–762.

Hoover, H.D., Dunbar, S.B., & Frisbie, D.A. (2001). *Iowa Tests of Basic Skills*. Rolling Itasca, IL: Riverside Publishing Company.

Hoover, W., & Gough, P. (1990). The simple view of reading. *Reading and Writing: An Interdisciplinary Journal, 2*, 127–160.

Hoxby, C.M. (2000). The effects of class size on student achievement: New evidence from population variation. *The Quarterly Journal of Economics, 115*(4), 1239–1285.

Hudson, A. (1999). Diglossia. In B. Spolsky (Ed.), *Concise encyclopedia of educational linguistics* (pp. 37–42). New York: Elsevier.

Huey, E. (1908/1968). *The psychology and pedagogy of reading*. Cambridge: The MIT Press.

Hunt, E. (1986). The next word on verbal ability. In P.E. Vernon (Ed.), *Reaction time and intelligence* (pp. 56–76). New York: Ablex.

Hyde, J.S. (2005). The gender similarities hypothesis. *American Psychologist, 60*(6), 581–582.

Hyde, J.S., & DeLameter, J. (2003). *Understanding human sexuality* (8th ed.). New York: McGraw-Hill.

Hyde, J.S., & Linn, M.C. (1988). Gender differences in verbal ability. *Psychological Bulletin, 104*, 53–69.

Indiana Phonics Taskforce. (n.d.). *Report of the Indiana Phonics Taskforce*. Retrieved from http://www.doe.state.in.us

International Dyslexia Association. (2002). *What is dyslexia?* Retrieved December 3, 2007, from http://www.interdys.org/FAQWhatIs.htm

Invernizzi, M., Abouzeid, M., & Gill, J.T. (1994). Using students' invented spelling as a guide for spelling instruction. *The Elementary School Journal, 95*(2), 155–167.

Irausquin, R.S., Drent, J., & Verhoeven, L. (2005). Benefits of computer-presented speed training for poor readers. *Annals of Dyslexia, 55*, 246–265.

Isaakson, M.B. (1992). Learning about reluctant readers through their letters. *Journal of Reading, 34*, 632–637.

Jacklin, C.N. (1989). Female and male: Issues of gender. *American Psychologist, 44*, 127–133.

Jackson, E. (1906). Developmental alexia (congenital word-blindness). *American Journal of Medical Sciences, 131*, 843–849.

Jahandire, K. (1999). *Spoken and written discourse: A multi-disciplinary perspective*. Greenwich, CT: Ablex.

Jean, G. (1992). *Writing: The story of alphabets and scripts*. New York: Henry Abrams.

Johns, J.L. (1980). First graders' concepts about print. *Reading Research Quarterly, 15*, 529–549.

Johns, J.L. (2005). *Basic Reading Inventory–Ninth Edition*. Dubuque, IA: Kendall/Hunt Publishing Co.

Johnson, D.D. (2001). *Vocabulary in the elementary and middle school*. Boston: Allyn & Bacon.

Johnston, P., & Allington, R. (1991). Remediation. In R. Barr, M. Kamil, P. Mosenthal, & D. Pearson (Eds.), *Handbook of reading research* (Vol. 2, pp., 88–112). New York: Longman.

Jones, C.J. (2001). Teacher-friendly curriculum-based assessment in spelling. *Teaching Exceptional Children, 34*(2), 32–38.

Jones, S.M., & Dindia, K. (2004). A meta-analytic study of perspective on equity in the classroom. *Review of Educational Research, 74*, 443–472.

Joshi, R.M. (1999). A diagnostic procedure based on reading component model. In I. Lundberg, F.E., Tonnessen, & I. Wusted (Eds.), *Dyslexia: Advances in theory and practice* (pp. 207–219). Boston: Kluwer Academic Publishers.

Joshi, R.M., & Aaron, P.G. (1991). Developmental reading and spelling disabilities: Are they dissociable? In R.M. Joshi (Ed.), *Written language disorders*. Boston: Kluwer Academic Publishers.

Joshi, R.M., & Aaron, P.G. (2000). The component model of reading: Simple view of reading made a little more complex. *Reading Psychology, 21,* 85–97.

Joshi, R.M., & Aaron, P.G. (2002). Naming speed and word familiarity as confounding factors in decoding. *Journal of Research in Reading, 25,* 160–171.

Joshi, R.M., & Aaron, P.G. (2003). A new way of assessing spelling and its classroom applications. In R.M. Joshi, B. Kaczmarek, & C.K. Leong (Eds.), *Literacy acquisition, assessment, and instruction: The role of phonology, orthography, and morphology* (pp. 153–161). Amsterdam: IOS Press.

Joshi, R.M., & Aaron, P.G. (Eds.). (2006). *Handbook of orthography and literacy.* Mahwah, NJ: Lawrence Erlbaum Associates.

Joshi, R.M., Aaron, P.G., Dean, E., & Rupley, E. (in press). Drop everything and write: An innovative program to improve literacy skills. *Learning Enquiry.*

Joshi, R.M., Dahlgren, M., & Boulware-Gooden, R. (2002). Teaching reading in an inner city school through multisensory approach. *Annals of Dyslexia, 52,* 229–242.

Joshi, R.M., Williams, K., & Wood, J. (1998). Predicting reading comprehension with listening comprehension: Is this the answer to the IQ debate? In C. Hulme & R.M. Joshi (Eds.), *Reading and spelling: Development and disorders* (pp 319–327). Mahwah, NJ: Lawrence Erlbaum Associates.

Juel, C. (1991). Beginning reading. In R. Barr, M.L. Kamil, P.B. Mosenthal, & P.D. Pearson (Eds.), *Handbook of reading research* (Vol. 2, pp. 759–788). New York: Longman.

Juel, C. (1994). *Learning to read and write in one elementary school.* New York: Springer Verlag.

Just, M.A., & Carpenter, P.A. (1987). *The psychology of reading and language comprehension.* Boston: Allyn & Bacon.

Kamhi, A.G., Pollock, K.E., & Harris, J.L. (1996). *Communication development and disorders in African American children: Research, assessment, and intervention.* Baltimore: Paul H. Brookes Publishing Co.

Kantrowitz, B., & Underwood, A. (1999, November 22). Dyslexia and the new science of reading. *Newsweek,* 72–78.

Karlsen, B., & Gardner, E.F. (1995). *Stanford Diagnostic Reading Test–Fourth Edition (SDRT-4).* San Antonio, TX: Harcourt Assessment.

Karmiloff, K., & Karmiloff-Smith, A. (2001). *Pathways to language.* Cambridge, MA: Harvard University Press.

Katz, S., Lautenschlager, G., Blackburn, A. & Harris, F.H. (1990). Answering reading comprehension items without passages on the SAT. *Psychological Science, 1,* 122–127.

Kaufman, A.S., & Kaufman, N.L. (2003). *Kaufman Test of Educational Achievement, Second Edition (KTEA-II).* Circle Pines, MN: AGS Publishing.

Kavale, K.A. (2005). Identifying specific learning disability: Is responsiveness to intervention the answer? *Journal of Learning Disabilities, 38,* 553–562.

Kavale, K.A., & Forness, S.R. (1987). Substance over style: Assessing the efficacy of modality testing and teaching. *Exceptional Children, 54,* 228–239.

Kavale, K.A., Holdnack, J.A., & Mostert, M.P. (2006). Responsiveness to intervention and the identification of specific learning disability: A critique and alternative proposal. *Learning Disability Quarterly, 29*(2), 113–128.

Keenan, J.M., Betjemann, R.S., Wadsworth, S.J., DeFries, J.C., & Olson, R.K. (2006). Genetic and environmental influences on reading and listening comprehension. *Journal of Research in Reading, 28*(1), 75–91.

Kessler, B., & Treiman, R. (2003). Is English chaotic? Misconceptions concerning its irregularity. *Reading Psychology, 24*(3), 267–290.

Kilpatrick, J.J. (1984). *The writer's art.* New York: Andrews, McMeel & Parker Co.

Kilpatrick, J.J. (2002, October 20). Growing the language with new uses. *Tribune Star,* Terre Haute, IN.

King, D.H. (2000). *English isn't crazy.* Baltimore: York Press.

Kirk, S. (1962). *Educating exceptional children.* Boston: Houghton Mifflin.

Kirk, S. (1963, April). *Behavioral diagnosis and remediation of learning disabilities.* Paper presented at the conference Explorations into the Problems of the Perceptually Handicapped Child, Chicago.

Kline, C., & Kline, C. (1978). Follow-up study of 216 dyslexic children. *Bulletin of the Orton Society, 25*, 127–144.

Konold, T.R., Juel, C., McKinnon, M., & Deffes, R. (2003). A multivariate model of early reading acquisition. *Applied Psycholinguistics, 24*, 89–112.

Kovaleski, J.F. (2004). Response to instruction, the identification of learning disabilities: A guide to school teams. *Communiqué, 32*(5), 2–5.

Kuo, L., & Anderson, R.C. (2006). Morphological awareness and learning to read: A cross language perspective. *Educational Psychologist, 41*(3), 161–180.

Labov, W. (1973). Language characteristics: Blacks. In R.H. Bentley & S.D. Crawford (Eds.), *Black language reader* (pp. 96–116). Glenview, IL: Scott Foresman & Co.

Labov, W. (1995). Can reading failure be reversed: A linguistic approach to the question. In V.L. Gadsen & D.A. Wagner (Eds.), *Literacy among African American youth: Issues in learning, teaching, and schooling* (pp. 39–68). Cresskill, NJ: Hampton Press Inc.

Lee, L. (1971). *Northwestern Syntax Screening Test (NSST).* Evanston, IL: Northwestern University Press.

Leith, D. (1996). The origins of English. In D. Graddol, D. Leith, & J. Swann (Eds.), *English: History, diversity, and change.* London: The Open University.

Leong, C.K., & Tamaoka, K. (1998). Cognitive processing of Chinese characters, words, sentences, and Japanese kanji and kana. *Reading and Writing: An Interdisciplinary Journal, 10*, 155–164.

Leopold, W.F. (1947). *Speech development of a bilingual child: A linguist's record* (Vol. II). Evanston, IL: Northwestern University.

Leslie, L., & Caldwell, J. (2006). *Qualitative Reading Inventory–Fourth Edition.* Boston: Allyn & Bacon

Leu, D.J., & Kinzer, C.K. (2003). *Effective literacy instruction*, K–8 (5th ed). Upper Saddle River: Prentice Hall.

Liberman, I.Y., Shankweiler, D., Liberman, A.M., Fowler, C., & Fischer, F.W. (1977). Phonetic segmentation and recoding in the beginning reader. In A.S. Reber & D. Scarborough (Eds.), *Towards a psychology of reading* (pp. 88–109). Mahwah, NJ: Lawrence Erlbaum Associates.

Lie, A. (1991). Effects of a training program for stimulating skills in word analysis in first-grade children. *Reading Research Quarterly, 26*, 234–250.

Lindamood, P., & Lindamood, P. (1998). *Lindamood Phoneme Sequencing Program for Reading, Spelling, and Speech.* Austin, TX: PRO-ED.

Lonigan, C.J. (2006). Conceptualizing phonological processing skills in pre-readers. In D.K. Dickinson & S.B. Neuman (Eds.), *Handbook of early literacy research* (Vol.2., pp 77–89). New York: Guilford Press.

Lord, E.E. (1925). The study and training of a child who was word blind. In E. Lord, L. Carmichael, & W. Dearborn (Eds.), Special disabilities in learning to read and write. *Harvard Monographs in Education: Vol. II*(1, Series 1).

Lovett, M.W., Ransby, M.J., & Barron, R.W. (1988). Treatment, subtype, and word-type effects on dyslexic children's response to remediation. *Brain & Language, 34*, 328–349.

Lubliner, S. (2005). *Getting into words: Vocabulary instruction that strengthens comprehension.* Baltimore: Paul H. Brookes Publishing Co.

Lundberg, I., Frost, J., & Peterson, P. (1988). Effects of an extensive program for stimulating phonological awareness in preschool children. *Reading Research Quarterly, 23*, 263–284.

Lyon, G.R., Fletcher, J.M., Shaywitz, S.E., Shaywitz, B.A., Torgesen, J.K., Wood, F.B., et al. (2001). Rethinking learning disabilities. In C.E. Finn, R.A. Rotherham & C.R. Hokanson, Jr. (Eds.), *Rethinking special education for a new century* (pp. 259–287). Washington, DC: Thomas B. Fordham Foundation and Progressive Policy Institute.

MacArthur, C.A. (2006). Understanding writing development and disabilities. *Perspectives*, *32*(2), 6–9.

MacArthur, C.A., Ferretti, R.P., Okolo, C.M., & Cavalier, A.R. (2001). Technology applications for students with literacy problems: A critical review. *The Elementary School Journal*, *101*, 273–301.

Maccoby, E.E., & Jacklin, C.N. (1974). *The psychology of sex differences*. Stanford, CA: Stanford University Press.

MacGinitie, W.H., MacGinitie, R.K., Maria, K., Dreyer, L.G., & Hughes, K.E. (2000). *Gates-MacGinitie Reading Tests, Fourth Edition*. Itasca, IL: Riverside Publishing Company.

Mair, V.H. (1996). Modern Chinese writing. In P.T. Daniels & W. Bright (Eds.), *The world's writing systems* (pp. 200–208). New York: Oxford University Press.

Makita, K. (1968). The rarity of reading disability in Japanese children. *American Journal of Orthopsychiatry, 38*, 599–614.

Malstrom, J. (1973). Dialects–Updated. In R.H. Bentley & S.D. Crawford (Eds.), *Black language reader* (pp. 13–22). Glenview, IL: Scott Foresman Co.

Malmquist, E. (1958). *Factors related to reading disabilities in first grade*. Stockholm: Almquist & Wiksell.

Mambretti, J. (1999). *Internet technology for schools*. Jefferson, NC: McFarland.

Mambretti, J., & Schmidt, A. (1999). *Next generation Internet: Creating advanced networks and services*. New York: John Wiley & Sons.

Manguel, A. (1996). *A history of reading*. Toronto: Random House of Canada.

Mann, V.A., Tobin, P., & Wilson, R. (1987). Measuring phonological awareness through the invented spellings of kindergarten children. *Merrill-Palmer Quarterly, 33*, 354–391.

Manzo, A.V., & Manzo, U.C. (1995). *Teaching children to be literate: A reflective approach*. New York: Harcourt Brace.

Markwardt, F.C. (1998). *Peabody Individual Achievement Test–Revised (PIAT-R)*. Circle Pines, MN: AGS Publishing.

Marshall, J.C., & Newcombe, F. (1973). Patterns of paralexia. *Journal of Psycholinguistic Research, 2*, 179–199.

Maslin, P. (2003). *Comparing basal programs*. Retrieved October 2007 from http://reading first.virginia.edu/pdfs/maslin_whitepaper.pdf

Massaro, D.W., & Jesse, A. (2005). The magic of reading: Too many influences for quick and easy explanations. In T. Trabasso, J. Sabatini, D. Massaro, & R.C. Calfee (Eds.), *From orthography to pedagogy* (pp. 37–62). Mahwah, NJ: Lawrence Erlbaum Associates.

McCarney, S.B. (2004). *Attention Deficit Disorder Evaluation Scale*. Columbia, MO: Hawthorne Educational Services.

McCarthy, S. (1995). The Cree syllabary and the writing system riddle: A paradigm in crisis. In I. Taylor & D.R. Olson (Eds.), *Scripts and literacy* (pp. 59–76). Boston: Kluwer Academic Publishers.

McConkie, G.W., & Rayner, K. (1975). The span of the effective stimulus during reading. *Perception and Psychophysics, 17*, 578–586.

McKeown, M.G., Beck, I.L., Omanson, R.C., & Pople, M.T. (1985). Some effects of the nature and frequency of vocabulary instruction on the knowledge and use of words. *Reading Research Quarterly, 20*, 522–535.

McLaughlin, M., & Allen, M.B. (2002). *Guided comprehension: A teaching model for grades 3–8*. Newark, DE: The International Reading Association.

Meek, C. (2003). Classroom crisis: It's about time. *Phi Delta Kappan, 84*, 592–595.

Meier, D. (2002). Standardization versus standards. *Phi Delta Kappan, 84*, 191–198.

Mezynski, K. (1983). Issues concerning the acquisition of knowledge: Effects of vocabulary training on reading comprehension. *Review of Educational Research, 53*, 253–279.

Michaels, S., & Collins, J. (1984). Oral discourse styles: Classroom interaction and the acquisition of literacy. In D. Tannen (Ed.), *Coherence in spoken and written discourse*. Norwood, NJ: Ablex.

Michalowski, P. (1996). Mesopotamian cuneiform. In P.T. Daniels & W. Bright (Eds.), *The world's writing systems* (pp.33–72). New York: Oxford University Press.

Miller, J., & Weinert, R. (1998). *Spontaneous spoken language: Syntax and discourse.* Oxford, United Kingdom: Clarendon Press.

Miller, J.F., & Chapman, R.S. (1981). The relation between age and mean length of utterance. *Journal of Speech and Hearing Research, 24,* 154–161.

Mitford, M. (1966). *Teaching to read: Historically considered.* Chicago: University of Chicago Press.

Moats, L.C. (1995). *Spelling, development, disabilities, and instruction.* Baltimore: York Press.

Moats, L.C. (2000). *Speech to print: Language essentials for teachers.* Baltimore: Paul H. Brookes Publishing Co.

Molfese, V., Modglin, A., & Molfese, D. (2003). The role of environment in the development of reading skills. *Journal of Learning Disabilities, 36,* 59–67.

Molfese, V., & Molfese, D. (2002). Environmental and social influences on reading as indexed by brain and behavioral responses. *Annals of Dyslexia, 52,* 120–137.

Monaghan, J.E., & Barry, A.L. (1999). *Writing the past: Teaching reading in Colonial America and the United States.* Newark, DE: International Reading Association.

Monroe, M. (1932). *Children who cannot read.* Chicago: University of Chicago Press.

Moody, S.W., Vaughn, S., Hughes, M.T., & Fischer, M. (1998). Broken promises: Reading instruction in resource rooms. *Learning Disability Quarterly, 64,* 211–215.

Morais, J., Bertelson, P., Cary, L., & Alegria, J. (1986). Literacy training and speech segmentation. *Cognition, 24,* 45–64.

Morais, J., Cary, L., Alegria, J., & Bertelson, P. (1979). Does awareness of speech as a sequence of phones arise spontaneously. *Cognition, 7,* 323–331.

Morgan, W.P. (1896). A case of congenital word-blindness. *British Medical Journal, 2,* 1368.

Morris, D., Bloodgood, J., & Perney, J. (2003). Kindergarten predictors of first-and second-grade reading achievement. *Elementary School Journal, 104*(2), 93–110.

Morrow, L.M. (1993). *Literacy development in the early years: Helping children read and write.* Englewood Cliffs, NJ: Prentice Hall.

Mufwene, S.S., Rickford, J.R., Bailey, G., & Baugh, J. (Eds). (1998). *African American English: Structure, history, and use.* London: Routledge.

Murray, B. (n.d.). *Adopting a reading series?* Retrieved January 14, 2008, from http://www.auburn.edu/academic/education/reading_genie.

Muter, V. (1998). Phonological awareness: Its nature and is influence over early literacy development. In C. Hulme & R.M. Joshi (Eds.), *Reading and spelling: Development and disorders* (pp. 113–125). Mahwah, NJ: Lawrence Erlbaum Associates.

Nagy, W.E. (1988). *Teaching vocabulary to improve reading comprehension.* Newark, DE: International Reading Association.

Nagy, W.E., & Anderson, R.C. (1984). How many words are there in the printed school English? *Reading Research Quarterly, 19,* 304–330.

Nagy, W.E., Anderson, R.C., Schommer, M., Scott, J.A., & Stallman, A.C. (1989). Morphological families in the internal lexicon. *Reading Research Quarterly, 24,* 263–282.

National Assessment of Educational Progress. (1995). *Reading: A first look: Findings from the National Assessment of Educational Progress* (Rev. ed.). Washington, DC: U.S. Government Printing Office.

National Center for Education Statistics. (2000). *Trends in educational equity for girls and women.* Washington, DC: U.S. Department of Education.

National Center for Education Statistics. (2004). *Internet access in U.S. public schools and classrooms: 1994–2002.* Retrieved December 24, 2006, from http://nces.ed.gov/surveys/frss/publications/2004011

National Commission on Excellence in Education. (1983). *A nation at risk: The imperative for educational reform.* Washington, DC: U.S. Department of Education.

National Commission on Teaching and America's Future. (2003). *No dream denied, A Pledge to America's Children.* Washington, DC: Author.

National Reading Panel. (2000). *Teaching children to read: An evidence-based assessment of the scientific research literature on reading and its implications for reading instruction. Reports of the subgroups.* Bethesda, MD: Author.

National Right to Read Foundation. (2000). *Analysis of grade 1 reading programs.* Retrieved November 8, 2007, from http://www.nrrf.org/analyses_grade1.htm

Nelson-Herber, J. (1986). Expanding and refining vocabulary in content areas. *Journal of Reading, 29,* 626–33.

Neuman, S. (1999). Creating continuity in early literacy: Linking home and school with a culturally responsive approach. In L. Gambrell, L. Moror, S. Neuman, & M. Pressley (Eds.), *Best practices in literacy instruction.* New York: The Guilford Press.

Newcomer, P. (2001). *Diagnostic Achievement Battery–Third Edition (DAB-3).* Austin, TX: PRO-ED.

Newman, A.P. (1980). *Adult basic education.* Boston: Allyn & Bacon.

Newman, J.M., & Church, S.M. (1990). Myths of whole language. *The Reading Teacher, 44*(1), 20–26.

No Child Left Behind Act of 2001, PL 107-110, 115 Stat. 1425, 20 U.S.C. §§ 6301 *et seq.*

Nye, B., Hedges, L., & Konstantopoulos, S. (2000). The effects of small classes on academic achievement. *American Educational Research Journal, 37*(1), 123–151.

O'Connor, J., & Wilson, B. (1995). Effectiveness of Wilson Reading System used in public school training. In C.M. McIntyre & J. Pickering (Eds.), *Clinical studies of multisensory structured language education* (pp. 88–112). Salem, OR: International Multisensory Structured Language Education Council.

Olinghouse, N.G. (2007). Student- and instruction-level predictors of narrative writing in third-grade students. *Reading and Writing: An Interdisciplinary Journal, 6,* 387.

Olson, D.R. (1977). The basis of language in speech and writing. *Harvard Educational Review, 47,* 257–281.

Olson, D.R. (1991). Literacy as metalinguistic activity. In D.R. Olson & N. Torrance (Eds.), *Literacy & Orality* (pp. 251–270). New York: Cambridge University Press.

Olson, R.K. (2002). Dyslexia: Nature and nurture. *Dyslexia, 8,* 143–159.

Olson, R.K., Wise, B., Ring, J., & Johnson, M. (1997). Computer-based remedial training in phoneme awareness and phonological decoding: Effects on the posttraining development of word recognition. *Scientific Studies in Reading, 1*(3), 235–253.

O'Neal, V., & Trabasso, T. (1973). Is there a correspondence between sound and spelling? Some implications for Black English speakers. In D.S. Harrison & T. Trabasso (Eds.), *Black English: A seminar* (pp. 171–190). Hillsdale, NJ: Lawrence Erlbaum Associates.

Ong, W.J. (1982). *Orality and literacy: The technologizing of the word.* New York: Methuen.

Oregon Reading First Center. (2004, March). *Review of comprehensive reading programs.* Retrieved December 10, 2007, from oregonreadingfirst.uoregon.edu/downloads/intro_summ_review_3-04.pdf

Orton, S.T. (1937). *Reading, writing, and speech problems in children.* New York: Norton.

Ourada, L.D. (2001). Five language arts "sponges." Retrieved October 2007 from http://www.education-world.com/a_lesson/TM/WS_sponges.shtml

Owens, R.E. (1988). *Language development* (2nd ed.). New York: Macmillan Publishing Co.

Palincsar, A.S., & Brown, A.L. (1984). Reciprocal teaching of comprehension fostering and monitoring activities. *Cognition & Instruction, 1,* 117–175.

Pelosi, P.L. (1977). The roots of reading diagnosis. In H.A. Robinson (Ed.), *Reading and writing instruction in the United States: Historical trends.* Newark, DE: International Reading Association.

Pennington, B.F., Groisser, D., & Welsh, M.C. (1993). Contrasting attention deficit hyperactivity disorder vs. reading disability. *Developmental Psychology, 29,* 511–523.

Philips, S. (1972). Participant structures and communicative competence: Warm Springs children in community and classroom. In C. Cazden, V. John, & D. Hymes (Eds.), *Functions of language in the classroom* (pp. 370–394). New York: Teachers College Press.

Pichert, J., & Anderson, R.C. (1977). Taking different perspectives on a story. *Journal of Educational Psychology, 69,* 309–315.

Pinker, S., & Bloom, P. (1990). Natural language and natural selection. *Behavioral and Brain Sciences, 13,* 707–784.

Pisecco, S., Baker, D., Silva, P., & Brooke, M. (2001). Boys with reading disabilities and/or ADHD: Distinctions in early childhood. *Journal of Learning Disabilities, 34,* 98.

Pitts, M.M. (1983). Comprehension monitoring: Definition and practice. *Journal of Reading, 26,* 516–523.

Pollock, J.S. (1996). *Final evaluation report: Reading Recovery Program 1993–94.* Columbus, OH: Department of Program Evaluation.

Pontecorvo, C., & Orsolini, M. (1996). Writing and written language in children's development. In C. Pontecorvo, M. Orsolini, B. Burge, & L. Resnik (Eds.), *Children's early text construction* (pp. 3–23). Mahwah, NJ: Lawrence Erlbaum Associates.

Poole, I. (1934). Genetic development of articulation of consonant sounds in speech. *Elementary English Review, 11,* 159–161.

Potts, M., Carlson, P., Cocking, R., & Copple, C. (1979). *Structure and development in child language: The preschool years.* Ithaca, NY: Cornell University Press.

Pressley, M. (2002). *Improving comprehension instruction: Rethinking research, theory, and classroom practice.* San Francisco: Jossey-Bass.

Pressley, M., El-Dinary, P., Gaskins, I., Schuder, T., Gergman, J., Almasi, J., et al. (1992). Beyond direct explanation: Transactional instruction of reading comprehension strategies. *Elementary School Journal, 92,* 511–554.

Preston, R.C. (1964). Ability of students to identify correct responses before reading. *Journal of Educational Research, 58,* 181–183.

RAND Reading Study Group. (2001). *Reading for understanding: Towards an R&D program in reading comprehension.* Santa Monica, CA: Author.

Rathvon, N. (2004). Early reading assessment: A practitioner's handbook. New York: Guilford Press.

Rayner, K. (1998). Eye movements in reading and information processing. *Psychological Review, 124*(3), 372–422.

Rayner, K., & Kaiser, J.S. (1975). Reading mutilated text. *Journal of Educational Psychology, 67,* 301–306.

Rayner, K., & Pollatsek, A. (1989). *The psychology of reading.* Englewood, NJ: Prentice-Hall.

Rayner, K., White, S., Johnson, R., & Liversedge, S. (2006). Raeding words with jumbled letters: There is a cost. *Psychological Science, 17*(3), 192–193.

Read, C. (1971). Pre-school children's knowledge of English phonology. *Harvard Educational Review, 41,* 1–34.

Read, C. (1975). *Children's categorization of speech sounds in English.* Urbana, IL: National Council of Teachers of English.

Reason, R. (1999). ADHD: A psychological response to an evolving concept (Report of a working party of the British Psychological Society). *Journal of Learning Disabilities, 32*(1), 85–91.

Redd, T.M., & Webb, K.S. (2005). *A teacher's introduction to African American English.* Urbana, IL: National Council of Teachers of English.

Reichter, G.M. (1969). Perceptual recognition as a function of the meaningfulness of the stimulus material. *Journal of Experimental Psychology, 81,* 275–281.

Reid, R., & Maag, W. (1994). How many fidgets is a pretty much: A critique of behavior rating scales for identifying students with ADHD. *Journal of School Psychology, 2,* 424–428.

Reutzel, D.R. (1999). Organizing literacy instruction: Effective grouping strategies and organizational plans. In L.B. Gambrell, L.M. Morrow, S.B. Neuman, & M. Pressley (Eds.), *Best practices in literacy instruction* (pp. 271–291). New York: Guilford Press.

Reutzel, D.R., & Cooter, R.B. (2003). *Strategies for reading assessment and instruction.* Columbus, OH: Merrill/Prentice Hall.

Rice, J.M. (1897). The futility of spelling grind. *The Forum, 23,* 163–172.

Rickford, J.R. (1999). *African American English: Features, evolution, educational implications.* Malden, MA: Blackwell.

Robinson, A. (1995). *The story of writing.* London: Thames & Hudson.

Rogers, H. (1994). Optimal orthographies. In I. Taylor & D.R. Olson (Eds.), *Scripts and literacy* (pp. 31–43). Boston: Kluwer Academic Publishers.

Rosenshine, B., Meister, C., & Chapman, S. (1996). Reciprocal teaching: A review of research. *Review of Educational Research, 66,* 181–221.

Roskos, K., & Neuman, S.B. (2001). Environment and its influences for early literacy teaching and learning. In S.B. Neuman & D.K. Dickinson (Eds.), *Handbook of early literacy research* (pp. 281–294). New York: Guilford Press.

Rothstein, R. (2004). A wider lens on the black–white achievement gap. *Phi Delta Kappan, 86*(2), 105–110.

Rotter, J.B. (1966). Generalized expectancies for internal vs. external control of reinforcement. *Psychological Monographs, 80*(No. 1).

Rupley, W.H., Willson, V.L., & Nichols, W.D. (1998). Exploration of the developmental components contributing to elementary school children's reading comprehension. *Scientific Studies of Reading, 2*(2), 143–158.

Sadoski, M., Goetz, E.T., & Fritz, J.B. (1993). Impact of concreteness on comprehensibility, interest, and memory for text: Implications for dual coding theory and text design. *Journal of Educational Psychology, 85,* 291–304.

Salvia, J., & Ysseldyke, J. (1991). *Assessment* (5th ed.). Boston: Houghton Mifflin.

Salvia, J., & Ysseldyke, J.E. (2004). *Assessment in special and inclusive education* (9th ed.). Boston: Houghton Mifflin.

Sampson, G. (1985). *Writing systems: A linguistic introduction.* Stanford, CA: Stanford University Press.

Samuels, M.L. (1969). Some applications of Middle English dialectology. In R. Lass (Ed.), *Approaches to English historical linguistics* (pp 33–66). New York: Holt, Rinehart, & Winston.

Sanders, J. (2002). Something is missing from teacher education: Attention to two genders. *Phi Delta Kappan, 84,* 241–244.

Sanders, W.L., Wright, P.S., & Horn, S.P. (1997). Teacher and classroom context effects on student achievement: Implications for teacher evaluation. *Journal of Personnel Evaluation in Education, 11*(1), 57–67.

Sanford, A.J., & Garrod, S.C. (1981). *Understanding written language: Explorations in comprehension beyond the sentence.* New York: John Wiley & Sons.

Savage, R. (2001). The 'simple view' of reading: Some evidence and possible implications. *Educational Psychology in Practice, 17,* 17–33.

Scarborough, H.S. (2005). Developmental relationships between language and reading: Reconciling a beautiful hypothesis with some ugly facts. In H.W. Catts & A.G. Kamhi (Eds.), *The connections between language and reading disabilities* (pp. 3–24). Mahwah, NJ: Lawrence Erlbaum Associates.

Scarborough, H.S. (1998). Early identification of children at risk for reading disabilities: Phonological awareness and some other promising predictors. In B.K. Shapiro, P.J. Accardo, & A.N. Capute (Eds.), *Specific reading disability: The spectrum* (pp. 160–188). Baltimore: York Press.

Scarborough, H.S., & Brady, S.A. (2002). Toward a common terminology for talking about speech and reading: A glossary of the "phone" words and some related terms. *Journal of Literacy Research, 34,* 299–336.

Schmandt-Besserat, D. (1992). *Before writing: From counting to cuneiform.* Austin: University of Texas Press.

Schmitt, C. (1918). Developmental alexia: Congenital word-blindness or inability to learn to read. *Elementary School Journal, 18,* 680–700.

Scholes, R.J., & Willis, B.J. (1991). Linguists, literacy, and the intentionality of Marshall McLuhan's Western man. In D.R. Olson & N. Torrance (Eds.), *Literacy and orality* (pp. 215–235). New York: Cambridge University Press.

Schweinhart, L.J., Weikart, D.P., & Larner, M.B. (1986). Consequences of three preschool curriculum models through age 15. *Early Childhood Research Quarterly, 1*(1), 15–45.

Scragg, D. (1975). *A history of English spelling.* New York: St. Martin's Press.

Scribner, S., & Cole, M. (1981). *The psychology of literacy.* Cambridge, MA: Harvard University Press.

Seligman, M.E. (1975). *Helplessness: On depression, development, and death.* San Francisco: Freeman.

Seymour, P.H. (2006). Theoretical framework for beginning reading in different orthographies. In R.M. Joshi & P.G. Aaron (Eds.), *Handbook of orthography and literacy* (pp. 441–462). Mahwah, NJ: Lawrence Erlbaum Associates.

Shanahan, T. (2003). Research-based reading instruction: Myths about the National Reading Panel Report. *The Reading Teacher, 56,* 646–655.

Shanahan, T., & Barr, R. (1995). Reading Recovery: An independent evaluation of the effects of an early instructional intervention for at-risk learners. *Reading Research Quarterly, 30*(4), 958–996.

Shanker, J.L., & Ekwall, E.E. (2002). *Ekwall/Shanker Reading Inventory–Fourth Edition.* Boston: Allyn & Bacon.

Share, D., Jorm, A., Maclean, R., & Matthews, R. (1984). Sources of individual differences in reading achievement. *Journal of Educational Psychology, 76,* 1309–1324.

Share, D.L., & Stanovich, K.E. (1995). Cognitive process in early reading development: Accommodating individual differences into a model of acquisition. *Issues in Education, 1*(1), 1–57.

Shaywitz, S. (2003). *Overcoming dyslexia.* New York: Alfred A. Knoff.

Shaywitz, S., Fletcher, J.M., & Shaywitz, B. (1994). Issues in the definition and classification of attention deficit disorder. *Topics in Language Disorders, 14,* 1–25.

Shaywitz, S., Mody, M., & Shaywitz, B. (2006). Neural mechanisms in dyslexia. *Current Directions in Psychological Science, 15*(6), 278–281.

Shearer, A.P., & Homan, S.P. (1994). *Linking reading assessment to instruction.* New York: St. Martin's Press.

Shefter, H. (1976). *Six minutes a day to perfect spelling.* New York: Pocket Books.

Short, E.J., & Ryan, E.B. (1984). Metacognitive differences between skilled and less skilled readers: Remediating deficits through story grammar and attribution training. *Journal of Educational Psychology, 76,* 225–236.

Short, K.G., Harste, J.C., & Burke, C. (1996). *Creating classrooms for authors and inquirers* (2nd ed.). Portsmouth, NH: Heinemann.

Silvaroli, N., & Wheelock, W. (2003). *Classroom Reading Inventory–Tenth Edition.* Monterey, CA: McGraw-Hill.

Simon, J. (1998–1999). Woodcock Diagnostic Reading Battery. *Diagnostique, 24*(1), 285–297.

Singapore Dyslexia Association. (n.d.). *What is dyslexia?* Retrieved December 3, 2007, from http://www.das.org.sg

Skinner, B.F. (1957). *Verbal behavior.* New York: Appleton-Century-Crofts.

Slingerland, B. (1974). *Screening tests for identifying children with specific language disabilities.* Cambridge, MA: Educators Publishing Service.

Slingerland, B. (1977). *A multi-sensory approach to language arts for specific language disability children.* Cambridge, MA: Educators Publishing Service.

Slosson, R.L., & Nicholson, C.L. (1990). *Slosson Oral Reading Test–Revised (SORT-R).* East Aurora, NY: Slosson Educational Publications.

Smith, N.B. (1965). *American reading instruction.* Newark, DE: International Reading Association.

Smith, R.S. (1990, December). *Developmental spelling and other language predictors of reading achievement*. Paper presented at the Annual meeting of the National Reading Conference, Miami, FL.

Snow, C.E. (1977). The development of conversation between mothers and babies. *Journal of Child Language, 4,* 1–22.

Snow, C.E. (1990). The development of definitional skill. *Journal of Child Language, 17,* 697–710.

Snow, C.E., Burns, M.S., & Griffin, P. (Eds.). (1998). *Preventing reading difficulties in young children.* Washington, DC: National Academies Press.

Spache, G.D. (1940). Characteristic errors of good and poor readers. *Journal of Educational Research, 34,* 182–189.

Spache, G.D. (1981). *Diagnostic Reading Scales.* Monterey, CA: CTB/McGraw-Hill.

Spalding, R.B. (2003). *The writing road to reading* (5th ed.). New York: Harper Collins.

Spalding, R.B., & Spalding, W.T. (1986). *The writing road to reading.* New York: Morrow.

Spann, M.B. (1999). *Portable file-folder word walls: 20 Reproducible patterns for thematic word walls to help kids become better readers, writers and spellers.* New York: Scholastic.

Spearman, C. (1904). "General intelligence" objectively determined and measured. *American Journal of Psychology, 15,* 201–293.

Sperling, G. (1960). The information available in brief visual presentations. *Psychological Monographs, 74*(No. 498).

SRA/McGraw-Hill. (2008). *Reading Mastery Signature Edition.* New York: Author.

Stahl, S.A. (1988). Is there evidence to support matching reading styles and remedial reading methods? A reply to Carbo. *Phi Delta Kappan, 70,* 317–322.

Stahl, S.A. (1992). Saying the "p" word: Nine guidelines for exemplary phonics instruction. *The Reading Teacher, 45*(8), 618–625.

Stahl, S.A. & Fairbanks, M. (1986). The effects of vocabulary instruction: A model-based meta-analysis. *Review of Educational Research, 56,* 72–110.

Stahl, S.A., & Miller, P.D. (1989). Whole language and language experience approaches for beginning reading: A quantitative research synthesis. *Review of Educational Research, 59,* 87–116.

Stahl, S.A., & Murray, B.A. (1993). Environmental print, phoneme awareness, letter recognition, and word recognition. In D.J. Leu & C.K. Kinzer (Eds.), *Examining central issues in literacy research, theory, and practice. Forty-second yearbook of the National Reading Conference* (pp. 227–233). Chicago: National Reading Conference.

Stahl, S.A., & Vancil, S.J. (1986). Discussion is what makes semantic maps work in vocabulary instruction. *The Reading Teacher, 40,* 62–69.

Stanovich, K.E. (1986). Matthew effects in reading: Some consequences of individual differences in the acquisition of literacy. *Reading Research Quarterly, 21,* 360–406.

Stanovich, K.E., Cunningham, A.E., & Cramer, B.R. (1984). Assessing phonological awareness in kindergarten: Issues of task comparability. *Journal of Experimental Child Psychology, 38,* 175–190.

Stanovich, K.E., Cunningham, A.E., & Feeman, D.J. (1984). Relation between early reading acquisition and word decoding with and without context: A longitudinal study of first-grade children. *Journal of Educational Psychology, 76,* 668–677.

Sternberg, R.J. (1985). *Beyond IQ: A triarchic theory of human intelligence.* New York: Cambridge University Press.

Stevenson, H.W., Stiegler, J.W., Luckner, G.W., Lee, S., Hsu, C., & Kitamura, S. (1982). Reading disabilities: The case of Chinese, Japanese, and English. *Child Development, 53,* 1164–1181.

Stewart, W.A. (1973). Sociolinguistic factors in the history of American Negro dialects. In R.H. Bentley & S.D. Crawford (Eds.), *Black language reader* (pp. 45–70). Glenview, IL: Scott Foresman & Co.

Stroop, J.R. (1935). Studies of interference in serial verbal reactions. *Journal of Experimental Psychology, 28,* 643–662.

Sulzby, E. (1996). Roles of oral and written language as children approach conventional literacy. In C. Pontecorvo, M. Orsolini, B. Burge, & L.B. Resnik (Eds.), *Children's early text construction* (pp. 25–46). Mahwah, NJ: Lawrence Erlbaum Associates.

Sulzby, E., Barnhart, J., & Hieshima, J. (1989). Forms of writing and rereading from writing: A preliminary report. In J. Mason (Ed.), *Reading/writing connections* (pp. 31–63). Boston: Allyn & Bacon.

Swanson, H.L. (1999a). Instructional components that predict treatment outcomes for students with learning disabilities: Support for a combined strategy and direct instruction model. *Learning Disabilities Research and Practice, 13,* 129–140.

Swanson, H.L. (1999b). Reading research for students with LD: A meta-analysis of intervention outcomes. *Journal of Learning Disabilities, 32,* 504–532.

Swanson, H.L., Carson, C., & Saches-Lee, C.M. (1996). A selective synthesis of intervention research for students with learning disabilities. *School Psychology Review, 25*(3), 370–391.

Swanson, H.L., Howard, C.B., & Saez, L. (2006). Do different components of working memory underlie different subgroups of reading disabilities? *Journal of Learning Disabilities, 39,* 252–269.

Sweet, A., & Snow, C. (2002). Metacognitive differences between skilled and less skilled readers: Remediating deficits through story grammar and attributions training. *Journal of Educational Psychology, 76,* 225–235.

Tan, L.H., & Perfetti, C.A. (1998). Phonological codes as early sources of constraint in Chinese word identification: A review of current discoveries and theoretical accounts. *Reading and Writing: An Interdisciplinary Journal, 10,* 165–200.

Tangel, D.M., & Blachman, B.A. (1995). Effect of phoneme awareness instruction on kindergarten children's invented spelling. *Journal of Reading Behavior, 24,* 233–261.

Taylor, I. (1976). *Introduction to psycholinguistics.* New York: Holt, Rinehart, & Winston.

Taylor, I., & Taylor, M. (1995). *Writing and literacy in Chinese, Korean, and Japanese.* Philadelphia: John Benjamins Publishing Co.

Teale, W.H. (1989). Language arts for the 21st century. In J.M. Jenson (Ed.), *Stories to grow on: Demonstration of language learning in K–8 classrooms* (pp. 1–34). Portsmouth, NH: Heineman.

Teale, W.H., & Sulzby, E. (1986). *Emergent literacy: Writing and reading.* Norwood, NJ: Ablex.

Templin, M.C. (1957). Certain language skills in children, their development and interrelationships. *Institute of Child Welfare Monograph Series.* Minneapolis, MN: University of Minnesota Press.

Thomas, C.J. (1905). Congenital word-blindness and its treatment. *The Ophthalmoscope, 3,* 380–385.

Thorndike, E. (1921). *The teacher's word book.* New York: Teachers College Press.

Thorndike, R.L. (1973). *Reading comprehension education in fifteen countries: An empirical study.* New York: John Wiley & Sons.

Tierney, R.J., Readence, J.E., & Dishner, E.K. (1995). *Reading strategies and practices* (4th ed.). Boston: Allyn & Bacon.

Tierney, R.J., & Shanahan, T. (1991). Research on the reading writing relationship: Interactions, transactions, and outcomes. In R. Barr, M.L. Kamil., P. Mosenthal, & P.D. Pearson (Eds.), *Handbook of reading research* (Vol.2, pp. 246–280). White Plains, NY: Longman.

Torgesen, J.K., & Bryant, B.R. (1995). *Test of Phonological Awareness.* Austin, TX: PRO-ED.

Torgesen, J.K., & Bryant, B.R. (2004). *Test of Phonological Awareness, Second Edition.* East Moline, IL: LinguiSystems.

Torgesen, J.K., Wagner, R.K., & Rashotte, C.A. (1997). Prevention and remediation of severe reading disabilities: Keeping the end in mind. *Scientific Studies of Reading, 1,* 217–234.

Torgesen, J.K., Wagner, R.K., & Rashotte, C.A. (1999). *Test of Word Reading Efficiency (TOWRE).* Austin, TX: PRO-ED.

Torgesen, J.K., Wagner, R.K., Rashotte, C.A., Alexander, A.W., & Conway, T. (1997). Preventive and remedial interventions for children with severe reading disabilities. *Learning Disabilities: A Multidisciplinary Journal, 8,* 51–61.

Tracey, D.H., & Morrow, L.M. (1998). Motivating contexts for young children's literacy development: Implications for word recognition. In J.L. Metsala & L.C. Ehri (Eds.), *Word recognition in beginning literacy* (pp. 340–356). Mahwah, NJ: Lawrence Erlbaum Associates.

Traugott, E.C. (1976). Pidgins, creoles, and the origins of vernacular black English. In D.S. Harrison & T. Trabasso (Eds.), *Black English: A seminar* (pp. 57–93). Mahwah, NJ: Lawrence Erlbaum Associates.

Treiman, R. (1993). *Beginning to spell*. New York: Oxford University Press.

Treiman, R. (1998). Why spelling? The benefits of incorporating spelling into beginning Reading instruction. In J.L. Metsala & L.C. Ehri (Eds.), *Word recognition in beginning literacy* (pp. 289–313). Mahwah, NJ: Lawrence Erlbaum Associates.

Treiman, R. (2004). Spelling and dialect: Comparisons between speakers of African American English and White speakers. *Psychonomic Bulletin & Review, 11*, 338–342.

Treiman, R., Mullennix, J., Bijeljae-Bubic, R., & Richmond-Welty, E.D. (1995). The special role of rimes in the description, use and acquisition of English orthography. *Journal of Experimental Psychology, General, 124*, 107–136.

Trelease, J. (1989). *The read-aloud handbook*. New York: Penguin Books.

Tuerk, P.W. (2005). Reach in the high-stakes era: Achievement, resources, and No Child Left Behind. *Psychological Science, 16*(6) 419–425.

Uhl, W.L. (1916). The use of the results of reading tests as bases for planning remedial work. *Elementary School Journal, 17*, 266–275.

Uhry, J. (2002). Finger-point reading in kindergarten: The role of phonemic awareness, one-to-one correspondence, and rapid serial naming. *Scientific Studies of Reading, 6*(4), 319–342.

United Nations Educational, Scientific, and Cultural Organization. (1953). *Progress of literacy in various countries*. Paris: Author.

U.S. Department of Education. (2001). *Early Reading First*. Retrieved December 24, 2006, from http://www.ed.gov/programs/earlyreading/index.html

Vaessen, A., Gerretsen, P., & Blomert, L. (2007, July). *The naming speed deficit is not what it looks like: Testing the assumptions of the double deficit hypothesis.* Poster presented at the Fourteenth annual meeting of the Society for the Scientific Study of Reading, Prague, The Czech Republic.

Vallins, G.H. (1954). *Spelling*. London: Andre Deutsch.

van Daal, H.P., & Reitsma, P. (1993). The use of speech feedback by normal and disabled readers in computer-based reading practice. *Reading and Writing: An Interdisciplinary Journal, 5*, 243–259.

van der Leij, A., & van Daal, H.P. (1999). Automatization aspects of dyslexia: Speed limitations in word identification, sensitivity to increasing task demands, and orthographic compensation. *Journal of Learning Disabilities, 32*, 417–428.

Vaughn, S., Gersten, R., & Chard, D.J. (2000). The underlying message in LD intervention research: Findings from research synthesis. *Exceptional Children, 67*, 99–114.

Vaughn, S., Levy, S., Coleman, M., & Bos, C. (2002). Reading instruction for students with LD and EBD. *Journal of Special Education, 36*, 2–13.

Vellutino, F.R. (1979). *Dyslexia: Theory and research*. Cambridge, MA: MIT Press.

Venezky, R. (1976). *Theoretical and experimental base for teaching reading*. St. Louis: Mosby.

Vukovic, R.K., & Siegel, L.S. (2005). The double-deficit hypothesis: A comprehensive analysis of evidence. *Journal of Learning Disabilities, 39*(1), 25–47.

Wagner, R.K., & Rashotte, C.A. (1993). *Does phonological awareness training really work? A meta-analysis.* Paper presented at the annual meeting of the American Educational Research Association, Atlanta, GA.

Wagner, R.K., Torgesen, J.K., & Rashotte, C. (1999). *Comprehensive Test of Phonological Processing (CTOPP)*. Austin, TX: PRO-ED.

Wagstaff, J.M. (1999). *Teaching reading and writing with word walls*. New York: Scholastic.

Wagstaff, J.M. (2005). *Word walls that work*. Retrieved March 2005 from http://content.scholastic.com/browse/article.jsp?id=4380

Walker, C.B. (1987). *Reading the past: Cuneiform*. Los Angeles: University of California Press.

Washburne, C. (1936). Ripeness. *Progressive Education, 13*, 125–130.

Washington, J.A., & Craig, H.K. (2001). Reading performance and dialectal variation. In J.L. Harris, A.G. Kamhi, & K.E. Pollock (Eds.), *Literacy in African American communities* (pp. 147–168). Mahwah, NJ: Lawrence Erlbaum Associates.

Waters, G., Bruck, M., & Seidenberg, M. (1985). Do children use similar processes to read and spell words? *Journal of Experimental Child Psychology, 39*, 511–530.

Waterson, B. (1997). *The Egyptians*. Malden, MA: Blackwell Publishing.

Wechsler, D. (1991). *Wechsler Intelligence Scale for Children–Third Edition (WISC-III)*. San Antonio, TX: Harcourt Assessment.

Wechsler, D. (2001). *Wechsler Individual Achievement Test–Second Edition (WIAT-II)*. San Antonio, TX: Harcourt Assessment.

Wellman, B., Case, I.M., Mengert, I.G., & Bradbury, D.E. (1931). Speech sounds of young children. *University of Iowa Studies in Child Welfare, 5*(2).

White, T.G., Graves, M.F., & Slater, W.H. (1990). Growth of reading vocabulary in diverse elementary schools: Decoding and word meaning. *Journal of Educational Psychology, 82*, 281–290.

Wiederholt, J.L., & Bryant, B.R. (2001). *Gray Oral Reading Tests, Fourth Edition (GORT-4), examiner's manual*. Austin, TX: PRO-ED.

Wilkinson, G.S. (1993). *Wide Range Achievement Test–Third Edition (WRAT-3)*. Wilmington, DE: Jastak Associates.

Willcut, E.G., Pennington, B.F., Boada, R., Ogline, J., Tunick, K., Chhabidas, N., et al. (2001). A comparison of deficits in reading disability and attention deficit/hyperactivity disorder. *Journal of Abnormal Psychology, 110*, 157–172.

Wilson, B. (1994). *The Wilson Reading System (WRS)*. Hopedale, MA: Educomp Publications.

Wilson, R.G., & Rudolph, M. (1986). *Merrill linguistic reading program*. Columbus, OH: Charles Merrill.

Wittrock, M.C. (1986). Students' thought processes. In M.C. Wittrock (Ed.), *Handbook of research on teaching* (pp. 297–314). New York: Macmillan.

Wleklinski, M.H. (1993). *Effectiveness of special education programs on the reading achievement of students with learning disabilities*. Unpublished doctoral dissertation, Indiana State University, Terre Haute, IN.

Wolf, M., & Bowers, P.G. (1999). The double-deficit hypothesis for developmental dyslexia. *Journal of Educational Psychology, 91*, 415–438.

Wolf, M., Goldberg, A., Cirino, P., Morris, R., & Lovett, M. (2002). The unique and combined contribution of naming speed and phonological processes in reading disability: A test of the double-deficit hypothesis. *Reading and Writing, 15*, 43–72.

Wolfram, W., & Schilling-Estes, N. (1998). *American English: Dialects and variation*. Malden, MA: Blackwell Publishing.

Wollman-Bonilla, J.E. (1989). Reading journals: Invitations to participate in literature. *The Reading Teacher, 43*, 112–120.

Wolraich, M., & Hannah, N. (1996). Comparison of diagnostic criteria for attention deficit hyperactivity disorder in a county-wide sample. *Journal of the American Academy of Child Development and Adolescent Psychiatry, 35*, 319–324.

Wong, W.L., & Ho, C.S. (2007, July). *Central executive speed of processing deficit in Chinese developmental dyslexia: Its impact on word decoding and reading comprehension*. Poster presented at the fourteenth annual meeting of the Society for the Scientific Study of Reading, Prague, The Czech Republic.

Woodcock, R.W. (1987). *Woodcock Reading Mastery Test–Revised (WRMT-R)*. Circle Pines, MN: AGS Publishing.

Woodcock, R.W. (1991/1994). *Woodcock Language Proficiency Battery–Revised*. Itasca, IL: Riverside Publishing Company.

Woodcock, R.W. (1997). *Woodcock Diagnostic Battery–Revised (WDRB-R)*. Itasca, IL: Riverside Publishing Company.

Woodcock, R.W., & Johnson, M.B. (1989). *The Woodcock-Johnson–Revised Tests of Achievement*. Chicago: Riverside.

Woodcock, R.W., McGrew, K.S., & Mather, N. (2001). *Woodcock-Johnson III Tests of Achievement*. Itasca, IL: Riverside Publishing Company.

Woods, M.J., & Moe, A.J. (2003). *Analytical Reading Inventory–Seventh Edition.* Upper Saddle River, NJ: Prentice Hall.

Wylie, R.E., & Durrell, D.D. (1970). Teaching vowels through phonograms. *Elementary English, 47*, 787–791.

Yap, R.L., & van der Leij, A. (1994). Word processing in dyslexics. *Reading and Writing: An Interdisciplinary Journal, 5*, 261–279.

Yatvin, J. (2000). Minority view. In *Report of the National Reading Panel* (pp. 1–3). Rockville, MD: National Institute of Child Health and Human Development.

Ysseldyke, J.E., & Algozzine, B. (1995). *Special education: A practical approach for teachers* (3rd ed.). Boston: Houghton Mifflin.

Ysseldyke, J.E., Algozzine, B., Shinn, M.R., & McGue, M. (1982). Similarities and differences between low achievers and students classified learning disabled. *Journal of Special Education, 16*, 73–85.

Glossary

acoustic memory Sound-based memory.

analytic phonics Children are taught to read a few words first without any phonetic analysis. After this, the sounds of letters in these words are taught.

attention-deficit/hyperactivity disorder (ADHD) An inability to pay sustained attention coupled with impulsive and hyperactive behavior are considered symptoms of ADHD. Furthermore, in order to make a clinical diagnosis, these symptoms should persist for more than 6 months and should interfere with daily functions such as learning and task performance. Even though inattentive/impulsive behavior and hyperactivity often occur together, they can also occur independent of each other. When inconsistent attention and impulsivity are the most readily observable symptoms, whereas hyperactive behavior is not the most obvious behavioral problem, the condition is referred to as ADHD, predominantly inattentive type (ADHD-I). Even though treatment with stimulant drugs is the most frequently adopted treatment plan, several authorities advocate the use of behavioral therapy instead. Inconsistent attention can lead to poor performance on tests of reading. In contrast, poor decoding and word recognition skills can also make attention wander.

auditory processing The ability of individuals with normal hearing and typical intelligence to differentiate, recognize, and process sounds, especially sounds of the language.

autism and autism spectrum disorder Autism is characterized by impaired social interaction and communication skills, along with a markedly restricted repertoire of activity and interests. Manifestations of the disorder vary greatly, and for this reason it is also referred to as autism spectrum disorder. A mild form is called Asperger syndrome. Autism is also sometimes referred to as early infantile autism, childhood autism, or Kanner's autism. It is generally believed that autism is associated with some biochemical abnormality in the brain. Some children with autism are precocious word callers.

basal readers A set of textbook materials produced by five or six major publishers in the United States. These are graded books meant for Grades 1–6. They come as a package that also includes teacher's guidebooks, workbooks for students, storybooks for extra reading.

behavioral psychology The school of psychology which proposes that behavior that is observable and measurable is the legitimate object of scientific study. Some behavioral psychologists insisted in the past that mental concepts such as reasoning and memory, which are not directly observable, are not part of the discipline of psychology.

biolinguistics The study of language from a biological perspective. Topics that are studied under this interdisciplinary branch of linguistics include evolution of language, comparison of animal and human communication, critical periods in the acquisition of different aspects of language, and the nature of language disorders caused by neural impairment.

clause A group of words (or grammatical unit) ordinarily consisting of a subject and a predicate. The subject is what the sentence is about and the predicate, which usually is a verb, tells something about the subject. Each complete sentence has a subject and a predicate. A sentence can have a main clause and more than one subordinate clause. In the sentence, "The sun is shining although it is late in the evening," *the sun is shining* is the main clause and *although it is late* is a subordinate clause. In the sentence, *the sun* is the subject and *is shining* is the predicate. In contrast to a clause, a phrase may or may not contain a subject or a verb. In the example sentence, *although it is late* is a phrase.

cognitive A term that describes mental processes by which the sensory input is transformed, stored, and retrieved. This is generally referred to as information processing.

cognitive behavior therapy A combination of cognitive therapy and behavior therapy. Cognitive therapy helps individuals learn to change their unproductive thought patterns, whereas behavior therapy helps individuals unlearn undesirable behaviors and learn new behaviors. Reasoning, visualization, and positive feelings are used in cognitive therapy, whereas reinforcement and modeling are the tools used in behavior therapy.

cognitive domain This is a part of the Component Model of Reading. Factors such as word recognition and linguistic comprehension are included in the cognitive domain.

cognitive psychology In contrast to behavioral psychology, cognitive psychology proposes that unobservable mental concepts such as reasoning, memory, problem solving, and creativity can be studied with the help of suitable experimental techniques. Reading is an area which lends itself well to the explorations of cognitive psychology.

cohort effect Peer influence.

co-morbid The phenomenon of two disorders co-existing in an individual. For example, a child may have both a reading disability and attention–deficit/hyperactivity disorder.

Component Model of Reading A model of reading that considers reading as being made up of three domains. Each domain, in turn, contains components that are independent of each other. When any one of these components fails, acquisition of literacy skills is affected.

congenital word blindness This term was first used in the English language by Pringle Morgan, a British physician, to describe unexpected reading difficulty in children who are otherwise developing typically. It describes an inability to learn to read that cannot be explained by any neurological or sensory impairment and that has existed from birth. The term *dyslexia* has replaced the term *congenital word blindness*. *See also* dyslexia.

connotative meaning Meaning of words that is dependent on the context in which the words appear.

consonant A speech sound that is produced by obstructing some part in the vocal tract. Consonants are classified on the basis of where the sound is obstructed and how it is obstructed.

constructivism The proposition that one's understanding of the world depends on one's own interpretation of it. Consequently, knowledge of the world varies from individual to individual.

content words Nouns, verbs, and adjectives.

correlation coefficient A measure of the degree of linear relationship between two variables, usually labeled x and y. Correlation coefficients can vary from minus one to plus one (-1 to $+1$). The correlation coefficient between height and weight is about $+0.6$ and 0.7, the coefficient between intelligence quotient (IQ) and reading comprehension is less than 0.5.

curriculum-based measurement (CBM) Tests constructed using the material taught in the classroom. These are brief tests and can be administered frequently in the classroom.

decoding The process of converting the written language into speech. Decoding eventually leads to comprehension.

deep orthography Orthography is the visual representation of a language. English orthography is considered to be "deep" because simply knowing the names of the letters will not help the reader to pronounce the written word correctly. In contrast, the orthographies of Italian and Finnish are considered "shallow" because words can be pronounced successfully by sounding out the names of the constituent letters. Orthographies fall on a continuum from English and French being deep and Italian and Spanish being shallow. The concept that the nature of orthography—deep or shallow—is a contributing factor to reading difficulty is referred to as the orthographic depth hypothesis.

denotative meaning Meaning of words as seen in dictionaries.

Diagnostic and Statistical Manual of Mental Disorders, Fourth Edition (DSM-IV) A manual, published by the American Psychiatric Association (1994), to be used for diagnoses related to mental health and to disorders such as attention-deficit/hyperactivity disorder. The *DSM* has gone through several editions; the most recent is the text revision of the fourth edition, published in 2000.

dialect A regionally or socially distinctive variety of a language with a particular type of pronunciation and grammar. It represents a variation of language, not a distinct language.

digraph two letters standing for one phoneme (e.g., /ch/ in *church*).

Direct Instructional System for Teaching Arithmetic and Reading (DISTAR) A highly structured program that is designed for preschool children and underachieving children in the early elementary grades.

direct vocabulary instruction Instructional efforts by the teacher to increase vocabulary knowledge of students by means of explicit instruction. This may include teaching words and their meanings directly and teaching strategies to understand the meaning of words. In addition, the teacher may encourage students to use the newly learned words in their writing assignments. This is in contrast to incidental learning of vocabulary.

discrepancy model A procedure for diagnosing learning disabilities based on the discrepancy between a student's intelligence quotient and his or her reading achievement score.

Down syndrome A group of symptoms associated with having an extra chromosome 21. The symptoms include intellectual disability, poor muscle tone, and often respiratory and cardiac disorders. The degree of the severity varies, with some individuals having cognitive impairments requiring limited support and others having cognitive impairments requiring extensive support.

DSM-IV *See Diagnostic and Statistical Manual of Mental Disorders, Fourth Edition.*

dyslexia An inability to learn to read easily despite typical intelligence, hearing, and vision. It is also described as "unexpected reading failure." *See also* congenital word blindness.

ecological domain One of the three domains of the Component Model of Reading. Factors such as family environment and classroom environment are included in the ecological domain.

emergent literacy Reading and writing behavior of children that precedes formal instruction.

environmental print Written language encountered in signs, directions, and billboard advertisements. Preschool children are exposed to written language in this fashion.

ESL Abbreviation for *English as a second language.*

etymology Word origin with reference to its history.

explicit instruction Used in the context of reading instruction, this refers to the teaching of phonics skills directly.

fluency The ability to read accurately at a fast rate with proper intonation. Fluency facilitates comprehension.

Four Blocks Model A framework that integrates skills and meaning for teaching children to read.

function words Grammar words such as prepositions and conjunctions.

grammar Rules that govern language usage.

grapheme A letter or a group of letters that stands for one phoneme. The letter *c* in the word *cat* is a grapheme. The four letters *ough* in the word *though* also represent a single grapheme.

homonym These are words which are pronounced the same way but have different meaning (e.g., *weak/week*). Homonyms may or may not share the same spelling (e.g., *post/post, alter/altar*).

hyperlexia The unexpected word reading skills of some individuals who otherwise have limited language skills. Hyperlexia is a pathological condition in which the individual starts to sound out words early in life, often at approximately 3 years of age, without any formal instruction. In contrast to word-reading ability, the comprehension of children with hyperlexia—for both reading and listening—is at the below-average level.

hypothesis A proposition or a suggestion advanced to explain a phenomenon. A hypothesis remains a hunch until it is verified or rejected. An example is the proposition that creating an awareness of phonemes in children increases their reading performance. When repeated experimental studies show this to be the case, the hypothesis is accepted and becomes part of a theory.

idiom A form of expression peculiar to a language. For example, the idiom "living on skid row" is peculiar to American English. Another example is "Once upon a time."

informal inventories Records of children's performance based on teacher observation of children as they read and write.

informal tests Quasi-standardized tests in the sense the classroom teacher can determine the average performance of children in his or her classroom on any literacy function by using tests that he or she has developed. As a result, the teacher can judge any student's performance as average, below average, or above average with reference to the average classroom performance. These tests are usually based on classroom curriculum and are frequently administered, enables the teacher to monitor students' progress. Examples of informal tests are words read in 1 minute, number of words misread, number of words spelled correctly on a spelling test, and so forth.

instant word reading Also known as sight word reading. Instant word reading is done quickly and automatically. It facilitates comprehension.

invented spelling Spontaneous attempts by young children, usually preschoolers, to "write" words.

John effect Stands for the high degree of correlation between vocabulary size and reading skill. Students with limited vocabulary knowledge cannot comprehend text well.

kinesthetic learning Learning activities that involve feeling of the movements of the limbs and body and that are designed to promote acquisition of literacy skills. Examples include tracing letter shapes with fingers and using plastic letters to form and learn to read words.

lateralization of the brain Although the two cerebral hemispheres of the brain are similar in appearance, they do not process information in an identical manner. It is thought that in most people, the left hemisphere handles grammar and speech better than the right hemisphere. Conversely, the right hemisphere is thought to be better suited for processing spatial information. It is also thought that this diversification of functions is more pronounced in the male brain than in the female brain.

learned helplessness A psychological condition in which a person comes to believe that he or she has no control over a certain situation and, therefore, whatever he or she does is futile. Some children who are poor readers eventually learn to be helpless after repeated failure.

learning disabilities Difficulties, specially in learning to read, spell, and write, by individuals whose development is otherwise typical. Learning disabilities do not include difficulties associated with visual or hearing impairments or caused by limited learning experience. For this reason, learning disabilities associated with reading are also described as unexpected reading failure; the term *dyslexia* is also used interchangeably.

learning style An individual's preferred way of processing information. Some learners prefer auditory input, whereas others prefer visual input. Although the notion of learning styles is appealing, research does not support the feasibility of incorporating learning styles in the classroom. Learning best occurs when all the modalities are used simultaneously.

letter names and letter sounds The English alphabet has 26 letters, and each one has a name. However, many of these letters have more than one sound. For example, the letter *a* is pronounced differently in words such as *alien, and,* and *all.*

linguistics The scientific study of languages. There are several specialty areas of linguistics. Examples include comparative linguistics, historical linguistics, sociolinguistics, evolutionary linguistics, and structural linguistics.

literacy The ability to read and write at a level adequate for communicating and processing written information.

literature circle Small groups of students who read and discuss books and work on classroom assignments.

locus of control A personality construct referring to a person's locus (the place or location) of control over life events. If the person feels that he or she is in control of the events, the locus of control is said to be internal. In contrast, if the person feels that he or she has little or no control over events and that external circumstances such as luck, fate, and other people determine the events, the control is said to be external. An individual may not be conscious of his or her locus of control.

LTM Abbreviation for *long-term memory.*

Matthew effect Refers to the observation that good readers read extensively and become increasingly better readers, whereas poor readers read little and become increasingly poor readers.

mean length of utterance (MLU) The average number of morphemes in a spoken sentence. It is a measure of language skill.

median The middle score in a distribution of scores; it is a measure of central tendency.

mental age A measure of mental maturity, usually expressed as the chronological age for which a given level of performance is average or typical. Thus, if a 8-year-old child's mental age is also 8, he has an intelligence quotient of 100.

mental lexicon A dictionary in the mind. What one knows is organized on different bases and is stored in one's memory. Mental lexicons can be organized chronologically (e.g., the months of the year), conceptually (e.g., mammals found in Africa), and so on.

meta-analysis A statistical procedure that combines the results of several studies that have addressed the same question. It is an analysis of analyses. Meta-analysis findings are more reliable than the findings of a single study.

metacognition Knowing what one knows and knowing what one does not know is metacognition. It is insight into one's own thinking. For example, a person may know that he or she can understand a book on dyslexia, but this person also knows that he or she cannot understand a book on quantum physics.

metaphor A figure of speech in which a word or a phrase is applied to someone or something to make a comparison but not in a literal sense. A metaphor has a meaning other than what the words in the sentence mean. Examples include "A mighty fortress is our God" and "He made a biting comment."

Middle English English used between approximately 1110 A.D. and 1450 A.D.

modality preference Refers to the means preferred for processing information. Some learners are visual learners who learn best by seeing, others are auditory learners who learn best by hearing, and others are kinesthetic learners who learn best by doing. Research shows that learning is most effective when teachers use all these modalities.

modeling and think-alouds These concepts form an important element in comprehension instruction. As a teacher reads a passage, he or she models what goes on in his or her mind by talking aloud. Students are expected to learn how to use these strategies by observing the teacher model.

morpheme The smallest unit of meaning in a language. The word *play* has one morpheme; the word *played* has two morphemes. The word *play* is a free morpheme and the *ed* is a bound morpheme.

morphology The study of the structure of words which includes prefixes and suffixes. The root word *morph* comes from the Greek word meaning "form." Morphology includes the basic morpheme such as nouns and verbs (e.g., *ball, walk*); it also includes prefixes and suffixes and (e.g., *[un]willing, walk[ed]*). Research shows that a knowledge of the structure of words is helpful in literacy acquisition. Such a knowledge is referred to as morphological awareness.

motherese A simplified version of language that mothers and caregivers use when they speak to children. It is characterized by the use of simple vocabulary and a slow pace of delivery.

multisensory approach Refers to multimodality teaching in which as many modalities as possible are used. The child hears words as they are pronounced, the child sees as the words are written, and the child feels the words by tracing written words with his or her fingers or by touching and feeling words constructed out of plastic letters.

Old English English used between approximately 450 A.D. and 1100 A.D.

onset and rime A consonant or consonant cluster that precedes a vowel is an onset; the vowel and the following consonants in a monosyllabic word constitute the rime. In words such as *strip, strong,* and *stream,* /str/ is the onset and *ip, ong,* and *eam* are the rimes, respectively. Many educators believe that practice in the use of onsets and rimes can improve the reading skills of children.

opaque orthography An orthography in which the letter–sound relationship is not straightforward. English is an example of opaque orthography.

orthographic depth hypothesis The proposition that deep orthographies such as English are harder to learn to read and write compared with shallow orthographies such as Italian and Finnish.

orthography Visual representation of language as influenced by phonology, morphology, and semantics. The word *spelling* is used to describe orthography of alphabetic writing systems. However, writing systems such as Chinese are not spelling based. In Chinese orthography, each character represents a syllable, but most Chinese characters are polysyllabic. Thus, *orthography* is a comprehensive term that includes alphabetic as well as non-alphabetic writing systems.

parallel processing Processing of two or more items of information simultaneously. An example is the processing of all the letters in a word at the same time.

pedagogy The art and science of teaching or educating. The original Greek word from which *pedagogy* comes means "to lead the child."

phoneme The basic unit of speech sound that can change a word. For instance, by changing the phoneme /r/ to /b/, the word *rat* can be changed to *bat*. Phonemes are not easily identifiable in normal speech because phonemes overlap each other like shingles on the roof. In addition, one strings phonemes together when one speaks. English language is said to have about 44 phonemes.

phonemic awareness The ability to differentiate phonemes, the basic sounds of speech. The ability to decode written words depends on a sensitivity to phonemes and the eventual association of the written letters of the alphabet with their sounds.

phonetics The science of the study of sound-making in languages. The nature, production, and perception of sounds in languages form the areas of study. Such study includes the description, classification, and transcription of sounds in languages.

phonics Any of the several methods of teaching reading that stresses the relationship between letters and their sounds.

phonological awareness The ability to identify and generate rhyming sounds, the ability to identify and separate syllables in words, and the ability to identify and manipulate phonemes. *Phonological awareness* is an umbrella term that includes phonemic awareness.

phonology The study of the sounds in any particular language. It includes an inventory of sounds of a given language and the rules that describe how sounds interact with each other in that particular language.

phrase A group of words that has either no subject or no predicate.

portfolio assessment Assessment based on a student's overall performance over time. Portfolios may include essays, reports of projects, and so forth. They usually do not include test scores.

pragmatics of a language Language use and its meaning with reference to the culture in which it is used and the context in which it is used. For instance, the sentence, "He is warm-hearted" may be a compliment in one language and the opposite in another language.

predicate *See* clause.

print awareness An understanding of the nature of written language; pertains mainly to preschool children.

processing speed The speed with which an individual takes in, stores, and recalls information. In the field of reading, processing speed, as a research topic, has attracted much attention. Poor readers invariably are slow processors.

procognition Being able to surmise the thoughts and feelings of other people. Also known as theory of mind, this is a sort of mind reading. Efficient teaching requires a good dose of precognition skills.

psycholinguistics A branch of linguistics that deals with psychological factors associated with the acquisition (and loss of) language. It is interdisciplinary in nature, involving fields such as psychology, cognitive science, artificial intelligence, and linguistics. Of particular interest to psycholinguists is finding an explanation for the speed with which children acquire language and syntax, all within a short period of 3–4 years, without being formally taught.

psychological domain One of the three domains of the Component Model of Reading. Factors such as motivation and locus of control are included in the psychological domain.

qualitative assessment of spelling Assessment of written spelling based on the degree of phonological proximity to the correct spelling. Qualitative assessment does not use the dichotomy of "correct" and "incorrect" as used in quantitative assessment of spelling.

rating scale An informal assessment procedure in which the parent or the teacher rates the performance or behavior of the student. This is usually expressed in quantitative terms such as *always, often,* or *never.*

r-controlled The presence of the letter *r* can change the pronunciation of the vowels in certain words (e.g., *can* and *car, bad* and *bar*).

read-aloud books Books that are interesting to children and are usually read to them by an adult. Use of read-aloud books provides an opportunity to share quality literature.

reading readiness The readiness to profit from reading instruction; a teachable moment.

Reading Recovery (RR) A remedial reading approach attributed to Marie Clay.

reciprocal Interchangeable, given, or owned mutually. The relationship between phonemic awareness and reading skill is reciprocal in the sense that phoneme awareness increases reading skill and increased reading skill results in higher level of phonemic awareness.

reciprocal teaching A form of comprehension strategy instruction wherein the teacher and the students interchange roles as instructional model and learner.

reinforcer Any event or object that makes an individual repeat what he or she did. This refers to the rewarding or unpleasant consequences of one's actions. Reinforcers can be pleasant tangibles, such as candy bars, or intangibles, such as praise, attention, or feedback. Or, reinforcers can be unpleasant, such as a failing grade or a reprimand from the teacher. The reinforcer is an important component of behavioral psychology.

reliability of a test A reliable test is one on which people score similarly on two different occasions. Tests that have a reliability of 0.7 and greater are considered generally reliable.

response to intervention (RTI) A model for addressing learning disabilities that differs from the discrepancy model. This is a multitiered model involving the repeated use of assessment, intervention, and monitoring until the student reaches an expected level of reading skill.

rote memorization A type of memorization which primarily occurs through repetition. There is little or no attempt to make the information meaningful or to understand it in terms of things one already knows.

scaffolding Providing step-by-step instructional support to a student.

schema Background knowledge that is a prerequisite for comprehension.

schwa sound The sound of the vowel in unstressed syllables in multisyllabic words is softened. For example, the second /e/ in the word *every* is glossed over.

semantic Meaning.

semantic memory Meaning-based memory.

simple view of reading The proposition that proficient reading requires two skills, decoding and linguistic comprehension.

sociolinguistics A branch of linguistics that studies language with reference to its relationship to social variables such as educational level, professional background, and ethnicity.

standard deviation (*SD*) A measure of variability of scores within a group. A high level of *SD* shows that the performance of the students in the particular group is very divergent; a low level of *SD* indicates that the performance of the children in the group is more or less homogeneous.

Standard English A dialect of English spoken by a majority of the people in an English-speaking nation.

standard error of measurement (*SEM*) A statistic that estimates the amount of error in a score. For example, a child's score in a test of reading comes mainly from the child's reading skill but is also due to factors such as luck and chance. The scores obtained because of luck and chance do not reflect true reading skill and are therefore called error.

standard score A score that is modified so that it has a set mean and standard deviation (*SD*) and can be compared with the score obtained from another standardized test. The intelligence (IQ) score is an example. It has a mean of 100 and a *SD* of 15. This makes it possible to compare a child's IQ score with his or her score on any other standardized test with the same mean and *SD*.

standardized test A test in which the administration, scoring, and interpretation procedures are set by administering the test to a large number of individuals and refining the test on the basis of the feedback obtained.

STM Abbreviation for *short-term memory.*

story grammar A knowledge of the structure of stories or passages—that they have a beginning, an end, and other information that is usually arranged in a logical manner.

syllabic writing A writing system in which each syllable is represented by a single written symbol. English does not use syllabic writing; it only has a few symbols (e.g., @ for *at*, & for *and*).

syllable A unit of speech that consists of one or more vowels occurring alone or in conjunction with one or more consonants. A syllable is uttered as a single unit of speech. A word is described as monosyllabic, bisyllabic, or polysyllabic depending on the number of syllables the word has. *Man* and *school* are monosyllabic words; *Christmas* and *teacher* are bisyllabic words; *fantastic* and *irregular* are polysyllabic words.

syndrome A collection of recognizable signs or symptoms. For example, the syndrome of dyslexia includes difficulty in decoding written words, slow reading, and imperfect spelling.

syntax The structure of sentences; the way in which words are put together to form sentences and phrases.

synthetic phonics A method of teaching reading in which letters of the alphabet and their sounds are taught first. Blending these sounds into syllables and words is introduced as the next step.

teacher expectation Certain preconceived beliefs teachers form about their pupils. On the basis of such beliefs, teachers expect their students to perform in a certain way. When the expectation is low, the pupils sense their teachers' attitude and fulfill such expectation.

transparent orthography Written language in which letters in words have one-to-one relationship with their pronunciations. In transparent orthography, words can be correctly pronounced even if the reader does not know the word but knows the names of the letters of the alphabet.

variance A statistical measure of variability or scatter seen in the test scores of a group of individuals. It is standard deviation squared (SD^2).

visual process In this book, this term refers to the physiological aspects of vision.

vocabulary knowledge The fund of words an individual can understand and use knowledgeably.

vowel A speech sound that is produced without any obstruction in the vocal tract.

wh- **words**: Words that start with a *wh-* notation. *What, where,* and *when* are examples of *wh-* words. The use of *wh-* words is an important milestone in language development because it is a sign of children's desire to acquire knowledge about the world. Not all *wh-* words are learned at the same time. For instance, children use *what* before *when*.

whole language A philosophy of literacy instruction, not a method of teaching. It emphasizes meaning, rather than skills such as decoding and word recognition, as the basic instructional approach.

word recognition A process made of two subprocesses, decoding and instant word reading. The term is used in this book to refer to the ability to pronounce written words quickly and effortlessly.

word wall Written words displayed in the classroom on charts or bulletin boards.

working memory As conceived in the 1950s, short-term memory (STM) was thought to have two components: acoustic STM and visual STM. Recently, a third component, executive STM, was added to the STM model, and the STM memory model came to be called the working memory. Executive STM plays an executive function by directing the acoustic and visual memories, by analyzing the nature of the function to be performed, by focusing on the task that is to be performed, and by screening out irrelevant stimuli. Children with attention-deficit/hyperactivity disorder are said to have a dysfunctional executive system of the working memory.

Review of Selected Basal Readers

Basal readers are packages of instructional materials published by five or six major companies and used for teaching literacy and reading skills to children in grades K–8.

HISTORY OF BASAL READERS

The origins of **basal readers** can be traced to the McGuffey Readers, which were introduced in the 1860s and continued to be published until the 1960s. The idea behind the McGuffey Readers was that having a standard book for each grade would make teaching and learning to read a well-regulated, streamlined, systematic endeavor. During the 1940s, Scott Foresman produced a basal series that was based on a philosophy similar to that of the McGuffey Readers. The stories in the Scott Foresman basal reader starred two children named Dick and Jane and described them and their activities in simple but repetitive sentences. These books encouraged memorizing words by sight using the "look and say" method. During the late 1950s, this basal reader and its predominantly "look and say" approach were criticized as being meaningless and dull. As a result, basal readers began to restructure their materials, using phonics-based instruction to teach literacy. Later, the phonics emphasis in turn was criticized, and meaning-based instruction was actively promoted. As a result, during the latter part of the 1980s, meaning-based whole language became the force behind literacy education, and basal readers had to adapt to this change in educational philosophy. The importance once given to basal readers declined, and trade books were used instead. Once again, things did not remain static for very long; the 1990s saw a renewed interest in phonics instruction and the resurgence of basal readers. Since the 1980s, more culturally diverse materials have been incorporated into the basal readers to reflect the changes in society. As this brief history indicates, educational philosophy has a strong impact on the methods and content of basal readers. However, basal readers can differ from one another in the emphasis placed on teaching methods, the selection of literacy pieces, and the quality of artwork.

Basal readers are produced by publishers in collaboration with educators, reading specialists, writers, and artists. A basal reader package usually contains text materials, previously published short stories, longer narratives, workbooks, assessment materials, and teacher guides. The materials follow a predetermined scope and sequence. In addition to teaching suggestions, the teacher's guide also contains pre- and postreading activities, assessment materials, and questions to ask students. The organization of the basal readers makes teaching somewhat systematic by targeting specific skills, such as vocabulary and spelling, for instruction and assessment. The structured nature of basal readers has also been the target of criticism; many feel that they are inflexible, do not allow for creative instruction, and are often not authentic. Another criticism is that basal readers are written as though all students have identical skills. This criticism can at least be partially deflected by using the basal readers flexibly and individualizing instruction.

During the 1980s, basal readers were criticized by proponents of both the code-emphasis and meaning-emphasis approaches of teaching reading. Educators who thought reading should focus on the development of decoding skills believed that basal readers fell short in the area of phonics instruction. Proponents of whole language alleged that basal readers were mechanical, meaningless, boring, uninspiring, and not authentic (Goodman, Shannon, Freeman, & Murphy, 1988).

However, Stahl and Miller (1989) noted that teaching reading through the basal series does not result in inferior reading achievement when compared to teaching reading through a meaning-based approach, such as whole language. It should also be noted that

> advocates of Whole language have yet to provide compelling research evidence demonstrating the effectiveness of such approaches in teaching children to read. Indeed research over the past 70 years shows that structured systematic teaching in the early grades produces the better results. (Chall & Squire, 1991, p. 138).

This statement is also supported by the meta-analyses done by the National Reading Panel (NRP; 2000).

In spite of these differences of opinion, basal readers are helpful in making reading instruction structured and systematic, particularly in the early grades. Resourceful professional reading teachers know how to use basal readers flexibly to make the program meet their students' instructional needs. Most of the basal reading programs have, over the years, enhanced the quality of the books used in their programs. In addition, the publishers tend to respond to and keep up with current developments in literacy education.

A large number of school systems currently make use of some form of basal reading program for kindergarten through grade 6. Although there are several companies that publish basal reading programs, about five of them account for nearly 80% of the total sales. Most of the basals present guidelines for teaching decoding, comprehension, and children's literature, although the programs have different emphases. The focus on different skills may also change according to age levels.

REVIEW OF MAJOR BASAL READER PROGRAMS

The Oregon Reading First Center (2004) examined various reading programs based on basal readers to see how they addressed three of the five components of reading recommended by the NRP. The three components were phonemic awareness, phonics, and fluency at the K–3 grade levels. Based on reviews by independent judges, the center's rank order of the basal reading programs was SRA-Reading Mastery, Houghton Mifflin, Open Court, Harcourt, Scott Foresman, and Macmillan/McGraw-Hill. It should be noted that this comprehensive report examined only how the three components were treated at the K–3 grade levels and did not evaluate the teaching of vocabulary and comprehension. Instructional materials for higher levels were also not examined.

Maslin (2003) examined the following five basal readers: Open Court, Macmillan/McGraw-Hill, Harcourt, Houghton Mifflin, and Scott Foresman. Maslin noted that although all of these basal reading programs present systematic phonics instruction in greater detail than their predecessors, Houghton Mifflin and Macmillan/McGraw-Hill provide good instructional scope and sequence for beginning reading instruction. Open Court, Houghton Mifflin, and Harcourt present phonics instruction based on their own decodable texts. Maslin measured "text engagingness" by asking students to rate the text selections for the quality of the pictures and subject matter content. Although students rated all the programs highly, Open Court was rated the highest for text quality and MacMillan/McGraw-Hill was rated the highest for pictures and stories.

Using a different set of criteria, Bruce Murray (n.d.) of Auburn University evaluated the following seven basal reading programs: McGraw-Hill; Houghton Mifflin; Scott Foresman; Scholastic; Harcourt; SRA-Reading Mastery, and Open Court. He looked at such aspects as how the programs introduce the short sounds of /a/ and /u/ at the beginning reading level; how they build fluency at the second-grade level, and how they teach comprehension in the fourth grade. Based on these criteria, Murray summarized his findings as follows.

The Harcourt series received the lowest ranking because the sequence of phonics instruction seemed haphazard and directions to the teachers were not systematic and explicit. Nevertheless, this series had good literature. The new Houghton Mifflin series seemed to provide more explicit, systematic phonics instruction than previous editions (see Aaron & Joshi, 1992). However, according to Murray, phonemic awareness—the basic building block of reading—was not addressed properly, as were guided practice and modeling. This series seemed to provide a sufficient amount of decodable texts and appeared to be a better series after the first grade, especially in providing explicit comprehension strategy instruction.

The McGraw-Hill series also provided good strategies for beginning reading instruction, especially in phonemic awareness and phonics instruction. However, vocabulary development and comprehension strategies were not very well covered.

Scholastic presented the phonics program in a systematic way, but the program moved rather slowly and phoneme awareness and blending programs were presented without much direction. At the first-grade level, there was not much direction for teaching guided practice and blending. Furthermore, at the first-grade level, predictable books were provided rather than decodable texts. However, vocabulary instruction was good.

Although the Scott Foresman series had tried to provide explicit phonics instruction, some problems remained, such as limited instruction in phonemic awareness and blending and stories that were not aligned with instruction. However, after the first grade, fluency training and comprehension instruction were relatively well presented.

SRA-Reading Mastery, based on the original DISTAR program, was explicit enough but moved very slowly. According to Murray, decoding a word (e.g., *am*) was not introduced until Lesson 28, and the lessons proceeded at an "excruciatingly slow pace."

Murray concluded that Open Court offered the best basal reading series for learning to read given a typical population of elementary school children; it offered more and better decodable texts and provided for good reading practice. Its fluency instruction for grade 2 and summarization instruction for grade 4 were well conceived.

CONCLUSIONS ABOUT BASAL READERS

Based on these evaluations of basal programs, some general conclusions can be drawn. First, all basal readers are not created equal; hence, it is not fair to make general criticisms of all basal readers. Their individual strengths and weaknesses must be weighed against students' needs. Second, there is no single basal reading program that addresses well all components at all grades and all skill levels; hence, teachers and administrators must be clear about the overall orientation of the basal readers and the academic needs of the students in the school system. Furthermore, basal readers must be supplemented by other literacy materials. As Maslin (2003) pointed out, the basal reader is a tool for delivering good instruction; it should not be the instruction.

An analysis of reading programs for grade 1 is provided by the National Right to Read Foundation's *Analysis of Grade 1 Reading Programs* (2000). Some of the basal readers compared are Open Court Reading, McGraw-Hill Reading, and Scott Foresman Reading. Please note that the comparison is limited to grade 1 and the focus is on phonics.

Technology Assistance and Computer Use in Literacy Instruction

Computer-assisted instruction has several advantages. Children are often motivated to work with computers; they can work at their own pace, yet the teacher can control the pace of the instruction; and feedback can be immediate (MacArthur, Ferretti, Okolo, & Cavalier, 2001). Further, several research studies have shown that computer-assisted instruction improves reading, writing, and spelling skills. Blok, Oostdam, Otter, and Overmaat (2002) reviewed 42 studies of computer-assisted instruction carried out since 1990 and concluded that computer programs generally tend to be effective, although they have only a small effect size. The important finding, however, is that computer programs improve literacy skills of both typical readers and students who lag behind in reading performance (Irausquin, Drent, & Verhoeven, 2005; van Daal & Reitsma,1993; van der Leij & van Daal, 1999; Yap & van der Leij, 1994).

Almost 99% of all public schools in the United States have Internet access, and about 92% of classrooms in these schools have access to the Internet. Further, according to Mambretti and Schmidt (1999), the Internet "is a revolutionary technology to change every aspect of society and, in particular, the educational system" (p. 17). Research also indicates that the Internet can be a very important and useful tool in producing written compositions, particularly in the upper grades.

WEB SITES FOR GENERAL LITERACY INSTRUCTION

One of the most useful web sites that the reading professional should be familiar with is the one developed by the Florida Center for Reading Research (http://www.fcrr.org). It provides up-to-date information for teachers, administrators, parents, and researchers. The web site also provides information about remedial programs. The site is recommended by the International Dyslexia Association.

The Blumberg Center web site (http://www.indstate.edu/soe/blumberg/reading), developed at Indiana State University by P.G. Aaron, provides useful information on all aspects of literacy skills. Based on the teacher-friendly Component Model of Reading, the web page provides information on resources for parents, teachers, and other school professionals. Its special focus is on reading disability.

Another web site based on a similar reading model was developed by Dr. James Royer. The Reading Success Lab (http://www.readingsuccesslab.com) provides information about assessment and intervention, and the software is based on the principle that reading consists of two components—decoding and comprehension.

The Reading Genie (http://www.auburn.edu/academic/education/reading_genie), developed by Dr. Bruce Murray at Auburn University, is a useful link that provides helpful materials for teaching literacy skills. It is well designed and is updated periodically.

Professional reading teachers should also check the web sites of the education administrative offices in their own state for information on literacy activities, policies, programs, and initiatives. Information follows regarding web sites from a few states.

> The official web site of the Texas Education Agency is http://www.tea.state.tx.us/curriculum/elar/index.html. It provides information on curriculum, assessment, and rules and regulations regarding educational policies.
>
> The site at http://www.texasreading.org/utcrla/ was developed by the Vaughn Gross Center for Reading and Language Arts of the University of Texas in Austin and provides valuable tips for improving reading skills for all students, especially struggling readers, English language learners, and special education students. The materials can be downloaded free of charge.
>
> The official web site of the California State Department of Education for reading and language arts is http://www.cde.ca.gov/ci/rl). It provides information on instructional materials and children's literature.
>
> The state of Indiana's web site is http://www.indianastandardsresources.org/standardsummary.asp. It provides information about the standards classroom teachers should meet; it also provides information regarding teaching materials suitable for kindergarten through grade 12. The site contains descriptions of teaching materials for each grade level on phonemic awareness, decoding, comprehension, and narrative and expository writing.
>
> An Oregon site, http://reading.uoregon.edu/curricula/index.php, is designed to provide information to teachers, administrators, and parents about teaching reading. The web site includes definitions and descriptions of reading-related research and the theories behind each of the components of reading. It also includes information about instruction and assessment. Ample examples are presented.

COMMERCIAL SITES FOR PURCHASING INSTRUCTIONAL MATERIALS

Reading A-Z (http://www.readinga-z.com) offers numerous teacher-friendly materials for teaching phonemic awareness, alphabet knowledge, fluency, vocabulary, and reading comprehension suitable for children from grades K–6 of all ability levels. The web site also includes children's books, leveled books, lesson plans, and printable worksheets. The program can be purchased for individual classrooms or for an entire school. Both individual and school subscriptions are available; the cost of school subscriptions depends on the number of classrooms that will use the material.

Reading Tutors (http://www.reading-tutors.com/main/ViewPage/name/Program_Overview) sells instructional resource packets in six categories: phonological awareness, alphabet, phonics, high-frequency words, fluency, and comprehension. Printable exercise sheets can also be obtained from this site.

Teachnology (http://www.teach-nology.com) provides worksheets, lesson plans, and other printable items for teachers. These easy-to-use materials are for instruction on phonics, reading comprehension, spelling, and other areas of reading, as well as language arts.

Lessons in Literacy (http://www.greatsource.com) provides instructional materials for grades 1–6 on print awareness, phonological awareness, phonics and word study, vocabulary, fluency, comprehension, and writing. Individual software can be purchased from this firm.

SELECTED LIST OF COMPUTER PROGRAMS FOR TEACHING LITERACY SKILLS

Probably one of the first published software programs was *Reader Rabbit,* which is produced by the Learning Company (http://www.learningcompany.com). The software has various programs for different age and grade levels and focuses on the alphabetic principle and vocabulary development. Many school districts have used this program.

Two software programs developed by Creative Education Institute (CEI) (http://www.ceilearning.com)—*Codebreakers* and *Essential Learning Systems* (ELS)—can be useful in the early elementary grades. The creators of these programs claim that they are derived from scientifically based reading research.

Reading Rockets (http://www.readingrockets.org) has software programs not only for children but also for parents, teachers, and educators. A desirable feature of the program for children is that it covers several reading and writing skills and is recommended by the International Dyslexia Association.

Accelerated Reader (http://www.renlearn.com/ar) can be accessed through the Internet. In addition to the use of literature, this software also tests for comprehension. It manages students' records and allows teacher input in drafting questions. Half of the schools in the United States are said to use some form of *Accelerated Reader.*

Earobics (http://www.earobics.com) is a software program that includes activities for all the components recommended by the National Reading Panel (NRP). It is recommended by the Florida Center for Reading Research and is claimed to have improved literacy skills, including phonological awareness and comprehension. This is a commercially available program.

Essential Skills (http://www.essentialskills.net) provides software programs that are designed to enhance early learning in the areas of phonemic awareness, phonics, vocabulary, fluency, reading comprehension, spelling, and writing.

ReadWriteThink (http://www.readwritethink.org/resources/index.asp) offers links to a number of useful resources on the Internet for language arts teachers. This web site was established by the International Reading Association and the National Council of Teachers of English. The site offers useful downloadable information and practical hints about every aspect of literacy learning. Lessons and lesson plans can also be downloaded free of charge. The site also lists resources such as *4Teachers.org* (http://www.4teachers.org), a free, multifaceted site that describes a variety of easy, ready-to-use tools for teachers and students.

OTHER SOURCES FOR COMPUTER-ASSISTED INSTRUCTION

A to Z Teacher Stuff (http://atozteacherstuff.com) provides teachers with free lesson plans, thematic units, and resources.

The Rosetta Project Library (http://www.childrensbooksonline.org/library.htm) provides text and illustrations taken from many classic books. The information can be used for teaching children of all ages. Books are arranged by age level. There are books for English language learners and information for home-school instructors.

Ebooks for Young Readers (http://etext.virginia.edu/ebooks/subjects/subjects-young.html) is a collection of electronic books available in ebook, Palm, and web versions prepared by the University of Virginia's Electronic Text Center.

Reading Is Fundamental (RIF; http://www.rif.org) is the largest children's literacy organization in the United States. Its aim is to expand and encourage children's literacy learning by providing free books and information about resources. This web site provides information on how to donate books or how to be a volunteer in a local RIF program. The RIF Reading Planet section of the site contains educational games and activities for children.

Reading Rainbow (http://pbskids.org/readingrainbow) complements the Public Broadcasting System (PBS) children's series of the same name by providing details on books featured on the television series. The site also offers online games and activities.

LDonline (http://www.ldonline.org) provides information and resources for parents, teachers, and individuals with learning disabilities. The web site is produced by WETA-TV, the PBS station in Washington, D.C., which also offers two other comprehensive educational sites: ReadingRockets.org and ColorinColorado.org. These web sites provide useful information for teachers, parents, and teachers. *Reading Rockets* (http://www.readingrockets.org) provides information about literacy learning and suggests strategies for supporting struggling readers. It offers news, practical information, expert advice, and resources for parents and teachers.

Another web site that provides information on software that can help individuals with reading and writing problems is http://www.gatfl.org/ldguide/default.htm.

Scholastic (http://www.scholastic.com) provides a large number of resources for teachers, specific to grade levels and subject areas, including information about authors.

Starfall (http://www.starfall.com) is a widely used program designed for the emergent reader. The web site provides information about interactive books and offers word family games that teach phonemic awareness, comprehension, vocabulary, and spelling skills. These materials can be downloaded for free. The illustrations are excellent and are often accompanied by questions that the child is expected to answer.

Success for All (http://www.successforall.com) is a program intended to teach literacy skills. Several studies have shown that this program is successful in helping students become better readers. Developed by Robert Slavin, formerly of Johns Hopkins University, and his colleagues, it has received support from research studies. The program is suitable for grades pre-K through 8 and provides materials for all aspects of literacy development for typical readers, English language learners, and students at risk.

Smart Kids Software (http://www.smartkidssoftware.com/home.shtml) offers software that enhances different aspects of literacy development. The professional reading teacher can use programs such as *Carmen Sandiego* and *Word Detective* for vocabulary development.

Oxton House Publishers (http://www.oxtonhouse.com/literacy.html) has materials for all five skills recommended by the NRP. The program begins with Dr. Fisher's *Concept Phonics*, initially focusing on phonemic awareness, and then moves on to decoding, spelling, vocabulary, fluency, comprehension, and handwriting. The materials have been recommended by the late Isabelle Liberman, one of the pioneering researchers who recognized the important role of phonology in reading, and by contemporary educator, author, and researcher Louisa Moats.

Mindplay (http://www.mindplay.com) has been developing software since 1986. The web site claims that research supports the programs' success. There are three programs:

My Reading Coach and *Embedded Teacher Intelligence* teach phonemic awareness, phonics sounds and rules, vocabulary, word structure, syntactic processing, and reading comprehension through a multisensory approach.

Reading Analysis and Prescription System is a computerized diagnostic system.

Fluent Reading Trainer is designed to develop fluent reading and comprehension.

A helpful book is R.L. Bender and W.N. Bender's *Computer-Assisted Instruction for Students at Risk* (Allyn & Bacon, 1996).

SOFTWARE DESIGNED TO IMPROVE SPECIFIC LITERACY SKILLS

The previous section described software programs intended to help develop overall literacy skills. This section presents software designed to develop specific literacy skills, such as phonics and vocabulary.

Software for Improving Phonological Awareness and Phonics

Reading Doctor (http://www.readingdoctor.com.au) software uses a multisensory technique to teach phonological awareness, phonemic awareness, and phonics skills. Developed by speech and language specialists, the program uses an interactive approach to teach letter–sound knowledge, word segmentation, word blending, and word recognition.

The Cognitive Concepts web site (http://cogcon.com/gamegoo/config.html) is similar to Starfall and has free, downloadable materials for teaching decoding and comprehension. Cognitive Concepts, a subsidiary of Houghton Mifflin, developed Earobics. The software is widely used in schools.

LinguiSystems (http://www.linguisystems.com/index.php) provides a commercial program that has been developed along the lines of software programs such as *Sounds Abound* to teach phonology-related skills.

DaisyQuest (http://www.metiri.com/Solutions/DaisyQuest.htm) is a stand-alone software package developed at the University of Florida. It is designed to improve prereading and early reading skills in students in grades pre-K–1. Skills improved through *DaisyQuest* are phonological awareness skills; rhyming; beginning, middle, and ending sounds; blending sounds; and others. *DaisyQuest* is designed to be used independently by young students and has an excellent research base.

The Waterford Early Reading Program (http://www.waterford.org) is designed as a complete computer-based program to teach phonological awareness, letter–sound correspondence, and comprehension from kindergarten through grade 2. Distributed by Pearson Digital Learning (http://www.pearsondigital.com), it is relatively expensive; however, the quality is good and the activities can be used during the entire school year. The web site claims that the materials are based on research recommended by organizations such as the Society for the Scientific Studies of Reading and the International Reading Association.

Earobics (http://www.earobics.com) is CD-ROM–based software with over 300 levels of instruction providing comprehensive training in auditory processing, phonological awareness, phonics, and spoken language processing. Earobics Step 1 is for developmental ages 4–7, Earobics Step 2 is for developmental ages 7–10, and Earobics Step 3 for Adolescents and Adults is aimed at older struggling readers.

Touchphonics Second Edition is a manipulative multisensory phonics system published by Educators Publishing Services (http://www.epsbooks.com). This multisensory program is designed to develop students' phonemic awareness and phonics knowledge. Educators Publishing Services publishes a variety of instructional materials for improving reading and spelling skills, and the professional reading teacher might benefit from browsing their web site.

Discover Intensive Phonics is published by Reading Horizons (http://www.readinghorizons .com). This is an individualized, interactive phonics program that uses a multisensory approach; the web site claims that it is systematic, explicit, direct, and research based. The program features a human voice soundtrack.

Webbing into Literacy (http://curry.edschool.virginia.edu/go/wil/home.html) was developed by Dr. Laura Smolkin at the University of Virginia. This software features downloadable nursery rhymes and alphabet books, along with related lesson plans, and a list of 101 books for children.

Words and Pictures (http://www.bbc.co.uk/schools/wordsandpictures/index.shtml) was developed by the British Broadcasting Corporation (BBC) and includes numerous interactive activities on phonics, word sounds, and high-frequency words. This site does use British spelling.

Software for Improving Word Recognition Skills

Preschool Rainbow (http://www.preschoolrainbow.org) is a recipient of an Academic Excellence award. It provides ideas for preschool teachers and early childhood education lesson plans, which are arranged by themes and can enrich classroom curriculum. The site also contains easy learning games. The Rainbow Resource Room has games that teach number and early math concepts.

Reading is Fundamental: Reading Planet (http://www.rif.org/readingplanet) is software that contains activities for creating print awareness, comprehension, and writing. It can be downloaded for free. The program has animation and sound.

Read, Write, & Type (http://www.readwritetype.com), also labeled Talking Fingers, is software that was developed with funding from the National Institute of Child Health and Human Development (NICHD). It has research support and is intended for children ages 6–9. The program uses a multisensory approach and teaches phonological awareness, letter–sound correspondence, and fluency. It has been recommended by several researchers as a supplementary program.

Software for Improving Vocabulary Knowledge

Smart Kids Software (http://www.smartkidssoftware.com/home.shtml) has software programs that teach phonics, vocabulary, and comprehension skills. The programs are organized by grade levels rather than subskills.

Super Kids Software (http://www.superkids.com/aweb/tools/words) has software programs to teach vocabulary words in a game-like format. Games include Hangman, Word Scrambler, and Hidden Word Puzzles.

Vocabulary Builder (http://www.esl.net/vocabulary_builder.html) is designed to meet the needs of children ages 5–12 years and combines pictures, text, and sound to make an interactive vocabulary building system. The page at http://www.eslcafe.com/search/Vocabulary/index.html has several activities designed to teach vocabulary words in a game-like format.

Vocabulary University (http://www.vocabulary.com) has interactive games for students to learn about word etymology and word meaning. Games are at different levels of difficulty. Level 1 is meant for upper elementary students and Level 2 for middle school students.

Software for Improving Comprehension Skills

Reading Quest (http://www.readingquest.org/strat) has a variety of activities designed to improve comprehension and uses strategies such as reciprocal teaching, question and answer techniques, graphic organizers, semantic feature analysis, and summarizing.

The web site http://www.abc.teach.com offers information relevant to teaching reading comprehension. The activities are grouped by grade levels, beginning with the kindergarten level and going up to the sixth-grade level.

Software for Improving Fluency

Soliloquy Reading Assistant (http://www.soliloquylearning.com) combines speech recognition and verification technology backed by reading research and educational science to help students develop fluency. Based on research by Marilyn Adams, the program traces children's errors and provides both visual and audio feedback help with these problem words.

The Read Naturally web site (http://www.readnaturally.com) claims to provide teachers with the tools they need to address the fluency needs of their students. The offered package includes books, tapes, CDs, and software programs. A reading fluency table can be downloaded for free. Read Naturally offers six phonics levels in the form of 24 nonfiction stories, and corresponding tapes, and CDs. All materials are sequenced for fluency assessment from grades 1 through 8.

Great Leaps Reading Program (http://www.greatleaps.com) is divided into three major areas: phonics, sight phrases, and reading fluency.

ASSISTIVE TECHNOLOGY

The professional reading teacher can examine the web site http://www.abilityhub.com/read/index.htm for information on assistive technology. The site also provides information for text-to-speech software, which is designed for individuals with reading difficulties. This software highlights and reads the text aloud at the same time.

Kurzweil 3000 (http://www.kurzweiledu.com/kurz3000.aspx) is another software application that reads text aloud, visually highlights the text being read, and employs a number of advanced techniques for making the material accessible to people with reading-related disabilities. It makes text available to users through multiple sensory channels, letting them simultaneously see, hear, and track words.

Road Runner by Ostrich Software is yet another text-to-speech software that reads aloud and highlights the text.

Because computer technology changes frequently, school personnel should check the Internet frequently for updated programs and materials.

CRITERIA FOR SELECTING SOFTWARE

The proliferation of educational software in recent years makes the task of choosing the appropriate software a challenging and time consuming undertaking. The major criteria to be used in selecting software are 1) the cost, 2) technical specifications, 3) student needs, and 4) instructional support. Additional information is provided in the following section.

1. Software should fit the curriculum, not the other way around.

2. Software should be evaluated for how it will be used in the curriculum, whether as part of the curriculum or as a stand-alone unit.

3. Software should meet the goals of instruction, whether it is improving comprehension skills, vocabulary, or general knowledge.

4. The teacher's instructional goals will help determine whether to purchase software that the entire class can use at the same time or students can use individually.

5. If students must quit the program before completing it, they should be able to come back and continue from where they left off.

6. Students should be able to log on easily and quit easily without losing their work.

7. The program should allow connection to the Internet at a reasonably fast rate.

8. The program should allow for easy recordkeeping so that individual students' performance can be kept as a cumulative record.

9. If students work on group projects, a "tool software" would be helpful. Software such as *HyperStudio* and *HyperCard* provide a platform for students to work collab-

oratively and build webbed projects. When a topic is chosen, each student can be responsible for researching one aspect of the topic. The software can then tie all the reports together into one product.

The web site Classroom Connect (http://corporate.classroom.com) contains tips on how to integrate technology with the general education classroom instruction. Also look for articles by Tammy Payton (http://www.tammypayton.net).

REVIEWS OF INSTRUCTIONAL SOFTWARE

The following web sites periodically review instructional software.

SuperKids Educational Software Review (http://www.superkids.com)

Discovery Education School Resources (http://school.discoveryeducation.com)

GameZone's KidZone (http://www.gzkidzone.com)

PROFESSIONAL ORGANIZATIONS AND JOURNALS WITH A FOCUS ON LITERACY

The International Reading Association (IRA) web site (http://www.reading.org/) gives information about the association, its publications, and other web resources. The organization has over 100,000 members. IRA also has regional and local branches that the professional reading teacher may want to join.

The IRA journal *The Reading Teacher* (http://www.reading.org/publications/journals/rt/index.html) can be used as a classroom resource. This journal is published eight times per year. It provides valuable hands-on ideas for classroom teachers.

Reading Online (http://www.readingonline.org/about/about_index.asp) is a free, online-only publication of the IRA. Its focus is on literacy practice and research in classrooms serving students ages 5 to 18. *Literacy* is broadly defined to include traditional print literacy as well as visual literacy, critical literacy, media literacy, and digital literacy.

The National Reading Conference (NRC) web site can be accessed at http://www.nrconline.org/. According to the site, NRC is a professional organization for individuals who share an interest in research and in the dissemination of information about literacy and literacy instruction. NRC publishes the *Journal of Literacy Research* (http://www.nrconline.org/jlr.html), a peer-reviewed quarterly journal that carries articles on all aspects of literacy, mostly based on empirical research.

The International Dyslexia Association (IDA) is dedicated to helping individuals with reading disabilities (dyslexia), their families, and their teachers. Its web site can be accessed at http://www.interdys.org/. IDA is the oldest learning disabilities organization in the nation. Its goal has been to provide the most comprehensive forum for parents, educators, and researchers for sharing their experiences, problems, and knowledge about remedial instruction.

Reading Research Quarterly is published by the International Reading Association (http://www.reading.org/publications/journals/rrq/index.html). It is a peer-reviewed journal and publishes articles mostly based on empirical research.

Scientific Studies of Reading (http://www.triplesr.org/journal/) is the official journal of the Society for the Scientific Study of Reading. It carries original empirical investigations of all aspects of reading and related areas and is published quarterly.

Reading and Writing: An Interdisciplinary Journal (http://www.springerlink.com/content/ 1573-0905/) is published nine times a year and is one of the premier journals in the field of literacy research. It publishes research articles pertaining to all aspects of literacy and has been especially known to attract readers and researchers from different countries.

Reading Research and Instruction (http://www.collegereadingassociation.org/rri.html) is a quarterly peer-reviewed journal published by College Reading Association. The articles deal with research and instruction in reading and literacy education. Its focus is on teacher education, college reading, clinical reading, and adult literacy.

Reading and Writing Quarterly (http://www.tandf.co.uk/journals/titles/10573569.asp) publishes information to "improve instruction for regular and special education students who have difficulty learning to read and write. Interdisciplinary in scope, the journal addresses the causes, assessment, prevention, and remediation of reading and writing difficulties in regular and special education settings."

Reading Psychology (http://www.tandf.co.uk/journals/titles/02702711.asp) is published five times per year. It contains original manuscripts in the fields of literacy and reading as well as related disciplines.

Suggested Reading

Lefever, D., & Pearman, C. (2005). Early readers and electronic texts: CD-ROM storybook features that influence reading behaviors. *The Reading Teacher, 58*(5), 446–454.

Picard, S. (2005). Collaborative conversations about second-grade readers. *The Reading Teacher, 58*(5), 458–464.

Author Index

Subject Index

Page numbers followed by *b*, *f*, and *t* indicate boxes, figures, and tables, respectively.